A COMPLETE GUIDE

THE NAPA &
SONOMA BOOK

A COMPLETE GUIDE

8TH EDITION

THE NAPA & SONOMA BOOK

Peg Melnik,
with Tim Fish

The Countryman Press
Woodstock, Vermont

We welcome your comments and suggestions. Please contact:
Great Destinations Guide Editor
The Countryman Press, P.O. Box 748, Woodstock, Vermont 05091

Eighth Edition

ISBN 978-1-58157-093-9

Cover photo © Thomas Hallstein/Outsight
Interior photos by the author unless otherwise specified
Book design by Bodenweber Design
Composition by Cantera Design
Maps by Mapping Specialists Ltd., Madison, WI © The Countryman Press

Published by The Countryman Press, P.O. Box 748, Woodstock, Vermont 05091

Distributed by W. W. Norton & Company, Inc., 500 Fifth Avenue, New York, NY 10110

Manufactured in the United States of America

10 9 8 7 6 5 4 3 2 1

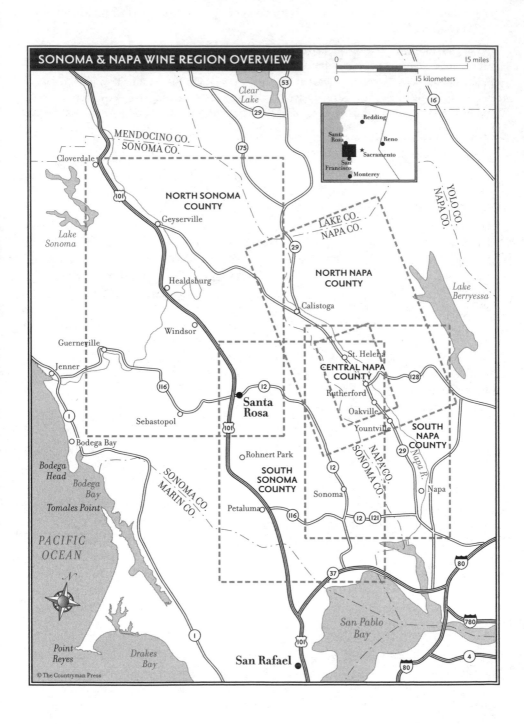

SONOMA & NAPA WINE REGION OVERVIEW

0   15 miles
0   15 kilometers

Clear Lake

MENDOCINO CO.
SONOMA CO.

Cloverdale

NORTH SONOMA
COUNTY

Lake Sonoma

Geyserville

LAKE CO.
NAPA CO.

YOLO CO.
NAPA CO.

NORTH NAPA
COUNTY

Healdsburg

Lake Berryessa

Calistoga

Windsor

Guerneville

St. Helena

Jenner

CENTRAL NAPA
COUNTY

Santa Rosa

Rutherford

Sebastopol

Oakville

Yountville

SOUTH NAPA
COUNTY

Bodega Bay

Rohnert Park

NAPA CO.
SONOMA CO.

Bodega Head

Bodega Bay

SOUTH
SONOMA
COUNTY

Sonoma

Napa R.

Napa

SONOMA CO.
MARIN CO.

Tomales Point

Petaluma

PACIFIC
OCEAN

San Pablo Bay

Point Reyes

Drakes Bay

San Rafael

© The Countryman Press

Redding

Santa Rosa

Reno

Sacramento

San Francisco

Monterey

Contents

ACKNOWLEDGMENTS

Many people made this book possible. We want to thank all the wineries, restaurants, inns, and businesses that have put up with all our phone calls, e-mail inquiries, and spontaneous visits. Numerous organizations proved to be great resources. In particular, the Napa County Historical Society and Sonoma County Museum supplied many of our priceless historical photographs.

We would also like to acknowledge the devoted team at the Countryman Press, particularly Jennifer Thompson, Elaine Cissi, Doug Yeager, Julie Nelson, Fred Lee, and Kermit Hummel. We'd also like to thank two publications that are dear to us: the *Press Democrat* and *Wine Spectator*. While this book is produced independently from both, we are grateful to be gainfully employed while we continue producing this guide in our off hours.

Finally, we want to thank our children, Sophie and Tucker, for putting up with us over the years. Sophie was born the week of our very first deadline in 1991 and has grown up with this book. Tucker followed eight years later, and as long as we bribed him with ice cream, he tagged along willingly as we traveled the trails of Napa and Sonoma.

Now, we would like to hear from you. What do you like and dislike about this book? Also, let us know about your experiences in Wine Country—both good and bad. We hope the inns, restaurants, wineries, and other businesses that are mentioned here live up to their recommendations. If they don't, let us know. Contact Tim Fish and Peg Melnik directly via e-mail at TimFish@comcast.net and Melniknote@aol.com.

The Carneros vineyards of Silverado—a typical vista in Wine Country. Courtesy Silverado

INTRODUCTION

This book is for tourists and natives alike who not only appreciate opinionated authors such as us, but also welcome our advice. We feel strongly that we want you to spend your time wisely: You shouldn't be wasting your time on tourist traps or even second-rate restaurants. After all, your time in Wine Country is precious, prime time.

Putting together the eighth edition of *The Napa and Sonoma Book* was quite a challenge. How do you improve a book that has already been called the best Wine Country guide by the *New York Times*, the *Los Angeles Times*, *Wine & Spirits*, *San Francisco* magazine, the *Orange County Register*, and the *California Grapevine*? But we gave it a shot and believe you'll be pleased with the results.

One thing hasn't changed since the first edition, of course. Napa and Sonoma counties are remarkable places. After a few days of sampling the cabernet sauvignons, zinfandels, and chardonnays, you may never go home. But as you read this book, you'll see that there's far more to Napa and Sonoma than wine. We're continually amazed at the beauty of this place. Merely driving to work remains a treat. There's a sense of mystery and strength in the surrounding mountains. The vineyards and fields take on a vibrant yellow in the spring as the wild mustard arrives with the fog and rain. In the summer, the vines grow bushy and green, weighed down with grapes, and in the fall, they take on the delicate reds and yellows of autumn leaves. The hills rolling to the coast assume a shimmering green in the spring, reminding us unmistakably of Ireland. With its cliffs and pounding shore, the coastline is dramatic and jagged. It rivals even the famed Big Sur to the south.

With this great outdoors comes a whirl of recreational activities—everything from tennis to tide pooling. For those who prefer pampering to a strenuous hike among redwoods, Napa and Sonoma will indulge. Health spas soothe the body and soul. The restaurants of Wine Country insist that you can be healthy and luxuriate at the same time, marrying the best of local meats and produce with just the right wine. The inns and bed-and-breakfasts appeal to every style, from easy country pleasure to posh extravagance.

How can you possibly know where to begin? That's where we come in. We've created a book to guide you through Wine Country with a minimum of fuss and a maximum of pleasure. We wish you a happy stay. Read on and enjoy.

—*Tim Fish and Peg Melnik, Santa Rosa, California*

The Way This Book Works

This book is divided into 10 chapters. Entries within each chapter are first divided into "Napa County" and "Sonoma County," and then each county is broken down geographically, according to the names of towns, moving generally from south to north.

Some entries include specific information—telephone numbers, addresses, business hours, and the like—organized for easy reference at the beginning of the entry. All information was checked as close to the publication date as possible. Even so, because details can change without warning, it's always wise to call ahead.

For the same reason, we have routinely avoided listing specific prices, indicating instead a range. Lodging price codes are based on a per-room rate, double occupancy during summer months. Off-season rates are often cheaper. Restaurant price ratings indicate the cost of an individual meal, including appetizer, entrée, and dessert but not cocktails, wine, tax, or tip.

Price Codes

	Lodging	Dining
Inexpensive	Up to $100	Up to $10
Moderate	$100 to $150	$10 to $22
Expensive	$150 to $250	$22 to $35
Very Expensive	More than $250	$35 or more

Credit Cards

The following abbreviations are used for credit card information.

AE: American Express   MC: MasterCard
DC: Diner's Club   D: Discover Card
CB: Carte Blanche   V: Visa

Towns in Napa and Sonoma Counties

Napa and Sonoma counties, you'll discover, resist being broken down into neat geographic areas. Easier to categorize is Napa Valley, with its strip of small towns and villages beginning in the south with the population center, the city of Napa. North from there is Yountville, a popular tourist mecca with shops and restaurants. The vineyard villages of Oakville and Rutherford come next, followed by St. Helena, with its lovely downtown storefronts. Finally, at the county's warm, northern end is the resort town of Calistoga. Sonoma County is larger and more varied. Sonoma Valley, narrow and somewhat separate, is home to the historical city of Sonoma and the vineyard communities of Kenwood and Glen Ellen. In south-central Sonoma County is the river town of Petaluma, bordered on the north by the village of Cotati and the ever growing bedroom community of Rohnert Park. Santa Rosa is Sonoma County's largest city as well as its business and cultural hub. To the north, surrounded by vineyards, is the chic country town of Healdsburg. The town of Sebastopol is in the region known as West County, which has a personality of its own. Its wild terrain makes it part "rugged individualist," but its popularity as an immigration spot for San Francisco's counterculturalists during the 1960s makes it part "earth child" as well.

The first public tour of Beringer Vineyards in 1934. Courtesy Beringer Vineyards

1

HISTORY

Wine Country Chronicles

History repeats itself; that's the one thing that's wrong with history.

—*Clarence Darrow*

Why was it, back in school, that the worst, most monotonous teachers taught history? It didn't take long before all those dates and wars and proclamations made your brain glaze over like an Easter ham. Well, that kind of history won't repeat itself here. It helps, of course, that Napa and Sonoma counties have a lively past, busy with fascinating people and places—and, yes, dates and wars and proclamations, too. From the thunderous tremors that raised the land out of a prehistoric sea to the chic winery life of today, Napa and Sonoma counties have been twins—fraternal, rather than identical. They share similar origins but have grown into distinctly different siblings.

NATURAL HISTORY

A vast inland sea once spanned Napa and Sonoma counties, the salt water nourishing the soil over the millennia. The Mayacamas Mountains as well as coastal and other mountain ranges attest to the land's violent origins. Continental plates have fought for elbow room here for millions of years, colliding and complaining, creating a tectonic furnace of magma and spewing forth volcanoes and towering mountain spines that now divide and surround the two counties.

The rolling hills of the Carneros mark the southern borders, where Napa and Sonoma counties meet San Pablo Bay. Between them looms the Mayacamas range with the peaks of Mount Veeder and Diamond Mountain. Low coastal hills border Sonoma to the west, and the Blue Ridge shoulders Napa to the east. On the northern edge begins a vast stair of ranges that lead to the California border and beyond.

At 4,344 feet, Mount St. Helena is the area's tallest remnant of the volcanic era. Magma still simmers below the hills, producing the area's powerful geysers and Calistoga's soothing mineral water. Other vivid reminders occur on occasion: earthquakes. The San Andreas Fault runs up the center of Bodega Head on the coast, and the more timid Rodger's Creek Fault sits beneath Santa Rosa and Healdsburg.

When the ancient sea receded, it left bays and lagoons that became fertile valleys. The Napa and Russian rivers formed and for eons roamed back and forth over the face of the Napa and Santa Rosa plains, mixing the soil and volcanic ash. Napa Valley, 5 miles wide and

In the early 1900s, beer hops were big business in Sonoma County, and hop kilns were abundant.

Courtesy Sonoma County Museum

40 miles long, lies east of the Mayacamas. The land to the west was vaster, with dozens of smaller valleys: the largest and most temperate Sonoma, the parched Alexander and Dry Creek valleys to the north, and near the ocean the lush Russian River Valley, where redwoods the width of two-car garages began to grow. All the while, the Pacific Ocean pounded western Sonoma, even today eroding its jagged coastline.

It's hard to imagine a land more made to order for wine. The soil is rich with minerals from ancient oceans and volcanic ash, and the rocky nature of the land creates excellent drainage. Cool air masses from the Pacific meet the dry desert air from the east, creating a unique climate. Fog chills the mornings, then burns off as the days turn ideally warm; as the sun sets, the crisp air returns. And perhaps most important: rain falls. Typically, Napa and Sonoma counties are drenched December through April; then things dry up until November. All in all, it's a perfect spot for wine.

As humans were entering stage right, Napa and Sonoma counties already pulsed with life. Cougars, lynx, rattlesnakes, wolves, elk, and deer roamed, along with the mightiest of all, grizzly bears. Hawks, buzzards, and eagles glided above the hillsides. Sturgeon and salmon swarmed in the rivers, and along the coast whales, otters, and sea lions prospered and the great white shark lurked. Many of these have survived the arrival of man, though in reduced numbers. Others were not so lucky.

SOCIAL HISTORY

First Inhabitants

Brave the occasionally harrowing California freeway system, and you'll inevitably see this bumper sticker: California native. How natives do moan about newcomers! It's rather silly, of course, because people are such a recent addition to northern California—five thousand years, in the big scheme of things, is hardly enough time to unpack.

The earliest "newcomers" crossed the land bridge that once connected Asia and Alaska, then wandered south. The first known inhabitants were the Pomo and Miwok tribes in Sonoma and the Wappo, who lived in Napa Valley and eastern Sonoma County. It was a plentiful place and allowed an unhurried way of life, the men hunting and the women gathering berries, mussels, and other food. They assembled near the streams when the salmon returned but were careful because the grizzly bears attracted by the salmon had a taste for human flesh, as well. Communities thrived. Most were small, but some villages had populations of one thousand or more. The coastal Miwok used shells as money, and Pomo women achieved great expertise as basket makers. Pomo men lived away from their wives in communal lodges, which also served as ceremonial sweat houses as well as impromptu schools for boys. These early inhabitants gave special names to this land of theirs, names that remain today. Not that historians agree particularly on what the words mean. Mayacamas is a Spanish adaptation of a Native American word that meant "howl of the mountain lion." Napa, depending on which story you believe, is Wappo for "grizzly bear," "fish," or "bountiful place." Petaluma, a city in southern Sonoma County, may be Pomo for "flat back" or Miwok for "behind the hill"—both referring to the Sonoma Mountains and the flat Petaluma plain. Cotati, another Sonoma County city, sounds poetic, but its possible Pomo meaning is anything but: "punch in the face." One name that didn't stick was Shabakai, or "long snake"—that's what Natives called the Russian River.

The first European arrivals were heavily outnumbered. As many as twelve thousand Wappo lived between Napa and Clear Lake to the north, and eight thousand Pomo prospered in what are now Sonoma, Lake, and Mendocino counties. That would quickly change.

Sonoma County was the first to be explored by the white man, and as explorers often seem to do, they stumbled onto it by accident. Lieutenant Francisco de Bodega y Cuadra was piloting his Spanish ship, the *Sonora,* along the coast in search of San Francisco Bay. Startled Indians paddled out in canoes to greet the *Sonora,* presenting the crew with elaborate feather and shell offerings. Rough seas and a damaged skiff prevented Bodega y Cuadra and crew from actually coming ashore, but the lieutenant's name nonetheless stuck: Bodega Bay. The first expedition actually to land in Sonoma County came the following year, when a small party of Spanish set out from their presidio, or military outpost, in San Francisco. Crossing the bay, they entered the mouth of the Petaluma River with the crazy notion that it ended up in Tomales Bay and the vast Pacific. (Always looking for shortcuts, those explorers.) It didn't, of course, so Lieutenant Fernando Quiros and his crew explored the Petaluma plain, instead.

Russians, however, not the Spanish were the first to establish an outpost in the area. By the early 1800s the Russian-American Company, a private entity supported largely by imperial Russia, was expanding south after the Alaskan fur trade began to play out. In 1809 Ivan Kuskov and crew landed in Bodega Bay and scouted the area. They returned in 1812 and established a colony they called Rumiantsev. Exploring the coastline further, Kuskov selected a blustery bluff a few miles to the north and established Fort Ross the following year. The fort became the hub of Russian activity, with Rumiantsev its major port. Though a prime location for fur trade, Fort Ross was not the most habitable place. Even today the bluffs overlooking the Pacific are fogged in much of the year, and the wind and dampness can be severe. One early visitor wrote: "It is so easy to catch cold here that even those inhabitants of Ross who were born here are sick almost every year." Later, ranches were established inland, where the climate was more moderate, and the Russians grew much-needed grain and produce for their Alaskan settlements. The slaughter of sea otters, meanwhile, was ruthless and devastating. By 1821 the annual catch had dropped from hundreds to 32.

For generations, Miwok Indian thrived along the Sonoma County coast. Courtesy Sonoma County Museum

*Immigrant Samuele Sebastiani labored from dawn to dusk quarrying cobblestones, eventually saving up
enough money to buy the vineyard and winery that still bear his name.* Courtesy Sebastiani

This Land Is Whose Land?

The Spanish weren't keen on the Russians hanging around just to the north. They were
determined that their presidio in San Francisco would be the dominant force in the area.
Even Mexico declaring independence from Spain in 1822 didn't lessen the importance of
the land north of San Francisco. California had been explored and established largely
through the mission system, which began in 1769 as a way to civilize the "heathen" Natives
and convert them to Catholicism. It was also a way to establish a Spanish presence and, if
the mission was successful, add greatly to the wealth and power of the church.

In 1823 Father José Altimira, an ambitious young priest at San Francisco's Mission
Dolores, became convinced that a new mission was needed in the northern territory. But
church authorities—cautiously considering their waning influence with the new Mexican
government balked, so Altimira turned to the Mexican governor of California, don Luis
Arguello. Seeing an opportunity to thwart the Russians, Arguello approved the idea.
Altimira set out that year with a party of 14 soldiers to explore the land north of the bay,
from Petaluma to Napa to Suisun. According to legend, he marked his path by sowing
mustard seed, which today blooms bright yellow every spring. Altimira was most
impressed by Sonoma Valley, with its mild climate and tall trees.

On July 7, 1823, with a makeshift redwood cross, Altimira blessed the mission site in
what is now the city of Sonoma, and the Mission San Francisco Solano was established. It
was California's last mission and the only one established under Mexican rule. In the early
years the mission was a great success, and despite having the reputation of being a harsh
taskmaster, Altimira converted more than seven hundred Native Americans. In the fall of
1826, Native laborers had just brought in a bountiful harvest when they staged a violent
uprising. The mission was partially burned, and Father Altimira fled for his life. He was
replaced and the mission was rebuilt, and in 1834 it was at the height of its prosperity

when the Mexican Congress secularized the mission system and returned the acquired wealth to the people. It was the beginning of a new era.

Lieutenant Mariano Guadelupe Vallejo was an enterprising 28-year-old officer given the opportunity of a lifetime. The Mexican government sent him to Sonoma to replace the padres and also to establish a presidio and thereby thwart Russian expansion. Vallejo's ambitions were far greater than even that; he soon became one of the most powerful and wealthy men in California. As commandant general, Vallejo ruled the territory north of San Francisco and eventually set aside more than 100,000 acres for himself. He laid out the town of Sonoma around an 8-acre plaza—the largest in California—and for himself built the imposing Petaluma Adobe in 1836. It was the largest adobe structure in northern California and the first crop-producing rancho in the area.

Vallejo pushed for the settlement of Napa and Sonoma counties, and he found an ally in frontiersman George Yount. Others had been exploring Napa Valley since 1831, but Yount was the first to explore with the notion of settlement. Befriending the already powerful Vallejo, Yount requested a land grant. Vallejo consented—but only after Yount converted to Catholicism and became a naturalized Mexican citizen. (Zoning laws were really tough then.) Yount never became an upstanding Catholic, but he did establish the 11,814-acre Rancho Caymus in 1836, now the Yountville area of central Napa County. About that same time, Vallejo was giving Sonoma land grants to family members, who established the rancho predecessors of Santa Rosa, Kenwood, and Healdsburg. Mexican influence continued to expand, particularly after 1839, when the Russians, having wiped out the otter population, gave up and sold Fort Ross.

Otters weren't the only inhabitants facing annihilation. Indian uprisings were not uncommon, and Yount's house in Napa Valley was half home, half fortress. Occasionally, Vallejo led campaigns against rebellious Indians, but perhaps the most devastating blow came in 1837 when a Mexican corporal inadvertently brought smallpox to Sonoma Valley. This white man's disease all but wiped out Sonoma County's Native population.

Bear Flag Revolt

Throughout the 1830s and early 1840s, American settlers streamed into California, lured by stories of free land. Mexican rule, however, denied Americans land ownership, and this led to confrontations. Tensions peaked in 1846, when rumors spread that Mexico was about to order all Americans out of California. At dawn on June 14, some 30 armed horsemen from Sacramento and Napa valleys rode into Sonoma. So began the Bear Flag Revolt, 25 eventful days when Sonoma was the capital of the independent Republic of California. Though significant, it was a revolution of almost comic proportions. Few soldiers still guarded the Sonoma outpost when the riders arrived, and the insurrectionists captured Sonoma without a single shot. Vallejo was roused from his bed and tied to a chair. One story has it that he tried sly negotiations with the rebels, freely offering the leaders his brandy and getting them drunk. Whether that's truth or folklore, the rebels prevailed. By noon, William Ide was elected leader of the new republic, and a makeshift flag was hoisted to the top of a pole in the plaza. Saddle maker Ben Dewel crafted this flag for the new government, using a grizzly bear as the chief symbol. (Some said it looked more like a prized pig, rather than a bear.) The Bear Flag Republic had a short reign. In July, an American navy vessel captured the Mexican stronghold of Monterey and claimed California for itself. The Bear Flag boys immediately threw in with the Americans, and four years later, in 1850, California became a state. Eventually, in 1911, the Bear Flag was adopted as the state flag.

The 1840s and 1850s were formative years for Napa and Sonoma counties. The Gold Rush of 1848 sent Americans by the thousands into the Sierras. Once-powerful Sonoma almost became a ghost town as residents left to pan gold and San Francisco achieved new significance. Other towns were born of miner commerce, such as the river ports of Napa and Petaluma.

A First Glass of Wine

During this time, California's wine industry was conceived. Oats and wheat had been the primary crops of Napa and Sonoma counties, and sheep and cattle were also dominant.

Vallejo and Yount grew the crude mission grapes brought north by the priests for sacramental wine, but it wasn't until 1856, when a Hungarian aristocrat named Agoston Haraszthy arrived in Sonoma, that the idea of a wine industry first took root. Haraszthy had attempted vineyards in San Diego and San Mateo and immediately recognized potential in the soil and climate of Sonoma and Napa valleys. Purchasing land and a winery northeast of the plaza, Haraszthy established Buena Vista—"beautiful view."

By 1858 Haraszthy had already surpassed Vallejo's accomplishments as a winemaker and even inspired a German apprentice named Charles Krug, who founded Napa Valley's first winery in 1861. That same year, convinced that the mission grape wasn't the only variety that would thrive in California, Haraszthy toured the wine regions of Europe and returned with cuttings from three hundred classic varieties. It was his experimentations with these grapes that brought Haraszthy fame and earned him the title Father of the California Wine Industry. Wineries began to spring up throughout Napa and Sonoma counties, the beginnings of wine dynasties such as Beringer and Inglenook that still live today.

The later part of the century was a boom period. Between 1850 and 1860 Napa County's population grew from 400 to almost 5,000. By 1869 Sonoma County's residents numbered 19,000. Petaluma, its largest city, was on its way to becoming the egg capital of the world. The burgeoning city of Santa Rosa had snatched the county seat from Sonoma in 1854, and with the completion of the San Francisco and North Pacific railroad line in 1870, its destiny as the North Bay's largest city was established. It was the era of the highwaymen, with the legendary Black Bart and others robbing stagecoaches around the North Bay. It was also

Fruit of the Vine—Who's on First

Spanish missionaries are usually credited with bringing the first wine grapes to Sonoma and Napa, but that might not really be the case. Apparently, Russian colonists at Fort Ross imported vines from Peru as early as 1817, predating the Spanish by a good seven years. But the padres made up for it in volume. Father José Altimira, founder of Mission San Francisco Solano in Sonoma, planted one thousand vines of mission grape, a rather coarse variety brought north from Mexico for sacramental wine.

Napa's first vineyard was planted in 1838 by Napa's first white settler, George Yount. He brought mission vines east from Sonoma and made wine for his own use. It didn't take long before the entrepreneurial spirit set in, and General Mariano Vallejo of Sonoma was the first to succumb. Vallejo became California's first commercial winemaker in 1841, eventually planting seventy thousand vines. His wine sold under the name Lachryma Montis, or "tears of the mountain," and became the toast of San Francisco. The winery was hardly a chic shop; his cellar, press, and sales outlet were housed in an army barracks. As for a tasting room . . .

an era of genius. Calling the area a "chosen spot," horticulturist Luther Burbank created varieties of fruit trees that brought the curious from around the country. And it was a time of pleasure—the resort town of Calistoga, founded by California's first millionaire, Sam Brannan, had become a vacation mecca—as well as a time of creativity—Robert Louis Stevenson was inspired by a stay in Napa Valley and called its wine "bottled poetry."

The wine industry was small but growing in the late 1800s, though it shared the land with other important crops: hops, timber, and apples in Sonoma and wheat in Napa. Winemaking and drinking in those days were anything but the chic activities they are today. Wine was sold almost exclusively in bulk and often wasn't even blended until it reached its selling point. It was vended from barrels in saloons and stores, with customers usually bringing their own containers. Gustave Niebaum of Inglenook and the old Fountaingrove Winery in Santa Rosa were among the first to bottle their own wines. Niebaum was also the first to use vintage dates on his wine and promote "Napa Valley" on his labels.

Winemaking received two blows late in the century: the depression of the 1870s and the aphid phylloxera. The wine industry somehow weathered the economic hard times, though people like Haraszthy were not so lucky. His winery failed, and business setbacks forced him to pursue dealings in Central America, where he met his death—accounts say he was devoured by an alligator while crossing a Nicaraguan river.

As for phylloxera, it attacked the vineyards of Napa and Sonoma counties with equal fervor. A voracious microscopic aphid that infests vine roots, phylloxera first appeared in Europe in the 1860s, devastating the vineyards of Chateau Margaux, Chateau Lafite, and others. Only by grafting their vines to American rootstock were the Europeans able to save their classic wines. While the European wine industry recovered, California wine began to receive its first world notice. Sonoma County—not Napa—had been the undisputed capital of California wine, but fate and phylloxera would change all that. Phylloxera surfaced first in Sonoma Valley in 1875, and it spread slowly north to the Russian River. By 1889, Sonoma County's vineyards were in ruin when the French invited American wines to compete in the World's Fair. Napa Valley's wines scored well, raising Napa from obscurity to fame. The crown had been snatched by the time phylloxera finally invaded Napa. Growers tried everything to kill the bug, from chemicals to flooding their fields, but nothing worked. Eventually, most were forced to pull out their vines. Some planted again, using resistant stock. Others gave up and planted fruit trees.

Not long after that, just after the turn of the 20th century, famed writer Jack London began buying property in Glen Ellen. Saying he was tired of cities and people, he retired to the mountain retreat he called Beauty Ranch, becoming the first of a long line of celebrities drawn to life in Wine Country.

A Complaint from Mother Nature

A new century brought new tragedy. Downtown Calistoga was leveled by a fire in 1901, and on April 18, 1906, what became known as the San Francisco Earthquake equally devastated Sonoma County, particularly Santa Rosa. Built on the loose foundation between two creek beds, Santa Rosa shimmied like gelatin. The earthquake laid waste to the downtown area and killed one hundred people. (It didn't help that the brick buildings were poorly constructed.) Three large downtown hotels, one reporter wrote, "fell as if constructed of playing cards." It would be years before Calistoga and Santa Rosa recovered, and San Francisco, of course, took a beating, but a fact not often reported was the impact that

The old bottling line at Buena Vista Winery. Courtesy Buena
Vista Winery

terrible event had on the California wine business. Many of the wineries stored their wine in the cooler climate of San Francisco, and the quake destroyed almost two thirds of the state's wine supply.

The castlelike wineries of Napa County—Greystone Cellars, Beringer, Inglenook, and the others that harked back to the grandeur of Bordeaux— were spared the earthquake. But looming even more dangerously on the horizon of the wine industry was something called Prohibition.

Prohibition had been a growing movement in the United States since the turn of the century, and by 1917, a majority of states had outlawed alcohol. The United States Congress cinched it with the Volstead Act, and on January 1, 1920, Prohibition began. In Sonoma County alone it left three million useless gallons of wine aging in vats. Sebastiani in Sonoma, Beaulieu in Rutherford, and a handful of other wineries survived by making religious wine and medicinal spirits. But most wineries closed—almost 200 alone in Sonoma County and more than 120 in Napa Valley. By the time Prohibition was repealed in 1933, the Great Depression was on, followed by World War II. Recovery of the wine industry took time.

A Resurgence

In 1937 the opening of a single bridge would forever change Sonoma County. It wasn't just any bridge, mind you, but the Golden Gate, spanning the mouth of San Francisco Bay. Sonoma County became part of a thoroughfare in California's major north–south corridor, the Redwood Highway. And Sonoma County became its own destination—for example, the Russian River area, already a popular resort spot for San Franciscans, boomed.

After World War II, the vineyards of Europe were once again devastated, and with the flow from Europe cut off, America turned to its own wine. The end of the war started the slow rebirth of the wine industry, and Napa and Sonoma began prospering in the 1950s and 1960s. By the early 1970s, a small tourist industry began forming around the wineries: Tourists were drawn to free wine tastings; restaurants and hotels began to appear. When corporations began eyeing the family-owned wineries, there was no question that Napa and Sonoma were ripe with potential and profit. Inglenook was the first to go corporate when United Vintners bought it in 1964; Beaulieu and others followed. In Napa Valley, new wineries began opening; some were small operations—called "boutiques" in industry lingo—others were more dramatic, such as Sterling, a towering, white villa perched on a hill south of Calistoga. Brash young winemakers such as Robert Mondavi promoted California wine like no one had in the past. By the 1970s even the French—who so often had turned up their noses at California wine—saw California's potential, particularly for sparkling wine. Moët Hennessy was the first to arrive, building Domaine Chandon in Yountville in 1975. Others followed.

Napa and Sonoma counties also became a favorite location for filmmakers. Alfred Hitchcock immortalized Bodega Bay in *The Birds;* thousands still stop each year for a photo of one of Sonoma County's most recognizable landmarks, the Bodega School House. Later, wine life at its most ruthless was portrayed in TV's *Falcon Crest*, which used Spring Mountain Vineyards in St. Helena as a backdrop.

Wine Country's greatest achievement and the final turning point for Napa and Sonoma came in 1976. At the now infamous Paris tasting (see the sidebar), French wine experts for the first time picked several California wines over the classic wines of Bordeaux and Burgundy in a blind tasting. History was made, and Napa and Sonoma counties' prominence in the world of wine was set.

Today Napa and Sonoma counties continue to grow, much to the chagrin of long-standing residents. The California Travel and Tourism Commission's most recent study reported 3.5 million people travel to Napa County, and seven million visit Sonoma County yearly, drawn increasingly by wine, landscape, and climate. Santa Rosa is a small but blossoming metropolis of suburbs. Highway 29, the main road through Napa Valley, pulses with activity. How different it is from the days of grizzly bears and the Wappo Natives. Yet Napa and Sonoma remain strikingly beautiful places.

Upstaging the French

California and French wine lovers have a long-standing love-hate relationship—California loves French wine and France hates California's. We exaggerate—but only somewhat. California winemakers have always aspired to the quality and reputation of Bordeaux and Burgundy wines, while French enthusiasts ignored the wines of California. That is, until May 24, 1976.

It began with British wine merchant Stephen Spurrier, who had a taste for California wine but had a difficult time convincing his English and European customers. Spurrier hit on the idea of staging a blind tasting of California and French wines, using the nine greatest palates of France. It was unheard of. California had beaten French wines in past tastings, but the judges were always American, and what did they know?

The French judges were aware that they were sampling both French and American wines, though the bottles were masked. As the tasting progressed, the tasters began pointing out the wines they believed were from California, and their comments about them grew increasingly patronizing. When the sacks were removed from the bottles, however, the judges were mortified: The wines they thought were classic Bordeaux or Burgundy were in reality from California. Six of the 11 highest-rated wines were, in fact, from California—almost entirely from Napa. The 1973 Stag's Leap cabernet beat 1970 vintages of Chateau Mouton-Rothschild and Chateau Haut-Brion, and a 1973 Chateau Montelena bested Burgundy's finest whites. France contested the findings, of course, but it was too late. California, particularly Napa, had earned its place on the international wine map.

The opening of the Golden Gate Bridge in 1937 made Napa and Sonoma counties easily accessible to and from San Francisco.

Courtesy Sonoma County Museum

2

TRANSPORTATION
Getting There

Gridlock is not the rarity it used to be in Wine Country, so it pays to know your way around. Highways 101 and 29, the main thoroughfares through Napa and Sonoma counties, are always hectic, especially on weekends. In addition, the terrain conspires against smooth travel—any approach requires a minor mountain expedition.

Perhaps that's why in the late 1700s the earliest explorers came by water. The Sonoma coast was the area's first highway marker, and as sailing ships from around the globe made for the New World, the Napa and Petaluma rivers, which connect with San Pablo Bay, allowed early settlers a fast way inland.

By the mid-1800s, trails from the Central Valley took travelers along Clear Lake to Bodega Bay as well as south and east along the bay to Benicia. Carts and stagecoaches brought folks along primitive roads, stirring up dust in the summer and churning up mud in the winter. By the 1860s, steamships were chugging up and down the Napa and Petaluma rivers, but soon railroads steamed onto the scene, with names like Southern Pacific and San Francisco North Pacific, connecting the towns of the two budding counties to the East Bay.

The automobile changed everything, for better and for worse. Sonoma County remained somewhat innocently isolated from San Francisco—it's a long loop around that bay—until the big day in May 1937, when the Golden Gate Bridge opened a speedier route north, and Napa and Sonoma counties became one of the travel destinations for San Francisco and for the world. Today, in fact, 50 percent of the people who visit Wine Country each year originate their getaway in San Francisco.

There are numerous ways to get to and get around Wine Country. Let us be your guide.

GETTING TO NAPA & SONOMA

By Air
Air travelers bound for Wine Country can arrive at and depart from one of three major airports handling numerous domestic and international airlines, and there's also a regional airport serving the area.

San Francisco International (SFO), Oakland International (OAK), and **Sacramento Metropolitan (SMF)** are all within easy driving distance of Napa and Sonoma counties. **Charles M. Schulz Sonoma County Airport** is a regional airport located just a few miles northwest of Santa Rosa: 707-546-7740. It's home to **Horizon Air**, which makes two daily flights to **LAX** in **Los Angeles** and a daily flight to Seattle/Tacoma. The regional airport is named after the famed cartoonist of the *Peanuts* comic strip, who lived and worked in Santa Rosa for more than 30 years.

Napa & Sonoma Access

Approximate mileage and times by car between towns and cities:

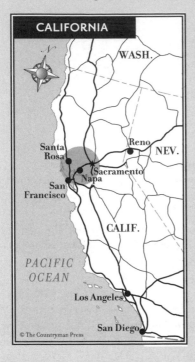

Napa County	Time	Miles
Napa (the city) to:		
Calistoga	30 min.	25
Eureka	4 hr.	255
Los Angeles	8 hr.	439
Oakland	I hr.	46
Reno	3.5 hr.	200
Rutherford	10 min.	II
Sacramento	I hr.	61
St. Helena	20 min.	18
San Francisco	I hr.	56
San Diego	II hr.	600
Santa Rosa	I hr.	36
Sonoma	15 min.	12
Yountville	10 min.	8

Sonoma County	Time	Miles
Santa Rosa to:		
Bodega Bay	45 min.	22
Eureka	4 hr.	219
Geyserville	25 min.	21
Healdsburg	15 min.	15
Jenner	45 min.	32
Los Angeles	8 hr.	431
Oakland	I hr.	60
Petaluma	20 min.	16
Reno	4 hr.	229
Sacramento	2 hr.	97
San Francisco	I hr.	56
San Diego	II hr.	600

Within Wine Country

Moving north or south in Napa and Sonoma counties is easy going. Highway 29, Napa Valley's main street, cuts a long and straight path from the San Pablo Bay north to Lake County. Most of Napa's wineries are along this two-lane road, so traffic can back up. Silverado Trail to the east is a quieter two-lane, though it has its share of wineries, as well. In Sonoma County, Highway 101 will take you north and south at interstate speeds. Moving between Napa and Sonoma generally takes more patience. Highway 12 offers the smoothest path, although it has its own winding hills. The Oakville Grade/ Trinity Road is a roller coaster around Mount Veeder that offers some of the best views of both counties. Petrified Forest and Spring Mountain roads scale the northern Mayacamas Mountains and, at the top, merge with Calistoga Road from Santa Rosa. Low gear on these roads is a good idea. Weather is never a problem. It rarely snows in Wine Country, and when it does it melts quickly, even in the highest elevations.

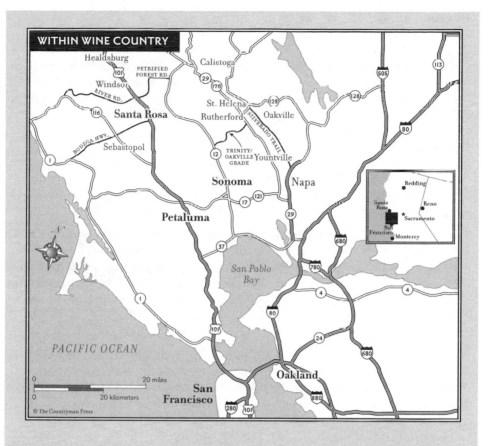

WITHIN WINE COUNTRY

From the north: Travelers from the north can reach Wine Country via two major roadways. Highway 101 brings visitors into the heart of Sonoma County. If Napa Valley is your destination, take the Highway 128 east exit at Geyserville; it's a beautiful route, a two-lane road that leads you right into Calistoga.

If you're arriving via Interstate 5 (I-5), connect with Interstate 505 (I-505) near Sacramento. For a scenic route or if upper Napa Valley is your destination, exit at Highway 128 in Winters. Follow it west along beautiful Howell Mountain. If you're in a hurry or Sonoma County is where you're headed, from I-505 connect with Interstate 80 (I-80) West; then take the Highway 12 exit, which leads to the cities of Napa and Sonoma.

From the south: Like visitors from the north, drivers arriving from Southern California can choose between Highway 101 and I-5. Traveling 101 brings you through the heart of San Francisco. Stay alert—101 empties onto the streets of the city and can be a bit confusing. Continue across the Golden Gate Bridge through Marin County and into central Sonoma County. To reach the city of Sonoma or Napa Valley, exit on Highway 37 in Novato, and connect with Highway 121. From I-5, connect with I-580, and continue into downtown Oakland. There, connect with eastbound I-80. Exit on Highway 12, which leads to the cities of Napa and Sonoma.

From the east: Wine Country is an easy jaunt from Sacramento or Reno. From I-80, connect with Highway 12. Take it west to Napa and then on to Sonoma Valley.

By Car

Although planes and trains will bring you to the threshold of Wine Country, a car is a necessity in Wine Country proper. Public transportation is limited, and the landscape is so vast that you'll need your own wheels. Traffic is common on Saturday and Sunday and during peak summer months, so an ambitious itinerary can be cut short by the weekend tourist crush. If you're close enough to drive to Wine Country, see the sidebar on pages 26–27 for information on finding Napa and Sonoma counties.

Renting a Car

Because a car is almost a requirement in Wine Country, visitors arriving by air inevitably rent a vehicle. Most major rental companies, of course, work out of the metro airports, and they're typically helpful in plotting routes and will often supply drivers with basic maps to reach their destinations. Just in case, here are a few directions:

San Francisco International Airport: To find your way to Wine Country from the Bay Area's largest airport, take Highway 101 north into San Francisco. The highway empties onto the streets, so watch the signs carefully. Continue through the city across the Golden Gate Bridge, and you'll soon find yourself in central Sonoma County. To reach the town of Sonoma or the Napa Valley, take Highway 37 in Novato, and connect with Highway 121.
　　Miles: 72 to central Sonoma County; 82 to Napa Valley.
　　Time: 90 minutes.

Oakland International Airport: To reach Napa County and the city of Sonoma, take I-80 north through Oakland, and connect with Highway 29 north. For Napa, stay on Highway 29, and for the city of Sonoma, take Highway 12/121. To reach central Sonoma County, take I-80 north through Oakland, exit on I-580, and then connect with Highway 101 north, which takes you into the heart of Sonoma County.
　　Miles: 82 to central Sonoma County; 46 to Napa Valley.
　　Time: 1 hour to Sonoma; 45 minutes to Napa.

Sacramento Metropolitan Airport: Take I-5 south, and connect with the I-80 west bypass. Follow the signs to San Francisco. Take Highway 12 to Napa, continuing west to the cities of Sonoma and Santa Rosa.
　　Miles: 61 to Napa; 97 to central Sonoma County.
　　Time: 90 minutes to Napa; 2 to 2.5 hours to central Sonoma County.

You can also rent a car after arriving in Napa and Sonoma counties. Local information and reservation numbers are listed below. Reservations up to a week in advance are recommended.

NAPA COUNTY
Budget Rent-A-Car (707-224-7845)
Enterprise Rent-A-Car (707-253-8000)
Hertz (800-654-3131)

SONOMA COUNTY
Avis (800-331-1212)
Budget Rent-A-Car (800-527-0700)
Enterprise Rent-A-Car (800-325-8007)
Hertz (707-528-0834 or 800-654-3131)

Airport Shuttle

Here's an alternative to renting a car at the airport: Reasonably priced express shuttle buses and vans operate to and from the San Francisco and Oakland airports. These comfortable vehicles operate 16 to 20 hours a day, seven days a week. Shuttles depart from airports about every one to two hours, depending on the operator, and deliver passengers to selected drop-off points in Wine Country.

One-way fares (cash only) range from $18 to $35, depending on the operator, the drop-off point, and any excess luggage requirements. Reservations are not usually required, but on weekends and in peak seasons buses fill up, and you may be forced to stand in the aisle. Schedules fluctuate, so it's smart to reserve shuttle services in advance.

Airport Express, SFO to Santa Rosa (707-837-8700, 800-327-2024)
Evans Airport Service, SFO and OAK (Oakland) to Napa (707-255-1559, 707-944-2025, 800-294-6386)
Sonoma Airporter, SFO to the town of Sonoma (707-938-4246)

By Bus

Greyhound bus service to Sonoma and Napa counties is very limited. It's also possible to ride Greyhound to San Francisco, and then make connections on Golden Gate Transit to reach Wine Country. A travel agent will have the most up-to-date information on Greyhound schedules and connections.

Greyhound in San Francisco (415-495-1569)
Golden Gate Transit (415-923-2000, 707-541-2000) For travel between San Francisco and Sonoma County; one-way fare from San Francisco to Santa Rosa is $7.25.

Once inside Wine Country, public bus service is available through **Sonoma County Transit** and **Napa Valley Transit.** This method of travel could be indispensable for the Wine Country visitor on a tight budget. One drawback: Bus stops, which can be few and far between, are usually not close to wineries and other tourist attractions.

One-way fares average between $1 and $2.50, and weekend service is limited. If buses will be your primary form of transportation, it may be essential to gather the most current timetables and route maps, which are updated frequently. The cities of Santa Rosa, Napa, Healdsburg, and Petaluma also offer bus service within their city boundaries.

Napa County

The V.I.N.E. (800-696-6443, 707-255-7631) The Napa city bus travels mainly along Highway 29 between Calistoga and Vallejo, with bus and ferry connections to and from San Francisco.
VineGo (707-252-2600) Offers limited service between most Napa Valley towns.

Sonoma County

Sonoma County Transit (707-576-7433, 800-345-7433) For travel within Sonoma County.
Santa Rosa Transit (707-543-3333) City bus.
Petaluma Transit (707-778-4460) City bus.
Healdsburg In-City Transit (707-431-3324) City bus.

By Train

Amtrak's westbound *California Zephyr* and north-to-south *Coastal Starlight* trains drop off Napa County-bound passengers in the city of Martinez, about 40 miles south of Napa. Amtrak has continuing ground transportation that delivers passengers directly to Napa but not Sonoma.

For **Amtrak** information and reservations, call 800-872-7245 or check their Web site at www.amtrak.com. It's advisable to consult a travel agent for assistance in booking Amtrak, 1151 Pearl St., Napa.

Just for the record, the **Napa Valley Wine Train** is actually a gourmet restaurant on rails and not a true form of transportation. (For details, see chapter 7, Recreation.)

By Limousine

The ultimate in personal transportation is the limousine, and for many visitors to Wine Country, chauffeured travel goes hand in hand with wine tasting. For others, the pricey, three-hour ride to the Sonoma coast can be a romantic and unforgettable luxury.

Both Napa Valley and Sonoma County have an abundance of professional limousine services that will map out wine-tasting itineraries for the novice or deliver connoisseurs to wineries of their choosing. Most also offer daylong, fixed-rate touring packages with extras, such as gourmet picnic lunches or evening dining, included in the price. Per-hour rates range from $45 to $165, depending on the limo and the tour. That doesn't include taxes, driver gratuities, parking fees, or bridge tolls. A three- or four-hour minimum is standard, and complimentary champagne is often served. Reservations are required at least two or three days in advance and as much as a week in advance during peak vacationing months. Some recommend booking at least a month ahead of time.

For your added safety, the limousine service you engage should be both licensed and insured. Ask your hotel concierge to recommend a service or talk to your travel agent. Listed below are some of Wine Country's most popular limousine services. Companies may be based in one county, but they frequently take passengers all over Wine Country and beyond.

NAPA COUNTY
Antique Tours (707-226-9227)
Evans Inc. (707-255-1559)
Executive Limousine (707-257-2949)

SONOMA COUNTY
California Wine Tours (800-294-6386)
Style N Comfort (707-838-3900, 800-ITS-LIMO)
Celebrity Star Limousine (707-542-5466)
Pure Luxury Limousine Service (707-795-1615)

By Taxi

When buses are too inconvenient and limousines too expensive, call for an old standby: a taxicab. The cab companies below are on duty 24 hours a day, seven days a week. Per-mile fares average $3.

NAPA COUNTY
Napa Valley Cab (707-257-6444)
Black Tie Taxi (707-259-1000)
1-800 Taxi Cab (707-257-6444)
Yellow Cab Napa (707-226-3731)

SONOMA COUNTY
Bill's Taxi Service (707-869-2177)
Vern's Taxi Service (707-938-8885)
George's Taxi Yellow (707-544-4444)
Santa Rosa Taxi (707-579-1212)

NEIGHBORS ALL AROUND

To the South

The striking countryside and tony hamlets of Marin County are directly south of Wine Country. In San Rafael, just east of Highway 101, don't miss the dramatic **Marin Civic Center**, one of the last buildings designed by Frank Lloyd Wright. If you're not in a hurry, consider trekking north or south on Highway 1, the winding two-lane road that hugs the rugged coast line. It will take you by **Muir Woods**, home to some of the tallest redwoods north of the Bay, and also to the majestic **Mount Tamalpais**. Drive to its 3,000-foot summit for a spectacular view of San Francisco (clear weather permitting, that is). **Point Reyes Lighthouse** is also worth a stop along Highway 1, as are the many oyster farms near Marshall.

Farther south—just a one-hour drive from Wine Country—is one of the most intriguing, romantic, and ethnically diverse cities in America: **San Francisco**. Ride a cable car, snack on scrumptious dim sum in Chinatown, gorge on culture and shopping, or just admire the view. (See chapter 4, Culture, for more suggestions.) Across the Bay are **Oakland** and the ever-eclectic **Berkeley**, both stops worth making.

To the East

While motoring your way to Sacramento along I-80, your thoughts may turn to . . . onions. The aroma of onions and other commercially grown produce fills the air in fertile Sacramento Valley, where fruits and vegetables are tended in endless flat fields. The city of **Sacramento**, the state capital and once a major hub for rail and river transportation, is proud of its historic center: **Old Town**, a faithful re-creation of the city's original town center, with a multitude of shops, restaurants, and museums.

To the North

Not to be outdone by Napa and Sonoma counties, Mendocino County is also a major player in the game of fine wine, with several premium wineries along Highway 101 and in beautiful Anderson Valley. The coastal hamlet of **Mendocino**, one of Hollywood's favorite movie locations, is also a treasure trove for shoppers. Its art galleries, antiques shops, and fine dining, and its New England-like atmosphere make it a popular second destination for Wine Country visitors.

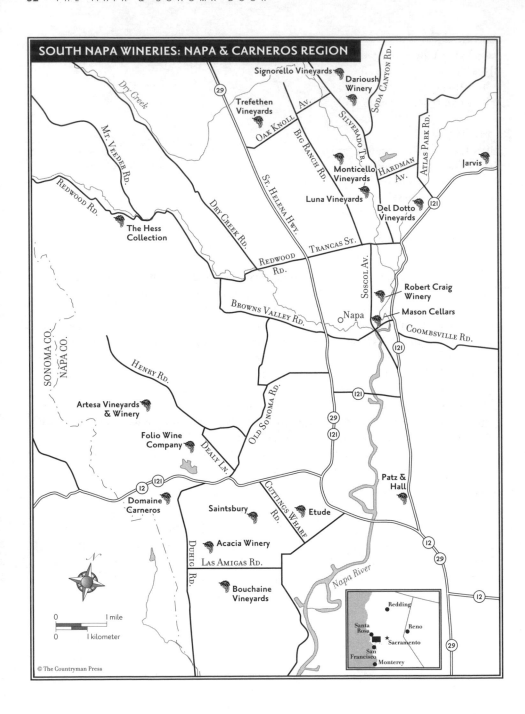

SOUTH NAPA WINERIES: NAPA & CARNEROS REGION

Dry Creek

Mt. Veeder Rd.

Signorello Vineyards

Darioush Winery

Soda Canyon Rd.

Trefethen Vineyards

Oak Knoll Av.

Silverado Tr.

Atlas Park Rd.

Redwood Rd.

Dry Creek Rd.

St. Helena Hwy

Big Ranch Rd.

Monticello Vineyards

Hardman Av.

Jarvis

121

The Hess Collection

Luna Vineyards

Del Dotto Vineyards

Trancas St.

Redwood Rd.

Browns Valley Rd.

Soscol Av.

Robert Craig Winery

Napa

Mason Cellars

Coombsville Rd.

121

Sonoma Co. / Napa Co.

Henry Rd.

Old Sonoma Rd.

121

121

29

121

Artesa Vineyards & Winery

Folio Wine Company

Dealy Ln.

12   121

Patz & Hall

Domaine Carneros

Saintsbury

Cuttings Wharf Rd.

Etude

Acacia Winery

Las Amigas Rd.

Duhig Rd.

12

29

Bouchaine Vineyards

Napa River

N

0   1 mile
0   1 kilometer

Redding

Santa Rosa

Reno

Sacramento

San Francisco

Monterey

12

29

© The Countryman Press

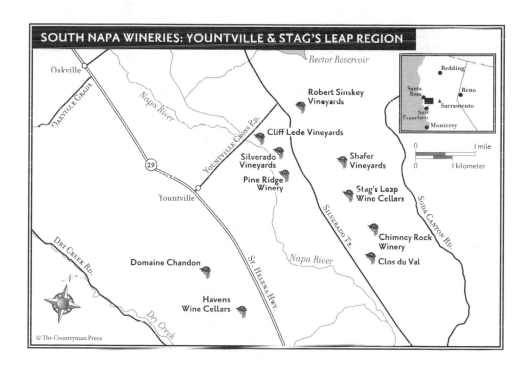

SOUTH NAPA WINERIES: YOUNTVILLE & STAG'S LEAP REGION

Oakville

Rector Reservoir

Napa River

OAKVILLE GRADE

YOUNTVILLE CROSS RD.

29

Robert Sinskey Vineyards

Cliff Lede Vineyards

Silverado Vineyards

Pine Ridge Winery

Shafer Vineyards

Stag's Leap Wine Cellars

SODA CANYON RD.

SILVERADO TR.

Yountville

Chimney Rock Winery

Clos du Val

DRY CREEK RD.

ST. HELENA HWY.

Napa River

Domaine Chandon

Havens Wine Cellars

DRY CREEK

N

Redding

Santa Rosa

Reno

Sacramento

San Francisco

Monterey

0   1 mile

0   1 kilometer

© The Countryman Press

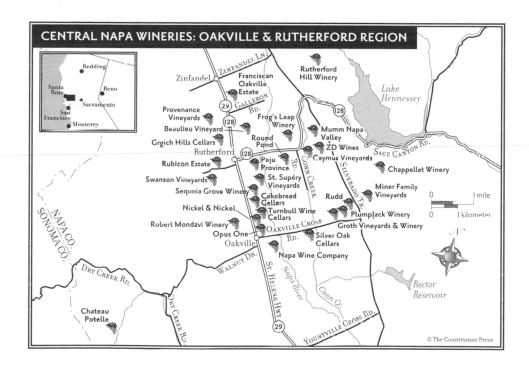

CENTRAL NAPA WINERIES: OAKVILLE & RUTHERFORD REGION

Redding

Santa Rosa

Reno

Sacramento

San Francisco

Monterey

Zinfandel

ZINFANDEL LN.

Franciscan Oakville Estate

Rutherford Hill Winery

Lake Hennessey

GALLERON RD.

29

128

Provenance Vineyards

128

Frog's Leap Winery

128

Beaulieu Vineyard

Mumm Napa Valley

Grgich Hills Cellars

Round Pond

ZD Wines

SAGE CANYON RD.

Rutherford

128

Rubicon Estate

Peju Province

Caymus Vineyards

Chappellet Winery

Swanson Vineyards

St. Supéry Vineyards

3RD.

CONN CREEK

SILVERADO TR.

Miner Family Vineyards

Sequoia Grove Winery

Cakebread Cellars

Rudd

Nickel & Nickel

Turnbull Wine Cellars

Plumpjack Winery

Robert Mondavi Winery

OAKVILLE CROSS

Groth Vineyards & Winery

Opus One

Oakville

RD.

Silver Oak Cellars

NAPA CO.

SONOMA CO.

WALNUT DR.

Napa Wine Company

ST. HELENA HWY.

DRY CREEK RD.

Napa River

Conn Cr.

Rector Reservoir

N

Chateau Potelle

DRY CREEK RD.

29

YOUNTVILLE CROSS RD.

0   1 mile

0   1 kilometer

© The Countryman Press

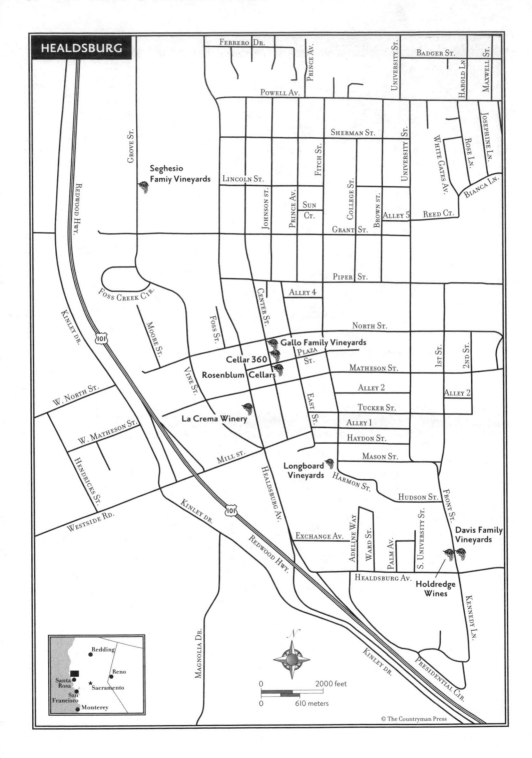

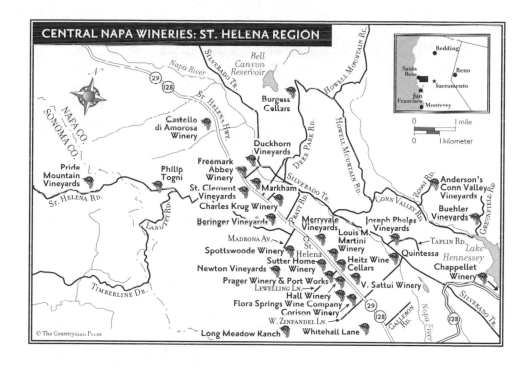

CENTRAL NAPA WINERIES: ST. HELENA REGION

Bell Canyon Reservoir

Napa River

Burgess Cellars

Castello di Amorosa Winery

Duckhorn Vineyards

Pride Mountain Vineyards

Phillip Togni

Freemark Abbey Winery

St. Clement Vineyards

Markham

Charles Krug Winery

Beringer Vineyards

Anderson's Conn Valley Vineyards

Buehler Vineyards

NAPA CO. SONOMA CO.

ST. HELENA RD.

ST. HELEN'S HWY.

DEER PARK RD.

HOWELL MOUNTAIN RD.

SILVERADO TR.

CONN VALLEY RD.

ROSSI RD.

GREENFIELD RD.

MADRONA AV.

St. Helena

Merryvale Vineyards

Louis M. Martini Winery

Joseph Phelps Vineyards

TAPLIN RD.

Quintessa

Lake Hennessey

Spottswoode Winery

Sutter Home Winery

Heitz Wine Cellars

Chappellet Winery

Newton Vineyards

Prager Winery & Port Works

LEWELLING LN.

V. Sattui Winery

Hall Winery

Flora Springs Wine Company

Corison Winery

W. ZINFANDEL LN.

Long Meadow Ranch

Whitehall Lane

TIMBERLINE DR.

LANG TEY RD.

BATTI RD.

CALLERON RD.

Napa River

SILVERADO TR.

Redding

Santa Rosa

Reno

Sacramento

San Francisco

Monterey

0 _____ 1 mile

0 _____ 1 kilometer

© The Countryman Press

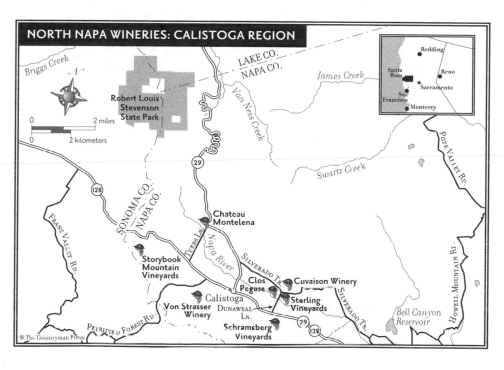

NORTH NAPA WINERIES: CALISTOGA REGION

Briggs Creek

LAKE CO. NAPA CO.

James Creek

Robert Louis Stevenson State Park

Van Ness Creek

POPE VALLEY RD.

SONOMA CO. NAPA CO.

Swartz Creek

FRANZ VALLEY RD.

Chateau Montelena

TEPES LN.

Napa River

SILVERADO TR.

HOWELL MOUNTAIN RD.

Storybook Mountain Vineyards

Clos Pegase

Cuvaison Winery

Calistoga

Von Strasser Winery

DUNAWEAL LN.

Sterling Vineyards

SILVERADO TR.

Bell Canyon Reservoir

PETRIFIED FOREST RD.

Schramsberg Vineyards

Redding

Santa Rosa

Reno

Sacramento

San Francisco

Monterey

0 _____ 2 miles

0 _____ 2 kilometers

© The Countryman Press

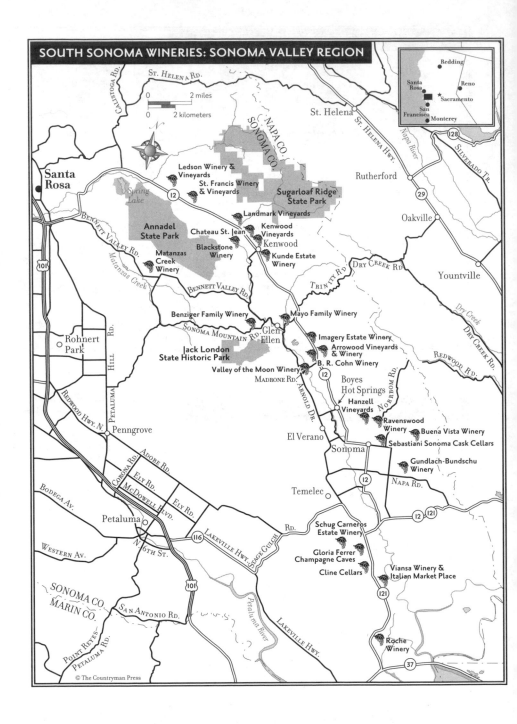

SOUTH SONOMA WINERIES: SONOMA VALLEY REGION

Redding

Santa Rosa   Reno

Sacramento

San Francisco   Monterey

St. Helena Rd.

0   2 miles

0   2 kilometers

Calistoga Rd.

St. Helena Rd.

NAPA CO.
SONOMA CO.

St. Helena

Rutherford

Santa Rosa

Spring Lake

Ledson Winery & Vineyards

St. Francis Winery & Vineyards

Sugarloaf Ridge State Park

Silverado Tr.

Napa River

St. Helena Hwy.

Oakville

Annadel State Park

Landmark Vineyards

Chateau St. Jean

Kenwood Vineyards

Kenwood

Blackstone Winery

Kunde Estate Winery

Bennett Valley Rd.

Matanzas Creek Winery

Matanzas Creek

Bennett Valley Rd.

Trinity Rd.

Dry Creek Rd.

Yountville

Dry Creek Rd.

Benziger Family Winery

Mayo Family Winery

Sonoma Mountain Rd.

Glen Ellen

Imagery Estate Winery

Arrowood Vineyards & Winery

Redwood Rd.

Rohnert Park

Jack London State Historic Park

Valley of the Moon Winery

B. R. Cohn Winery

Madrone Rd.

Arnold Dr.

Boyes Hot Springs

Hanzell Vineyards

Narbom Rd.

Petaluma Hill Rd.

Redwood Hwy. N.

Penngrove

Ravenswood Winery

Buena Vista Winery

El Verano

Sebastiani Sonoma Cask Cellars

Sonoma

Gundlach-Bundschu Winery

Adobe Rd.

Corona Rd.

Ely Rd.

McDowell Blvd.

Ely Rd.

Temelec

Napa Rd.

Bodega Av.

Petaluma

Lakeville Hwy.

Sage Gulch Rd.

Schug Carneros Estate Winery

Western Av.

N. 6th St.

Gloria Ferrer Champagne Caves

Cline Cellars

Viansa Winery & Italian Market Place

SONOMA CO.
MARIN CO.

San Antonio Rd.

Petaluma River

Lakeville Hwy.

Point Reyes–Petaluma Rd.

Roche Winery

© The Countryman Press

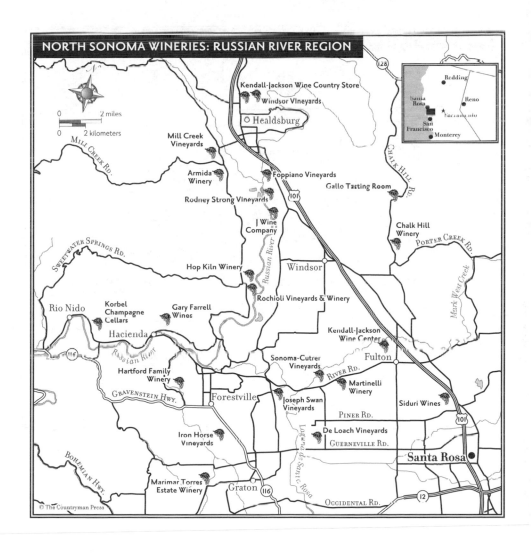

NORTH SONOMA WINERIES: RUSSIAN RIVER REGION

0 ————— 2 miles
0 ————— 2 kilometers

Kendall-Jackson Wine Country Store
Windsor Vineyards
Healdsburg
Mill Creek Vineyards
MILL CREEK RD.
Armida Winery
Foppiano Vineyards
Rodney Strong Vineyards
Gallo Tasting Room
J Wine Company
Chalk Hill Winery
SWEETWATER SPRINGS RD.
Russian River
Hop Kiln Winery
Windsor
PORTER CREEK RD.
Rochioli Vineyards & Winery
Rio Nido
Korbel Champagne Cellars
Gary Farrell Wines
Mark West Creek
Hacienda
Russian River
Kendall-Jackson Wine Center
Hartford Family Winery
Sonoma-Cutrer Vineyards
Fulton
RIVER RD.
GRAVENSTEIN HWY.
Forestville
Martinelli Winery
Joseph Swan Vineyards
Siduri Wines
PINER RD.
Iron Horse Vineyards
De Loach Vineyards
GUERNEVILLE RD.
Laguna de Santa Rosa
Santa Rosa
BOHEMIAN HWY.
Marimar Torres Estate Winery
Graton
OCCIDENTAL RD.
© The Countryman Press

Redding
Reno
Santa Rosa
Sacramento
San Francisco
Monterey

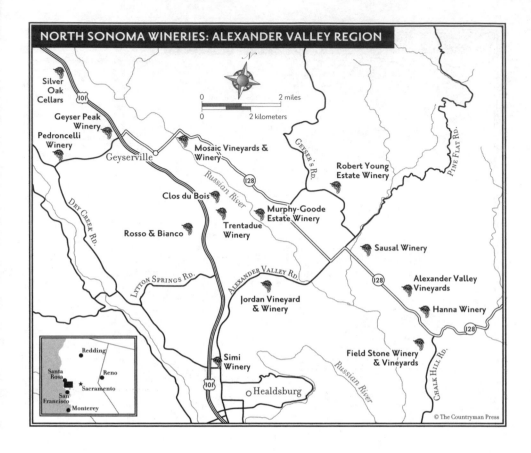

NORTH SONOMA WINERIES: ALEXANDER VALLEY REGION

Silver Oak Cellars

Geyser Peak Winery

Pedroncelli Winery

Geyserville

Mosaic Vineyards & Winery

Russian River

Robert Young Estate Winery

Clos du Bois

Murphy-Goode Estate Winery

Rosso & Bianco

Trentadue Winery

Dry Creek Rd.

Lytton Springs Rd.

Alexander Valley Rd.

Sausal Winery

Alexander Valley Vineyards

Hanna Winery

Jordan Vineyard & Winery

Simi Winery

Field Stone Winery & Vineyards

Russian River

Chalk Hill Rd.

Healdsburg

Redding

Reno

Santa Rosa

Sacramento

San Francisco

Monterey

© The Countryman Press

0   2 miles

0   2 kilometers

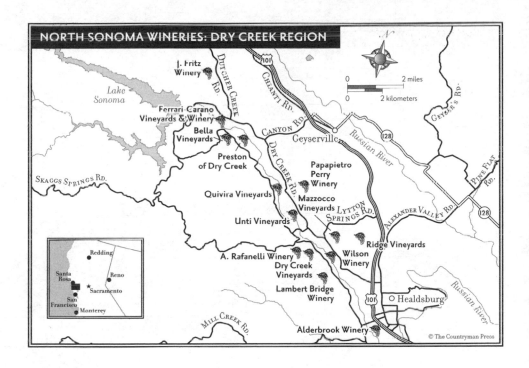

NORTH SONOMA WINERIES: DRY CREEK REGION

Take a rest from wine tasting and just watch the grapes grow. Courtesy Carneros Inn

3

LODGING

Home Away from Home

Just 30 years ago there were only 50 bed-and-breakfast inns in California; today there are more than eight hundred, with new ones hanging out shingles every year. One of the largest concentrations of B&Bs in the state is in Wine Country, where they're scattered through towns and vineyards.

The list of amenities at finer inns includes private balconies and decks, pools and saunas, evening wine tastings, home-baked chocolate chip cookies, and the like. These days private baths are not only standard, but are often equipped with whirlpool tubs for two. Plus the morning meal has evolved from "light Continental" fare to a breakfast that is often a gourmet delight, including creative egg entrées, quiches, sausages, waffles or pancakes, oven-fresh breads with homemade jams, fresh fruit, and champagne.

If you're more at ease staying at a familiar motel chain, or if your budget is your first consideration, Wine Country offers delightful options. Many of these are listed in the motel section included at the end of this chapter.

Don't expect a B&B to be less expensive than a conventional hotel or motel. Unlike its budget-wise British cousin, the Wine Country B&B is an intimate, serene, and often pricey luxury accommodation—and almost always worth it. Keep in mind that over time, policies, amenities, and even furnishings may change at some inns, as will the complimentary goodies.

NAPA AND SONOMA LODGING NOTES

Minimum stay: A majority of inns and B&Bs require a two-night minimum stay on weekends, while a three-night minimum stay is the norm on holiday weekends. (Virtually all inns and B&Bs are open year-round in Wine Country.)

Reservations/cancellations: Make reservations at popular inns and hotels several weeks in advance, because most fill up on weekends even in the off-season. A deposit by credit card for the first night is usually required. Expect a charge for last-minute cancellations.

Restrictions: Smoking is not permitted inside most inns, and pets are prohibited almost unanimously. As a general rule, children under 12 are discouraged, but some inns welcome kids and infants. In-room telephones and televisions are not usually furnished at B&Bs; likewise, room service is limited. Always ask about restrictions before booking.

Rates and credit cards: High season for Wine Country innkeepers is generally from April to October; off-season runs November to March. Many inns, however, make no distinction between the seasons and may charge the same rate year-round. At those that do recognize the off-season, expect to pay 20 percent to 30 percent less. Likewise, midweek rates may be significantly less than weekend rates. The following price codes are based on per-room, double-occupancy, high-season weekend rates at B&Bs and better lodgings.

Lodging Price Codes

Inexpensive:	Up to $100
Moderate:	$100 to $150
Expensive:	$150 to $250
Very Expensive:	Over $250

Credit Cards

The following abbreviations are used for credit card information.
AE: American Express
DC: Diner's Club
CB: Carte Blanche
MC: MasterCard
D: Discover Card
V: Visa

The Beazley House in a 1902 charmer in downtown Napa. Tim Fish

Lodging in Napa County

NAPA
BEAZLEY HOUSE

Innkeepers: Jim and Carol Beazley
707-257-1649, 800-559-1649; fax 707-258-1518
www.beazleyhouse.com
innkeeper@beazleyhouse.com
1910 1st St., Napa, CA 94559 (1st St. exit east off Hwy. 29)
Price: Expensive to Very Expensive
Credit Cards: MC, V

One of Napa's first B&Bs, this shingled, circa-1902 mansion has six charming and cozy rooms. Even more desirable is the carriage house, built in 1983, with a fireplace and two-person spa standard in each of its five rooms. The main house is a beauty; the dining and common rooms have coved ceilings and oak floors with mahogany inlays. The Sherry Room is pleasantly done in blue wallpaper and rich cherrywood, but if you're sensitive to street noise, request a room in the carriage house. The garden is a peaceful refuge with an old-fashioned swing. The Beazleys offer a warm welcome at breakfast, and Carol—a former nurse—concocts healthy but tasty fare served buffet style. The Beazleys also run the nearby Daughter's Inn.

CANDLELIGHT INN OF THE DUNN LEE MANOR

Innkeepers: Wendy and Mark Tamiso
707-257-3717, 800-624-0395; fax 707-257-3762
www.candlelightinn.com
mail@candlelightinn.com
1045 Easum Dr., Napa, CA 94558 (1st St. exit west off Hwy. 29)
Price: Expensive to Very Expensive
Credit Cards: AE, D, MC, V
Special Features: Pool

This 1929 English Tudor-style mansion is in the heart of suburbia, but the 1-acre grounds along Napa Creek are beautifully

parklike. The inn has a total of nine
rooms—six of them romantic suites with
two-person whirlpool baths, balconies or
decks, and fireplaces—and the decor is
comfortable but not overly fussy. One suite
has a cathedral ceiling and a stained-glass
window. A three-course breakfast is served
overlooking the lovely gardens that surround the house.

CARNEROS INN

General Manager: Joe Fairchild
707-299-4900, 800-400-9000; fax 707-
299-4950
www.thecarnerosinn.com
info@thecarnerosinn.com
4048 Sonoma Hwy., Napa, CA 94559
Price: Very Expensive
Credit Cards: AE, D, DC, MC, V
Special Features: Pool, health spa, restaurant

Situated on the beautiful rolling hills of the
Carneros grape-growing region just outside
the city of Napa, this luxury Plumpjack
resort opened in 2004 and includes 86
individual cottages that range in size from
975 to 1,800 square feet. The inn also has
12 vacation homes, popular for travelers
staying two or more nights. The decor is
rustic-meets-chic, with corrugated metal
roofs, Brazilian cherry floors, and wood
burning fireplaces in stone hearths.
Bathrooms feature limestone and tile plus
heated slate floors, and most feature soaking tubs and alfresco showers for those who
want to experience the outdoors. Each cottage also has a private patio garden, and
many have striking views of the surround
ing hillsides and vineyards.

COTTAGES OF NAPA VALLEY

Innkeeper: Mike Smith
General Manager: Mary Stevens
707-252-7810, 866-900-7810
www.napacottages.com
info@napacottages.com
1012 Darms Ln., Napa, CA 94558

Price: Expensive to Very Expensive
Credit Cards: AE, CB, D, DC, MC, V
Special features: Privacy; outdoor fireplaces; fireplace, whirlpool tub, and kitchenette in each cottage

These cozy cottages are the ultimate in private getaways. Each of the eight rooms, 500
to 600 square feet of space, has a fireplace,
a whirlpool tub, a kitchenette, a deck, and
an outdoor fireplace. Spa services include a
relaxing, in-room massage. Breakfast—
delivered to your front porch—is a basket
that features pastries from Bouchon Bakery.
Sweet.

CHURCHILL MANOR

Innkeepers: Joanna Guidotti and Brian
Jensen
707-253-7733, 800-799-7733
www.churchillmanor.com
bc@churchillmanor.com
485 Brown St., Napa, CA 94559 (1st St. exit
east off Hwy. 29)
Price: Expensive to Very Expensive
Credit Cards: AE, D, MC, V

From the moment you spy Churchill Manor,
you'll know it's special. Now a National
Historic Landmark, the inn was built in
1889 on a lush acre, and it has the Greek
Revival columns, wraparound verandas,
and grand parlors of days gone by. If you
like antiques, this is your place. The 10
guest rooms are located on all three floors
of this graceful mansion, and all have private baths and queen- or king-sized beds.
Hand-painted Delft tiles, 24-carat-gold
trim, and an antique beaded opera gown
are among the rich details in the rooms. A
generous, buffet-style breakfast is served
in the marble-tiled solarium, where wine
and cheese are offered in the evening.

ELM HOUSE INN, BEST WESTERN

Manager: Tom Kearns
707-255-1831, 888-849-1997; fax 707-255-
8609

800 California Blvd., Napa, CA 94559 (1st
St. exit east off Hwy. 29)
Price: Moderate to Expensive
Credit Cards: AE, MC, V
Special Features: Whirlpool
This wood-shingled inn is modern but
done in the style of an old European village.
Italian marble fireplaces adorn some of the
22 rooms (all with private baths), and each
has a TV, phone, and stocked refrigerator.
There's also a honeymoon suite with high
ceilings, a chandelier, and a private
whirlpool. The inn's elevator makes it
accessible to wheelchairs. A breakfast buffet is served in the courtyard when weather
permits. It's located at a busy intersection.

EMBASSY SUITES NAPA VALLEY
Manager: Reynaldo Zertuche
707-253-9540; fax 707-253-9202
www.embassynapa.com
info@embassynapa.com
1075 California Blvd., Napa, CA 94559 (1st

St. exit east off Hwy. 29)
Price: Expensive to Very Expensive
Credit Cards: AE, D, DC, MC, V
Special Features: Indoor and outdoor pools,
sauna, whirlpool, and restaurant

All 205 rooms in this hotel are two-room
suites with French country furnishings and
are equipped for light cooking with minire-
frigerators, coffeemakers, and microwave
ovens. In addition, all rooms have wet bars,
phones, and TVs. A daily complimentary full
breakfast is cooked to order, and two hours
of complimentary cocktails are served each
evening. Outside, enjoy a pond with swans
and ducks and a tropical atrium with a skylight for dining. This is an elegant, busi-
ness-class hotel that's also ideal for leisure
travelers. A $6.2-million renovation was
completed in 2007.

HENNESSEY HOUSE
Innkeepers: Kevin and Lorri Walsh
707-226-3774; fax 707-226-2975

Hennessey House is an 1889 Eastlake-style Queen Anne. Tim Fish

www.hennesseyhouse.com
inn@hennessyhouse.com
1727 Main St., Napa, CA 94559 (Lincoln
Ave. exit east off Hwy. 29)
Price: Moderate to Very Expensive
Credit Cards: AE, D, MC, V
Special Features: Sauna

This home—on the National Register of
Historic Places—is a stunning example of a
perfectly restored 1889 Eastlake-style
Queen Anne. The main house has six
rooms, all appointed with antiques and private baths. The four carriage-house rooms
are larger and more luxurious, and each is
equipped with a two-person whirlpool tub.
The Bridle Suite is done in masculine tones
and has a fireplace and skylight. A full
breakfast is served in the dining room, with
its restored, hand-painted and stamped tin
ceiling. The neighborhood is urban but
quiet and is a short walk to downtown Napa.

LA BELLE EPOQUE

Innkeepers: Roxann and Derek Archer
707-257-2161, 800-238-8070
www.labelleepoque.com
Roxann@napabelle.com
1386 Calistoga Ave., Napa, CA 94559 (1st St.
exit east off Hwy. 29; the Petite Maison
annex is at 1406 Calistoga Ave.)
Price: Expensive to Very Expensive
Credit Cards: AE, D, MC, V

The stained-glass windows and fine
Victorian furniture in this nine-room inn
will transport you to another time and
place. Built in 1893, this gingerbread
beauty is near downtown, which has wit-
nessed a rebirth in recent years, with a
horde of new restaurants and activities.
Family-heirloom antiques and collectibles
are scattered throughout the guest rooms
and the common parlor. All rooms have
private baths, and several have a whirlpool
tub. Most rooms have a fireplace. The inn
has two additional rooms tucked away in an
annex called the Petite Maison. Breakfast is
served in the dining room or on the sun
porch or is delivered to the room.

LA RÉSIDENCE COUNTRY INN

Innkeepers: Craig and Kathryn Hall
707-253-0337, 800-253-9203; fax 707-
253-0382
www.laresidence.com
4066 St. Helena Hwy., Napa, CA 94558 (on
Hwy. 29)
Price: Expensive to Very Expensive
Credit Cards: AE, DC, MC, V
Special Features: Pool, whirlpool

Built in 1870 by a New Orleans riverboat
pilot who arrived in San Francisco during
the Gold Rush, this Gothic Revival inn still
has the flavor of the Old South, with its
plantation shutters and parklike setting.
Twenty-five rooms are in a modern building styled after a French country barn.
Between the two buildings are a garden
with a pool and white gazebo. Nineteenth-
century antiques and chandeliers decorate
the rooms, many of which have fireplaces.
The pace is slow and easy, with lots of
porches and decks and a jogging and bicycling trail. A full breakfast is served in the
dining room, where guests dine privately at
small tables near a fireplace.

THE MAGNOLIA NAPA

Innkeeper: Reina Aguiniga
707-253-2583, 800-959-2583; fax 707-
257-8205
www.napamagnolia.com
info@napamagnolia.com
443 Brown St., Napa, CA 94559 (1st St. exit
east off Hwy. 29)
Price: Expensive to Very Expensive
Credit Cards: AE, MC, V, D, DC

This graceful Queen Anne Victorian, built
in 1886, is situated on a lush acre with a
pool, a hot tub, and a spa on the property.
It's on a quiet, tree-lined street, just a short

walk from downtown Napa. There are 17 guest rooms; all have private baths and all but one have a fireplace. A full breakfast is included in the room rate, and dinner is available—a perk because the inn's signature dish is Rock Cornish Game Hens stuffed with wild rice, honey, and curry dressing.

MERITAGE

General Manager: Michael Palmer
707-259-0633
www.themeritageresort.com
mpalmer@themeritageresort.com
875 Bordeaux Way, Napa, CA. 94558
Price: Expensive to Very Expensive
Credit Cards: AE, D, MC, V
Special Features: Underground Spa, underground wine cave, restaurant (The Siena)

The most unique feature of Meritage, situated on 8 acres of private vineyards, is its 22,000-square-foot cave, which includes a spa, banquet facility, and a wine tasting bar.

Above ground, the Meritage has 158 rooms, a gourmet restaurant called The Siena, a vineyard with walking trails, and even a wedding chapel that seats 60. The business center offers high-speed Internet access and conference and banquet rooms. The restaurant, with its Tuscan-inspired decor, has a menu to match. It features California cuisine with an Italian twist—great pastas and pizzas.

MILLIKEN CREEK INN & SPA

General Manager: Connie Gore
707-255-1197, 800-835-6117;
fax 707-255-3112
www.millikencreekinn.com
info@millikencreekinn.com
1815 Silverado Tr., Napa, CA 94558 (north on Hwy. 29, to Trancas exit)
Price: Expensive to Very Expensive
Credit Cards: AE, D, DC, MC, V

Milliken Creek Inn is located at the base of

The Napa River Inn in downtown Napa is a great hub for wine touring. Tim Fish

Wine Country. Nestled between the Silverado Trail and the Napa River, this boutique luxury inn beckons you to relax and unwind with the amenities of a large resort and the intimacy of a B&B. This place is set up to pamper: spa and massage services, yoga, jazz, private wine tastings, breakfast in bed, Italian linens, and Napa River views. Great for a romantic getaway.

NAPA RIVER INN

General Manager: Sara Brooks
707-251-8500, 877-251-8504
www.napariverinn.com
500 Main St., Napa, CA 94559
Price: Expensive to Very Expensive
Credit Cards: AE, D, MC, Visa

Once a mill, later a warehouse, this lovely old brick building right on the Napa River is now a luxury boutique hotel. The inn was built in the 1800s, and many of the rooms are filled with antiques and furnishings from that period. Some rooms have a California Wine Country look, while others have a nautical theme. The 66-room inn, which spreads through three adjacent buildings, has the charm of a fine B&B but the privacy of a hotel. Located in the heart of Napa's downtown, which is now bustling with new shops and restaurants, the inn is not far from COPIA (The American Center for Wine, Food, and the Arts) as well as the historic Napa Valley Opera House. Two of the city's top restaurants—Angele and Celadon—are on the property, and guests receive a complimentary breakfast at Sweetie Pie Pastries.

NAPA VALLEY MARRIOTT

General Manager: Michael George
707-253-8600, 800-228-9290;
fax 707-258-1320
www.marriotthotels.com/sfonp
3425 Solano Ave., Napa, CA 94558 (Hwy. 29 at Redwood Rd.)
Price: Expensive to Very Expensive
Credit Cards: AE, CB, D, DC, MC, V

Special Features: Pool, whirlpool, tennis courts, fitness room, two restaurants

With 297 rooms and suites, the Marriott is one of the largest inns in the valley. Nicer than a motel, it's not quite a hotel, either, but it's comfortably appointed and has the usual services you would expect from a chain hotel. On the north edge of the city, it's convenient to most of the valley.

The Poetry Inn is one of the most exclusive lodgings in Napa Valley. Courtesy Poetry Inn

THE POETRY INN

Innkeeper: Chris Parkes
707-944-0646; fax 707-944-9188
www.poetryinn.com
visitus@poetryinn.com
6380 Silverado Trail, Stag's Leap District, Napa CA., 94558 (just south of the Yountville Crossroad)
Price: Very Expensive
Credit Cards: AE, MC, V
Special Features: Spa services, indoor and outdoor showers for every room, private balconies

Cliff Lede, a Canadian businessman, established Cliff Lede Vineyards in 2002 and opened the nearby Poetry Inn in 2005. The inn, on a hillside in the Stag's Leap District, has stunning views of the Napa Valley. The three rooms have king-sized beds, private balconies, and wood-burning fireplaces. A popular spa treatment is a massage in the open air. Breakfasts include Brie and Strawberry stuffed French Toast—decadence at its best.

THE OLD WORLD INN
Innkeepers: Sharon and Russ Herschelmann
707-257-0112, 800-966-6624; fax 707-257-0118
www.oldworldinn.com
theoldworldinn@aol.com
1301 Jefferson St., Napa, CA 94559 (1st St. exit east off Hwy. 29)
Price: Expensive to Very Expensive
Credit Cards: AE, D, MC, V
Special Features: Whirlpool

A charming 1906 Victorian, this inn received a face-lift in recent years, and it's more beautiful than ever. The interior is impeccably designed, done in tastefully dramatic pastels and draped fabrics. The dining and common rooms on the first floor have gorgeous redwood woodwork and polished wood floors. Each of the 10 guest rooms is individually decorated: The Starry Night Room has skylights and a deck with a spa, while the Secret Garden Room has a secluded garden spa and a canopy bed, and most have fireplaces and claw-foot tubs. There's a two-course gourmet breakfast. Though on a busy street, the inn is surprisingly quiet.

RIVER TERRACE INN
General Manager: Sam Schorr
707-320-9000, 866-627-2386; fax 707-258-1236
www.riverterraceinn.com
1600 Soscol Ave., Napa, CA 94559 (1st St. exit off 29, left on Soscol)
Price: Moderate to Very Expensive
Credit Cards: AE, MC, V
Special Features: Whirlpool tubs, river views

Opened in 2003, this is the latest addition to the burgeoning tourist scene along the river in downtown Napa, which includes COPIA (The American Center for Wine, Food, and the Arts) as well as a new wave of hotels and restaurants. This three-story hotel, with an exterior design that's both stylish and rustic, appeals to vacationers and business travelers alike. The 106 rooms and 28 junior suites all have a touch of luxury, with crown moldings, ceiling fans, and granite bathrooms with whirlpool tubs. Most of the rooms have balconies, many of which overlook the river.

SILVERADO RESORT
Manager: Kirk Candland
707-257-0200, 800-532-0500; fax 707-257-2687
www.silveradoresort.com
resv@silveradoresort.com
1600 Atlas Peak Rd., Napa, CA 94558 (1 mile northeast of Napa)
Price: Very Expensive
Credit Cards: AE, CB, D, DC, MC, V
Special Features: Two 18-hole golf courses, eight pools, tennis, restaurant, room service, spa, salon

Golf is king at Silverado. Its two courses—which underwent a $3.5-million face-lift in 2003—are considered the best in Napa Valley. With more than 750 regular members, the resort is constantly bustling with activity. The main house, an imposing mansion built just after the Civil War, was remodeled in 1992. Today, there are 280 rooms scattered over the 1,200-acre estate, ranging in size from studios to three-bedroom suites. The units are individually owned by members but rented out like hotel rooms. (The Oak Creek East section is the most secluded; the Clubhouse side is convenient to the tennis courts and golf courses.) All rooms are comfortably furnished to feel like home, and the kitchenettes contain just about everything you need for light cooking. The concierge staff is perhaps the best in the valley.

Silverado Resort recalls an old southern plantation. Tim Fish

STAHLECKER HOUSE

Innkeepers: Ron and Ethel Stahlecker
707-257-1588, 800-799-1588;
fax 707-224-7429
www.stahleckerhouse.com
stahlbnb@aol.com
1042 Easum Dr., Napa, CA 94558 (1st St. exit west off Hwy 29)
Price: Expensive
Credit Cards: AE, D, MC, V

This 1948 ranch-style house seems more like a home than a B&B, situated on one and a half acres of landscaped grounds embellished with a creek and mature trees. It has four appealing guest rooms with canopy beds, antique furniture, fireplaces, and private baths. Two rooms have whirlpool spas and private patios. Relax on the immense sun deck surrounded by gardens and oak and laurel trees or read in the gathering room. The hosts serve a gourmet candlelight breakfast in the dining room and complimentary beverages around the clock.

THE WESTIN VERASA NAPA RESIDENCES

800-937-8461
www.westinnaparesidences.com
1314 McKinstry St., Napa CA., 94559
Price: Expensive
Credit Cards: AE, CB, D, MC, V
Special Features: Restaurant, fitness center, conference room, bocce ball court

The hotel has 160 suites—studios, one-bedroom or two-bedroom—with kitchenettes. This kind of condo hotel has been around for decades in resort towns, but visitors are just starting to see more of them in northern California. The hotel is set to open in January of 2008.

Yountville

BORDEAUX HOUSE

Innkeeper: Jean Lunney
707-944-2855, 800-677-6370;
fax 707-945-0471
www.bordeauxhouse.com
6600 Washington St., Yountville, CA 94599
(off Hwy. 29 at Washington St.)
Price: Moderate to Expensive
Credit Cards: MC, V

The inn—a modern, distinctive redbrick building—is a far cry from the usual cozy Victorian inn. Likewise, the furnishings have an eclectic style, with a mix of antiques and modern pieces. Eight of the seven guest rooms in this inn have fireplaces, most have balconies or patios, and all have private baths. A full breakfast is served in the common room. Close to all of Yountville's shops and restaurants, it's a good choice for those on a budget.

LAVENDER

Manager: Rachel Retterer
707-944-1388, 800-522-4140; fax 707-944-1579
www.foursisters.com
2020 Webber St., Yountville, CA 94599
(one block east of Washington St.)

Price: Moderate to Very Expensive
Credit Cards: AE, MC, V

The inn is a little bit of Provence in the heart of Napa Valley. Surrounded by its namesake flowering herb, the inn has eight guest rooms in all, including two in the main house—a lovely old farmhouse with a wide porch—and the others in three cottages. The decor is done in French country furnishings and fabrics, and all rooms have fireplaces. The layout of the grounds allows for a great deal of privacy, but there's plenty of room for guests to mingle in the gardens or in the breakfast room, where a Parisian-style bistro breakfast is served. Guests have pool privileges at nearby sister inn Maison Fleurie. The innkeepers are exceptionally friendly.

MAISON FLEURIE

Manager: Rachel Retterer
707-944-2056, 800-788-0369;
fax 707-944-9342
www.foursisters.com
6529 Yount St., Yountville, CA 94599
(one block east of Washington St.)
Price: Moderate to Very Expensive
Credit Cards: AE, D, MC, V
Special Features: Pool, whirlpool

French for "flowering house," Maison Fleurie is a lovely complex of vine-covered buildings blessed with a colorful past—built in 1873, it was a bordello and a speakeasy. Today, it is a 13-room inn in the heart of the increasingly chic burg of Yountville, but it has the feel of a French country inn, featuring provincial antiques and reproductions. Six rooms have fireplaces, while the pool and whirlpool offer relaxation in a private setting. A full breakfast is served family-style in the fireside dining room.

NAPA VALLEY LODGE

Manager: Valerie Raven
707-944-2468, 800-368-2468; fax 707-944-9362

www.woodsidehotels.com
jwolfe@napavalleylodge.com
2230 Madison St., Yountville, CA 94599
(one block off Hwy. 29)
Price: Very Expensive
Credit Cards: AE, D, DC, MC, V
Special Features: Pool, whirlpool, sauna, fitness room, bocce ball court and courtyard

This delightful lodge has 55 well—appointed and spacious rooms and suites—33 with fireplaces-decorated with wicker and tropical plants and offering postcard views of the valley. It is styled as a Spanish hacienda, with a red-tile roof and balconies and a pool and whirlpool spa in a pleasant courtyard. In-room coffeemakers and cooler/ refrigerators are provided, and a champagne breakfast buffet is included—poolside if weather permits. This is a restful location surrounded by ripening grapes in the vineyards, and it's an easy walk to Yountville's shops. Special golf packages are also available. The inn had a $6-million remodel in 2007.

OAK KNOLL INN

Innkeepers: Barbara Passino and John Kuhlmann
707-255-2200; fax 707-255 2296
www.oakknollinn.com
oakknollinn@aol.com
2200 E. Oak Knoll Ave., Napa, CA 94558
(3 miles south of Yountville)
Price: Very Expensive
Credit Cards: MC, V
Special Features: Pool, whirlpool

Oak Knoll Inn is a treasure, perhaps our favorite B&B in Napa Valley. It's intimate—only four guest suites—but the rooms are spacious and luxurious, with tall French windows, rustic fieldstone walls, and vaulted ceilings. The rooms have king-sized beds, Italian marble fireplaces, private baths, and sitting areas with overstuffed chairs and sofas. Surrounded by gardens and 600 acres of merlot and syrah vine-

yards, the inn is well off the bustle of Highway 29; the setting is peaceful and the view, magnificent—plus, the innkeepers are gracious and unstuffy. The phrase "gourmet breakfast" is used loosely at many B&Bs, but not here. Barbara Passino creates truly magnificent breakfasts, including poached eggs in puff pastry and an indulgence called a chocolate taco stuffed with fresh sorbet. Breakfast is served in the dining room or on the veranda near your room. There's also quite a spread set out for the nightly wine-and-cheese hour.

PETIT LOGIS INN

Innkeepers: Jay and Judith Caldwell
877-944-2332; fax 707-944-2338
www.petitlogis.com
jay@petitlogis.com
6527 Yount St., Yountville, CA 94599
Price: Moderate to Expensive
Credit Cards: AE, D, MC, V
Special Features: Fireplaces, 6-foot whirlpool tubs, patios

This inn has a culinary edge. It's within walking distance of The French Laundry—by many accounts the best restaurant in America—and it's also near some other top-rated restaurants, including Bouchon and Bistro Jeanty. All five guest rooms feature a fireplace and a 6-foot double Jacuzzi. The shingled lodge with a trellis of vines has a French country, minimalist feel. The inn is simple and lovely, and the price is right. Wireless Internet is available.

VILLAGIO INN & SPA

Manager: Mary Crow
707-944-8877, 800-351-1133; fax 707-944-8855
www.villagio.com
reservations@villagio.com
6481 Washington St., Yountville, CA 94599
Price: Very Expensive
Credit Cards: AE, DC, MC, V
Special Features: Spa with 10 treatment rooms, lap pool, fitness room

The 3,500-square-foot spa is the drawing card at the Villagio Inn & Spa in Yountville. Tim Fish

Villagio Inn & Spa has 112 guest rooms, and each features a wood-burning fireplace, a patio or balcony, a refrigerator, and a bottle of chilled chardonnay. Of course, the drawing card here is the 3,500-square-foot spa with 10 treatment rooms, and a 40-foot lap pool. Yet another plus is the V Marketplace, featuring upscale specialty shops, galleries, cafés, a complete wine cellar, and a hot-air balloon company—all housed within a 130-year-old restored brick winery. A new spa on the facility will open in 2008.

VINTAGE INN

General Manager: Mary Crow
707-944-1112, 800-351-1133;
fax 707-944-1617
www.vintageinn.com
reservations@vintageinn.com

6541 Washington St., Yountville, CA 94599
(Washington St. exit off Hwy. 29)
Price: Very Expensive
Credit Cards: AE, D, MC, V
Special Features: Pool, children welcome, pet friendly

This is an exceptional inn designed with villa-style units clustered around a common waterway. The 80 spacious and beautifully decorated rooms have oversized beds, whirlpool-spa tubs, ceiling fans, in-room coffeemakers and refrigerators, private verandas, and wood-burning fireplaces. Second-story rooms cost a little more but are worth it for the vaulted ceilings and, especially, the views. California bubbly is served with the breakfast buffet. The V Marketplace shopping complex is next door.

YOUNTVILLE INN

Manager: Joan Torassa
707-944-5600; fax 707-944-5666
www.yountvilleinn.com
info@yountvilleinn.com
6462 Washington St., Yountville, CA 94599
Price: Expensive to Very Expensive
Credit Cards: AE, D, MC, V
Special Features: Fireplaces, pool,
whirlpool, patios

Prefer a full-service hotel but can't afford
the sky-high premiums of some of the
nearby lodgings? This inn is a good alternative. Set on a peaceful creek and featuring mature landscaping, the hotel has an
elegantly rustic feel to it. There are 51
rooms, each featuring a fieldstone fireplace. Many of the top rooms have vaulted
ceilings and private patios. A Continental
breakfast is served.

RUTHERFORD

AUBERGE DU SOLEIL

Manager: Bradley Reynolds
707-963-1211
www.aubergedusoleil.com

info@aubergedusoleil.com
180 Rutherford Hill Rd., Rutherford, CA
94573 (off Hwy. 29)
Price: Very Expensive
Credit Cards: AE, D, MC, V
Special Features: Restaurant, pool,
whirlpool, tennis court, health spa

Auberge du Soleil is Napa Valley's most lux
urious experience. Fifty-two rooms and
suites are nestled in olive trees on a remote
33-acre hillside. The style throughout the
inn is distinctly southern France, with
deep-set windows and wood shutters and
doors. Each room or suite has a terrace and
private entrance, and most have spectacular
views of the valley. All furnishings are chic
yet casual, and terra-cotta tiling is used
generously throughout on floors and coun-
tertops, helping to keep rooms cool during
Napa Valley's toasty summer days. The
rooms range from standard bedroom and
bath to deluxe suites with fireplaces and
whirlpool baths. There are also two private
luxury cottages, each with whirlpool tub
and fireplaces. After indulging yourself in
the 7,000-square-foot Spa du Soleil—one of

Southern France melds with California at Auberge du Soleil, Napa Valley's most luxurious experience.
Courtesy Auberge du Soleil

the most luxurious in the valley—take in the sculpture garden set along a half-mile path. The restaurant is also not to be missed (see chapter 5, Restaurants).

RANCHO CAYMUS INN
Innkeeper: Otto Komes
707-963-1777, 800-845-1777
www.ranchocaymus.com
info@ranchocaymus.com
1140 Rutherford Rd., P.O. Box 78, Rutherford, CA 94573 (from Hwy. 29, east on Rutherford Rd.)
Price: Moderate to Very Expensive
Credit Cards: AE, CB, DC, MC, V

This romantic hacienda may recall the film *Like Water for Chocolate* (rose petals are optional). The stucco inn, with a red-tile roof, is built around a serene court-yard garden, and it's clear an artist's hand was involved in the design. The original owner, sculptor Mary Tilden Morton, cre-ated an inn distinguished by stained-glass windows, hand-hewn beams, hand-thrown stoneware, and tooled wooden lamps. Ecuadorian and Guadalajaran craftsmen made the elegant yet unique furnishings. All 26 rooms are split level, most have private balconies and adobe beehive fire-places, and four suites have whirlpool

The classic Art Deco El Bonita Motel is Napa's best bargain. Tim Fish

baths. A generous Continental breakfast is served either in the dining room by the fireplace or out in the courtyard. The staff is obliging. Restaurant La Toque serves French cuisine (see chapter 5, Restaurants) and is one of the best in Napa.

ST. HELENA
ADAGIO INN
Innkeeper: Polly Keegan
707-963-2238, 888-823-2446;
fax 707-963-5598
www.adagioinn.com
innkeeper@adagioinn.com
1417 Kearney St., St. Helena, CA 94574 (two blocks off Main St.)
Price: Very Expensive
Credit Cards: MC, V

The sun-soaked porch at this 1904 Victorian cottage offers relaxation after a day of shopping and wine tasting. The three guest rooms are spacious and done in romantically antique decor, and two of the rooms have large whirlpool tubs. The two-room Sonata Suite has a private entrance, while Prelude has a private deck with a two-person hot tub. The Concerto Suite has a window seat framed with stained glass and a brass bed. The location is nearly ideal, in a quiet residential neighborhood a few steps from St. Helena's Main Street.

EL BONITA MOTEL
Manager: Pierrette Therene
707-963-3216, 800-541-3284;
fax 707-963-8838
www.elbonita.com
195 Main St., St. Helena, CA 94574
Price: Moderate to Expensive
Credit Cards: AE, D, DC, CB,MC, V
Special Features: Pool, whirlpool, sauna, garden

Don't let the "motel" in its name fool you. The 1950s meets the new millennium at El Bonita, a chic, art deco, pastel-hued clas-

The Harvest Inn in St. Helena seems like a European village. Tim Fish

sic. It's also Napa's best bargain. Built in 1953, the motel was renovated and newly landscaped in 1992. With a new wing of deluxe rooms, El Bonita now has 41 units, all cheerfully appointed; a few have kitchens and whirlpool baths. The garden and lawn span 2.5 acres, all sheltered from busy Highway 29. Trees and hedges also help cushion the steady hum of traffic. There's Continental breakfast service in the lobby or—weather permitting—on the patio.

HARVEST INN
General Manager: Jennifer Moss-Clay
707-963-9463, 800-950-8466;
fax 707-963-4402
www.harvestinn.com
reservations@harvestinn.com
1 Main St., St. Helena, CA 94574 (on Hwy. 29 south, off St. Helena)
Price: Expensive to Very Expensive
Credit Cards: AE, D, DC, MC, V
Special Features: Two pools, whirlpools

There's a bit of Old England in Napa Valley at the Harvest Inn, a stately English Tudor-style lodge built from the bricks and cobblestones of old San Francisco homes. Most of the 54 guest rooms have king sized beds, brick fireplaces, wet bars, and refrigerators, and all are furnished with antiques or reproductions. Several suites have whirlpool tubs. The lush landscaping also helps to create the aura of another time and place. The inn's Harvest Centre has a wine bar and dance floor, and a complimentary Continental breakfast is served in the dining hall. The inn overlooks a 14-acre working vineyard and is within strolling distance of many wineries.

HOTEL ST. HELENA
Innkeeper: Mary Haney
707-963-4388, 888-478-4355;
fax 707-963-5402
www.hotelsthelena.com
1309 Main St., St. Helena, CA 94574
Price: Inexpensive to Expensive
Credit Cards: AE, MC, V

In the thick of St. Helena's shopping and dining, this hotel on the town's Main Street is richly furnished with antiques. Built in 1881, the hotel has 17 rooms and one suite; 14 have private baths. Its turn-of-the-20th-century charm makes it especially homey. There's a wine bar, and a Continental breakfast is served every morning. The hotel is air-conditioned.

INK HOUSE BED & BREAKFAST

Innkeeper: Kevin Outcalt
707-963-3890; fax 707-968-0739
www.inkhouse.com
inkhousebb@aol.com
1575 St. Helena Hwy., St. Helena, CA 94574
(on Hwy. 29, 1 mile north of Rutherford)
Price: Moderate to Expensive
Credit Cards: MC, V
Special Features: Garden, observatory

A glass-enclosed rooftop observatory with a 360-degree view of vineyards distinguishes this yellow, 1884 Italianate Victorian listed on the National Register of Historic Places. Each of the seven second-story guest rooms has a vineyard view and period furnishings. Two rooms share a bath; five have private baths. Just for fun, take a lesson on the antique pump organ in the parlor, or take in a sunset from the wraparound porch. A full gourmet breakfast is served, plus wine and hors d'oeuvres at night. This is an exceptional location and setting. Though it's right on Highway 29, the inn is remarkably quiet.

THE INN AT SOUTHBRIDGE

Hotel Manager: Don Lynch
707-967-9400, 800-520-6800
www.innatsouthbridge.com
southbridge@slh.com
1020 Main St., St. Helena, CA 94574 (on Hwy. 29, just south of downtown)
Price: Very Expensive
Credit Cards: AE, CB, DC, MC, V
Special Features: Restaurant, health spa

A classy addition to St. Helena, this inn complex is a sleekly modern Italianate design. All 20 rooms are on the second floor and done in handsome ivory white and cream and hues with sophisticated wood accents. Each of the rooms feature a fireplace, oversized tub, and French doors that open onto a private balcony. A few of the rooms are rather close to Main Street. Just off the lobby is a family-style Italian restaurant called Pizzeria Tra Vigne; it's not bad for a quick pizza (see chapter 5, Restaurants). Also part of the complex is the Health Spa Napa Valley (see chapter 7, Recreation). A Continental breakfast is included.

MEADOWOOD NAPA VALLEY

707-963-3646, 800-458-8080;
fax 707-963-3532
www.meadowood.com
900 Meadowood Ln., St. Helena, CA 9457 (east of St. Helena)
Price: Very Expensive
Credit Cards: AE, DC, MC, V
Special Features: Health spa, croquet, restaurants, golf, pool, tennis; children welcome

Meadowood never falters in its interpretation of luxury. Its white-trimmed buildings, tiered with gabled windows and porches, are reminiscent of New England's turn-of-the-20th-century cottages. The staff pampers with style, and a soothing sense of privacy prevails. Most of the resort's 85 cottages, suites, and lodges—scattered around a gorgeous, wooded 250-acre property—have cathedral ceilings, skylights, ceiling fans, and air-conditioning. Rooms range in size from one-room studios with fireplaces to four-bedroom suites with sitting rooms. Each room has a private deck with a view of pine trees or gardens, and a queen- or king-sized bed with a goose-down comforter. Breakfast is not included; however, a Continental repast can be delivered to your door, or a full feast is available at the Grill. Better yet, try a light breakfast by the pool, surrounded by lush lawns and trees. Meadowood also has one of the finest health facilities in the valley, with aerobic and exercise rooms and a full spa (see chapter 7, Recreation).

SHADY OAKS COUNTRY INN

Owners: Lisa Wild-Runnells and John Runnells
707-963-1190; fax 707-963-9367
www.shadyoakscountryinn.com
info@shadyoakscountryinn.com
399 Zinfandel Ln., St. Helena, CA 94574
(2 miles south of St. Helena)
Price: Expensive
Credit Cards: D, MC, V

Oak and walnut trees surround this friendly country inn consisting of five guest rooms with private baths, all furnished with antiques. The main house, built in the 1920s, has three lovely rooms. The old stone winery, dating from the 1880s, has two more luxurious rooms, one with a vineyard view from a private deck, the other with a distinct stone interior. A full gourmet champagne breakfast—eggs Benedict or Belgian waffles are the norm—is served in your room or in the dining room and garden patio, which is guarded by Roman columns. Wine and cheese are served in the evening. For those who are up for a little recreation, there's a new bocce ball court in front of the inn.

VINEYARD COUNTRY INN

Innkeepers: Pat and Ortwin Krueger
707-963-1000; fax 707-963-1794
www.vineyardcountryinn.com
201 Main St., St. Helena, CA 94574
Price: Expensive to Very Expensive
Credit Cards: AE, MC, V
Special Features: Pool, whirlpool

This lovely inn takes its inspiration from a French country village. Surrounding a central court, the buildings are crowned with steeply pitched roofs and intricate brick chimneys. There are 21 elegant suites, with exposed-beam ceilings, redbrick fireplaces, king- or queen-sized beds, and wet bars with refrigerators. Many have balconies with vineyard views. For the breakfast buffet, small tables are grouped around the large dining room fireplace. The inn is on busy Highway 29, but the rooms are relatively quiet.

WINE COUNTRY INN

Innkeeper: Jim Smith
707-963-7077, 888-465-4608;
fax 707-963-9018
www.winecountryinn.com
romance@winecountryinn.com
1152 Lodi Ln., St. Helena, CA 94574
Price: Expensive to Very Expensive
Credit Cards: MC, V
Special Features: Pool, whirlpool

This guest house is modern, but a tall stone tower gives it an Old World feel. There are 29 rooms, each decorated with country-style quilts and antiques; all have private baths, and many have fireplaces and decks or balconies with lush views. Five cottages are a recent edition, and each has wooden floors, fireplaces, private patios, and two-person whirlpool tubs. A buffet-style breakfast is served daily.

ZINFANDEL INN

Innkeepers: Diane and Jerry Payton
707-963-3512
www.zinfandelinn.com
800 Zinfandel Ln., St. Helena, CA 94574
(1 mile south of St. Helena on Hwy. 29)
Price: Expensive to Very Expensive
Credit Cards: MC, V
Special Features: Garden, pool, whirlpool

A striking example of a modern English Tudor, this luxury getaway is planted in the heart of Wine Country. A fountain and an arched doorway crowned with fieldstone greet you, while the dining room has a beautifully inlaid oak floor. The three guest rooms are all named for grape varieties. The Chardonnay Room may be the most elegant, with its stone fireplace, king-sized bed in a bay window, and private entrance. The romantic Zinfandel Room has a private balcony, wood-burning stove, and whirlpool tub. The Chablis Room offers Victorian inspiration with a panoramic view of vineyards and mountains.

CALISTOGA

BRANNAN COTTAGE INN

Innkeepers: Doug and Judy Cook
707-942-4200; fax 707-942-2507
www.brannancottageinn.com
brannancottageinn@sbcglobal.net
109 Wapoo Ave., P.O. Box 81, Calistoga, CA 94515 (just off Hwy. 29, near Brannan St.)
Price: Moderate to Expensive
Credit Cards: MC, V
Special Features: Garden

Built around 1860 by Calistoga founder Sam Brannan, this inn is listed on the National Register of Historic Places and is the only guest house constructed for Brannan's Hot Springs Resort, which still stands on its original site. Not surprisingly, it's also the oldest building in town. Restoration began in the 1980s: Reconstruction of the gingerbread gable was based on enlarged vintage photographs. Today, an eclectic collection of furnishings, including plush and comfortable antiques, finishes the six guest rooms. All have private baths, private entrances, and air-conditioning. The house is surrounded by gardens—weather permitting, the generous breakfast may be served in the courtyard under trees—so guests can always find a private, quiet spot to read and relax, and the sunny courtyard beckons after a day of "spa-ing."

CALISTOGA RANCH

General Manager: Philip Kendall
707-254-2800, 800-942-4220;
fax 707-254-2888
www.calistogaranch.com
580 Lommel Rd., Calistoga, CA 94515
Price: Very Expensive
Credit Cards: AE, D, DC, MC, V
Special Features: Pool, health spa, restaurant, hiking trails

Set on a 157-acre spread in the forested hills outside Calistoga, this luxury resort opened in the summer of 2004. It includes 47 individual guest lodges ranging in size from 600 to 2,400 square feet and constructed of cedar, stone, and other natural materials that create an elegant yet casual atmosphere. The living areas open up onto mahogany decks that have retractable roofs, which lend an indoor-outdoor atmosphere. Activities center on the pool and health-spa bathhouse, but there are also 4 miles of hiking trails.

CARLIN COTTAGES

Innkeeper: Larry & Georgene Costello
707-942-9102, 800-734-4624;
fax 707-942-2295
www.carlincottages.com
1623 Lake St., Calistoga, CA 94515 (Hwy. 29 north through town, west on Lake)
Price: Moderate to Expensive
Credit Cards: AE, MC, V
Special Features: Pool, whirlpool

Remember the old auto court motels of the 1950s? Well, Carlin Cottages is a souped-up version of those vanishing classics. There are 15 cottages—ranging from studios to two-room suites—and each is minimally but agreeably appointed with country, Shaker-style furniture. Most of the cottages have kitchenettes, and seven cottages have whirlpool tubs with water fed by a mineral spring. There's a pool in the center of the courtyard, and mature trees shade the entire property. Located on a quiet residential street, Carlin Cottages is a good spot for families. A good value.

CHATEAU DE VIF

Innkeepers: Felipe Barragan and Peter Weatherman
707-942-6446, 877-558-2513;
fax 707-942-6456
www.cdvnapavalley.com
info.cdvnapavalley.com
3250 Hwy. 128, Calistoga, CA 94515
Price: Expensive to Very Expensive
Credit Cards: AE, MC, V
Special Features: Eight-person Jacuzzi outside by the garden, 40-foot heated lap pool

Surrounded by 2 acres of vineyards, this B&B has an understated elegance appreciated by the discerning. (Ted Kennedy has reportedly been a guest.) The inn has excellent views of Mount St. Helena and great gourmet breakfasts: fresh-baked scones, breads, and muffins; country sausage; and vegetable quiches. All three rooms have queen-sized beds and private baths. An eight-person whirlpool spa sits outside by the garden. A perk for wine-lovers: The inn produces its own Chateau de Vie label for its guests.

CHELSEA GARDEN INN

Innkeeper: Connie McDonald
707-942-0948, 800-942-1515;
fax 707-942-5102
www.chelseagardeninn.com
innkeeper@chelseagardeninn.com
1443 2nd St., Calistoga, CA 94515
(near downtown)
Price: Expensive
Credit Cards: AE, D, MC, V
Special Features: Pool

Formerly known as Scott Courtyard, this stylish inn has a lushly landscaped courtyard that lends a wonderfully secluded feel. All five accommodations are one-bedroom suites, each with a private entrance and air-conditioning—a real comfort on those Calistoga summer days. Breakfast is served in the common room warmed by a stone fireplace or in the courtyard by the pool. This inn is near downtown but quiet, and the hospitality is first-rate.

CHRISTOPHER'S INN

Innkeepers: Christopher and Adele Layton
707-942-5755; fax 707-942-6895
www.christophersinn.com
christophersinn@earthlink.net
1010 Foothill Blvd., Calistoga, CA 94515
(on Hwy. 29 just south of Lincoln Ave.)
Price: Expensive to Very Expensive
Credit Cards: AE, MC, V

This stylish inn has 22 rooms, all with private baths, and its rich antiques and Laura Ashley wallpaper and curtains evoke an English country inn. An architect by trade, Christopher Layton renovated three old summer cottages. The grounds are impeccably tended, bright with color and shaded by tall trees; one room has a private garden patio, and another has a porch shaded by star jasmine. A wing was added in 1997, and many of the new rooms feature fireplaces and whirlpool tubs. A modest Continental breakfast is delivered to your room or served in the garden. Location is both an advantage and a bit of a disadvantage. Guests can walk to town, but Highway 29 can be noisy during the day. It's practically a moot point, however, because all the rooms are soundproofed.

CHANRIC INN

Innkeepers: Ric Pielstick and Channing McBride
707-942-4535, 877-281-3671;
fax 707-942-4557
www.thechanric.com
info@thechanric.com
1805 Foothill Blvd., Calistoga, CA 94515
(on Hwy. 128 north of Lincoln Ave.)
Price: Expensive
Credit Cards: AE, D, MC, V
Special Features: Pool, whirlpool

Cottage Grove offers guests their own little world. Tim Fish

Set on a shady hillside, the Chanric Inn is an easy walk to Calistoga's main-street dining and shopping. All rooms have private baths and guests are pampered with fluffy down comforters, high-thread-count Egyptian cotton sheets, and plush bathrobes. The pool and spa boasts a view of the Palisades Mountains. A full breakfast emphasizes ingredients from local organic farms, and it can be served at an intimate table or at the big table where guests gather. The grounds are lovely, with beautiful roses and a trellised ancient grape vine.

COTTAGE GROVE INN

Innkeeper: Donna Johnson
707-942-8400, 800-799-2284
www.cottagegrove.com
innkeeper@cottagegrove.com
1711 Lincoln Ave., Calistoga, CA 94515
(a few blocks north of downtown)
Price: Very Expensive
Credit Cards: AE, D, DC, MC, V

This classy inn is actually a group of 16 California Craftsman-style cottages, built on the site of Brannan's original Calistoga resort. The cottages, nestled in a grove of old elms, are a short walk to Calistoga's many spas. Each cottage features skylights, hardwood floors, a covered front porch with wicker rockers, ceiling fans, a wood-burning fireplace, air-conditioning, and a two-person whirlpool tub. Each has a distinct design theme. The Nautical Cottage, for example, takes New England as its inspiration. The Gardener's Cottage sports a picket-fence headboard and floral prints. The inn also offers wifi Internet access and flat screen televisions. Some cottages are situated close to the street, but Lincoln Avenue is considerably quieter at night.

FOOTHILL HOUSE

Innkeeper: Darla Anderson
707-942-6933, 800-942-6933;
fax 707-942-5692
www.foothillhouse.com
info@foothillhouse.com
3037 Foothill Blvd., Calistoga, CA 94515
(on Hwy. 128 north of Petrified Forest Rd.)

Price: Expensive to Very Expensive
Credit Cards: AE, D, MC, V

This cozy inn is a find. Shaded by tall trees and set amid lush gardens, the modest turn-of-the-20th-century farmhouse is a soothing getaway. Foothill House offers three elegant suites and a private cottage. All have private baths (three with whirlpool tubs), private patio-door entrances, refrigerators, and wood-burning stoves or fireplaces. Laura Ashley prints and antiques furnish the rooms, including queen- or king-sized four-poster beds. The cottage, called Quail's Roost, is accented in white-washed pine and equipped with a kitchenette and a two-person whirlpool that looks out to a waterfall. Guests are pampered with a generous, gourmet breakfast delivered to their room or taken on the terrace. Afternoon wine and cheese in the sun room is an extravagant spread.

GARNETT CREEK INN

Innkeepers: Kenneth Lavin and Jerry Tatum
707-942-9797; fax 707-942-8021
www.garnettcreekinn.com
garnettcreekinn@gmail.com
1139 Lincoln Ave., Calistoga, CA 94515
Price: Expensive to Very Expensive
Credit Cards: MC, V

A 19th-century Victorian with a wrap-around porch, this charming inn is located in the heart of Calistoga. There are five rooms in all, each with private bath and gas fireplace and tastefully decorated with elegant country fabrics and New England antiques and period reproductions. The Lucinda Suite offers a deep, soaking tub and sitting room with a bay window overlooking the garden. A Continental breakfast is served in your room or on the porch, weather permitting.

HIDEAWAY COTTAGES

Manager: Ren Ta
707-942-4108

www.hideawaycottages.com
1412 Fairway, Calistoga, CA 94515 (just off Lincoln Ave.)
Price: Moderate to Very Expensive
Credit Cards: AE, MC, V
Special Features: Pool, whirlpool

These 17 units are comfy but utilitarian, and all are set amid tall, mature trees on 2 acres on a quiet residential street close to Lincoln Avenue restaurants and shops. It's a good spot if you're planning an extended stay. Three deluxe cottages are available, and one of the cottages can accommodate groups of four or six. Air-conditioning and televisions are standard, and most units have kitchenettes.

MEADOWLARK

Innkeeper: Kurt Stevens and Richard Flynn
707-942-5651, 800-942-5651
www.meadowlarkinn.com
info@meadowlarkinn.com
601 Petrified Forest Rd., Calistoga, CA 94515
Price: Expensive to Very Expensive
Credit Cards: AE, MC, V
Special Features: Mineral pool and clothing optional for hot tub and sauna

This luxurious inn is just 2 miles outside Calistoga, and it has plenty of land to roam: 20 acres. There's a mineral pool on the property and a clothing-optional policy for the hot tub and sauna. The bedrooms all have private baths and queen-sized beds, and all have private decks or terraces to take advantage of the views. Gourmet breakfasts are served, and guests are encouraged to enjoy the vistas from their terraces or decks. Well-behaved dogs are welcome.

MOUNT VIEW HOTEL

Manager: Andrea Detrinidad
707-942-6877, 800-816-6877;
fax 707-942-6904
www.mountviewhotel.com
info@mountviewhotel.com

1457 Lincoln Ave., Calistoga, CA 94515
Price: Expensive to Very Expensive
Credit Cards: AE, MC, V
Special Features: Health spa, pool,
whirlpool, restaurant

Restored Mission Revival and on the
National Register of Historic Places, this
elegant lodge was originally a European-
style hotel built in 1917. There are 29 units
and three cottages, including nine luxurious suites, one of which is furnished in art
deco-period pieces. It's in the heart of
Calistoga shopping and dining. The hotel
has its own superb spa (see chapter 7,
Recreation), and others are just a step
away.

THE PINK MANSION
Innkeepers: Toppa and Leslie Epps
707-942-0558, 800-238-7465
www.pinkmansion.com
pink@napanet.net
1415 Foothill Blvd., Calistoga, CA 94515
(on Hwy. 128—near Hwy. 29)
Price: Expensive to Very Expensive
Credit Cards: D, MC, V
Special Features: Indoor pool, whirlpool,
garden

Postcard views of Napa Valley and lush
forests await visitors who stay at this 1875
Victorian. The home's pink exterior will
catch your attention, while the flowers, rare
plants, and exotic palms will hold your
interest—the estate grounds include 3 acres
of landscaped gardens. The inn features two
rooms and four suites with fireplaces. Two
of the suites have whirlpools, and all are
done in grandmotherly antiques. There is
also a 1,000-square-foot cottage with a loft
and fireplace. The inn also has an indoor
pool. Wine and cheese cap off the afternoon.

SOLAGE CALISTOGA
Innkeeper: Richard Hill
707-226-0800; fax: 707-226-0809

www.solagecalistoga.com
info@solagecalistoga.com
755 Silverado Trail, Calistoga, CA. 94515
Price: Very Expensive
Credit Cards: AE, D, MC, V
Special Features: Solbar restaurant, Spa
Solage, 130-foot swimming pool

A 22-acre complex includes 89 accommodations, from one-room studios to deluxe
suites, as well as the Spa Solage and the
restaurant Solbar. The hip bistro offers
healthful entrees as well as rich comfort
food. Breakfasts are not part of the room
rate, but include decadent dishes such as
Double Decker French Toast and Made-
From-Scratch Blueberry Buckwheat
Pancakes. This is a green resort, which
means all the water is recycled and all the
cleaning products are environmentally
friendly. Solage Calistoga offers great views
of the Palisades and the Mayacama
Mountains.

Calistoga Spa Lodging
Many spas offer lodging/spa treatment discount packages. For complete spa treatment
information, see chapter 7, Recreation.

Calistoga Spa Hot Springs (707-942-6269,
www.calistogaspa.com, 1006 Washington
St., Calistoga, CA 94515; Moderate; MC, V)
Relaxed and unpretentious, this inn has the
amenities of a resort but at more affordable
prices. All 57 family-oriented units have
kitchenettes, air-conditioning, TVs, and
telephones. Features include a fitness room
and four outdoor mineral pools. Children
are welcome.

Calistoga Village Inn and Spa (707-942-
0991, www.greatspa.com, 1880 Lincoln
Ave., Calistoga, CA 94515; Moderate to
Expensive; AE, D, MC, V) This inn has
been everything from a motel to a Moonie
camp. Rooms are pleasant but modestly
appointed. Some suites have whirlpool

tubs. Two outdoor mineral pools offer an expansive view of the mountains. There are an inside mineral whirlpool and sauna.

Dr. Wilkinson's Hot Springs (707-942-4102, www.drwilkinson.com, 1507 Lincoln Ave., Calistoga, CA 94515; Expensive; AE, MC, V) This spa has 42 spacious and functional motel-type rooms, many with kitchenettes. There are two outdoor mineral pools plus an indoor mineral whirlpool. Shopping and dining are within walking distance. Rooms, grounds, and pools have recently been polished up.

Eurospa & Inn (707-942-6829, www.eurospa.com, 1202 Pine St., Calistoga, CA 94515; Moderate to Expensive; AE, D, MC, V) Each of the 13 rooms at this inn and spa is decorated in a different theme. Many rooms have private whirlpools and gas-burning stoves. There are an outdoor pool and whirlpool. It's close to downtown yet away from the main-street bustle.

Golden Haven Hot Springs Spa and Resort (707-942-8000, www.goldehaven.com, 1713 Lake St., Calistoga, CA 94515; Inexpensive to Expensive; AE, MC, V) Amid towering oak trees and lush gardens, this inn and spa isn't fancy but offers 28 rooms, several of them two-room suites, five with kitchenettes, and all with refrigerators. Rooms with whirlpools and saunas are also available.

Indian Springs Spa and Resort (707-942-4913, www.indianspringscalistoga.com, 1712 Lincoln Ave., Calistoga, CA 94515; Expensive to Very Expensive; D, MC, V) Eighteen whitewashed bungalow-style cottages—one is a three-bedroom that sleeps six—overlook 16 acres of palm trees and views of Mount St. Helena. There's a gorgeous Olympic-sized mineral pool. It's an easy walk to downtown shopping and dining.

Roman Spa (707-942-4441, 800-820-4461, www.romanspahotsprings.com, 1300 Washington St.; Inexpensive to Expensive; AE, D, MC, V) Lushly landscaped grounds surround this older but well-tended 60-room motel-type resort. Half of the units have kitchenettes. There's an outdoor mineral pool and whirlpool plus a large indoor whirlpool and sauna.

Lodging in Sonoma County

SONOMA VALLEY

BELTANE RANCH
Manager: Ann Soulier
707-996-6501
www.beltaneranch.com
11775 Sonoma Hwy., P.O. Box 395, Glen Ellen, CA 95442 (on Hwy. 12 between Kenwood and Glen Ellen)
Price: Moderate to Expensive
Credit Cards: None
Special Features: Tennis, hiking trails, working vineyard

This former bunkhouse was built in 1890 and has been everything from a turkey farm to a historic farmhouse with ties to the Underground Railroad. The ranch was even rumored to be a brothel, but now it's a quiet and unpretentious B&B. It sits on 1,600 acres of land, amid vineyards and olive trees. (The inn even makes its own Beltane Ranch Olive Oil.) A stylish porch and veranda with an elaborate gingerbread railing were added to the house years ago. There are five guest rooms, each with a private entrance and bath and one with a wood-burning stove. There's also a new cottage with one bedroom and a private garden. A full breakfast is served in the wood-paneled dining room or on the wraparound veranda. An added bonus is the remarkable hiking trail on the property, which takes you past vineyards.

BUNGALOWS 313

Innkeepers: Denise and Tony Salvo
707-996-8091; fax 707-996-7301
www.bungalows313.com
info@bungalows313.com
313 1st St. E., Sonoma, CA 95476 (a half
block north of Sonoma Plaza)
Price: Expensive to Very Expensive
Credit Cards: D, MC, V
Special Features: Garden

Located just a half block from the Sonoma
Plaza, this inn is near the best restaurants,
shops, and historical sites but is hidden in a
secluded compound. There's a lovely little
garden with a stone fountain, perfect for
relaxing in a chair with a good book. There are
five bungalows in all, each with a kitchenette
and a distinct personality and modern furnishings. The Brick House bungalow was built
in 1907 and recalls an Italian farmhouse. It
has 20-inch-thick stone walls, tile floors, a
fireplace, and a claw-foot tub. Dolce bungalow
and Vita bungalow both have two-story lofts,
and each overlooks a private garden.

THE COTTAGE INN AND SPA/THE MISSION BED-AND-BREAKFAST

Innkeeper: Anne Labarre
707-996-0719, 800-944-1490
www.cottageinnandspa.com
info@cottageinnandspa.com
302 1st St. E., Sonoma, CA 95476
(one block north of Sonoma Plaza)
Price: Moderate to Very Expensive
Credit Cards: MC, V

These two inns are side by side on 1st Street
East, not far from the downtown plaza, but
still a quiet oasis. A Mediterranean-style
courtyard is enclosed by a high stucco wall
and features a fountain and whirlpool. The
two inns have eight rooms total between
them, all done with Mexican tile floors. Many
have private entries or patios; some have
fireplaces and whirlpool baths. Fresh-baked
goodies are delivered each morning, allowing
guests a private Continental breakfast.

EL DORADO HOTEL

Manager: Jens Hoi
707-996-3030, 800-289-3031;
fax 707-996-3148
www.hoteleldoradosonoma.com
info@eldoradosonoma.com
405 1st St. W., Sonoma, CA 95476 (on the
downtown plaza)
Price: Moderate to Expensive
Credit Cards: AE, MC, V
Special Features: Restaurant, pool

The El Dorado is a special hotel. Restored
to its original elegance, it has 27 rooms, all
with private baths. All of the rooms are
done in elegantly modern decor and have
four-poster beds and terraces that offer
views of the hotel's Spanish courtyard or
the historic plaza. The lobby restaurant, El
Dorado Kitchen, serves California cuisine.

FAIRMONT SONOMA MISSION INN AND SPA

Manager: Kelly Cosgrove
707-938-9000, 800-862-4945
www.fairmont.com
100 Boyes Blvd., Boyes Hot Springs, CA
95416 (just north of Sonoma on Hwy. 12)
Price: Very Expensive
Credit Cards: AE, DC, MC, V
Special Features: Health spa, golf course,
pool, exercise rooms, two restaurants

Sonoma County's premier hotel, and now
part of the prestigious Fairmont chain, the
Sonoma Mission completed an impressive
$60-million face-lift in 2005. The inn was
built on a site once considered a sacred healing ground by Native Americans. By the turn
of the 20th century, the area had become a
getaway for well-heeled San Franciscans,
who came to Boyes Hot Springs Hotel to "take
the waters." It has been a destination ever
since, and the rich and famous who have
stayed here include Sylvester Stallone, Billy
Crystal, and Tom Cruise.

From the impressive Mission-style façade
to its health-spa pamper palace, the inn

The rooms are so cozy at the Fairmont Sonoma Mission Inn, you'll find it hard to leave. Courtesy Sonoma Mission Inn

exudes luxury. The 228 rooms and suites are all elegantly done in warm wood highlights and pastel hues, and many have fireplaces, whirlpool tubs, and plantation shutters and offer views of the inn's shady grounds. The spa has also received a complete makeover and is among the most luxurious in Wine Country. (See chapter 7, Recreation, for more details.) The 10-acre grounds also include two restaurants (see chapter 5, Restaurants). Santé is the inn's upscale eatery, but sadly the food is not quite up to the price tag; The Big 3 is an adequate spot for breakfast and lunch. If there's a drawback to the Sonoma Mission Inn, it's location. Though convenient to wineries and historic sites of Sonoma Valley, it's located along a hectic and well-developed thoroughfare. The grounds, however, remain peaceful.

GAIGE HOUSE INN

Hotel Manager: Nico Hallwass
707-935-0237, 800-935-0237;

fax 707-935-6411
www.gaige.com
gaige@Thompsonhotels.com
13540 Arnold Dr., Glen Ellen, CA 95442
(off Hwy. 12)
Price: Very Expensive
Credit Cards: AE, D, MC, V
Special Features: Pool, whirlpool tub

This exceptional inn is a sanctuary off the beaten path. A Queen Anne Italianate built in the 1890s, it has 23 guest rooms, all elegantly done in modern tones. All the rooms have private baths and air-conditioning, and many have private entrances, whirlpool tubs, and fireplaces. The best is the Gaige Suite, which has a canopied king-sized bed, a whirlpool tub, and a private balcony with a grand view. A new addition contains eight Zen suites done in sleek Asian design, some overlooking the nearby creek. Breakfast, which is serious business here, is optional and costs $15 per person. Favorite dishes include the artichoke and pistachio blini with home-smoked salmon. The pool is a lovely setting, and there's a whirlpool tub in the garden. It's in an ideal location for wine touring and Sonoma dining.

GLENELLY INN & COTTAGES

Innkeeper: Kristi Hallamore Jeppesen
707-996-6720; fax 707-996-5227
www.glenelly.com
glenelly@glenelly.com
5131 Warm Springs Rd., Glen Ellen, CA 95442 (off Hwy. 12 at Arnold Dr.)
Price: Expensive
Credit Cards: MC, V
Special Features: Whirlpool

Originally established in 1916 as a railroad inn, this French Colonial has grand verandas on both floors and six rooms, with two additional garden cottages nearby. All rooms have stylish country furnishings that recall grandmother's house, and most have claw-foot tubs with showers. All rooms open to the veranda or deck in this quiet, wooded setting with nearby wineries and restaurants. A generous buffet breakfast is served near the stone fireplace in the dining room. A favorite is salsa-jack soufflé. This is that rare B&B that's family friendly.

THE INN AT RAMEKINS

Innkeeper: Marilyn Piraino
707-933-0452; fax 707-933-0451
www.ramekins.com
inn@ramekins.com
450 W. Spain St., Sonoma, CA 95476
Price: Moderate to Expensive
Credit Cards: AE, D, MC, V
Special Features: Culinary school, restaurant

This has to rate as one of the most food-savvy B&Bs of all. The six guest rooms are on the second floor of Ramekins Sonoma Valley Culinary School, well within reach of delectable aromas. All rooms have private baths, antique-pine furniture, custom-made down comforters, and oversized bathrooms, and one room has a fireplace. Ramekins is also just a few blocks from the historic Sonoma Plaza.

KENWOOD INN AND SPA

General Manager: Karl Bruno
707-833-1293, 800-353-6966;
fax 707-833-1247
www.kenwoodinn.com
10400 Sonoma Hwy., Kenwood, CA 95452 (1 mile south of Kenwood, on Hwy. 12)
Price: Very Expensive
Credit Cards: AE, MC, V
Special Features: Heated pool, health spa

This intimate resort looks like a small Tuscan village in a grove of oak trees. The inn includes 29 rooms situated around three courtyards on the 2.5-acre property. The second-story suites offer dramatic views of the Valley of the Moon and its many vineyards. The rooms are large and have a casual luxuriousness to them. At the heart of the compound are the pool, gardens, and spa facility. A full country breakfast is included, and a lunch menu is also offered poolside. Dinner—Italian fare—is offered to guests Thursday, Friday, and Saturday. Traffic along Highway 12 quiets dramatically at night.

LEDSON HOTEL AND HARMONY LOUNGE

General Manager: Meghan Ainsworth
707-996-9779
www.ledsonhotel.com
480 1st St. E., Sonoma, CA 95476
Price: Expensive
Credit Cards: AE, D, MC, V
Special Features: Wine bar, restaurant

This luxury two-story hotel is situated on the charming Sonoma Plaza. Six individually decorated rooms are on the upper floor, while the Harmony Lounge and Wine Tasting Bar covers the entire ground floor.

Rooms have king-sized beds, whirlpool spas, fireplaces, and balconies. Three of the rooms overlook Sonoma Plaza, offering a delightful view. The heart of Wine Country appears to be shifting from Sonoma Valley to Healdsburg and St. Helena, making retail shops on Sonoma Plaza less vibrant than in years past, but this hotel is still a lovely place to stay.

THE LODGE AT SONOMA RENAISSANCE RESORT AND SPA

General Manager: David Dolquist
707-935-6600, 888-710-8008;
fax 707-935-6829
www.thelodgeatsonoma.com
1325 Broadway, Sonoma, CA 95476 (1 mile south of Sonoma Plaza)
Price: Expensive to Very Expensive
Credit Cards: CB, D, DC, AE, MC, V
Special Features: Restaurant, pool, whirlpool, bar, fireplaces, health spa

One of the newest and largest hotels in Sonoma Valley, this 182-room inn is part of the Renaissance/Marriott family of hotels. The 9-acre complex features a main lodge and 18 cottages. Many of the rooms and suites have private entrances and fireplaces. The inn is elegantly designed in classic California Mission style. The courtyard is impressive, with its towering Canary Island date palms. The health spa features private cabanas and a mineral water pool. Be sure to check out Carneros Bistro and Wine Bar, the inn's restaurant (see chapter 5, Restaurants), a handsome space that features fresh pastas, pizzas, and steaks, and other treats from the rotisserie.

MACARTHUR PLACE

Manager: Bill Blum
707-938-2929, 800-722-1866;
fax 707-933-9833
www.macarthurplace.com
info@macarthurplace.com
29 E. MacArthur St., Sonoma, CA 95476

(four blocks south of Sonoma Plaza)
Price: Very Expensive
Credit Cards: AE, MC, V
Special Features: Restaurant, pool, whirlpool, health spa, garden

MacArthur Place is Wine Country living at its most luxurious. Sixty-four rooms and suites are set in a private 7-acre compound lush with gardens and sculptures. The property was once a working vineyard and ranch, and the original house—a grand Victorian built in the 1850s—includes 10 rooms. Twenty-nine deluxe suites were recently added, and each includes a wood-burning fireplace, king-sized bed, whirlpool tub, and TV with DVD player with six-speaker sound. The inn's Garden Spa offers a range of treatments, from a rose-petal bath to an olive-oil body polish. The property's historic barn is now home to a conference center as well as a cocktail bar and the valley's premier steak house, Saddles. (See chapter 5, Restaurants).

SONOMA VALLEY INN, BEST WESTERN

Manager: Alexis Swan
707-938-9200, 800-334-5784;
fax 707-938-0935
www.sonomavalleyinn.com
550 2nd St. W., Sonoma, CA 95476 (one block west of Sonoma Plaza, off Hwy. 12)
Price: Moderate to Very Expensive
Credit Cards: AE, CB, D, DC, MC, V
Special Features: Pool, whirlpool, fitness room

An intimate motel may be the best way to describe this exceptional lodge just a block from Sonoma Plaza. Rooms and furnishings are well above average for a motel, and many are equipped with kitchenettes, wet bars, whirlpools, and fireplaces. Most of the rooms open onto a lovely courtyard. It's ideal for families visiting the valley. Complimentary Continental breakfast is included and delivered to the rooms.

THISTLE DEW INN
Innkeepers: Jan Rafiq and Gregg Percival
707-938-2909, 800-382-7895; fax: 707-
938-2129
www.thistledew.com
info@thistledew.com
171 W. Spain St., Sonoma, CA 95476 (a half
block from Sonoma Plaza)
Price: Moderate to Expensive
Credit Cards: AE, MC, V, D
Special Features: Whirlpool

This inn is decorated throughout with vintage
Arts and Crafts furniture and decor. Each
of the six guest rooms (two in the main
house and four in the adjacent cottage) has
a private bath, air-conditioning, and a
ceiling fan. Five rooms have private decks
and entrances. Three rooms have gas fireplaces, and three are equipped with large
whirlpool tubs. Another whirlpool tub is in
the garden. A full gourmet breakfast is
served in the dining room or on the deck.
This is a charming inn, reasonably priced
and in an excellent location for strolling to
all of Sonoma's finest.

Petaluma
SHERATON SONOMA COUNTY
General Manager: Tom Buckley
707-283-2888; fax 707-283-2828
www.sheraton.com/petaluma
745 Baywood Dr., Petaluma, CA 94954
Price: Inexpensive to Very Expensive
Credit Cards: AE, MC, V
Special Features: Restaurant, pool,
whirlpool

Located on the Petaluma River marina, and
centrally located to wine touring in both
Sonoma and Napa, this inn is a good choice
for travelers who prefer the ease and
amenities of a business hotel. Designed
with peaked roofs and porches, it looks like
something from a New England port town.
The 183 rooms are well appointed, if a bit
generic, and have a certain masculine elegance to them.

Santa Rosa
FLAMINGO RESORT HOTEL
General Manager: Foriann Bynum
707-545-8530, 800-848-8300
www.flamingoresort.com
info@flamingoresort.com
2777 4th St., Santa Rosa, CA 95405 (at
Farmers Ln.)
Price: Inexpensive to Very Expensive
Credit Cards: AE, DC, MC, V
Special Features: Pool, whirlpool, tennis,
fitness center, restaurant

French country furnishings and mature
landscaping make this 170-room resort
hotel friendly and comfortable in an
unfussy way. Sonoma Valley's premium
wineries are just minutes east on Highway
12. Guests have access to an adjacent fitness
center, and the 25-meter outdoor pool is
heated year-round. Specialty shops and
excellent restaurants are just blocks away
on Farmers Lane. It's popular with both
business travelers and tourists.

FOUNTAINGROVE INN HOTEL
Manager: Ken Murakami
707-578-6101, 800-222-6101;
fax 707-544-3126
www.fountaingroveinn.com
101 Fountaingrove Pkwy., Santa Rosa, CA
95403 (off Hwy. 101 at Old Redwood Hwy.
exit)
Price: Inexpensive to Very Expensive
Credit Cards: AE, D, DC, MC, V
Special Features: Heated pool, whirlpool,
restaurant, conference center

The redwood-and-stone exterior of this
luxury hotel is modern but blends harmo-
niously with the landscape, and the delib-
erately low sweep of the architecture
affords an unobstructed view of the
Round Barn historical landmark just up
the hill. The 124 rooms are elegantly simple and decorated with tasteful furnishings. Each room has a king-sized or two
queen-sized beds and a small refrigera-

The Hotel La Rose is located in historic Railroad Square, Santa Rosa. Tim Fish

tor. Continental buffet breakfast is included for business travelers, and standard hotel services are available. The hotel offers wine-touring packages as well as golf packages.

THE GABLES

Innkeepers: Pam and Mike Stanbrough
707-585-7777, 800-GABLESN;
fax 707-584-5634
www.thegablesinn.com
innkeeper@thegablesinn.com
4257 Petaluma Hill Rd., Santa Rosa, CA 95404 (Rohnert Park Hwy., east exit off Hwy. 101)
Price: Expensive
Credit Cards: AE, D, MC, V

The 15 gables over keyhole-shaped windows lend the name to this 1877 high-Victorian Gothic Revival inn. Other features include ceilings that soar to 25 feet, a mahogany staircase, and three Italian marble fireplaces. The seven spacious guest rooms (all with private bath, featuring a claw-foot tub) include four suites. The separate William and Mary's Cottage is furnished with a kitchenette, a woodstove, a two-person whirlpool tub, and a queen-sized bed in the loft. The inn is air-conditioned throughout. A full gourmet breakfast and afternoon snacks are included.

HILTON

General Manager: Lowell Johnson
707-523-7555; fax 707-569-5555
www.winecountryhilton.com
3555 Round Barn Blvd., Santa Rosa, CA 95403 (off Hwy. 101 at Old Redwood Hwy. exit.; also off Mendocino Ave.)
Price: Moderate to Expensive
Credit Cards: AE, D, MC, V
Special Features: Pool, whirlpool, fitness center, restaurant, lounge, banquet facilities

This pleasant hotel, with views of Santa Rosa and easy access to Highway 101 and the local wineries, had a $6-million face-lift in 2004. The 250 spacious guest rooms and suites are scattered over 7 acres, and though the rooms aren't lavish, they are quite comfortable. The hotel caters to business travelers; all rooms have telephone-equipped desks. There are full hotel services, and the pool area is refreshing and upscale. Ask for a room with a view when making your reservation.

HOTEL LA ROSE

General Manager: Laura Knipping
707-579-3200, 800-527-6738;
fax 707-579-3247
www.hotellarose.com
reservations@hotellarose.com
308 Wilson St., Santa Rosa, CA 95404
(downtown Santa Rosa exit off Hwy. 101)
Price: Moderate to Very Expensive
Credit Cards: AE, CB, D, DC, MC, V
Special Features: Restaurant

This historic hotel—built in 1907 from stone extracted from the mountain ridges east of Santa Rosa—is in Railroad Square, once the hub of commerce in Sonoma County. Now, the square is an eclectic urban area busy with bohemian coffee-houses, nightclubs, and a few street folks. Reconstructed in 1985, the hotel and adjacent carriage house have a total of 49 rooms, with English country interiors, private baths renovated in 1998, and televisions. Twenty of the rooms have patios or balconies overlooking a courtyard garden. A European breakfast is included. Josef's Restaurant in the hotel is recommended.

HYATT VINEYARD CREEK

General Manager: Keo Hornbostel
707-636-7100; fax 707-636-7130
www.hyatt.com
170 Railroad St., Santa Rosa, CA 95401
Price: Moderate to Expensive

Credit Cards: AE, MC, V
Special features: Pool, health spa, restaurant

A recent addition to downtown Santa Rosa, this hotel appeals to conventioneers more than tourists. Still, it's a pleasing if somewhat generic hotel, with 155 rooms on three floors. The decor is standard, but many rooms overlook courtyards and the pool area, which is situated along a bucolic creek. Highway 101 is nearby, making it easily accessible to Wine Country touring, but traffic can be noisy, even at night. Many of Santa Rosa's best restaurants are within walking distance.

SAFARI WEST WILDLIFE PRESERVE AND TENT CAMP

Owners: Nancy and Peter Lang
707-579-2551, 800-616-2695;
fax 707-579-8777
www.safariwest.com
info@safariwest.com
3115 Porter Creek Rd., Santa Rosa, CA 95404
Price: Expensive to Very Expensive
Credit Cards: AE, MC, V
Special Features: African wilderness experience with exotic animals

This is no Jurassic Park—no danger lurks—but it's based on the same idea: Making the wild accessible. At Safari West you can now stay overnight in authentic, canvas African safari tents with hardwood floors, in close proximity to but separated from exotic wildlife. Each tent has a king-sized bed or two doubles and a bathroom with a shower. A three-hour tour, scheduled separately, will take you through the 400 acres of wilderness, revealing some of the three hundred exotic mammals and birds. (The tour is not included in the price for an overnight stay.)

VINTNERS INN

Manager: Percy Brandon
707-575-7350, 800-421-2584;
fax: 707 575-1426

The rooms at Vintners Inn in Santa Rosa offer comfort and luxury. Courtesy Vintners Inn

www.vintnersinn.com
info@vintnersinn.com
4350 Barnes Rd., Santa Rosa, CA 95403
(off Hwy. 101)
Price: Expensive to Very Expensive
Credit Cards: AE, D, DC, MC, V
Special Features: Whirlpool, restaurant

Surrounded by a 92-acre vineyard, Vintners Inn is one of Sonoma County's finest establishments. It's a European-style hotel with an Old World atmosphere, from its French country decor to the central plaza with a fountain. The 44 guest rooms are separated into three buildings that ring the courtyard. Climbing the staircase in each building is akin to going upstairs to bedrooms in an elegant farmhouse. The oversized rooms in this Provençal-influenced inn have beamed ceilings and pine furni-

ture, some dating back to the turn of the previous century. Many rooms have fireplaces. Ground-floor rooms have patios; second-floor rooms have balconies with vineyard or courtyard views. Continental breakfast is included; room service is also available. The inn is convenient to both Sonoma and Napa Valley wineries. Next door is the superb John Ash & Company restaurant. (See chapter 5, Restaurants.)

HEALDSBURG
BELLE DE JOUR INN
Innkeepers: Tom and Brenda Hearn
707-431-9777; fax 707-431-7412
www.belledejourinn.com
16276 Healdsburg Ave., Healdsburg, CA
95448 (1 mile north of Dry Creek Rd.,
across from Simi Winery)

In a former incarnation, the 1869 Camellia Inn was Healdsburg's first hospital. Tim Fish

Price: Expensive to Very Expensive
Credit Cards: AE, MC, V

A peaceful B&B inn on the northern out-skirts of Healdsburg, Belle de Jour is set on a tranquil 6-acre hilltop with lovely views of rolling hills and distant mountains. The Italianate main farmhouse, built around 1873, is where the innkeepers live and pre-pare scrumptious breakfasts. The five guest suites, all decorated with French-country-inspired furniture, are set behind the main house. Two of the rooms have whirlpool tubs for two. The Terrace Room has an intimate whirlpool tub with views of the countryside. There's also a large suite in the carriage house equipped with whirlpool tubs for two as well as a gas fireplace. The Caretaker's Suite has a king-sized canopy bed, a big whirlpool tub, and French doors leading to a trellised deck. The inn is centrally located for touring Napa and Sonoma, and the Hearns are superb hosts.

CAMELLIA INN

Innkeepers: Ray, Del, and Lucy Lewand
707-433-8182, 800-727-8182
www.camelliainn.com
211 North St., Healdsburg, CA 95448 (two blocks east of Healdsburg Ave.)
Price: Moderate to Expensive
Credit Cards: AE, MC, V, D
Special Features: Pool, garden, fishpond

This 1869 Italianate Victorian home entered the turn of the 20th century as Healdsburg's first hospital. It's now a magnificent inn with nine guest rooms and still has many of its original and unique architectural details, including the twin marble fireplaces in the double parlor. All the rooms in the air-conditioned inn have private baths and are furnished with antiques and accented with chandeliers and Oriental rugs. On a quiet residential street just two blocks from the plaza, the inn is named for the 50 or so varieties of camellias that grace its gardens. A full breakfast buffet is served in the dining room, dominated by a mahogany fireplace mantel. The innkeepers are very friendly.

DRY CREEK INN, BEST WESTERN

General Manager: Aaron Krug
707-433-0300, 800-222-5784;
fax 707-433-1129
www.drycreekinn.com
198 Dry Creek Rd., Healdsburg, CA 95448 (off Hwy. 101 at Dry Creek Rd. exit)

Price: Inexpensive to Expensive
Credit Cards: AE, D, DC, MC, V
Special Features: Pool, whirlpool, exercise room

This motel is distinguished by its outstanding location for wine touring. There is fairly standard motel decor throughout, but a spectacular view of Dry Creek Valley is the payoff in many rooms. Rooms are equipped with refrigerators and coffeemakers, and a Continental breakfast is included—great for families. It's well situated for a day of wine tasting followed by dining downtown on the plaza. The downside: The inn fronts busy Highway 101, but the road quiets considerably at night.

GRAPE LEAF INN

Innkeepers: Richard and Kae Rosenberg
707-433-8140; fax 707-433-3140
www.grapeleafinn.com
info@grapeleafinn.com
539 Johnson St., Healdsburg, CA 95448 (two blocks east of Healdsburg Ave.)
Price: Expensive to Very Expensive
Credit Cards: MC, V

The 12 elegant guest rooms in this 1900 Queen Anne Victorian are furnished with cast-iron beds, armoires, and warm oak accents, and all are named for grape varietals. Seven of the rooms have skylights, and nine have tubs for two. The Chardonnay Suite is appealing, with stained-glass windows and cedar-paneled walls. The Syrah Suite is one of the most luxurious, with a Japanese soaking tub and a skylight. The inn's quiet porch is perfect for unwinding after a day of wine touring. A full country breakfast is served in the dining room. Wine is served nightly, and the inn is within walking distance of Healdsburg's historic downtown plaza. For those who prefer a more exotic setting, the innkeepers have a unique offering: three guests cottages seven minutes from the inn, located amid a 10-acre, old vine zinfandel vineyard.

HAYDON STREET INN
Innkeepers: John Harasty and Keren Colsten
707-433-5228, 800-528-3703; fax 707-433-6637
www.haydon.com
innkeeper@haydon.com
321 Haydon St., Healdsburg, CA 95448 (off Hwy. 101 at Central Healdsburg exit)
Price: Moderate to Very Expensive
Credit Cards: AE, D, MC, V

In a quiet residential area and surrounded by trees, this Queen Anne Victorian inn has nine charming guest rooms, all with hardwood floors, antiques, down comforters, and private baths. More romantic are the three cottage rooms, all with king-sized beds, fireplaces, and large whirlpool tubs. A generous breakfast buffet is crafted by owner John, a retired chef, and served in the dining room. The inn is a short walk to Healdsburg's plaza.

HONOR MANSION
Innkeepers: Steve and Cathi Fowler
707-433-4277, 800-554-4667; fax 707-431-7173
www.honormansion.com
innkeeper@honormansion.com
14891 Grove St., Healdsburg, CA 95448
Price: Expensive to Very Expensive
Credit Cards: AE, MC, V
Special Features: 100-year-old magnolia trees, lap pool, koi pond, putting green, bocce court, tennis court, and spa services

Honor Mansion has—appropriately—won its share of honors. It was named one of the most romantic inns by American Historic Inns. Built in 1883, this Victorian mansion attributes its name to Dr. Herbert Honor, whose family owned the property for more than one hundred years. The Fowlers bought the inn in 1994 and remodeled the entire building—and these innkeepers will spoil you outright, from mints on your pillow to scrumptious afternoon appetizers.

There's a breakfast buffet, and you'll want to check out the inn's Honor Mansion Cookbook. Most of the guest rooms and suites feature queen-sized beds, comfy sitting areas, claw-foot tubs, and great views. The inn is near the Healdsburg plaza and a short drive from many wineries in the area.

HEALDSBURG INN ON THE PLAZA
Innkeeper: Genny Jenkins
707-433-6991, 800-431-8663; fax 707-433-9513
www.healdsburginn.com
110 Matheson St., Healdsburg, CA 95448 (off Healdsburg Ave.)
Price: Very Expensive
Credit Cards: AE, D, MC, V
Special Features: Art gallery

Right on Healdsburg's delightful downtown plaza, this 12-room inn welcomes guests through the main-floor gift shop. Four rooms in the front have bay windows and overlook the plaza with its bevy of shops, restaurants, and tasting rooms. They have king-sized beds, fireplaces, and whirlpool tubs for two in their private baths. The back rooms open on to a balcony, and most have king-sized beds, private baths with old-fashioned soaking tubs, and fireplaces. The solarium and roof garden is the common area where guests take breakfast and afternoon refreshments. In-room TVs and phones are available on request.

HOTEL HEALDSBURG
General Manager: Aziz Zhari
707-431-2800, 800-889-7188; fax 707-431-0414
www.hotelhealdsburg.com
frontoffice@hotelhealdsburg.com
25 Matheson St., Healdsburg, CA 95448
Price: Expensive to Very Expensive
Credit cards: AE, DC, MC, V

This contemporary, three-story hotel is right on the main square of Healdsburg, a

The Hotel Healdsburg imparts a sense of cosmopolitan style. Tim Fish

small town that manages to be both quaint and cosmopolitan. The hotel is modern in decor but remains warm and inviting, with a stone fireplace in the lobby and—for those who like to people-watch—a screened-in porch. Hotel Healdsburg has 55 rooms, all designed to pamper: oversized bathrooms done in Italian glass mosaic tile, 6-foot soaking tubs, private balconies, down comforters. In addition, a Continental breakfast is delivered to your door. Right off the lobby is Dry Creek Kitchen, a restaurant owned by star chef Charlie Palmer—best known for his Aureole restaurants in New York and Las Vegas. Showcasing American cuisine and wine from Sonoma County, the restaurant serves lunch and dinner. The Healdsburg's location on the downtown square can be a drawback for guests sensitive to noise.

LES MARS

Owners: Sarah and David Mars
877-431-1700
www.lesmarshotel.com

27 North St. Healdsburg, CA. 95448
Price: Expensive to Very Expersive
Credit Cards: AE, V, MC.

Les Mars feels like a European hotel on American turf. Its front lobby is elegant, with 17th and 18th century antiques, warm wood and soft colors. It offers Old World luxury and 21st century technology—such as entertainment amenities housed within a Louis XV armoire. The hotel has 16 individual guest rooms, many of which have high ceilings and fireplaces. Outdoors there's a pool with a French limestone fountain nearby. Les Mars is one of the most decadent hotels in Wine Country, particularly for the palate. The restaurant with a buzz – Cyrus – is on the hotel's premises and it has quite a draw. Cyrus is as close to the French Laundry experience as you can get in Sonoma County. The hotel was wise to make it a power partner. If you want the ultimate in pampering, choose Les Mars and make a reservation – quick as you can – at Cyrus.

MADRONA MANOR

Innkeepers: Bill and Trudi Konrad
707-433-4231, 800-258-4003
www.madronamanor.com
info@madronamanor.com
1001 Westside Rd., Healdsburg, CA 95448
(Central Healdsburg exit; west 1 mile off
Hwy 101)
Price: Expensive to Very Expensive
Credit Cards: MC, V
Special Features: Pool, restaurant

This country inn and restaurant is the
grande dame of Sonoma County. With its
mansard roof, expansive porch, and surrounding lush gardens, this three-story
Victorian built in 1881 is a majestic sight
amid a glade of trees. Large and ornate
antiques decorate most of the mansion's
formal guest rooms. Its 22 rooms have 18
fireplaces, many graced with delicate hand-
painted borders, and eight of the rooms
have balconies or decks. All rooms are air-
conditioned and include private baths.
Three smaller buildings house five suites
and two Jacuzzi tubs. In the Carriage House,
ask for Suite 400, which has a fireplace and
whirlpool tub. For seclusion, try the Garden
Suite, with a fireplace, rattan furniture, and
private deck. Well off the main road,
Madrona Manor guarantees an unhurried
stay and a return to the slower pace of the
home's Victorian heyday. Buffet breakfast is
included. The restaurant is also first rate.
(See chapter 5, Restaurants).

GEYSERVILLE
HOPE-MERRILL HOUSE AND HOPE-BOSWORTH HOUSE

Innkeepers: Ron and Cosette Scheiber
707-857-3356, 800-825-4233
www.hope-inns.com
moreinfo@hope-inns.com
21253 Geyserville Ave., Geyserville, CA
95441 (1 mile north of Geyserville exit off
Hwy. 101)
Price: Moderate to Expensive
Credit Cards: AE, D, MC, V

Special Features: A quarter acre of vines on
the premises, pool

The Hope-Merrill House offers something
rare among inns: "Pick and Press for a
Crushing Good Time," a two-day stay in the
fall to harvest wine and in the spring to bottle wine. Guests are guided through virtually
every step of winemaking by Graham
Parnell, a former instructor in the Enology
Department at Santa Rosa Junior College.
Perks of the working vacation include brag-
ging rights, two cases of wine to take home,
and a chance to inhabit a historic treasure.
A stagecoach stop in the 1870s and now an
enchanting inn, Hope-Merrill House is
listed on the Sonoma County Landmarks
Register. Aficionados of architectural details
will enjoy the historical significance of the
structure: A striking example of 19th-century
Eastlake Stick style, the home was built
entirely of redwood. Notice the authentic
Victorian hand-screened wallpaper. Its
eight rooms all have private baths; two have
whirlpool tubs. A generous country-style
breakfast is served in the dining room. The
innkeepers also run the less formal Hope-
Bosworth House across the street. Built in
1904, it's a Queen Anne Craftsman style,
and it has four guest rooms.

SONOMA WEST COUNTY
APPLEWOOD INN

Innkeepers: Jim Caron and Darryl Notter
707-869-9093, 800-555-8509;
fax 707-869-9170
www.applewoodinn.com
stay@applewoodinn.com
13555 Hwy. 116, Guerneville, CA 95446
(a quarter mile south of Guerneville on
Hwy. 116)
Price: Expensive to Very Expensive
Credit Cards: AE, MC, V
Special Features: Restaurant, pool, hot tub

This Mission-style inn hidden in a stand of
redwoods is one of Sonoma County's
finest. It's romantic and formal yet familiar,

like a wealthy grandmother's house. The site was originally an apple orchard and now harbors a circa-1922 mansion with nine rooms and Piccola Casa, a matching house added in 1995, with seven rooms. Three new suites and an additional building called The Gatehouse were added in 1999. There are no stuffy Victorian-era museum furnishings here—the rooms have been decorated to feel like a private home, blending antiques with contemporary pieces and family heirlooms. Rich fabrics drape windows and upholstered furniture, and beds are dressed in fine pastel linens. All rooms have private baths, TVs, and phones. The new rooms have private decks, fireplaces, and whirlpool tubs and showers for two. The common area is centered on a huge double-sided stone fireplace. Breakfast is served in the inn's freestanding restaurant, Applewood, and the inn also has a cooking school. (See Chapter 5, Restaurants).

BODEGA BAY LODGE AND SPA

Manager: Tim McGregor
707-875-3525, 800-368-2468
www.bodegabaylodge.com
rooms@bodegabaylodge.com
103 Hwy. 1, Bodega Bay, CA 94923
Price: Expensive to Very Expensive
Credit Cards: AE, CB, D, DC, MC, V
Special Features: Restaurant, fitness room, whirlpool, sauna, pool, full-service spa, complimentary wifi Internet access

This wood-shingled seaside lodge—well appointed and intimate—is sheltered from coastal winds but close enough for the sound of the surf. All rooms have ocean or bay views and private balconies, and many feature fireplaces, vaulted ceilings, spa baths, refrigerators, wet bars, and coffeemakers. Even the pool and whirlpool offer breathtaking views. The Duck Club restaurant is expensive, but it's one of the best on the Sonoma coast. (See chapter 5, Restaurants.)

THE FARMHOUSE INN RESTAURANT & SPA

Innkeeper: Catherine Bartolomei
707-887-3300, 800-464-6642;
fax 707-887-3311
www.farmhouseinn.com
innkeep@farmhouseinn.com
7871 River Rd., Forestville, CA 95436
(9 miles west of Hwy. 101)
Price: Expensive to Very Expensive
Credit Cards: AE, MC, V
Special Features: Pool, restaurant, and spa

Built as a farmhouse in 1878, this inn later became a horse ranch and later still, a roadhouse lodge. Today, not only is it one of the most stylish inns in Sonoma County, but it's also home to one of the finest restaurants in Wine Country. (See chapter 5, Restaurants.) Each of the 10 rooms has a private entrance, and the decor is right out of *Architectural Digest*—elegant and modern yet warm. Many of the rooms have fireplaces, whirlpool tubs, and private saunas. The interior of the main house sets a distinct New England tone, with a long, Shaker-style dining room

Stay in luxury at the Farmhouse Inn in Forestville.
Courtesy Farmhouse Inn

where a rich breakfast feast is spread. The din of traffic on River Road may jangle some nerves, but noise drops considerably at night. The innkeeper and staff are exceptionally friendly.

INN AT OCCIDENTAL
Innkeepers: Jerry and Tina Wolsborn
707-874-1047, 800-522-6324
www.innatoccidental.com
innkeeper@innatoccidental.com
3657 Church St., Occidental, CA 95465
(one block off Bohemian Hwy.)
Price: Expensive to Very Expensive
Credit Cards: AE, MC, V

Perched on a hill overlooking the quiet village of Occidental, this comfortable, three-story Victorian inn is a jewel, one of Wine Country's best. It is well off the beaten path and delightfully so. Guarded by fruit trees and a lush courtyard garden with a fountain, the inn was built in 1876. The 16 rooms and the vacation rental called Sonoma Cottage all have private baths, fireplaces, and feather beds. All are sumptuously furnished with antiques, and the color palette of each room is designed around a specific collectible. The Wolsborns are exceptional hosts, offering wine, cheese, and homemade cookies by the living room hearth each evening. A superb gourmet breakfast is served in the dining room or on the porch.

INN AT THE TIDES
General Manager: Carlo Galazzo
707-875-2751, 800-541-7788;
fax 707-875-2669
www.innatthetides.com
iatt@monitor.net
800 Hwy. 1, P.O. Box 640, Bodega Bay, CA 94923
Price: Moderate to Very Expensive
Credit Cards: AE, D, MC, V
Special Features: Indoor-outdoor pool, whirlpool, sauna, workout room, two restaurants

Six coastal acres with natural landscaping surround this inn—actually 12 separate lodges scattered over a hillside. The 86 guest rooms are agreeably designed, and each has a bay or ocean view, with a refrigerator, coffeemaker, and a hide-a-bed. The inn is home to Sonoma County's leading winemaker dinner; if interested, inquire when making your reservations. Continental breakfast is served across Highway 1 at The Tides.

The Inn at the Tides offers guests views of Bodega Bay and the Pacific Ocean. Tim Fish

RAFORD HOUSE INN
Innkeepers: Dane Pitcher and Rita Wells
707-887-9573, 800-887-9503;
fax 707-887-9597
www.rafordhouse.com
10630 Wohler Rd., Healdsburg, CA 95448
Price: Moderate to Expensive
Credit Cards: AE, D, MC, V

In the heart of rural Sonoma County, this inn is ideally located for touring the wineries of Russian River and Dry Creek valleys. An 1880 Victorian, it sits like a jewel on a gentle slope overlooking vineyards and tall redwoods. Stately palm trees stand as sentinels on the front lawn, and at the end of a tall staircase is a wide porch, an ideal place to kick off your shoes and watch the hummingbirds flitter by. Two of the six guest rooms have fireplaces, and all have private baths. Each room is decorated in a dominant color; the Blue Room is furnished with a four-poster bed and armoire. The Strawberry Room has a private entrance that opens onto the garden.

SONOMA ORCHID INN

Innkeepers: Brian Siewert and Dana Murphy
707-887-1033, 888-877-4466
www.sonomaorchidinn.com
innkeeper@sonomaorchidinn.com
12850 River Rd., Guerneville, CA 95446
(12 miles west of Hwy. 101)
Price: Moderate to Expensive
Credit Cards: AE, MC, V
Special Features: Redwood hot tub

Within walking distance of Korbel Champagne Cellars and the Russian River, this circa-1906 inn is built of redwood and has 10 guest rooms, each with a private bath. The rooms are decorated with English and American antiques, and some have forest or garden views. Hawthorn Cottage has a king-sized bed, a fireplace, and a cozy window seat. Madrone has a king-sized bed, a sitting area with a sofa, and a private brick patio. The inn serves decadent "skip-lunch breakfasts," replete with caloric dishes such as stuffed French toast soufflé.

SANTA NELLA HOUSE

Innkeepers: Bob Reeves and Betsy Taggart
707-869-9488, 887-869-9488
www.santanellahouse.com
info@santanellahouse.com
12130 Hwy. 116, Guerneville, CA 95446
(2 miles southeast of Guerneville)
Price: Moderate to Expensive
Credit Cards: AE, MC, V

Special Features: Hot tub

Nestled in a quiet redwood forest, this inn is an 1870 Victorian with a grand wrap-around veranda. There are four guest rooms, all with private baths and furnished with functional antiques and queen-sized beds. All have wood-burning fireplaces. A full breakfast—artichoke soufflé with basil-chive roasted potatoes is just one of many specialties—is served in the kitchen by the wood-burning stove. The parlor/music room is a favorite gathering place.

SEA RANCH LODGE

General Manager: Greg Harin
707-785-2371, 800-732-7262
www.searanchlodge.com
inquiry@searanchlodge.com
60 Sea Walk Dr., P.O. Box 44, Sea Ranch,
CA 95497 (29 miles north of Jenner on Hwy. 1)
Price: Expensive to Very Expensive
Credit Cards: AE, MC, V
Special Features: Restaurant

On bluffs above the Pacific Ocean, this lodge has one of the best vistas in Wine Country. All but one of the 20 rooms face the sea—cozy window seats offer front-row viewing for spectacular sunsets—and some of the rooms have fireplaces. The location is remote, but if you're in need of a peaceful getaway, this is it. Outside, the weathered wood recalls New England, and the interior feels like a rustic cabin, with knotty pine, cathedral ceilings, and quilted bedspreads. Some rooms have fireplaces and hot tubs. Three caveats: The lodge is historic, so the walls are a bit thin; locate your room's flashlight immediately because lighting is poor outside at night; and bring a sweater because fog keeps the locale cool even in summer. The restaurant is adequate but pricey—but, oh, that view! Hiking trails are well marked along the bluffs, and the inn is dog friendly.

SONOMA COAST VILLA & SPA

Innkeeper: Ingrid and Johannes Zachbauer
707-876-9818, 888-404-2255;
fax 707-876-9856
www.scvilla.com
reservations@scvilla.com
16702 Hwy. 1, Bodega, CA 94922
Price: Expensive to Very Expensive
Credit Cards: AE, MC, V
Special Features: Swimming pool, indoor
whirlpool, health spa, putting green

This Mediterranean-style resort on 60
acres is great for roaming. The pastoral
hillsides are lovely, and there are plenty
of meandering gardens. The inn's 18
rooms are furnished with modern
Mediterranean decor, including Italian
slate floors; all the rooms have fireplaces,
and many have whirlpool tubs and private
patios. A Continental breakfast is served
in the dining room.

Motels

NAPA VALLEY

Best Western Inn At The Vines (707-257-
1930, 877-846-3729,
www.innatthevines.com, 100 Soscol Ave.,
Napa, CA 94559; Inexpensive to Expensive;
AE, D, DC, MC, V) It has 69 rooms, some
wheelchair accessible. It also has a heated
pool and spa and restaurant; loft suites are
available.

Chablis Inn (707-257-1944, 800-443-
3490, www.chablisinn.com, 3360 Solano
Ave., Napa, CA 94558; Inexpensive to
Moderate; AE, MC, V) This is a basic 34-
unit motel. All rooms have a coffeemaker, a
refrigerator, and either a wet bar or a kitchenette. The rooms have all been renovated.

The Chateau (707-253-9300,
www.thechateauhotel.com, 4195 Solano
Ave., Napa, CA 94558; Inexpensive to
Expensive; AE, D, DC, MC, V) This is a
well-appointed inn in the heart of the valley. Six suites are available, and there's a
pool and whirlpool.

The Lodge of Calistoga (707-942-9400,
1865 Lincoln Ave., Calistoga, CA 94515;
Moderate to Expensive; AE, CB, D, DC, MC,
V) This offers 55 rooms; a hot mineral-
water swimming pool, a hot mineral-water
whirlpool, a sauna, a steam room, a
Continental breakfast.

John Muir Inn (707-257-7220, 800-522-
8999, www.johnmuirnapa.com, 1998
Trower Ave., Napa, CA 94558; Moderate to
Expensive; AE, D, DC, MC, V) This is a bet-
ter-than-average, 59-room motel built in
1986 and redecorated in 2000. Many rooms
have kitchenettes and overlook the garden
courtyard. Included are a pool, whirlpool,
and Continental breakfast.

SONOMA COUNTY

Bodega Coast Inn (707-875-2217, 800-
346-6999, www.bodegacoastinn.com, 521
Hwy. 1, Bodega Bay, CA 94923; Moderate to
Very Expensive; AE, D, DC, MC, V) Once a
Holiday Inn, this inn has 45 attractively
appointed rooms and suites, with balconies
offering lovely views of Bodega Bay harbor.
A few rooms have fireplaces, whirlpool
tubs, and vaulted ceilings. Some rooms
have two-person whirlpools.

Bodega Harbor Inn (707-875-3594,
www.bodegaharborinn.com, Bodega Ave. at
Coast Hwy. 1, Bodega Bay, CA 94923;
Inexpensive; MC, V) This offers 14 rooms, 2
suites, cottages, and vacation homes. Some
rooms have bay views, decks, fireplaces, and
kitchens. It's a bit funky, but comfortable.

El Pueblo Inn (707-996-3651, 800-900-
8844, www.elpuebloinn.com, 896 W. Napa
St., Sonoma, CA 95476; Inexpensive to Very
Expensive; AE, D, DC, MC, V) This 53-
room motel has a pool and a hot tub. There
are restaurants nearby. It's located at a busy
intersection.

Fairview Motel (707-433-5548, 74 Healdsburg Ave., Healdsburg, CA 95448; Inexpensive to Moderate; AE, D, MC, V) Included are 37 rooms, a pool, a whirlpool, and complimentary coffee. There are restaurants nearby.

Geyserville Inn (707-857-4343, 877-857-4343, www.geyservilleinn.com, 21714 Geyserville Ave., Geyserville, CA 95441; Inexpensive to Expensive; AE, D, MC, V) This is a recently built 38-room inn, pleasantly designed and comfortable. Many rooms have fireplaces and patios. Included are a pool and whirlpool.

Holiday Inn Express (707-829-6677, 800-465-4329, 1101 Gravenstein Hwy. S., Sebastopol, CA 95472; Inexpensive to Expensive; AE, D, DC, MC, V) Completed in late 1998, this pleasant, 82-room inn is just one of two hotels Sebastopol offers. Included are a pool, spa, gym, and Continental breakfast. Each room has a refrigerator and coffeemaker. Wifi Internet access is available.

Santa Rosa Courtyard by Marriott (707-573-9000, 175 Railroad St., Santa Rosa, CA 95401; Moderate to Expensive; AE, D, DC, MC, V) It has 138 nonsmoking rooms—plus a swimming pool, spa, café, lounge, and room service. It's handicapped accessible and is close to downtown and historic Railroad Square shopping area.

Timber Cove Inn (707-847-3231, 800-987-8319, www.timbercoveinn.com, 21780 N. Coast Hwy. 1, Jenner, CA 95450; Moderate to Very Expensive; AE, MC, V) This inn is charming but funky, with a breathtaking location perched on a rocky cliff overlooking the ocean. Many of the 50 rooms have ocean views; some have fireplaces and private hot tubs. Included are a restaurant and lounge.

Wine Country Travel Lodge (707-433-0101, www.winecountrytravelodge.com, 178 Dry Creek Rd., Healdsburg, CA 95448; Inexpensive to Expensive; AE, MC, V) This is a pleasant motel close to wineries. There are 22 rooms plus 1 suite—all non-smoking—with refrigerators and whirlpool tubs. Included is an indoor whirlpool and sauna and Continental breakfast.

SEBASTIANI·BUILDING·
1933

SEBASTIANI THEATI

The Sebastiani Theater is one of the oldest movie houses in Wine Country. Tim Fish

4

CULTURE

Life Is Sweet!

Blue jeans mingle with black tie in the Wine Country cultural scene, and that's the way we like it. Nearby San Francisco, of course, is a world-class cultural city, and though Napa and Sonoma counties can't compete with the City by the Bay's museums, opera, and ballet, Wine Country is more than just wineries, food, and scenic views.

Wine Country's literary heritage dates back to writer Robert Lewis Stevenson, who brought a touch of civilization to St. Helena in the 1880s. Later, Jack London, author of *The Call of the Wild*, retired to Glen Ellen and became a gentleman farmer. Carefully preserved historical sites, such as Sonoma's Mission San Francisco Solano, built in 1825, are reminders that Wine Country citizens have long honored their culture.

Music, as it always seems to, helped lead the way. In 1927, the Santa Rosa Symphony was the first to be organized, followed a few years later by the Napa Valley Symphony. As the communities began to grow after World War II and with the renewal of the wine industry in the 1960s, Napa and Sonoma's cultural landscape began to flourish as well.

Artists weary of the city and drawn to the beauty of Wine Country began moving north, making Napa and Sonoma the popular artistic havens they are today. Art galleries appeared, and wineries began to display art in their tasting rooms. The first theater companies formed in the early 1970s, and theaters have proliferated in Sonoma County to become a dominant force in local arts. Wineries have played a special role in this cultural expansion, promoting the arts as one of life's necessities as well as the perfect accompaniment to wine.

The following pages will give you some idea of the arts and entertainment possibilities in Napa and Sonoma. The best place to find current happenings are the entertainment pages of the *Napa Register* and Santa Rosa's *Press Democrat*. The arts councils of both counties are also good sources of information. For Napa, phone 707-257-2117, www.artscouncilnapavalley.org, and for Sonoma, phone 707-579-2787, www.sonomaarts.com.

Architecture

While Napa and Sonoma may not have the strong architectural traditions found in the East and Midwest, Wine Country has its own grand style. Plain and practical dried-brick buildings called adobes ruled until the first buildings in a European style were built in the 1860s, and many of those—particularly in Sonoma County—were lost in the earthquake of 1906. Architectural gems remain, however, and newer ones have been added.

The 1889 Gothic fortress of Greystone Cellars, once the winery for Christian Brothers, is now home to the Culinary Institute of America. Courtesy Culinary Institute of America, Greystone

The most obvious treasures are the castlelike wineries of Napa Valley. Most notable is **Beringer's** stately, German-style mansion called **Rhine House**, built in the late 1800s. Nearby is the Gothic fortress of **Greystone Cellars**, built in 1889. It was once the winery for Christian Brothers but is now home to the **Culinary Institute of America at Greystone.** **Inglenook's** grand chateau was built in 1887. In Sonoma, **Hop Kiln Winery** along the Russian River is inside a towering hop kiln built in 1880. The building with three tall spires was used to dry beer hops, back when the area was a center for growing that commodity. **Korbel Champagne Cellars** is an ivy-covered brick beauty with a brandy tower.

There are also newer winery wonders. Most striking is the **Sterling Vinyards** white hilltop villa south of Calistoga. Nearby is the postmodern temple to wine and art, **Clos Pegase,** designed by Princeton architect Michael Graves. Across Napa Valley is the distinctive shake-roofed **Rutherford Hill Winery**, which recalls an early Wine Country barn. The chateaux of **Domaine Carneros**, near Napa and Jordan in Sonoma's Alexander Valley, are extravagant reminders of France. Open since 1991, the high-tech **Artesa** is spectacularly understated. Built into the side of a Carneros hillside and nearly impossible to make out from the road, it recalls a buried temple. Not too far away is **Viansa**, built to look like a Tuscan village. **Opus One** winery, a joint venture between Robert Mondavi and France's Chateau Mouton-Rothschild, is another extravagant facade, designed by the firm that created San Francisco's Transamerica Pyramid.

The oldest city in the area, Sonoma, also has many of the oldest buildings, including *adobes* like the simple but majestic **Mission San Francisco Solano.** Surrounding the Sonoma Plaza are a number of historic buildings, including the fading but still regal **Sebastiani Theatre,** built in 1933.

The cities of Napa and Petaluma offer self-guided walking tours of downtown Victorian neighborhoods. (Check at visitor centers for maps.) Napa's tour includes the **Napa Opera House,** 1018 Main St., an Italianate beauty built in 1879 and now being refurbished. At the corner of 3rd and Randolph streets there's also the **First Presbyterian Church**, a Victorian Gothic built in 1874. Walking tour maps are available at the **Napa Valley Conference and Visitors Bureau** (1310 Napa Town Center, Napa; 707-226-7459).

A thriving river port in the 1870s, Petaluma has retained many of its beautiful homes, and the downtown is beautifully preserved—amazingly, the city was spared during the 1906 quake. Browse along Petaluma Boulevard and Kentucky Street, taking in the antiques shops and admiring the classic architecture. Drive through the Victorian neighborhoods and check out the majestic Queen Anne styling of the old **Gilger House** at 111 6th St. or the intricately ornate Spanish Colonial at 47 6th St. **The Petaluma Area Chamber of Commerce** is another great resource (799 Baywood Dr., Petaluma; 707-762-2785).

Many of Santa Rosa's great buildings were lost in the 1906 earthquake, though **McDonald Avenue on the west edge of downtown** has survived. Alfred Hitchcock filmed *Shadow of a Doubt* in Santa Rosa. Downtown has changed considerably since then, but the **McDonald Avenue residential area**, shown extensively in the film, remains the city's architectural prize. Just west of downtown is a lovely neighborhood of large homes, wide streets, and tall trees. The centerpiece is **Mableton**, at 1015 McDonald. Built in 1878, it was inspired by the plantation homes of Mississippi. Perhaps Sonoma County's most famous edifice was also popularized by Hitchcock: the **Bodega School House.** Featured prominently in the 1963 movie *The Birds*, it's located in the small burg of Bodega in West County. Movie buffs are constantly stopping by for a photo out front. It's a private home now, but it's occasionally open for private tours.

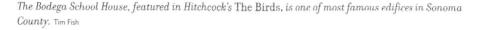

The Bodega School House, featured in Hitchcock's The Birds, *is one of most famous edifices in Sonoma County.* Tim Fish

Cinema

Although few of Napa's or Sonoma's grand old movie houses still stand—blame it on urban renewal or earthquakes—movie going remains an ardent passion in the area. **The Wine Country Film Festival**, a month-long celebration of the latest foreign and art films, is small but respected. **The Sonoma Film Institute**, staged in a classroom at Sonoma State University but open to the public, is low on atmosphere but high on quality. Finally, Sonoma and Napa are home to many top-name stars, and the two counties' landscapes are cinema stars in their own right: Both are favorite locations for Hollywood feature films and commercials.

Napa County

Cameo Cinema (707-963-9779, 1340 Main St., St. Helena, CA 94574) This charming theater in downtown St. Helena was completely refurbished in 1997. It shows first-run films—but as you might expect for a small town, a few weeks after release. The fare is mostly American, though occasional art and foreign films come for a stay.

Century Cine Dome (800-326-3264, extension 911, 825 Pearl St., Napa, CA 94559) This modern, eight-theater complex shows first-runs in downtown.

Sonoma County

Airport Cinemas (707-522-0330, 409 Aviation Blvd., Santa Rosa, CA 95403) This 12-screen complex has stadium seating and is one of the best in Wine Country. It even has a café.

The Raven Film Center (707-433-5448, 415 Center St., Healdsburg, CA 95448) The

The Raven Film Center shows both art films and Hollywood blockbusters. Tim Fish

main Raven Theater is easily the finest movie house in Wine Country, but sadly, the downtown Healdsburg theater seldom shows films these days. Four smaller theaters were added behind the original theater, and they show first-run movies and the occasional art film.

Rialto Cinemas (707-525-4840, 551 Summerfield Rd., Santa Rosa, CA 95405) Here's a rarity: a theater that devotes itself to foreign and cutting-edge art films.

Roxy (707-522-0330, 85 Santa Rosa Ave., Santa Rosa, CA 95404) This state-of-the art cinema has it all: great sound and projection plus stadium seating with rocking chairs. The place to see the latest action blockbuster.

Sebastiani Theatre (707-996-2020, 476 1st St. E., Sonoma, CA 95476) This is a delightful old theater that's slowly being restored. It shows first-run films.

Sebastopol Cinemas (707-829-3456, McKinley St. & Petaluma Ave., Sebastopol, CA 95472) This five-theater cinema is inside a refurbished brandy distillery. It shows first-run films.

Sonoma Cinemas (707-935-1234, 200 Siesta Way, Boyes Hot Springs, CA 95476) This four-plex theater shows first-run movies.

Galleries

Whether your thing is abstract expressionism or dolphins jumping through rainbows, there's an art gallery for you somewhere in Napa and Sonoma counties. A new gallery seems to open every weekend. The hills of northern California shelter some of the finest artists in the country. Each of the galleries has its own specialty. Some galleries are cooperatives, owned and operated by local artists. Others specialize in ceramics or offer paintings and prints of nationally known artists.

Napa County
CLOS PEGASE WINERY
707-942-4981; fax 707-942-4993
www.clospegase.com
info@clospegase.com
1060 Dunaweal Ln., Calistoga, CA 94515
Open: 10:30–5 daily, tours 11 & 2 daily
Admission: None

This winery is a work of art in itself. Designed by the award-winning architect Michael Graves, it looks like a postmodern Babylonian temple. A commanding edifice of tall pillars and archways done in bold hues of cream and terra cotta, Clos Pegase is an eye-catcher. The lawn and courtyard serve as a sculpture garden, which includes Richard Serra's provocative "Twins," a minimalist masterpiece. The regular winery tour offers a glimpse of owner Jan Shrem's impressive art collection, including 17th- and 18th-century French statuary artfully displayed in the winery's massive underground cave. Also, a casual browse in the visitors center reveals more treasures.

DI ROSA PRESERVE
707-226-5991; fax 707-255-8934
www.dirosapreserve.org
5200 Carneros Hwy. 121, CA 94559
Open: By Appointment
Admission: $12

Di Rosa Preserve is both an art gallery and nature preserve. The nationally known collection includes more than two thousand works of San Francisco Bay Area art: sculpture, paintings, and so forth. All's on display in a former stone winery and even outdoors, amid 35 acres of the rolling meadows of the scenic Carneros district of southern Napa Valley.

THE GALLERY AT CLIFF LEDE VINEYARDS
800-428-2259
1473 Yountville Cross Rd., Yountville, CA 94599
Open: 10–4 daily
Admission: None

The gallery, in the winery's original fermentation room, has a contemporary feel, with concrete floors and crisp walls. The permanent art includes Keith Haring's untitled sculpture of three dancing figures and Jim Dine's *Twin 6' Hearts*. A bronze sculpture by Lynn Chadwick right outside the gallery sets the stage for the work inside. Various shows open at the gallery, including the recent "Images from the Garden," featuring nine artists' botanical imagery.

Franz Gertsch is one of the many artists featured at the Hess Collection. Courtesy the Hess Collection

THE HESS COLLECTION

707-255-1144; fax 707-253-1682
www.hesscollection.com
4411 Redwood Rd., Napa, CA 94558
Open: 10–4 daily
Admission: None

If there's a gallery in Wine Country that deserves the title museum, it's the Hess Collection. Swiss entrepreneur Donald Hess transformed the old Mont La Salle Winery into an ultra-modern showcase for his two great passions: art and wine. Built on the rugged slopes of Mt. Veeder, the Hess Collection opened to the public in 1989.

The entrance opens onto a dramatic three-story staircase. The 130-piece collection spans the upper two floors and features the works of internationally know artists such as Francis Bacon, Robert Motherwell, and Frank Stella. A mix of paintings and sculpture, the works are provocative and often haunting, though humor plays a role, too.

I. WOLK GALLERY

707-963-8800
www.iwolkgallery.com
1354 Main St., St. Helena, CA 94574
Open: 10–5:30 daily
Admission: None

This is an excellent gallery with serious intentions about art, specializing in contemporary paintings, photography, and crafts by emerging American artists. *Contemporary* does not necessarily read *abstract* because the emphasis is on realist imagery. Exhibitions feature single artists, but a wide range of artists is shown continuously.

JESSEL GALLERY

707-257-2350; fax 707-257-2396
www.jesselgallery.com
jessel@napanet.net
1019 Atlas Peak Rd., Napa, CA 94558
Open: 10–5 daily
Admission: None

Jessel is the essence of what northern California galleries are all about. The art is not particularly challenging, but is lovely nonetheless, and the atmosphere is laid-back, almost meditative. If you're weary of the bustle of Highway 29, Napa's main drag, make a detour to this delightful gallery. Jessel, an artist who prefers just one name, opened the gallery in 1987, and offerings include gorgeous pastels and watercolors as well as jewelry and ceramics.

SONOMA COUNTY
LISA KRISTINE
707-938-3860
www.migrationphotography.com
453 First St. East
Open daily from 10 a.m. to 6 p.m.
Admission:

Honored by the United Nations, photographer Lisa Kristine captures indigenous people and the lives they lead. Her gallery on the Sonoma Square is a popular place to peruse. The striking pictures, both large and small, chronicle her travels. In the past two decades, she's documented more than 55 countries on six continents. Kristine says she wants to "open a dialogue about the diversity, beauty and hardship of our interlocking world."

SPIRITS IN STONE
707-938-2200, 800-4874-6624; fax 707-938-2263
www.spiritsinstone.com
452 1st St. E., Suite A, Sonoma, CA 95476
Open: 10–6 daily
Admission: None

If you think African art is just masks and primitive carvings, think again. The members of the Shona tribe in Zimbabwe, "the people of the mist," carve extraordinary stone sculptures. They believe that each stone hides a unique spirit, and the sculptor's task is to remove what has been hiding the spirit. The sculptures—which depict gods, people, and animals—reveal both vivid talent and primitive charm. A second Shona gallery is in Village Outlets, 3111 N. St. Helena Hwy. (Hwy. 29), St. Helena.

On the Trail of Art

ARTrails (707-579-ARTS) This is a Sonoma County tradition every October. For two weekends, dozens of artists open their studios to the public. It's a rare chance to see artists in their natural habitat, not to mention an opportunity for a bargain because there's no art-gallery middleman. It's sponsored by the Cultural Arts Council of Sonoma County; handy tour maps are available.

Other Galleries

NAPA COUNTY
Artesa Vineyards & Winery (707-224-1668, 1345 Henry Rd., Napa, CA 94559) This winery is an architectural work of art: Built into a hillside, it looks like a lost tomb. Contemporary art is on display throughout the winery.

Lee Youngman Galleries (707-942-0585, 1316 Lincoln Ave., Calistoga, CA 94515)

Walk through the gallery at Mumm Napa Valley. Courtesy Mumm

Included are "California style" art from nationally known artists, oils, watercolors, and metal and wood sculptures.

Mumm Napa Valley (707-967-7730, 8445 Silverado Trail, Rutherford, CA 94573) The long hallways of this winery are devoted to art, and it's a lovely space. Revolving shows are featured and Ansel Adams's "Story of a Winery" is on permanent display.

Raku Ceramics Collection (707-944-9211, 6540 Washington St., Yountville, CA 94599) Raku is a distinctive Japanese style of ceramics that creates a rustlike glaze. You can find some beautiful pieces here.

RASberry's Art Glass Gallery (707-944-9211, 6540 Washington St., Yountville, CA 94599) This is a gift shop disguising itself as a gallery. You may consider these garish creations art. We don't.

Robert Mondavi Winery (888-766-6328, 7801 St. Helena Hwy., Oakville, CA 94562) This is one of the first wineries to show art. Rotating shows are on display in the Vineyard Room.

SONOMA COUNTY

Bodega Landmark Studio (707-876-3477, 17255 Bodega Hwy., Bodega, CA 94923) West County artists a specialty here, including oils, watercolors, and ceramics.

Erickson Fine Art Gallery (707-431-7073, 324 Healdsburg Ave., Healdsburg, CA 95448) This attractive gallery is just off the square in downtown Healdsburg. It has a fine collection of serious art with only a smattering of frivolous landscapes.

Ren Brown Collection (707-875-2922, 1781 Hwy. 1, Bodega Bay, CA 94923) Modern Japanese prints are the focus of this gallery.

Santa Rosa Junior College Gallery (707-527-4298, 1501 Mendocino Ave., Santa Rosa, CA 94503) Here you'll find group shows by faculty and students.

Snoopy's Gallery (707-546-3385, 1667 W. Steele Ln., Santa Rosa, CA 94503) This is more of a museum and gift shop than a gallery, but it's worth checking out if you're a *Peanuts* fan. Creator Charles Schulz was a local, and many of his originals are on display.

Sonoma State University Gallery (707-664-2295, E. Cotati Ave., Rohnert Park, CA 49428) Included here are traveling exhibits of nationally known painters and sculptors as well as student and faculty group shows.

Built in 1846, the huge waterwheel at the historic Bale Grist Mill is still turning. Tim Fish

Sonoma Valley Museum of Art (707-939-7862, 551 Broadway, Sonoma, CA 95476) This is a pleasant gallery devoted to the works of Sonoma Valley artists.

Historic Places

NAPA COUNTY
BALE GRIST MILL
707-963-2236, 707-942-4575;
contact: Silverado District Headquarters,
20 E. Spain St., Sonoma, CA 95476
3369 St. Helena Hwy, St. Helena, CA 94574
Open: 10–5 daily
Admission: $4
Special Features: Gifts

Just think: If wheat had caught on in Napa Valley, you might be cruising Highway 29 in search of the perfect loaf of bread. When settlers first began arriving in Napa in the 1830s and 1840s, wheat, corn, and wild oats—not grapes—were the crops of choice. Mills, of course, were a necessity—not only as places to grind grain into meal and flour, but also as social centers for the community. Edward Turner Bale's gristmill, built in 1846, was one of three in Napa and the only one that survives.

If traffic or the glitz of wineries gets on your nerves, take an hour for a quiet getaway at the Bale Grist Mill State Historic Park. It seems miles and generations away. The mill is at the end of a short path, a refreshing walk through dense woods and across a lively brook. The first thing you'll notice is the 36-foot-high wooden waterwheel, rolling at a leisurely pace, water trickling down its curved steps. Inside the three-story wood mill house, a woman in a bonnet and period dress greets visitors. She might even offer you a slice of dense bread, made on-site with grain from the mill. The miller may actually crank up the giant millstones and grind flour.

The mill has a colorful past. Its builder, Dr. E. T. Bale, had a reputation as a rogue and scoundrel. He was fond of the bottle and refused to pay his debts. Jailed on a number of occasions, he was publicly whipped and once nearly lynched for shooting a relative of the important general Mariano Vallejo. Finally, Bale settled down and built the mill. It became the gathering spot for the north valley, where friends could exchange gossip and even stage dances. In those days, a miller was a leading citizen in the community, and his counsel in business matters was highly respected.

With the coming of new technology at the turn of the 20th century, the mill fell into neglect. It was restored by the Native Sons of the Golden West in 1925 and then again in 1967. It became a state historic park in 1974.

SONOMA COUNTY
FORT ROSS
707-847-3286; fax 707-847-3601
www.parks.sonoma.net/fortross.html
19005 Coast Hwy. 1, Jenner, CA 95450
Open: 10–4:30 daily
Admission: $2 per car
Special Features: Picnic area, gifts, camping

A quick history quiz: Who were Sonoma's first settlers (besides the Indians, of course)? If you said the Spanish, you're wrong. It was actually the Russians, who established Fort Ross, which predated the Sonoma Mission by 11 years.

The Russian-American Trading Company, a firm controlled largely by the Imperial Russian government, came to California to escape the cruel winters of Alaska and to hunt for valuable sea otters. Its workers landed south in Bodega Bay, which they called Rumiantsev, and explored to the north. On a windy bluff overlooking the Pacific, they built their fort and community, now the centerpiece of Fort Ross State Historic Park.

Under the Russians, the fort thrived for 30 years as a major trading center for trappers and explorers. The Spanish and, later, Mexican settlement of Napa and Sonoma was established largely to thwart the Russian presence at Fort Ross. By 1830 the sea otter population was decimated, and Fort Ross fell into decline. The Russians sold Fort Ross in 1839. It's certainly off the beaten path—miles from the nearest winery—but history buffs won't want to miss it, and the drive along Highway 1 is spectacular.

One structure built by the Russians still stands: the Commandant's House. The two blockhouses, the stockade, and the Russian Orthodox chapel have been carefully rebuilt. The visitors center and museum offer a look at the fort's past as well as a peek at Russian and Indian artifacts.

LUTHER BURBANK HOME AND GARDEN

707-524-5445
www.ci.santa-rosa.ca.us/rp/burbank
burbankhome@flash.netdex.com
Corner of Santa Rosa & Sonoma Aves.,
(Mail: P.O. Box 1678), Santa Rosa, CA 95402
Open 10–4 Wed.–Sun.; garden 8–7 (summer), 8–5 (winter)
Admission: $4 for adults, $3 for youth and seniors for docent-led house tour; no fee for garden
Special Features: Gifts

Plant genius Luther Burbank remains Santa Rosa's favorite son. Seventy-five years after his death, buildings and businesses bear his name. At the turn of the 20th century his fame was international. Burbank arrived from his native Massachusetts in 1877. In a letter home he wrote—and Santa Rosans love to quote this: "I firmly believe . . . this is the chosen spot of all this earth as far as nature is concerned."

From his Santa Rosa garden, Burbank developed more than eight hundred new strains of fruits, flowers, vegetables, and grasses. Burbank, along with other geniuses such as George Washington Carver, transformed plant breeding into a modern science. So great was Burbank's fame that by 1900, 150 people a day came to see the man and his garden. Among his visitors one day in 1915 were Thomas Edison, Henry Ford, and Harvey Firestone.

The house was built in about 1870 and is rather small, a modified Greek Revival cottage. Burbank lived there from 1884 to 1906, when the earthquake damaged the house and Burbank moved. When Burbank died in 1926, his wife, Elizabeth, returned to the cottage. The property was designated a National Historic Landmark in 1964, and upon Elizabeth's death in 1977, the house and garden became city property.

The half-hour tour of the house is full of facts and artifacts and includes a glimpse inside one of Burbank's original greenhouses. The garden, as you might expect, abounds in Burbank creations, particularly the Paradox Walnut Tree and the Burbank Rose.

Mission San Francisco Solano is Wine Country's most popular historic attraction. Tim Fish

MISSION SAN FRANCISCO SOLANO

707-938-9560 (mission); contact: Parks & Recreation Dept.,
20 E. Spain St., Sonoma, CA 95476
Corner of Spain St. & 1st St. E., Sonoma Plaza, Sonoma CA 95476
Open: 10–5 daily
Admission: $1—also good toward entry to Petaluma Adobe and Vallejo House; other historic
sites are also along the Plaza.

This is where European settlement in the area truly began. Though technically, the
Russians established the first outpost at Fort Ross, the true origins of Napa and Sonoma lie
at Sonoma's Mission San Francisco Solano. The white adobe mission with a red-tile roof is
probably the most popular historic attraction in Wine Country.

To appreciate its significance, it's helpful to understand the history of California's mission system. The Spanish government and Catholic Church began establishing California
missions in 1769, both as a way of converting "heathen" Indians and claiming land for
Spain. There were already 20 missions when the young and ambitious Father Jose Altimira
received permission from the Mexican governor of California to establish a new one north
of the San Francisco Bay. On July 4, 1823, Altimira celebrated Mass here with a makeshift
redwood cross and blessed the site.

The Sonoma Mission was the last to be established, and the mission system was dis-
solved in 1833. It became a center of religion and culture under General Mariano Vallejo's
rule, but it was sold by the Catholic Church in 1881. Used over the years as a blacksmith
shop and hay barn, the mission was nearly lost until the state intervened in 1906; restoration began three years later.

Today, only the long, low building to the east of the present chapel is original, although the current chapel was only built a few years later, in 1841. Displays explain how adobe buildings are constructed and how the mission was restored. The chapel is decorated with 14 Stations of the Cross, authentic relics of the mission period. The chapel decor is also patterned after mission interiors of the period, highly stylized primitive renderings by Christianized Indians.

PETALUMA ADOBE
707-762-4871
3325 Adobe Rd., Petaluma, CA 94954
Open: 10–5 daily
Admission: $2-admission also good toward entry to Mission San Francisco Solano and Vallejo House.
Special Features: Picnic tables

Once the heart of General Mariano Vallejo's sprawling 100-square-mile rancho, the Petaluma Adobe is the area's most meticulously restored adobe. The commanding two-story house was built in 1836 and has 3-foot-thick mud walls and a redwood veranda all around.

Authentic is the key word here. The rooms are furnished to the period, and goats and chickens roam the outdoor corridors. Outdoor displays include working replicas of a forge and a large oven for baking bread.

The tour is self-guided; the museum details the history of the adobe and how it was restored.

GENERAL VALLEJO HOME
707-939-6188; contact: Parks & Recreation Dept.,
Third St. and W. Spain St., Sonoma, CA 95476
1/2 mi. west of Sonoma Plaza
Open: 10–5 daily
Admission: $2-admission also good toward entry to Mission San Francisco Solano & Petaluma Adobe.
Special Features: Picnic tables

General Mariano Vallejo may have been the most powerful man in northern California in the 1850s, but he had a sense of poetry about him when he named his house Lachryma Montis. Latin for "tears of the mountain," the name was derived from a mountain spring on the property.

Vallejo was born in Monterey in 1807. His father was a Spanish soldier, and following his father into military service, Vallejo was commander of the presidio, the Spanish fort and settlement in San Francisco, when he was sent north in 1834. He commanded the northern frontier for 14 years and was largely responsible for encouraging the settlement of both Sonoma and Napa counties.

Vallejo's home, finished in 1852, reflects his embrace of the American culture. Instead of an adobe house, he built a two-story Gothic Victorian. The house was prefabricated—designed and built on the East Coast and shipped around Cape Horn. Vallejo and his family lived in the house for 35 years; the state bought the property in 1933.

The house and grounds are gorgeous, a quiet stop if you need relief from the bustle of Sonoma Plaza. The long driveway is flanked by tall cottonwood trees, and the gardens and vineyards are carefully tended. The self-guided tour begins in a large warehouse, where displays detail Vallejo's life and the history of the house. One detraction: Instead of tasteful ropes in the doorways guarding the rooms as in most historic homes, ugly white metal bars and cages have been installed to protect the considerable collection of artifacts and personal effects on display.

JACK LONDON STATE HISTORIC PARK
707-938-5216
www.parks.sonoma.net/JLStory.html
2400 London Ranch Rd., Glen Ellen, CA 95442
Open: 10–5 daily (park); 10–5 daily (house)
Admission: $6 per car
Special Features: Picnic tables, barbecue pits, hiking, horseback riding

"When I first came here, tired of cities and people," Jack London wrote of Glen Ellen, "I settled down on 130 acres of the most beautiful land to be found in California." The writer, famed for *The Call of the Wild* and other adventure stories, called his home in the Sonoma Mountains Beauty Ranch.

Today his ranch is in the heart of Wine Country's most beautiful state park, now a vast 880 acres of woodlands, fields, and hiking trails. The remains of the Wolf House is perhaps the park's most prominent feature. The massive castlelike stone building, four stories tall, was the culmination of Jack and Charmian London's dreams. On the night of August 22, 1913, only days before they were to move in, Wolf House mysteriously burned. The ruins remain today, although it requires a hike to see it. London died in 1916, reminding many of words he once said: "The proper function of man is to live, not exist. I shall not waste my days in trying to prolong them. I shall use my time."

London's grave along the half-mile trail to Wolf House is another popular stop. You can also visit London's ranch house, his stone barn, and pig palace. The House of Happy Walls, built by Charmian after London's death, serves as a museum, displaying an eighteen thousand-volume library, original furnishings, memorabilia, and the Londons' collection of South Pacific artifacts.

Libraries
Wine Country has two distinguished libraries: the Napa Valley Wine Library and the Sonoma County Wine Library. Both are exceptional resources.

The Napa Wine Library is inside St. Helena Public Library (707-963-5244, 1492 Library Ln., St. Helena, CA 94574). It has a vast collection, including more than six thousand books, tapes, and so forth, detailing everything from the art of winemaking to the history of Napa wine to the current community of wineries throughout the valley.

The Sonoma County Wine Library occupies a small wing inside the Healdsburg branch of the Sonoma County Public Library (707-433-3772, 139 Piper St., Healdsburg, CA 95448). Its collection is similar but somewhat smaller, though no less impressive. The library also subscribes to nearly 75 wine magazines and newsletters.

Museums

NAPA COUNTY
COPIA: THE AMERICAN CENTER FOR FOOD, WINE, AND THE ARTS
707-259-1600
www.copia.org
mail@copia.org
500 First St., Napa, CA 94559
Open: 10–5 PM daily (winter), 10–9 daily
(summer)
Admission: $12.50; half price on Wed.

COPIA is the brainchild of vintner Robert
Mondavi, who said he wanted to create a
place to celebrate and explore the abundance
and diversity of America's fine food, wine,
and art. The word *copia* means "abundance"
in Italian. The idea is to show how food,
wine, and the arts have played a role in people's lives, from the most primitive civilization to the present and into the future.

There are art displays, music, dance
and drama performances, wine classes,
restaurants, and more. A notable long-
term exhibit is called "Forks in the Road:
Food, Wine, and the American Table." It
explores the diversity of food and wine in
American life. It includes historic and
geographical influences as well as information on how sheer individuality helped
shape America's food culture.

*COPIA is a museum that celebrates America's food,
wine, and the arts.* Tim Fish

NAPA VALLEY MUSEUM
707-944-0500; fax 707-945-0500
www.napavalleymuseum.org
55 Presidents Circle, Yountville CA 94599
Open: 10–5 daily; closed Tues.
Admission: $4.50 adults, $3.50 seniors and students, free age six and younger

Since its debut in 1997, this has been an impressive addition to the valley. A stylishly modern take on an old California barn, the $3.5 million museum is devoted to the history, cul-
ture, and art of Napa, with standing and touring exhibits. One of the standing exhibits is
"California Wine: the Science of an Art," a highly interactive education in the making of
wine. Another permanent exhibit is "The Land and People of the Napa Valley," an overview
of how the valley came to be, from its geological beginnings to the time of the Wappo
Indians to its crowning as America's capital of wine.

SHARPSTEEN MUSEUM

707-942-5911; fax 707-942-6325
www.napanet.net/vi/sharpsteen/
1311 Washington St., P.O. Box 573, Calistoga, CA 94515
Open: 11–4 daily
Admission: Donation is appreciated

If you want a quick lesson in early Napa life, this quaint museum is the place to go. Ben and Bernice Sharpsteen created the museum almost as a hobby after Ben retired as a producer for Walt Disney and the couple moved to Calistoga. Before long, it became a community project, and today it's run by volunteers.

The first section of this museum is devoted to the Sharpsteens themselves, and frankly, it's rather dull. But the miniature model of early Calistoga that follows is delightful. The town was founded in 1859 as a resort by the flamboyant Sam Brannan. Brannan was a man of many firsts: California's first newspaper publisher, banker, and land developer. He built the first railroad and telegraph. He was also California's first millionaire. His elegant Hot Springs Resort was a gathering place for California's rich and famous, and his vision of Calistoga as a haven of healing waters and relaxation still lives today. Only one tiny Victorian cottage remains from Brannan's resort; it was moved in 1977 and is attached to the museum. Step inside the wonderfully ornate cottage, and you'll step back into the 1860s.

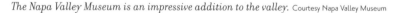

The Napa Valley Museum is an impressive addition to the valley. Courtesy Napa Valley Museum

The museum also details a great deal of northern California history. One display, a Napa Valley timeline, is particularly intriguing, dating back to the first explorers and the Sonoma Mission through the turn of the 20th century. There are also lessons about the early stagecoach days—a restored coach is on display—the first railroad, Robert Louis Stevenson's days in Napa, and more. There are enough old photos, newspapers, and artifacts to keep any history buff happy.

SILVERADO MUSEUM

707-963-3757; fax 707-963-0917
1490 Library Ln., P.O. Box 490, St. Helena, CA 94574
Open: Noon–4 daily; closed Mon.
Admission: Free

Writer Robert Louis Stevenson was taken with Napa Valley. In 1880, the author of *Dr. Jekyll and Mr. Hyde* and *Treasure Island* honeymooned with his wife in a cabin near the old Silverado Mine. He wrote about the area in *The Silverado Squatters.* He called Napa's wine "bottled poetry," and Mount St. Helena was the inspiration for Spyglass Hill in *Treasure Island.* Although Stevenson spent only a few months in Napa Valley, he has been accepted as an adopted son.

Part of the St. Helena Library Center, the museum has the feeling of a small chapel. Founded in 1969, on the 75th anniversary of Stevenson's death, Silverado is more a library than a museum. It contains more than eight thousand artifacts, including dozens of paintings and photographs, as well as original Stevenson letters and manuscripts. There are also hundreds of books and first printings.

SONOMA COUNTY

SONOMA COUNTY MUSEUM

707-579-1500
scm@pon.net
425 7th St., Santa Rosa, CA 95401
www.pressdemo.com/scmuseum
Open: 11–4 Wed.–Sun.
Admission: $5 adults, $2 students & seniors
Special Features: Gifts

The Sonoma County Museum building, a classic post office from early in the century, was saved from an insidious fate: progress. When the building was slated for demolition, preservationists prevailed, and it was moved to its present site in 1979. Now on the National Register of Historic Places, the structure is beautifully restored. A mix of Spanish and Roman influences, it's considered one of the few remaining examples of classic Federal-style architecture in California. Inside the two-story stucco building are marble floors and rich oak paneling—no better setting for a museum. Lobby displays detail the history of the building and its laborious move two blocks north. The main exhibit room offers rotating displays keyed to Sonoma history. This building also houses the Museum of Contemporary Art, formerly housed in the Wells Fargo Center of the Arts.

Other Museums

Napa County
Napa Firefighters Museum (707-259-0609, 1201 Main St., Napa, CA 94559; Mon.–Sat., 11–4) Antique firefighting equipment is on display.

Napa Valley Historical Society (707-224-1739, 1219 First St., Napa, CA 94558; Tues.–Sat., noon–4) This is a research, archival, and educational organization dedicated to the discovery and preservation of the people and history of Napa County. It has old photographs, old directories, and so forth.

Sonoma County
Healdsburg Museum (707-431-3325, 221 Matheson St., Healdsburg, CA 95448; Tues.–Sun., 11–4) This museum is devoted to early Healdsburg history, including Indian artifacts and five thousand photographs.

Native American Art Museum (707-527-4479, 1501 Mendocino Ave., Santa Rosa Junior College, Santa Rosa, CA 95401) Holdings here include artifacts and current works by Native American artisans.

Petaluma Historical Museum and Library (707-778-4398, 20 4th St., Petaluma, CA 94952; Wed.–Sat. 10–4, Sun. noon–3) This museum and library is devoted to early Petaluma history. It's located inside a classic 1903 Carnegie Library, and is a good place to begin a walking tour of Petaluma's classic Victorians.

Sonoma Depot Museum (707-938-1762, 270 First St. W., Sonoma, CA 95476; Wed.–Sun., 1–4:30) This rebuilt train depot, home to the Sonoma Valley Historical Society, features a permanent exhibit devoted to the 1846 Bear Flag Revolt plus exhibits detailing the Miwok Indian period and more.

Music

Napa County
NAPA VALLEY SYMPHONY
707-226-8742; fax 707-226-3046
www.napavalleysymphony.org
Lincoln Theater, California Veteran's Home, Yountville (Mail: 1100 Lincoln Ave., Suite 108, Napa, CA 94558)
Season: Pops concerts all year
Tickets: $10–$75

Asher Raboy is the conductor for this symphony that dates to 1933, when Luigi Catalano first gathered a cadre of amateur and professional musicians. Today, the orchestra includes more than 75 musicians from Napa Valley and the Bay Area.

Each of the season's five concerts features guest artists performing the great music of the classical repertoire. Past soloists have included pianist Philippe Bianconi and violinist Robert McDuffie. Each summer since 1969, the lovely Robert Mondavi Winery has played host to the symphony's Wine Country Pops, a warm and delightful June evening.

SONOMA COUNTY
SANTA ROSA SYMPHONY
707-546-8742; fax 707-546-0460
www.santarosasymphony.com
info@santarosasymphony.com
The Wells Fargo Center for the Arts, 50 S.R. Ave., Santa Rosa, CA 95404
Season: Oct.–May
Tickets: $27–$50

Bruno Ferrandis is the conductor. Musicians—all of respectable talent—come from around the Bay Area. Some are semiprofessionals with day jobs; others keep busy roaming from one orchestra to another. Guests of emerging musical reputation are featured in each concert. Recent soloists have included guitarist David Tanenbaum, pianist Andre Watts, and famed cellist Yo-Yo Ma, a close friend of Kahane.

The Wells Fargo Center for the Arts, a former church, is a large hall of about fifteen hundred seats. The acoustics aren't what they might be, but the symphony strives to overcome the limitations.

Other Music

NAPA COUNTY

Chamber Music in Napa Valley (707-963-1391, the Napa Valley Opera House, 1030 Main St., Napa, CA 94559) This winter series features top chamber performers in intimate settings.

Music in the Vineyards (707-258-5559, various locations and sponsors) This festival of chamber music happens every August and draws musicians from around the country.

Robert Mondavi Summer Music Festival (888-766-6328, 7801 Hwy. 29, P.O. Box 106, Oakville, CA 94562) A tradition since 1969, these June-through-August concerts on the lush lawns of Mondavi's winery bring in top names in popular music, including Tony Bennett, David Benoit, and the Preservation Hall Jazz Band.

SONOMA COUNTY

Cotati Jazz Festival (707-795-5508, run by Cotati Chamber of Commerce, downtown Cotati, CA 94931) During this late-June festival, jazz lovers hop between nightclubs listening to the best jazz musicians the Bay Area has to offer.

Healdsburg Plaza Tuesday Concert Series (707-433-6935, downtown Healdsburg, CA 95448) Held June through August, this series offers an eclectic array of music and livens Tuesday afternoons from 6 to 8 PM on this lovely plaza.

Petaluma Summer Music Festival (707-763-8920, Petaluma, CA 94952; various locations) This is Cinnabar Theater's annual ode to music and musical theater. Concerts and performances are staged throughout Petaluma during this August series.

Rodney Strong Music Series (707-433-0919, 11455 Old Redwood Hwy., Healdsburg, CA 95448) There's a summer long series of concerts on this winery's lawn.

Russian River Blues Festival (707-869-3940, Johnson Beach, Guerneville, CA 95446) Blues takes its turn at this annual two-day festival in June. The lineup of blues greats has recently included Taj Mahal, Joe Lewis Walker, and Dr. John.

Jazz on the River (707-869-1595, Johnson Beach, Guerneville, CA 95446) Jazz along the lazy Russian River has made this the most popular music festival in Wine Country. For two days every September, music lovers sun on the beach or listen from floating inner tubes. The lineup of jazz greats has recently included Larry Carlton, Grover Washington, Jr., David Benoit, and Etta James.

Wine Country Vintage Jazz Festival (707-869-1595, Doubletree Hotel, Rohnert Park, CA 94928) Sonoma County swarms with Dixie jazz nuts for one weekend every September This is a big event, bringing in bands from around the world. Don't ask them to play "When the Saints Go Marching In."

Nightlife

If you're cruising for a good time in Napa Valley at night, you'll discover quickly that things are rather sleepy. It's the nature of the beast. Napa is largely a haven for visitors seeking quiet and relaxation. Tourists, on the other hand, have less of an impact on Sonoma, which has its own large population to entertain. There's plenty to do after 10 PM, particularly in Santa Rosa. The Friday edition of Santa Rosa's *Press Democrat* is a good source for what's happening.

NAPA COUNTY

Downtown Joe's (707-258-2337, 902 Main St., Napa, CA 94559) and **Silverado Brewing Co.** (707-967-9876, 3020 St. Helena Hwy., N, St. Helena, CA 94574) are two brewpubs that have fun atmospheres, live music, and good beer. A great Calistoga hot spot is **BarVino** (707-942-9900, 1457 Lincoln Ave., Calistoga, CA 94515). It has a big city feel and great décor, with a sophisticated interplay of light and mirrors. It serves Italian trattoria fare plus great drinks, and its sidewalk seating is also a perk, if you like to people-watch. On a warm evening, try the beer garden at **Calistoga Inn** (707-942-4101, 1250 Lincoln Ave., Calistoga, CA 94515). They brew their own, and it's great stuff; also, a band is often playing in the bar. The historic **Napa Valley Opera House** (707-226-7372, 1030 Main St., Napa, CA 94559) brings in a variety of theater, as well as classical and popular music performances.

SONOMA COUNTY

Sonoma County's club scene is thriving. Live music can be found somewhere every night, and deejays seem to be spinning discs in a corner of every bar.

Santa Rosa is the center of Sonoma County's nightlife, although the outlying areas have a number of fine night spots. Sonoma County's premier stage is the **Wells Fargo Center for the Arts** (707-546-3600, 50 Mark West Springs Rd., Santa Rosa, CA 95403) Once a sprawling church complex, the center's main stage is the largest hall in the area, seating about fifteen hundred people. Recent headliners have included k.d. lang, Collective Soul, Tori Amos, Bonnie Raitt, and B.B. King.

Try the **Last Day Saloon** (707-545-2343, www.lastdaysaloon.com/; 120 Fifth St., Santa Rosa, CA 95401), which has the best Bay Area rock and blues bands. **Seven Ultra Lounge & Restaurant** (707-528-4700, 528 7th St., Santa Rosa, CA 95401) This place draws a post-high school, college crowd with its entertainment, music, beer, alcoholic beverages and wine.

Santa Rosa's hotels are another good source for late-night fun. Try **The Flamingo** (707-545-8530, 2777 4th St., Santa Rosa, CA 95405) and **Equus Lounge** of Fountain Grove Inn (707-587-0149, 101 Fountain Grove Pkwy., Santa Rosa, CA 95403) There are happening pubs in Santa Rosa. Try **Third Street Aleworks** (707-523-3060, 610 Third St., Santa Rosa, CA 95404). Check out the second floor of **The Cantina** (707-523-3663, 500 4th St., Santa Rosa, CA 95404) if you like to dance to deejays playing 1970s tunes and modern R&B. The crowd is young.

In Sonoma Valley, **Murphy's Irish Pub** (707-935-0660, 464 First St. E., Sonoma, CA 95476) is small but cozy, and it offers a great selection of imported ales. A different crowd entirely hangs out at **Little Switzerland** (707-938-9990, Grove & Riverside, El Verano, CA 95433). This place is a kick! Polka is king at Little Switzerland, a club and restaurant that dates from 1906. The crowd is made up of older, largely serious polka dancers, but they don't care if you show up for a kitsch thrill and make a fool of yourself on the dance floor. The place is delightfully tacky, with plastic flowers and Swiss Alps murals. Little Switzerland also has other music, such as Salsa.

Petaluma has one of Sonoma County's most active nightlife scenes. **Mystic Theater and Music Hall** (707-765-2121, 21 Petaluma Blvd. N., Petaluma, CA 94952) is another former movie house that has discovered live music. Recent acts have included Train and Joan Osborne. Next door is **McNear's** (707-765-2121, 23 Petaluma Blvd. N., Petaluma, CA 94952), a comfortable gathering spot with video games, pool tables, and live music on weekends. It's also one of the few places that serves food late.

West County has other popular stops. **Jasper O'Farrell's** (707-829-2062, 6957 Sebastopol Ave., Sebastopol, CA 95472) is another pub that makes you feel at home. There's live music almost every night and it's a potpourri: jazz, bluegrass, folk, rock. Darts are also a serious passion. In Healdsburg, **Bear Republic Brewing Co.** (707-433-BEER, 345 Healdsburg Ave., Healdsburg, CA 95448) may be Healdsburg's hottest night spot, featuring live music and some excellent hand-crafted beers. The **Raven Theater** (707-433-5448, 115 North St., Healdsburg, CA 95448) seldom plays movies anymore, but it brings in some excellent musical acts—everything from rap to Bo Diddley and Taj Mahal.

Theater

Theater is just taking root in Napa County; there are only a few community theaters and outdoor Shakespeare festivals. Sonoma, on the other hand, boasts a long tradition of theater. It has one professional company and several highly regarded semiprofessional groups—plus, a vastly successful summer stock repertory series brings in top college talent from around the country every year. As one local director said of the Sonoma drama scene: "I think there are more people who *do* theater than *see* theater."

SONOMA COUNTY
CINNABAR THEATER
707-763-8920; fax 707-763-8929
www.cinnabartheater.com
info@cinnabartheater.com
3333 Petaluma Blvd. N., Petaluma, CA 94952
Season: Year-round
Tickets: Various

Opera is a scary prospect for a lot of people. Perhaps it's the elitist air that surrounds it, the assumption that it's only for the wealthy and educated. Or perhaps singing in a foreign language turns people off. Whatever the reason, the late Marvin Klebe came to Petaluma in the early 1970s to change the perception of opera. From that began Sonoma County's most eclectic and dynamic theater. "Our main goals are to explore opera as an immediate and human experience to an audience that is not necessarily highbrow," Cinnabar's Elly Lichenstein commented.

Klebe, a powerful baritone, bought the old Cinnabar School on the northern outskirts of Petaluma and set about transforming it into a studio theater. (Luckily, he was also a master carpenter.) Soon, others—musicians, dancers, actors, technicians—got involved, and Cinnabar became a small, thriving performing arts center.

The heart of the place is Cinnabar Opera Theater. There's not a more intriguing theater company north of San Francisco. No, you won't find a tenor from San Francisco Opera on stage here, but you will see the finest singers hovering on "the outskirts" of Bay Area opera fame. Productions have run the gamut from *The Magic Flute* to musical chestnuts such as *Fiddler on the Roof.*

PACIFIC ALLIANCE STAGE COMPANY
707-588-3434 (box office); fax 707-588-3430
Spreckels Performing Arts Center, 5409 Snyder Ln., Rohnert Park, CA 94928
Season: Sept.–May
Tickets: Call for prices

Pacific Alliance is the county's first professional Actor's Equity company. The company also has the backing of Spreckels Center, which in turn is backed by the city of Rohnert Park. The theater continues to bring superior talents from around the Bay Area. A few talented local "amateurs" are also earning that all-important union card.

While acting approaches the level found in San Francisco, production values reveal a limited budget. Spreckels is also experimenting with a few offbeat productions in its small studio. It's all very refreshing.

SONOMA COUNTY REPERTORY THEATRE
707-823-0177 (Sebastopol)
104 N. Main St., Sebastopol, CA 95472
www.the-rep.com
Season: Year-round
Tickets: $18

Since its inception in 1995, this company has quickly become the area's leading theater, staging a mix of classics and cutting-edge dramas, comedies, and occasionally a musical.

Performances are in a small Sebastopol theater. Executive artistic director Jennifer King and producing artistic director Scott Phillips are a hurricane of energy and real talent. Top productions have included Shakespeare's *The Tempest* and *Hamlet* as well as *The Glass Menagerie*, *A Streetcar Named Desire*, *Tuesdays With Morrie* and *Assassins*.

SUMMER REPERTORY THEATER

707-527-4418; fax 707-524-1689
www.santarosa.edu/srt
1501 Mendocino Ave., Santa Rosa, CA 9540
Season: June–Aug.
Tickets: $8–$14

No one has a bigger local following than SRT. Every summer, the Santa Rosa Junior College organizes this three-ring circus of theater, bringing in talented student actors and technical people from around the country. Opening several major productions in four weeks and performing them in a repertory format packs a year's experience into two months.

Performance of The Mystery of Edwin Drood *by Summer Repertory Theater.* Courtesy Summer Repertory Theater, Jeff Thomas

Some summers are better than others, of course—it all depends on the show and the talent pool—but SRT is always worth a try. The play selection is generally rather safe, but SRT has proved its mettle with every genre: comedy, musical, and drama. Highlights have included sparkling productions of *Evita* and *The Mystery of Edwin Drood* and an entertaining version of Steve Martin's *Picasso at the Lapin Agile.*

SRT's production values are the highest in the area. Sets are always dynamic, on a par with many professional theaters. It's also significant that SRT is one of the few local companies performing in the summer—thus a perfect choice for tourists looking for a pleasurable evening on the town.

Other Theater
There are more than a dozen other theater companies in Napa and Sonoma. Many are community theaters. We include a selection of the best.

NAPA COUNTY
Dreamweavers (707-255-LIVE, 1637 Imola Ave., Napa, CA 94559) This is a community theater performing favorites such as *Same Time Next Year.*

Magical Moonshine Theater (707-257-8007, P.O. Box 2296, Yountville, CA 94599) Here's an internationally known puppet theater that doesn't have a regular Napa performance space. Look for them locally when they're not away on tour—they're charming and great for the family.

SONOMA COUNTY
6th Street Playhouse (707-523-4185, 52 West 6th St., Santa Rosa, CA, 95401) This is a relatively new addition to the Sonoma theater scene but many of the players involved are veterans. Recent productions include *The Grapes of Wrath.*

Sonoma State University (707-664-2353, Rohnert Park, CA 94928) SSU also has a talented theater department, and the new performing arts center has the county's best stage for theater.

Sonoma Community Center (707-938-4626, 276 E. Napa St., Sonoma, CA 95476) This is the stage for regular performances.

Seasonal Events
If there's one thing they know how to do in Wine Country, it's throw a party. If you live in or are visiting Napa or Sonoma counties and find that you have an open weekend in the summer, then maybe there's something wrong with you. There are enough festivals and fairs to keep you busy all year. Here, we list some of the most popular seasonal attractions. The agricultural products of the Napa and Sonoma region shine forth at the many county fairs. Wine, of course, is the centerpiece of many festivals; we've included wine events in a separate section that follows.

Bodega Bay Fisherman's Festival (707-875-3866, Bodega Bay, CA 94923) This is a decades-old tradition for this coast town made famous by Alfred Hitchcock's *The Birds.* This mid-April celebration includes bathtub races, harbor tours, kite flying, a golf tournament, and a boat parade. The high point of the weekend is the annual blessing of the fleet.

Calistoga Downtown Jazz & Blues (707-942-6333, Napa County Fairgrounds, Calistoga, CA 94515) This event happens in early October, and tickets range from $40 to $165.

Gravenstein Apple Fair (707-824-1765, Ragle Ranch Park, Sebastopol, CA 95472) Sebastopol, once the apple capital of the world, today specializes in the distinctive Gravenstein variety. There's a potpourri at this mid-August event: arts and crafts, music, hay rides, storytelling, and, of course, apple treats of all kinds. Admission.

Harmony Festival (707-542-4200, Sonoma County Fairgrounds, Santa Rosa, CA 95401) An only-in-California type of event, this celebration of food, music, and "lifestyle"—an annual June fair—includes everything from puppet theater to psychic palm readers. Admission.

Hometown Harvest Festival (707-963-5706, downtown St. Helena, CA 94574) A rich Napa tradition, celebrating the end of the growing season and the summer's bountiful harvest. One weekend in late October, there's scads of food, arts and crafts, music, and even a parade.

Napa County Fair (707-942-5111, fairgrounds, Calistoga, CA 94515) Every July, this has the usual down-home fun, but with a twist of chic Napa style that includes social gatherings and wine tastings. There are the usual rides, animals, produce, and music, plus wine, wine, wine. Admission.

Napa Town and Country Fair (707-253-4900, Napa Exposition Center, Napa, CA 94559) It has the usual every August: livestock, food and wine tasting, arts and crafts displays, a carnival, and entertainment. Admission.

Napa Valley Mustard Festival (707-259-9020, various locations) Mustard, the beautiful yellow wildflower that blooms throughout Wine Country every winter, is the focus of this late-winter series of food and wine events. Admission.

Petaluma Butter & Eggs Day (707-762-9348, downtown Petaluma, CA 94952) This is a celebration of this South-County town's early reputation as "the egg basket of the world." Poultry, milk, and eggs remain a strong presence in Sonoma. One Sunday every April, the town celebrates with a parade, music, and food.

Sebastopol Apple Blossom Festival (707-823-3032, 877-828-4748, downtown Sebastopol, CA 95472) When the apple trees are in striking form in April, you won't find a more beautiful place than Sebastopol. Apples rule, of course. Eat apple fritters, cobbler, and pies, plus enjoy music, games, and arts and crafts.

Sonoma County Fair (707-545-4200, fairgrounds, Santa Rosa, CA 95401) Sonoma County practically shuts down for two weeks every July as thousands pour in from the countryside for food, music, rides, blue-ribbon animals, and produce. You can even bet on horse races. Admission.

Yountville Days Festival (707-944-0904, downtown Yountville, CA 94599) Celebrate the history of Napa Valley's first settlement. This event, held the first Sunday in October, includes a parade, music, food.

Wine Events

We're still waiting to see this sign along a Napa or Sonoma road: GARAGE SALE & WINE TASTING. Wine events are everywhere and all the time in Napa and Sonoma. There's also considerable appeal to sampling and comparing all sorts of wine in one sitting. Most of the following events are staged outside.

The Sonoma County Harvest Fair attracts wine experts from around the country. Tim Fish

Napa Valley Wine Auction (707-963-3388, Meadowood Resort, St. Helena, CA 94574) The chic wine outing, this three-day June event is busy with extravagant parties, dances, and dinners. Auction tickets cost a fortune but are in high demand. All the big names of the Napa wine industry and elsewhere attend, and the auction raises millions for local charities.

Napa Valley Wine Festival (707-253-3563, Napa Exposition Center, Napa, CA 94559) The November wine tasting, dinner, and auction raises money for a local charity and marks the end of the wine season. Admission.

Napa Wine Festival and Crafts Fair (707-252-7142, downtown Napa, CA 94559) This busy event draws wine as well as arts and crafts buffs from around the county every September. Tasting fee.

Barrel Tasting Weekend (707-433-4335, Russian River Wine Rd., countryside surrounding Healdsburg, CA) Always the first event of the wine season, this event helps lift wine lovers out of the winter doldrums. Besides, everyone loves a sneak preview of wine that hasn't been bottled yet. Best of all: It's free.

Salute to the Arts (707-938-1133, Sonoma Plaza, Sonoma, CA 95476) This July event is a showcase for local artists, writers, restaurants, and wineries. Roam the beautiful historic square, and browse the many booths. Fee for wine and food.

Sonoma County Harvest Fair (707-545-4200, fairgrounds, Santa Rosa, CA 95401) This event could easily be listed with the regular seasonal offerings, but the wine tasting is the

Both building and contents are cutting edge at the San Francisco Museum of Modern Art. Courtesy SFMOMA, Richard Barnes

most important in Sonoma County. The fair brings in top wine experts from around the country. Then local wine buffs gather to compare their taste buds to those of the judges. This is great fun in October. There's also plenty of food, and the annual grape stomping contest is a crazy attraction. Admission.

Sonoma County Showcase of Wine & Food (800-935-7666, various locations) A bit less chichi than its Napa counterpart, this remains quite an elegant affair. The gala July weekend includes tastings, parties, and the auction itself. The event is usually sold out weeks in advance, despite steep ticket prices.

Sonoma Valley Harvest Wine Auction (707-935-0803, various locations) This casual and fun weekend affair every September includes winery parties, a main auction, and even a golf tournament.

Neighbors

With San Francisco so close, it's impossible to talk of culture without mentioning what that world-class city has to offer.

Museums are one of the most popular excuses for the pleasant hour's drive south. Best known is **The Exploratorium** (415-EXPLORE, exploratorium.edu, 3601 Lyon St.,

San Francisco, CA 94123), a magnetic place for families because of its hands-on science displays. Likewise, The **California Academy of Sciences** (415-750-7145, www.calacademy.org, 875 Howard St., San Francisco, CA 94103; in Golden Gate Park) is a popular spot for kids and families. Art museums include the cutting edge **San Francisco Museum of Modern Art** (415-357-4000, www.sfmoma.org, 151 3rd St., San Francisco, CA 94103) and the graceful **Palace of the Legion of Honor** (415-750-3600, www.legionofhonor.org, 100 34th Ave., San Francisco, CA 94122; at Clermont St., in Lincoln Park), which specializes in Rodin sculpture.

The performing arts are still another of San Francisco's many lures. The **San Francisco Ballet** (415-865-2000, www.sfballet.org, War Memorial Opera House) is one of the best in the country. The **San Francisco Symphony** (415-552-8000, sfsymphony.org, Davies Symphony Hall) is gaining a national reputation as well, and the **San Francisco Opera** (415-864-3330, www.sfopera.com, War Memorial Opera House) is one of the Bay Area's great artistic traditions. And while San Francisco is hardly Broadway, the theater district around Union Square is a happening place. The **American Conservatory Theater** (415-834-3200, 30 Grant Ave., San Francisco, CA 94133) is the city's most respected, and small off-Broadway-style theaters abound. For something uniquely San Francisco, don't miss the wacky musical revue *Beach Blanket Babylon* (415-421-4222, Club Fugazi, 678 Green St., San Francisco, CA 94133).

As for nightlife, San Francisco offers some top clubs. The **Fillmore** (415-346-6000, www.thefillmore.com, 1805 Geary St., San Francisco, CA 94115) brings in musical acts such as Crosby, Stills, and Nash, Counting Crows, and Megadeath. At **The Warfield** (Ticketmaster: 415-775-7722, 415-421-TIXS, 982 Market St., San Francisco, CA 94102) recent acts have included P. J. Harvey and David Byrne of Talking Heads fame. San Francisco's South of Market District is the place to be seen, a former industrial area with nightclubs on almost every corner.

The bounty of local artisan food producers is featured at West Country Grill. Courtesy West County Grill

5

Restaurants &
Food Purveyors

Bon Appétit!

If wine is "bottled poetry," as novelist Robert Louis Stevenson wrote, then fine dining in Wine Country is its culinary equivalent. As wineries have encroached on the farmland of Napa and Sonoma counties, gourmet restaurants have overtaken the burger joints. But the urban sprawl of fine dining hasn't upset the natives and certainly not the tourists. Today, Wine Country is widely known as a delicious place.

There are more restaurants than ever that are worth a visit, running the gamut from palatial chateaux to storefront bistros, along with ethnic eateries offering Mexican, Chinese, and Thai fare. There is more to dining out than just the food, of course. We also consider atmosphere. Does a restaurant set the tone for the meal to come? Is it warm, interesting, or unique? Most of all, does it work? Service is also key—after all, you're on vacation and deserve to be pampered. We are most interested in knowing how well the servers know the menu and can make intelligent comments about particular dishes. Each restaurant is given a price code, signifying the cost of a single meal including appetizer, entrée, and dessert, but not cocktails, wine, tax, or tip. Reviews are organized first by county, then by city or region, and then alphabetically. Food purveyors are grouped alphabetically by type, then by name of establishment. Every restaurant appears in the general index, too.

Dining Price Codes

Inexpensive:	Up to $20
Moderate:	$20 to $30
Expensive:	$30 to $40
Very Expensive:	$40 or more

The following abbreviations are used for credit card information.
AE: American Express
CB: Carte Blanche
D: Discover
DC: Diner's Club
MC: Master Card
V: Visa

Napa County Restaurants

NAPA
ANGELE
707-252-8115
www.angelerestaurant.com
540 Main St., Napa, CA 94558
Price: Expensive
Credit Cards: AE, MC, V
Cuisine: French
Serving: Lunch, Dinner
Reservations: Recommended
Special Features: Outdoor dining

This French-style bistro, located in a former boathouse on Napa's booming riverfront, has an elegant but unstuffy atmosphere, with concrete floors and walls and rough-hewn wood rafters. There are some serious players behind it; owners include Claudia Rouas, who built Auberge du Soleil, and Bettina Rouas, the former manager of The French Laundry. The chef is Christophe Gerard, who trained at Taillevent in Paris. The menu is classic to a tee, with petrale sole, pan-seared salmon, steamed mussels, and chicken with chanterelle mushrooms. Don't miss the immaculate *blanquette de veau*, an old-fashioned veal stew with a creamy white sauce. The wine list is modest but deftly selected, with a fine selection of French and Napa wines.

BISTRO DON GIOVANNI
707-224-3300
www.bistrodongiovanni.com
4110 St. Helena Hwy., Napa, CA 94558 (on Hwy. 29)
Price: Moderate to Expensive
Credit Cards: AE, D, DC, MC, V
Cuisine: Italian
Serving: Lunch, Dinner
Reservations: Recommended
Special Features: Outdoor dining

The seduction begins the moment you approach Bistro Don Giovanni. In the evening, when the porch and the lawn are filled with voices and the air is rich with aromas and music, you feel as though you've been invited to an extravagant party. Inside, the setting is romantic, a high-ceilinged room done in warm tones, white linen, and modern art with vineyard views through tall windows. The perfume from the open kitchen makes you anxious to get down to business: eating—and what fine business it is! Bistro Don Giovanni is Napa's most popular Italian restaurant for good reason.

Chef Donna Scala is a passionate chef. With roots in the country cooking of Italy and France, the food is delightfully straightforward. The menu includes the requisite salads, pasta, and risotto as well as pizza from a wood-burning oven. Salads are first-rate, and the antipasto is a generous and flavorful plate. House specialties include silk handkerchiefs (thin sheets of pasta with pesto), a robust braised lamb shank, and fillet of salmon pan seared for a thin crust to protect its moist and flaky heart. The wine list is mostly Napa and Italian and rather pricey. Service is attentive. This place is a find. Don't miss it!

BOON FLY CAFE (AT THE CARNEROS INN)
707-299-4900
4048 Sonoma Hwy., Napa, CA 94559
Price: Moderate to Expensive
Credit Cards: AE, D, MC, V
Cuisine: American
Serving: Breakfast, Lunch, Dinner
Reservations: Recommended

Location is this café's major appeal—it's in the heart of rural Carneros Wine Country—but the food is stylish and hearty, perfect for a wine-tasting lunch or dinner in shorts or jeans. The interior is high-tech, retro California barn, with towering ceiling, exposed metal beams, tin table tops, and wood floors. The food shares similar sensi-

The restaurant is high-tech, California barn at the Carneros Inn in Napa Valley. Courtesy Carneros Inn

bilities: modern yet full of comfort, stocked with artsy BLTs, Kobe burgers, grilled mahi-mahi, and towering stacks of French fries and onion rings. (Breakfast is rich enough to feed a farmhand, with eggs benedict, corned beef hash, and the like.) The wine list is modest and focused largely on wines from the surrounding Carneros region, and the prices are generally a steal.

BOUNTY HUNTER WINE BAR
707-255-0622
975 First Strt, Napa, CA 94559
Price: Moderate to Expensive
Credit Cards: AE, MC, V
Cuisine: California
Serving: Lunch, Dinner
Reservations: Not accepted

This is a popular hangout for Napa's wine savvy. Located in a circa-1888 building on the river downtown, the wine bar has a comfortably eccentric atmosphere, with exposed brick walls; a towering, tin-covered ceiling; and various bear and ram heads decorating the walls. Wine is the key player here, but the food hardly plays second fiddle. There are more than 50 wines available by the glass, and many are available in themed flights of three-Rhone-style reds, for example. The wine list is international and there are about four hundred selections, ranging from bargains to major investments. The menu is wine friendly, as you might expect, ranging from small plates of olives and charcuterie to Caesar salads and grilled skewers of tiger prawns with Cajun citrus marinade to pulled pork sandwiches.

CELADON

707-254-9690; fax 707-254-9692
www.celadonnapa.com
500 Main St., Napa, CA 94559
Closed: Sun.
Price: Expensive
Credit Cards: AE, D, DC, MC, V
Cuisine: California
Serving: Lunch, Dinner; closed Sun.
Reservations: Recommended
Special Features: Creekside dining room

Celadon has mastered the art of balance in its food, service, and décor. Tim Fish

Celadon masters the art of balance better than most restaurants. Its food is top rate, its service is intelligent and well paced, and its décor is refreshing. It's unfortunate but true that most restaurants don't manage to pull it all together and struggle with at least one of the three. Most impressive at Celadon is the food. Some top-rate dishes include the Maine crab cake and the

Moroccan-inspired braised lamb shank, and desserts include delectable items such as mango-and-nectarine fruit crisp. The wine list has a good selection by the glass, and prices across the board are reasonable. The restaurant's name refers to a type of pottery with a pale green glaze, and throughout the smart restaurant there are touches of pale green, pleasing and subtle.

COLE'S CHOP HOUSE

707-224-6328; fax 707-254-9692
www.coleschophouse.com
1122 Main St., Napa, CA 94559
Price: Very Expensive
Credit Cards: AE, DC, MC, V
Cuisine: Steak house
Serving: Dinner
Reservations: Recommended
Special Features: Creekside patio dining

Cole's Chop House is slick. A quiet storefront from the outside, inside it's a bustling, cosmopolitan nightclub with a jazz trio playing in the balcony. This place has a pulse. Located inside a circa-1886 building with loftlike 35-foot ceilings, it's a big restaurant with lots of tables and lots of people, but the service is seamless. Besides, Napa is cabernet country, and that's a wine that demands a slab o' meat. The beef is all top-of-the-line, dry-aged Chicago. Real grill masters, of course, are convinced the best steaks are made at home, but it's hard to deny the appeal of Cole's. The menu isn't cheap. A rib eye will run you $33—and that's just the steak. Even a potato is extra. But the à la carte side dishes are family-style huge, so two people can share. Appetizers are typical steakhouse fare: Oysters Rockefeller and the like. The grilled Mexican prawn cocktail has plenty of gusto, although the prawns can be overcooked. The center-cut pork chop is nicely done—savory, but it lacks a little something. On the other hand, Cole's "famous" porterhouse steak is a huge piece of meat, and it's tender, juicy, and powerfully flavored. The wine list has a good selection of half bottles and more than a dozen offerings by the glass. There's a good showing of French wines and some older California library wines.

FARM (AT THE CARNEROS INN)

707-299-4870
www.thecarnerosinn.com
Napa, CA 94559
Price: Very Expensive
Credit Cards: AE, MC, V
Cuisine: American
Serving: Lunch, Dinner
Reservations: Recommended
Special Features: Outdoor dining

Farm, the restaurant at the Carneros Inn, is rustic chic. The building is barnlike, with a high-pitched ceiling, exposed rafters, and windows, but it also has a contemporary feel, with clean lines and dramatic lighting. As for the food, it's quite good. Impressive are the wood stone oven pizza, the pork chop, and the carnoli risotto. Farm also has a decent wine list, focusing on Napa and Sonoma bottlings, and it has 21 wines by the glass. The bar is upscale with an urban feel. Best of all, the inn offers a place to stay after dinner.

JULIA'S KITCHEN

707-265-5700
www.juliaskitchen.org
At COPIA, 500 1st St., Napa, CA 94558
Price: Very Expensive
Credit Cards: AE, MC, V
Cuisine: California, French
Serving: Lunch, Dinner Wed.–Mon. Dinner Wed.–Sun.
Reservations: Recommended
Special Features: Outdoor dining

The late Julia Child lent her name to this restaurant, which is located in COPIA: The American Center for Wine, Food, and the Arts (see Museums in chapter 4, Culture).

COPIA has been struggling to find an audience, but the restaurant has become a true destination. The dining room is elegantly understated, and the best locale for a table is outside overlooking COPIA's impressive gardens. Freshness is key to the kitchen's success. Much of the produce comes from the garden. The kitchen is devoted to local producers, and the plate is filled with creative variations on pork chops, fish, and salads. The wine list is superb, and the restaurant offers tasting flights to go with the menu.

PIZZA AZZURRO

707-255-5552
1400 2nd St., Napa, CA 94559
Closed: Sun., Sat. Lunch
Price: Moderate
Credit Cards: MC, V
Cuisine: Italian
Serving: Lunch (closed Sat.), Dinner; closed Sun.
Reservations: Not accepted
Special Features: Outdoor dining

If only more casual Italian restaurants had food this tasty, and the price is *so* right. Azzurro is a good idea for lunch or for those much-needed low-achievement dinners during your Wine Country vacation. Located in a storefront in downtown Napa, Azzurro has a smart, functional atmosphere and limited sidewalk dining. There's a short list of salads, pasta, and pizzas, and so far, we haven't found a dud on the menu. The roasted mushroom, taleggio, and thyme is addicting and salads such as Caesar or chilled asparagus with creamy mustard dressing are light but flavorful. The wine list is small but well suited to the menu.

TUSCANY

707-258-1000
1005 1st St., Napa, CA 94559
Price: Moderate to Expensive

Credit Cards: AE, D, MC, V
Cuisine: Italian
Serving: Lunch Mon.–Fri., Dinner daily
Reservations: Only for parties of six or more

Tuscany is a bustling, bright-lights kind of stop in the city of Napa. With a full bar the length of one side of the restaurant, it has a nightclub feel: lots of people with drinks in hand making noisy conversation. The food is good, not great. For Italian, it's a good second choice after nearby Bistro Don Giovanni. The menu is big—and so are the portions—and all the Italian classics are offered. Start with roasted fresh vegetables served with various sauces and you won't regret it. The wine list has a good selection of wines by the glass for both reds and whites, and prices are standard. As for décor, the restaurant—complete with fake windows, a fake tile roof, and murals—emulates a Tuscan village. The big dining room is done up in clay and tan colors, and an open kitchen runs along one side.

UBUNTU RESTAURANT AND YOGA STUDIO

707-251-5656
www.ubuntunapa.com
1140 Main St., Napa CA. 94559
Price: Moderate
Credit Cards: AE, D, MC, V
Cuisine: Garden-inspired vegetarian
Serving: Breakfast, Lunch, Dinner
Reservations: Recommended
Special Features: biodynamic dishes, yoga studio

This unique restaurant focuses on biodynamic dishes, drawing from its own gardens and the labors of local farmers. Ubuntu—in a nutshell—means "humanity toward others," and this is a center for folks in touch with their spiritual side. In the loft above the restaurant, with soundproofed doors, is the yoga studio, and Ubuntu has a calendar with scheduled lectures, films, and music. Chef Jeremy Fox, who's worked at Rubican and the four-star Charles Nob

Hill in San Francisco, makes highly spiced dishes that appeal to both omnivores and herbivores. Popular entrees include the cauliflower in an iron pot, roasted, pureed, and raw, and the fig pizza.

YOUNTVILLE
AD HOC

707-944-2487; fax: 707-944-2275
www.adhocrestaurant.com
6476 Washington St., Yountville, CA 94599
Price: Expensive; Prix Fixe: $45
Credit Cards: AE, MC, V
Cuisine: California comfort
Serving: Dinner
Reservations: Recommended

Celebrity chef Thomas Keller, best known for his award-winning restaurant The French Laundry, is also behind this first-rate eatery. Here, comfort food reigns—favorites from Keller's childhood. Irresistible dishes served in generous portions include the fried chicken, the spiced hanger steak, and the braised beef short ribs. The menu is limited to a single hree-course meal and food is served family style. The wine list includes imports but focuses on Napa Valley labels, with a few bottlings from Sonoma. The atmosphere has a crisp, clean look, with the walls in light green and off white. The wooden tables have stainless steel accents which resemble mirrors, a smart touch. This is great spot in wine country—and it may be as close as you can get to Thomas Keller's ingenuity, given that The French Laundry requires a two-month wait.

BISTRO JEANTY

707-944-0103
www.bistrojeanty.com
6510 Washington St., Yountville, CA 94599
Price: Expensive
Credit Cards: MC, V
Cuisine: French
Serving: Lunch, Dinner

Bistro Jeanty in Yountville offers French county cuisine—comfort food with panache. Tim Fish

Reservations: Yes
Special Features: Outdoor dining

After preparing for years the meticulously elaborate creations at Domaine Chandon, chef Philippe Jeanty returned to his roots in 1998 and opened this delightful bistro. The idea, he said, was to create the French country comfort food he grew up with in Champagne. It's hard not to be won over by Jeanty's menu, which is ripe with classics such as *cassoulet, daube de boeuf,* and escargots. A favorite is *coq au vin,* a hearty red wine stew of moist chicken and mushrooms: delicious. Pâtés are a specialty of the house, and be sure to try the *rillettes de canard,* a blend of duck and goat cheese. For dessert, go with a sure thing: crêpe Suzette. There's a reason it's a classic. The restaurant is a clay-colored storefront in the heart of Yountville. The interior sets a soothing tone with antiques, French restaurant signs, and plenty of elbow room. The wine list won't impress stuffy collectors; it's a small and impeccable list selected strictly with the menu in mind.

BOUCHON

707-944-8037
6534 Washington St., Yountville, CA 94599
Price: Expensive
Credit Cards: AE, MC, V
Cuisine: French
Serving: Lunch, Dinner
Reservations: Yes
Special Features: Outdoor dining

If Bistro Jeanty down the road is trying to corner the market on French country bistros, then Bouchon has Paris in mind.

For a taste of Paris in Wine Country, head to Bouchon in Yountville. Tim Fish

The mood is distinctly urban. Noted New York designer Adam Tihany—famous for Cirque 2000, among others—has created a chic den with burgundy, velvet, bold mosaics, and a zinc raw bar handcrafted in France. If this sounds elaborate even by Napa Valley standards, there's good reason: The man behind it is Thomas Keller of The French Laundry in Yountville and Per Se in New York. Bouchon is truly one of the best dining experiences in Wine Country.

If Bouchon has the authentic feel of an upscale brasserie, it has a menu to match. Specialties include an incredible *steak frites* (French for "steak with fries") and an equally addictive *poulet à la Niçoise* (roasted chicken with a ragout of artichokes, onions, and olives). The terrine of duck foie gras is an indulgence worthy to begin any meal, but for something lighter, sample from the raw bar. The oysters are impeccable. The wine list is sharply focused on wines that bring out the menu's best, and prices are average. Service is first-rate, and Bouchon stays open late; the bar is one of the busiest and classiest in the valley.

BRIX

707-944-2749
www.brix.com
7377 St. Helena Hwy., Yountville, CA 94599
Price: Expensive
Credit Cards: AE, MC, V
Cuisine: California
Serving: Lunch, Dinner
Reservations: Recommended

The food here is reliable if a bit unexciting compared to the valley's top kitchens, but the atmosphere is soothing, and wine is taken seriously—a wine shop is just inside the front door. With its peaked wood ceiling and warm, earthy tones, the dining room recalls a private ski lodge. Through a wall of windows, the view is gorgeous—a garden, vineyards, and the rugged Mayacamas Mountains—and lovely sunsets are staged nightly. The service—professional, experienced, and attentive—is so skilled that it's almost inconspicuous. The menu is a bit too vast for our taste, and it shows: Everything is good, never great. We prefer a kitchen that focuses on a few entrées and does them well.

Enjoy a glass of bubbly on the terrace before dining at Domaine Chandon in Yountville. Tim Fish

ETOILE AT DOMAINE CHANDON

707-204-7529, 800-736-2892
www.chandon.com
1 California Dr., Yountville, CA 94599
Price: Very Expensive
Credit Cards: AE, D, DC, MC, V
Cuisine: California, French
Serving: Lunch, Dinner; closed Tues. and Wed. winter
Reservations: Required
Special Features: Jacket requested for men at dinner; outdoor dining

Domaine Chandon is not the consummate experience it once was—The French Laundry has stolen that thunder—and in fact it's downright disappointing at times, particu-

larly for the price. Housed in a modern, curved-concrete building with terrace views of the landscaped grounds, the restaurant is elegant but not pretentious. Servers dote over the table; we don't mind being pampered.

Being part of the Domaine Chandon winery, the emphasis here is naturally on sparkling wine. The superb wine list covers America and France with a surprisingly modest markup. The menu, which changes with the seasons, combines California creativity with the great traditions of French cooking. The menu changes with the seasons and the kitchen is generally more successful with seafood dishes—not surprising because bubbly plays such a crucial role at Chandon.

THE FRENCH LAUNDRY

707-944-2380
6640 Washington St., Yountville, CA 94599
Price: Very Expensive; Prix Fixe: $240
Credit Cards: AE, M, V
Cuisine: California-French
Serving: Lunch, Dinner
Reservations: Required
Special Features: Outdoor dining, garden; jackets required for men at both lunch and dinner

Not only is The French Laundry the best restaurant in Wine Country, it's one of the best in the country—period. Owner-chef Thomas Keller has become a celebrity, and there's a two-month waiting list for reservations (if you can get them to answer the phone!). The rich and famous flock here; Robert Redford is a regular. This place is hot. Is it worth all the fuss? Yes, if you can afford it. It's easily the most expensive restaurant in Wine Country—a dinner for two with a bottle of wine, tax, and tip approaches $500!

The grand, stone house, which was built in 1900, was a bar and brothel before becoming a French-style laundry. It was a restaurant of considerable distinction even before Keller took over in 1994. He

Food lovers line up to eat at The French Laundry. Tim Fish

expanded the gardens and the kitchen. The atmosphere is formal—okay, frankly, it's a little stuffy. You're there to worship the food quietly, and we can live with that. You might call Keller's cuisine "California labor-intensive." Every dish is an artistic feat as well as a culinary joy, and when it comes to butter, the kitchen's motto is: No fear. At night there are two menus: a five-course prix fixe and a nine-course chef's tasting menu. If money is no object, opt for the chef's tasting menu; you won't regret it. Portions are sized appropriately, but be prepared to indulge yourself. The kitchen's pace is unhurried, although service is attentive. Allow at least two or three hours for the meal.

There isn't a false step on the menu, and it's impossible to recommend a particular dish because we've seldom had the same thing twice. That's just how creative this kitchen is. And while the food is serious, Keller reveals his sense of humor in naming certain dishes. You might find macaroni and cheese on the menu, but it won't be like anything your mom or Kraft ever made. Then there's the signature dessert, coffee and doughnuts: You've never had cinnamon-sugared doughnuts so good, and they're

served with a cup of coffee—flavored mousse complete with foam. The wine list is impressive and expensive, with a superb offering of California and French wines. Wines by the glass are lacking. Save up your allowance, and make reservations at The French Laundry.

MUSTARDS GRILL

707-944-2424
www.mustardsgrill.com
7399 St. Helena Hwy., Napa, CA 94599
Price: Moderate
Credit Cards: D, DC, MC, V
Cuisine: California
Serving: Lunch, Dinner
Reservations: Recommended

After all these years, Mustards Grill still lives up to its reputation. Open since the early 1980s, it was one of the earliest players in Napa's burgeoning restaurant boom. The secret of Mustards isn't actually a secret at all: hearty bistro food prepared with style, at a moderate price and in a lively atmosphere. "Truck-stop deluxe" they call it. The open kitchen takes center stage, dominating an intimate dining room that's rich with dark wood; black-and-white tile;

and broad, open windows. The tables are close, but the din becomes so loud that it lends an air of privacy. While servers seem harried, they're efficient and friendly.

Chef-owner Cindy Pawlcyn, who also runs Cindy's Backstreet Kitchen and Go Fish up the road, creates comfort food with flair. House specialties include a juicy Mongolian pork chop, pan-roasted liver (yes, liver!), plus braised lamb shanks and grilled rabbit. A must are the onion rings, a heaping pile that comes thinly sliced and highly seasoned. In the summer, don't miss the first-class, heirloom tomato salad with goat cheese toast. For dessert, try the Jack Daniels Cake. Though rich and deadly, thankfully it carries nowhere near the kick of its namesake. The wine list is well focused and priced fairly. The wine-by-the-glass selection is also first-rate.

REDD

707-944-2222
www.reddnapavalley.com
6480 Washington St., Yountville CA 94599
Price: Very Expensive
Credit Cards: AE, MC, V
Cuisine: California
Serving: Lunch, Dinner
Reservations: Required
Special Features: Outside dining

Richard Reddington made a name for himself at Masa's and Jardiniere in San Francisco and Auberge du Soleil in Napa Valley, and then struck out on his own with this classy restaurant. From the atmosphere to the food to the service and the wine list, there isn't a false note. The interior is sleekly urban, with polished wood and aqua-blue highlights.

The menu shows Asian and French influences and showcases Reddington's passion for putting a high polish on what's ordinarily considered rustic comfort food. Signature dishes include glazed pork belly with apple purée, burdock, and soy caramel, as well as Liberty Farms duck breast and Swiss chard crepes on celery root and chocolate sauce. The wine list is on the expensive side, but it's loaded with collectibles from California and France, and the wine service is first rate. If you're in the mood to splurge, Redd is an excellent choice.

OAKVILLE/RUTHERFORD
AUBERGE DU SOLEIL

800-348-5406
www.aubergedusoleil.com
180 Rutherford Hill Rd., Rutherford, CA 94573
Price: Very Expensive
Credit Cards: AE, D, DC, MC, V
Cuisine: California, French
Serving: Breakfast, Lunch, Dinner
Reservations: Required
Special Features: View, outside dining

If you want a postcard view of Napa Valley, a tapestry woven of vineyards, make a reservation at Auberge du Soleil. Then, make sure you slip in early enough to grab a table on the outside deck. The check may cause a double take, but the experience is worth it. Auberge du Soleil, or "inn of the sun," is Wine Country's most luxurious resort (see chapter 3, Lodging). The restaurant—a page from *Metropolitan Home* magazine—suggests a villa in southern France, done in soft pastels and accented with rough-hewn wood, a large hearth, and bold arrangements of fresh

The deck of Auberge du Soleil offers the best views for dinner in Napa Valley. Tim Fish

flowers. What arrives on the plate rivals the atmosphere, with rich dishes such as roasted Liberty Farms duck and seared ahi tuna. Although pricey, the wine list is one of the best in northern California, with an extensive selection of wine by the glass, including champagne. Service, too, is impeccable but never overly attentive.

LA TOQUE

707-963-9770
www.latoque.com
1140 Rutherford Rd., Rutherford, CA 94573
(at Rancho Caymus)
Closed: Mon., Tues.
Price: Very Expensive; Prix Fixe: $98
Credit Cards: AE,D, MC, V
Cuisine: Contemporary French
Serving: Dinner; closed Mon. and Tues.
Reservations: Yes
Special Features: Outdoor dining

Following the lead of other star chefs, Ken Frank said goodbye to Los Angeles and transplanted to Napa Valley a decade ago. The result was La Toque, a romantically chic restaurant that makes you feel like you're in the French countryside. At press time La Toque was planning a move to the Westin in the city of Napa. Check restaurant website for details. The five-course prix fixe menu includes a series of indulgences such as duck breast, striped bass, and Niman Ranch beef. Don't pass on the additional cheese course, an exceptional offering of *fromage*. The wine list is practically a book put together by a very wine-savvy team. The service is also top rate, intelligent, and nimble. The restaurant is a great addition to Napa Valley, clearly one of Wine Country's finest.

RUTHERFORD GRILL

707-963-1792
1180 Rutherford Rd., Rutherford, CA 94523
Price: Moderate to Expensive
Credit Cards: AE, MC, V
Cuisine: American
Serving: Lunch, Dinner
Reservations: None for lunch, limited for dinner
Special Features: Outdoor dining

So you discovered a big burly cabernet sauvignon while wine tasting. What do you eat with it? California cuisine is not always cabernet friendly, but this restaurant fills that niche: steak. The prime rib and filet mignon may not be the best you've ever had, but the beef is tasty and generally tender, and the portions are generous. Steaks and baby-back ribs are grilled over hardwood, and even the hamburgers are worth trying. Appetizers include Maytag blue-cheese potato chips, a less-than-impressive mound of plain chips topped and quickly saturated with warm cheese. Be sure to try the homemade Oreo ice cream sandwich with chocolate sauce. A modern facade along Highway 29, Rutherford Grill says "chain," and is one of 30 similar eateries. The atmosphere is classy in a casual sort of way, with a decor that's steak-house-meets-nightclub: dark wood and leather. The wine list is narrow but well focused on Napa, and the service is deft.

ST. HELENA
CINDY'S BACKSTREET KITCHEN

707-963-1200
www.cindysbackstreetkitchen.com
1327 Railroad Ave, St. Helena, CA 94574
Price: Expensive
Credit Cards: D, DC, MC, V
Cuisine: California
Serving: Lunch, Dinner
Reservations: Recommended
Special Features: Full bar, patio seating

Cindy's has quickly becoming our favorite restaurant in Wine Country. We always feel welcome, and we love the atmosphere: It's light and breezy, with exposed rafters, soothing hues, pine floors, and a distinct, zinc bar. The restaurant is owned by Cindy Pawlcyn, the grande dame of Napa Valley and owner of Mustards Grill down the road and Go Fish.

The food is comforting but infused with flavor and is generally a welcome retreat from the traditional Wine Country cuisine. A dish such as spice-rubbed quail threatens to overwhelm your taste buds with its juicy intensity. We're a sucker for the grilled hanger steak and the Chinatown duck burger. Be sure to start with the backstreet fry, a crispy collection of calamari and fresh vegetables. The wine selection isn't large, but it has everything you need and is largely focused on Napa. The bar also has a fine list of ales and creative drinks such as a wild-apple martini.

GO FISH

707-963-0700
www.gofishrestaurant.net
641 Main St., St. Helena, CA
Price: Very Expensive
Credit Cards: AE, D, DC, JCB, MC, V
Cuisine: California
Serving: Lunch, Dinner
Reservations: Recommended
Special Features: Outside dining

This house of fish is a smart addition to Wine Country. The clever woman behind it knows that wine lovers can't subsist on red meat alone. The menu has a range of tasty offerings, including the option of "fish cooked your way," whether sautéed, wood grilled, or poached. Every dish we tried exceeded our expectations.

The wine list is fairly priced and appropriately weighted to whites. The service is knowledgeable, efficient, and friendly, while the décor is a feng shui haven. Go Fish is modern and clean yet cozy, as if it were a high-end home. The sushi bar dominates, running the length of the dining room. Good tip: If they offer the lobster roll sushi, don't hesitate to order it.

Sushi is prepared with extravagance at Go Fish in St. Helena. Tim Fish

MARTINI HOUSE

707-963-2233
www.martinihouse.com
1245 Spring St., St. Helena, CA 94574
Price: Very Expensive
Credit Cards: D, V, MC, DC
Cuisine: California
Serving: Lunch Fri.–Sun. only, Dinner daily
Reservations: Recommended
Special Features: Full bar, patio seating

If you've ever been to a Pat Kuleto-designed restaurant, you never forget it. The innovative restaurant designer and owner of such top San Francisco dining rooms as Boulevard, Farallon, and Jardinière is the man behind Martini House. Set in a 1923 Craftsman bungalow, the restaurant is dramatically stylish, with a design inspired by Napa history, including Indian-basket light fixtures, yet it remains as comfortable as an old leather coat. The patio is one of the valley's best outdoor dining experiences.

Chef and partner Todd Humphries, formerly of San Francisco's Campton Place, creates a menu of what Kuleto calls Napa Cuisine: hearty creations that focus on local, seasonal ingredients such as pan-roasted duck breast and seared sea bass, although the kitchen can be maddeningly inconsistent. The wine list is one of the best in the valley, however, with a wide range of varietals and regions.

PIZZERIA TRA VIGNE

707-967-9999
1016 Main St., St. Helena, CA 94574
Price: Moderate
Credit Cards: AE, D, MC, V
Cuisine: Italian
Serving: Lunch, Dinner
Reservations: Only for parties of eight or more

This family-friendly house of pizza has a stylishly casual atmosphere and reasonable prices, which make it a good lunch stop while you're touring the valley. The dining room is big and airy, with a brick, wood-fired pizza oven in full view. There are cozy booths and large communal tables that seat 12 or more. Don't let the laid-back veneer fool you, though: The people behind this pizzeria are the same savvy folks behind the restaurant Tra Vigne. The menu is the same at lunch or dinner, and if you don't feel like eating the usual pizza, try something called *piadine,* a basic pizza topped with salad, which you fold and eat like a taco. The grilled chicken version is wonderful. The wine list is appealingly no-nonsense.

PRESS

707-967-0550
www.presssthelena.com
587 Hwy. 29, St. Helena, CA
Price: Very Expensive
Credit Cards: AE, D, DC, MC, V
Cuisine: Steakhouse
Serving: Dinner
Reservations: Recommended
Special Features: Outside dining

This is a first-class steakhouse. In fact, the 20-ounce, dry-aged "cowboy" bone-in rib eye is one of the best steaks we've ever tasted. It's pricy at nearly $50, but decadence this tasty is hard to resist, plus it's big enough for two.

The menu is a carnivore's delight, with seven hearty steak options, including the dry-aged porterhouse for two, a hearty 32-ounce slab of meat. There are also a couple of tasty seafood options. The classic wedge salad is crisp yet savory with bite-sized bits of bacon, and crab cakes burst with the flavors of the sea.

The eclectic wine list is impressive but fairly expensive. The service is first class and the décor is inviting, uncluttered sophistication at its best—high ceilings, expansive glass, and black walnut accents. Good tip: If it's warm enough, sit outdoors by the fireplace.

TERRA

707-963-8931
www.terrarestaurant.com
1345 Railroad Ave., St. Helena, CA 94574
Closed: Tues.
Price: Very Expensive
Credit Cards: AE, CB, DC, MC, V
Cuisine: California-Asian
Serving: Dinner; closed Tues.
Reservations: Required

At Terra, East meets West, and the restaurant's Asian influence leaves an indelible mark on California cuisine. Terra's chef, Hiroyoshi Sone, is a superb talent and adds a little daring to each dish. The setting is the historic Hatchery Building, and the décor is crisp and elegant: high ceilings; tall, arched windows; and fieldstone walls. The duo behind Terra has an impressive resume: Sone led the kitchen at Wolfgang Puck's Spago in Los Angeles, and his wife, Lissa Doumani, was a pastry chef. While the black cod marinated in sake is a menu staple and the best entrée in the house, any variation on squab or pork chop is worth a try. For dessert, the tiramisu is a knockout. The wine list is superb, and the by-the-glass selection has improved recently. The service at Terra is always attentive, gracious, and knowledgeable. Terra is a rare find, indeed.

TRA VIGNE

707-963-4444
www.travignerestaurant.com
1050 Charter Oak Ave., St. Helena, CA
94574
Price: Expensive
Credit Cards: D, DC, MC, V
Cuisine: Italian, California
Serving: Lunch, Dinner
Reservations: Preferred
Special Features: Outdoor dining

One of Napa Valley's most popular restaurants, Tra Vigne is a sensory delight, from
the fragrance of roasted garlic wafting
through the courtyard and the neo-Gothic
atmosphere of the tall, stone building to the
pool of herb-infused olive oil at your table.
The food is generally cooked with a fiery
passion. Most dishes linger on the palate
(though a few muster only a mediocre rat-
ing). The odds are truly in your favor.
Worthy dishes include the classic antipasto
plate, roasted garlic polenta, and the
restaurant's signature short ribs.

Everything is made at the restaurant,
including prosciutto, breads, pastas,
cheeses, and gelato. Tra Vigne, which
means "among the vines," charms its guests
with rows of grapevines just outside the
courtyard. Inside, the decor is part Italian
villa, part Hollywood, with gold stripes on
the molding softened by earth tones. The
restaurant swarms with beeper-clad wait-
ers, and the service is impeccable.

The wine list offers a solid selection
from Napa and Italy. For fun, stop in for a
drink before dinner at the Cantinetta Tra
Vigne across the patio. There are more than
100 wines by the glass.

WINE SPECTATOR GREYSTONE
RESTAURANT

707-967-1010
www.ciachef.edu/greystone/spectator/
index.html
2555 Main St., St. Helena, CA 94574

Price: Expensive
Credit Cards: AE, CB, DC, MC, V
Cuisine: Mediterranean
Serving: Lunch, Dinner
Reservations: Recommended

You expect to be impressed by a restaurant
affiliated with the Culinary Institute of
America (CIA). Perhaps our expectations
are too high, but we've always been disappointed by this restaurant. It's a beautiful
spot and it's popular, but the weak link,
ironically, is the food. The kitchen has
recently shown improvement, but it can't
yet compete with Napa Valley's finest.

The atmosphere is promising if not
downright dramatic. The restaurant is in
the north wing of the recently restored
Greystone Cellars, a historic Wine Country
castle once known as Christian Brothers
and now home to the West Coast campus of
the CIA. With stone walls and a towering
ceiling, the room is cavernous and a bit
noisy. The decor is accented with bright
colors, and three open kitchen stations
lend energy. The recent addition of a grand
fireplace with a casual seating area has
warmed the interior significantly.

After a shaky start, the wine list has
come into its own, with an increasingly
wide selection and an adequate offering by
the glass. Service is professional but slow.

CALISTOGA
ALL SEASONS BISTRO

707-942-9111
www.allseasonsnapavalley.net
1400 Lincoln Ave., Calistoga, CA 94515
Price: Expensive
Credit Cards: MC, V
Cuisine: California, Mediterranean
Serving: Lunch (closed Mon., Tues.,
Thurs.), Dinner (closed Mon.)
Reservations: Recommended

All Seasons has a soothing bistro menu
matched with a modest but urbane setting.
Ceiling fans spin slowly over stained-glass

lights; the floor is done in black, white, and green tile; and two walls of windows let you watch downtown Calistoga go by. The lunch menu focuses on salads, pizzas, pastas, and sandwiches, while dinner emphasizes upscale comforts of grilled fish, duck, beef, and chicken. After a meal, linger over the dessert menu. Try something indulgent, such as an individual deep-dish berry pie. The wine selection is fabulous, and service is professional and warm.

BOSKOS TRATTORIA

707-942-9088
www.boskos.com
1364 Lincoln Ave., Calistoga, CA 94515
Price: Moderate
Credit Cards: AE, MC, V
Cuisine: Italian
Serving: Lunch, Dinner
Reservations: Not accepted

This Italian eatery serves basic and hearty food, and the price is right. The atmosphere is warm but casual and perfect for families. Lunch and dinner menus are the same and portions are generous. Pastas range from the basic spaghetti and meatballs to an enjoyable fettuccine Alfredo. There are also sandwiches—Italian sausage, *capicolla,* and the like—and pizza from a wood-burning stove. The beer and wine list is adequate.

BRANNAN'S GRILL

707-942-2233
www.brannansgrill.com
1374 Lincoln Ave., Calistoga, CA 94515
Price: Expensive
Credit Cards: AE, MC, V
Cuisine: California, American
Serving: Lunch, Dinner
Reservations: Recommended

Brannan's Grill is more adventuresome than it seems at first glance. With seating for two hundred, we expected the menu to be less exciting and the service to be any-

thing but meticulous. Happily, we were wrong on both counts. The food is lively and the atmosphere has a clublike coziness, with large windows that swing wide open when the weather is right.

Seafood is something Brannan's does particularly well; consider starting your meal with a selection of local oysters on the half shell. For hearty eaters, there's a good selection of steaks and a decadent Point Reyes blue cheese burger. The wine list showcases Napa Valley wines, but it's careful to include some less-traditional varietals. Rhone reds and whites, in particular, have a nice showing. The list is a bit pricey, but there's a good by-the-glass selection.

WAPPO BAR AND BISTRO

707-942-4712
www.wappobar.com
1226 Washington St., Calistoga, CA 94515
Price: Moderate to Expensive
Credit Cards: AE, MC, V
Cuisine: Eclectic
Serving: Lunch, Dinner; closed Tues.
Reservations: Recommended
Special Features: Outdoor dining

The world beat is pounding at this warm-blooded bistro. It's suited for adventurous souls prepared for an eclectic trip around the culinary world, from Latin America to the Mediterranean to who knows where. Although the kitchen often goes too far, we don't mind going along for the ride. The narrow dining room with reddish brown wainscoting and copper-covered tables and lights blends European bistro with southwestern warmth. If the weather is warm, the brick courtyard patio, covered with a grapevine arbor, is a must.

Owners Aaron Bauman and Michelle Mutrux share kitchen duties. The menu finds an eccentric match in the wine list, which offers more than the usual chardonnay, and at fair prices. Service is efficient and enthusiastic. Smart dishes to order include the festive Brazilian seafood chowder, the Thai noodle salad, and an addictive duck carnitas. Lunch includes sandwiches, salads, and Thai sweet potato fries—a yummy creation made clumsy by thick breading but saved by an addictive coconut-and-peanut dipping sauce.

Wappo Bar and Bistro in Calistoga offers a shady spot for lunch or dinner. Tim Fish

Sonoma County Restaurants

SONOMA VALLEY
CAFÉ CITTI
707-833-2690
9049 Sonoma Hwy., Kenwood, CA. 95452
Price: Moderate
Credit Cards: MC, V
Cuisine: Italian
Serving: Lunch, Dinner
Reservations: Only for parties of six or more
Special Features: Outdoor dining, deli

A trattoria in the strictest Italian sense—casual atmosphere with hearty wine and yummy, inexpensive pasta—Café Citti is a pleasure. There's a menu, but most people rely on the chalkboard on the wall. Customers order from the counter, cafeteria style. Lunch includes sandwiches: sweet Italian sausage and the usual cold deli fare. Pasta is mix and match; choose penne, linguine, and the like, and pair it with your sauce (marinara or Bolognese, to name a couple) of choice. Other offerings include a zesty Caesar salad and homemade focaccia, plus a luxurious risotto with mushrooms and garlic and a traditional Italian herb-roasted chicken that is to die for. For dessert, don't miss the crème brûlée or the tiramisu. For those traveling with kids, this is a perfect place to stop.

CAFÉ LA HAYE
707-935-5994
www.cafelahaye.com
140 E. Napa St., Sonoma, CA 95476
Price: Expensive
Credit Cards: AE, MC, V
Cuisine: California
Serving: Dinner; closed Sun. and Mon.
Reservations: Recommended
Special Features: Close to the Sonoma Square

Café la Haye is classy yet simple in its sophistication. More important, the food stands up to the best in Wine Country. If you're looking for a great meal on Sonoma Square, this is the spot.

A dependable starter is one of the house-smoked fish appetizers; salmon may come with a scallion pancake or trout with red onion relish. The seared black pepper lavender fillet of beef is perfectly cooked—a rich, juicy concoction, served with a tasty dollop of Gorgonzola-potato gratin. The pan-roasted chicken breast with a goat cheese herb stuffing is so good that you'll be tempted to set the fork and knife aside and attack it fried-chicken style. The wine list complements the menu, and it's well focused with a good selection of wines from Sonoma County and Napa Valley. As for the decor, the restaurant is tiny but seems spacious, with high, wooden rafters and an upper level of seating—yet it still manages to feel cozy.

CARNEROS BISTRO AND WINE BAR

707-931-2042
www.carnerosrestaurant.com
1325 Broadway, Sonoma, CA 95476
Price: Expensive
Credit Cards: AE, D, MC, V
Cuisine: Wine Country bistro
Serving: Breakfast, Lunch, Dinner
Reservations: Recommended
Special Features: Patio dining, live music in the hotel on Friday and Saturday nights

Carneros aspires to be a serious dining destination, and it nearly pulls it off. The food is good and the service shows promise. The restaurant is part of the Lodge at Sonoma, a 182-room complex owned by Renaissance Hotels (see chapter 3, Lodging). Carneros is the wine-growing region at the southern base of Napa Valley and Sonoma County, and the restaurant emphasizes wines produced from Sonoma County's 11 appellations.

The portions are big and so are the flavors. Just consider one of the menu trademarks: Sonoma duck patty melt, a decadently rich sandwich made with foie gras and onion rings. Bring your cholesterol medicine!

Prices on the wine list are the going rate and it's a good selection that emphasizes wines of the region. The room itself has a large and airy atmosphere, with an open kitchen and cathedral ceiling, but there's something rather generic about the place.

DELLA SANTINA'S

707-935-0576
www.dellasantinas.com
133 E. Napa St., Sonoma, CA 95476
Price: Moderate
Credit Cards: AE, D, MC, V
Cuisine: Italian
Serving: Lunch, Dinner
Reservations: Recommended
Special Features: Patio dining

Ah, the mighty aromas that escape from this café! Don't overlook this Italian trattoria just off bustling Sonoma Plaza. The food is as authentic and unfussy as the best from Mama's kitchen. The Della Santina family first opened shop in 1990. In summer, the intimate dining room gives way to a glorious garden patio, shady and green. The warm din of the kitchen mingles with Puccini and Verdi.

Appetizers include a Caesar salad that's a vibrant cut above the usual, and the antipasto plate is everything it should be: fat with prosciutto and olives. Pastas are first-rate, and roasted meats—particularly chicken and rabbit—are a specialty yet quality varies. At one meal the chicken is dry and flavorless, but at the next, it's tender and heavenly. The wine list is modest but well suited to the food.

DEUCE

707-933-3823
www.dine-at-deuce.com
691 Broadway, Sonoma, CA 95476
Price: Expensive
Credit Cards: AE, MC, V
Cuisine: Contemporary American
Serving: Lunch, Dinner
Reservations: Recommended
Special Features: Patio and garden area

The charming, 116-year-old Victorian farmhouse that's home to Deuce has a morbid past—it was a mortuary years ago—but that doesn't scare off customers. It's one of

Owner Pete Stewart welcomes diners to Deuce in Sonoma. Tim Fish

the most popular restaurants in the valley, and rightly so. The menu offers both comfort and adventure, with hearty fare such as grilled lamb, roasted quail, and crispy duck. The wine list is wisely focused on Sonoma wines, with more than one hundred labels and more than a dozen offerings by the glass. The prices are fair and service is friendly and well paced. If the weather is warm, ask for a table on the garden patio.

THE GENERAL'S DAUGHTER

707-938-4004
www.thegeneralsdaughter.com
400 W. Spain St., Sonoma, CA 95476
Price: Expensive
Credit Cards: AE, MC, V
Cuisine: California
Serving: Dinner; closed Mon.
Reservations: Recommended
Special Features: Outdoor dining

This 1883 farmhouse is a true showplace. Former owner Suzanne Brangham revitalized this once-dilapidated pink house, which belonged to General Mariano Vallejo's daughter Natalia, and opened the restaurant in 1994. The place is gorgeous, with lush landscaping; a wide porch; and a

classic interior of hardwood floors, antiques and lively murals. The bar is done in rich Honduran mahogany.

Chef Preston Dishman focuses on local ingredients and serves them with a southern flare. The restaurant maintains its own gardens, growing produce from lettuce to asparagus. Some favorite dishes include shrimp with grits and seared duck breast with corn and bacon risotto. One of its most decadent desserts is the Valrhona chocolate and gianduja with crème anglaise.

THE GIRL & THE FIG

707-938-3634
www.thegirlandthefig.com
110 W. Spain St., Sonoma, CA 95476
Price: Expensive
Credit Cards: AE, D, MC, V
Cuisine: French country food
Serving: Lunch, Dinner, Sunday Brunch
Reservations: Recommended
Special Features: Located on Sonoma Square, patio dining

The Girl & the Fig has its fans, even though the food and service are maddeningly inconsistent. Certainly, the restaurant is both appealing and convenient on Sonoma Plaza, adjacent to the lobby of the Sonoma Hotel, and with its tall, broad, wood-framed windows and light, mustard-colored walls, it's a pretty stop to spend a couple of hours here. The whole place feels breezy.

The menu offers plenty of comfort, ranging from a salami and brie sandwich and sirloin burger to duck confit and grilled polenta. Be sure to sample something from the cheese cart. The wine list is refreshing, even daring, and fairly priced. It focuses on California-produced, Rhone-style wines, with an emphasis on California syrahs. Few will complain that it's limited in scope, because there's plenty to choose from, and Rhone-style wines are food friendly.

GLEN ELLEN INN

707-996-6409
www.glenelleninn.com
13670 Arnold Dr., P.O. Box 1593, Glen
Ellen, CA 95442
Price: Expensive
Credit Cards: AE, MC, V
Cuisine: California fusion
Serving: Lunch (closed Mon. and Tues.),
Dinner Reservations: Recommended
Handicapped Access: Yes
Special Features: Outdoor dining

The Glen Ellen Inn is not the quaint little
dining room we once loved, but owners
Chris and Karen Bertrand have added some
sophistication to its small-town charm—
and in this quiet corner of the world, Chris
holds his own with Wine Country's finest
chefs. The Bertrands have continually
expanded their restaurant over the years,
adding an oyster grill, martini bar, and collection of cottages in recent years. The food
certainly hasn't suffered from the expansion. As for service, it's still first-rate, and
the wine list specializes in the best Sonoma
Valley wines. It includes a smart list by the
glass.
    Bertrand, schooled at the Fifth Avenue
Grill in Manhattan, cooks with a French
accent, relying on fresh, local ingredients.
Salads are exceptional. Specialties include
luscious Dungeness crab pot stickers and
just about anything Bertrand does with filet
mignon and salmon. For dessert, give in to
the ever-popular Glen Ellen Inn sundae or
the warm bread pudding.

HARVEST MOON CAFE

707-933-8160
www.harvestmoonsonoma.com
487 First St. W., Sonoma CA 95476
Price: Expensive
Credit Cards: MC, V
Cuisine: California
Serving: Lunch, Dinner
Reservations: Recommended
Handicapped Access: Yes
Special Features: Outdoor dining

This café on Sonoma Plaza Square is a cozy
retreat with sidewalk seating as well as a
patio out back. Inside, rich warm colors
and great aromas make you feel like you're
dining at a friend's house. Harvest Moon is
comfort food at its best, with dishes such as
the pork shoulder. Tasty lighter fare
includes the grilled California white bass.
The wine list has a good showing of local
wines with a strong sampling of imports.

KENWOOD RESTAURANT AND BAR

707-833-6326
www.kenwoodrestaurant.com
9900 Sonoma Hwy., Kenwood, CA 95452
Price: Expensive
Credit Cards: MC, V
Cuisine: California.
Serving: Lunch, Dinner; closed Mon. and Tues.
Reservations: Recommended
Handicapped Access: Yes
Special Features: Outdoor dining

This bistro, a California roadhouse turned
upscale, is in the heart of the Valley of the
Moon, one of the most beautiful spots in
Wine Country. The patio offers marvelous
views of Sugar Loaf Ridge, where vineyards
rib the lower slopes. The charm of sipping
wine made nearby should not be underesti-
mated, and Kenwood's wine list is a Who's
Who of Sonoma Valley vintners.
    The décor and chef-owner Max
Schacher's food are well matched: Both
paint a refined picture with subtle strokes.
The dining rooms have steep wood ceilings
and are done in muted tones brightened by
colorful paintings. Likewise, Schacher
believes in artistic presentation paired with
a sense of understatement, with dishes that
emphasize the quality of local duck or fish
rather than exotic creations. Frankly, we'd
like more adventure. Also, the same menu
is served lunch and dinner, which makes
for a pricey lunch.

MAYA

707-935-3500
www.mayarestaurant.com
101 East Napa St., Sonoma, CA 95476
Price: Moderate to Expensive
Credit Cards: MC, V
Cuisine: Mexican
Serving: Lunch (closed Sun.), Dinner
Reservations: Recommended
Handicapped Access: Yes

This place is fun, plain and simple. The atmosphere is festive, with warm wood accents, colorful Mexican décor, and artifacts, and a bar stacked as high as a Mayan temple with upscale tequilas. The food is not your typical Mexican cuisine, and it's generally quite appealing. It takes its inspiration from the Mayan region in southern Mexico, but the kitchen also offers its own take on dishes such as hanger steak, babyback ribs, and even spaghetti. Signature dishes include a luscious grilled chicken breast stuffed with habanero jack cheese and *mole rojo*. The wine list is limited, but there's a creative offering of drinks such as Margaritas, Sangria, and specialty tequilas.

SADDLES

707-933-3191
www.macarthurplace.com
29 E. MacArthur St., Sonoma, CA 95476
Price: Moderate to Expensive
Credit Cards: AE, MC, V
Cuisine: Steak and seafood
Serving: Lunch, Dinner
Reservations: Recommended
Handicapped Access: Yes
Special Features: Patio dining; part of MacArthur Place resort

If you want to order up a 10-ounce martini and a steak on the side, this is the place to go. Saddles is located in the MacArthur Place resort (see chapter 3, Lodging), In Wine Country, a good steak house is a rare find, and the prime-cut meats here are outstanding—but don't expect to be wowed by the service. The western theme, a bit overdone, carries throughout the restaurant: cowboy boots, hats, and branding irons. The steaks are good, but oh, that price tag! The 10 ounce filet mignon, the 14-ounce New York strip, and the 24-ounce porterhouse for two are solid cuts of meat, proficiently cooked, but ultimately the experience is rather ordinary. The wine list has a solid selection of newer, mostly California wines. Prices are reasonable. A plus: great martini offerings!

SANTÉ-FAIRMONT SONOMA MISSION INN

707-938-9000
www.fairmont.com/sonoma
18140 Sonoma Hwy., Sonoma, CA 95416
Price: Very expensive; Prix Fixe: $95
Credit Cards: AE, MC, V
Cuisine: California, Oriental
Serving: Dinner
Reservations: Recommended
Special Features: Poolside setting, handsome dining room

Santé is a handsome, Mission-style dining room, with dark wood beams, iron chandeliers, and wooden floors—but it's never a good sign when the best thing you can say about a restaurant involves its décor. The food doesn't live up to the price, though that isn't unusual at many hotel restaurants (see chapter 3, Lodging). The menu promises rich and deeply flavored dishes but the result is too often ill-conceived and boring. The wine list is one of the best in Sonoma County, although it comes at premium. If you're a hotel guest and prefer to eat in rather than out, this is a comfortable spot, but if you have the energy, there are far better places to dine nearby.

SHISO

707-933-9331
www.shisorestaurant.com
522 Broadway, Sonoma, CA 95476
Credit Cards: AE, MC, V
Cuisine: Modern Asian

Serving: Lunch, Dinner
Reservations: Recommended
Special Features: Fresh sushi, hot sake

This place is refreshing, with its cool, clean atmosphere and its impressive menu. Two crowd favorites are the lettuce cup and the banana mousse crepes with rum butter. The fresh sushi and hot sake are also popular. An inventive dish is the soft-shell crab BLT. *Shiso* refers to the Japanese mint brought over by the Japanese immigrants in the early 1800s. Owners say the goal of the restaurant is to offer that clean, refreshing "mint-like" quality to it's healthy cuisine.

SANTA ROSA
FLAVOR

707-573-9600
www.flavorbistro.com
96 Old Courthouse Square, Santa Rosa, CA 95404
Price: Moderate to Expensive
Credit Cards: AE, MC, V
Cuisine: California.
Serving: Lunch, Dinner; closed Sun.
Reservations: Recommended
Special Features: Outdoor dining

If you're exploring downtown Santa Rosa, this easygoing bistro is a good choice, particularly if you have kids. The dining room is big and roomy, and there are plenty of tables right out front to watch the tykes play on the lawn of Courthouse Square. The menu is family-friendly, offering a little of everything: salads, sandwiches, pastas, pizzas. Most menu items are available in small and large portions, and the kitchen seldom produces a miss. The food is rich and full of flavor—thus the name—with standouts that include Molly's chicken, slow roasted and seasoned with Middle Eastern spices. There's a good wine list that emphasizes local wines, and the service is generally sharp and attentive.

JOHN ASH & COMPANY

707-527-7687
www.vintnersinn.com/dining
4330 Barnes Rd., Santa Rosa, CA 95403
Price: Very Expensive
Credit Cards: AE, D, MC, V
Cuisine: California
Serving: Dinner
Reservations: Recommended
Special Features: Outdoor dining

Chef John Ash continues to pioneer Wine Country cuisine, but today, he has nothing to do with the daily operation of the restaurant. His protégé, Jeff Madura, lacks Ash's brilliance, but the restaurant remains a destination. Madura emphasizes local ingredients and strives to make each entrée beautiful visually.

The menu is ever changing but offers imaginative salads and pastas, lighter seafood dishes, and hearty steak and pork chops. The wine list is one of the best in Wine Country, and the by-the-glass selection is excellent. The service is attentive and pampering. The setting is a bucolic site next to Vintners Inn (see chapter 3, Lodging), with vineyard views through French windows and plenty of outdoor dining when weather permits. The multilevel dining room is done in elegant tones—try to grab a table by the fire—and the bar offers a more casual and energetic atmosphere for dining.

SYRAH

707-568-4002
www.syrahbistro.com
205 5th St., Santa Rosa, CA 95401
Price: Expensive
Credit Cards: AE, MC, V
Cuisine: French and American
Serving: Lunch, Dinner; closed Sun. and Mon.
Reservations: Recommended
Handicapped Access: Yes
Special Features: Courtyard dining

Syrah will delight serious syrah drinkers who spend as much time lingering over the wine list as they do the menu. Of course, the wine list has a fine selection of syrahs, with key French Rhone wines, even though it's weighted to California. The prices are fair, but there could be a better selection by the glass.

Situated in the historic City 205 Building, the restaurant is rustic-chic, with a peaked ceiling, wooden beams, modern art, and an open kitchen. The food, on the whole, is impressive. Good picks include the pan-roasted Petaluma chicken breast and the grilled lamb sirloin. There's always a good selection of local artisan cheeses, and desserts are well executed. Service couldn't be better—prompt and intelligent. Syrah is a fine addition to the dining scene in Wine Country, particularly with the addition of its new Petite Syrah Wine Shop attached to the restaurant. It's fun to order and then shop while you're waiting for dinner.

WILLI'S WINE BAR
(707) 526-3096
www.williswinebar.net
Price: Expensive
Credit Cards: D, MC, V
Cuisine: Eclectic
Serving: Lunch (closed Sun. and Mon.), Dinner
Reservations: Recommended
Handicapped Access: Yes
Special Features: Outdoor dining

This roadhouse-style restaurant is always packed with locals and tourists alike. The interior, done in dark wood and warm colors, fits like a pair of jeans, and there's a soothing patio out back when the weather cooperates. The kitchen offers a large menu of small plates and takes influence from Asia and the Mediterranean . There's always something intriguing and intensely flavored on the table, whether it's Tuscan pork

riblets, Dungeness crab tacos, or foie gras "poppers." There's a fine wine list, which also has an international point of view, and many wines are available by the glass. Our only gripe: the service. We always feel like we're doing them a favor by eating here.

ZAZU
707-523-4814
www.zazurestaurant.com
3535 Guerneville Rd., Santa Rosa, CA 95401
Price: Expensive
Credit Cards: AE, D, MC, V
Cuisine: Northern Italian, California
Serving: Dinner; closed Mon. and Tues.
Reservations: Recommended

ZaZu might as well post a sign out front: UPSCALE COMFORT FOOD. From this funky little roadhouse in the heart of the Russian River Valley chef-owners John Stewart and Duskie Estes produce hearty yet sophisticated fare. The menu blends delicious American classics such as butter-milk mashed potatoes and grilled sweet corn with creative variations on lamb, seafood, and duck. Be sure to try the slow-roasted balsamic pork shoulder with caramelized onions if it's on the menu. The chefs, who also run the equally good Bovolo in Healdsburg, are passionate about rustic Italian food, making *sopressata* and *coppa* by hand, for example. There are about 150 wines on the list, and local producers are featured extensively. Prices range from moderate to expensive. The decor of ZaZu is country chic with eclectic furnishings, and the service is warm but crisply attentive.

HEALDSBURG
BARN DIVA
707-431-0100
www.barndiva.com
231 Center St., Healdsburg, CA 95448
Price: Very Expensive
Credit Cards: AE, MC, V

Barn Diva is the hippest hangout in Healdsburg.
Tim Fish

Cuisine: California
Serving: Lunch, Dinner
Reservations: Recommended
Special features: Outdoor dining

In Wine Country, Barn Diva is known as a hip restaurant with late-night appeal where you can order exotic drinks from the bar until midnight. It's also known for its eclectic small plates and entrees, which are cleverly categorized in the menu under light, spicy, or comfort.

Whether you opt for lunch, an early dinner, or a nightcap, you won't be disappointed. The food is tasty, the drinks are festive, and though the waitstaff may be young, they're dedicated. What's more, the décor charms. The restaurant is rustic-chic, a cedar barn with a 14-foot ceiling and a sleek mahogany bar.

The wine list is sophisticated and fairly priced, with 150 bottles and 14 specialty cocktails at the going rate. The menu fol-

lows suit. Good picks include fish and duck entrees. Tip: on a warm summer's night, the back patio is perfect.

BISTRO RALPH

707-433-1380
109 Plaza St., Healdsburg, CA 95448
Price: Expensive
Credit Cards: MC, V
Cuisine: California
Serving: Lunch, Dinner
Reservations: Recommended
Special Features: Outdoor dining

Bistro Ralph recalls a Greenwich Village café: elegant in a spare, smartly industrial sort of way. Some might consider the atmosphere chilly, but it's never bothered us. Situated on the Healdsburg plaza, it's a handy spot for lunch or dinner.

The food by chef-owner Ralph Tingle is typically excellent, particularly if Tingle is in the kitchen, although there's an occasional miss. At lunch the CK Lamb burger is a must and the Caesar salad is dependable, and Tingle does particularly creative things with duck. Bistro Ralph has an efficient and modestly priced wine list that plays up the area's best producers. Service is always relaxed and attentive.

BOVOLO

707-431-2962
www.bovolorestaurant.com
Plaza Farms, 106 Matheson St., Healdsburg, CA 95448
Price: Moderate to expensive
Credit Cards: AE, D, MC, V
Cuisine: Northern Italian, California
Serving: Lunch (closed Wed.), Dinner (closed Wed. and Thurs.)
Reservations: Recommended
Special Features: Outdoor dining

Named for an Italian snail, Bovolo is not much to look at. It's little more than a glorified deli, but don't expect the usual soups and sandwiches. The rustic Italian food is prepared from scratch and with fervor. Chef John Stewart, who shares duties with chef/wife Duskie Estes, is a pork fanatic and cures his own sopressata, coppa, bacon and more. Pizza, pasta, and salads are also on the menu, and savory pork cheek and other hearty sandwiches are sold at lunch, while at night, there's a three-course prix fixe dinner. The wine selection is quite small—a few dozen are on the list—but it's loaded with gems.

There's always something interesting on the menu at Bovolo. Tim Fish

CYRUS

707-433-3311
www.cyrusrestaurant.com
29 North St., Healdsburg, CA 95448
Price: Very expensive
Credit Cards: AE, MC, V
Cuisine: California, French, Asian
Serving: Dinner
Reservations: Required

This is not only the top restaurant in Sonoma County, it's one of the best in northern California, giving competition to The French Laundry across the mountain and the top kitchens in San Francisco. Cyrus partners Nick Peyton and Douglas Keane have created an extravagant and formal food and wine experience, but somehow the mood is never stuffy. The dining room, with its textured yellow walls and arched pillars and vaulted ceiling, is at once dramatic and warmly inviting.

With Peyton working the front of the house, service is crisp and intuitive. Guests are greeted with Cyrus's trademark champagne and caviar cart, a piece of showmanship that's quite tempting. The wine list has more than seven hundred selections. It's worldly and expensive, but ripe with gems and classics. Wine pairings are available with each course, a good choice for a leisurely paced evening.

The menu is prix fixe but organized loosely. There are nine categories—from soup to foie gras, to fish, cheese and dessert—and guests can choose three-, four-, or five-course meals. Chef Keane's dishes are rich and deeply flavored yet never over the top, even when he adds elements of Asia and American comfort foods. If you want to experience a taste of Cyrus without the full price tag, each course is available á la carte in the bar, although reservations are not accepted, so arrive early.

DRY CREEK KITCHEN

707-431-0330
www.charliepalmer.com/dry_creek/home.
html
317 Healdsburg Ave., Healdsburg, CA
95448 (in the Hotel Healdsburg)
Price: Expensive
Credit Cards: AE, DC, MC, V
Cuisine: California
Serving: Lunch (closed Mon.–Thurs.),
Dinner
Reservations: Recommended

Given chef-owner Charlie Palmer's track record with his ever-expanding restaurant empire, it's not surprising that Dry Creek

Kitchen has raised the culinary bar in Sonoma County. Palmer, who moved his family to Sonoma a few years back, divides his time between Wine Country and his restaurants in New York and Las Vegas.

The decor is contemporary, with big columns that sweep dramatically toward the ceiling and subtle colors: cream with pear-green trim. It's comfortable, clean, and simple.

The menu follows the seasons and features local products almost exclusively: meat, seafood, produce, artisan cheeses, and, of course, wine. Palmer never gets in the way of these fine ingredients yet somehow finds a way to give them an intriguing twist. The wine list is extensive and has a particularly good offering of pinot noirs and zinfandels, and though prices are generally high, there's no corkage fee for guests who bring in their own bottle of Sonoma wine.

MADRONA MANOR

707-433-4231, 800-258-4003
www.madronamanor.com
1001 Westside Rd., Healdsburg, CA. 95448
Price: Very Expensive
Credit Cards: MC, V
Cuisine: French, California
Serving: Dinner
Reservations: Recommended
Special Features: Outdoor dining

It's a shame to approach this 1881 Victorian in the dark. Rising three stories to a steep mansard roof, this inn is a majestic sight set in a quiet glade, amid lush gardens (see Chapter 3, Lodging). The dining rooms, which used to be as stark and formal as a starched white shirt, now have warmer yet elegant tones. Service is very attentive, and Madrona Manor has one of the best wine cellars around, particularly if you like newer "blue chip" wines. The location is the main reason for coming to the manor. The food is dependably good, if rather uninspired, and the evening overall is

enjoyable. Perhaps the experience simply pales next to all the new competition in Healdsburg.

RAVENOUS

707-431-1302
420 Center St., Healdsburg, CA 95448
Price: Expensive
Credit Cards: MC, V
Cuisine: California
Serving: Lunch, Dinner; closed Mon. and Tues.
Reservations: Recommended
Special Features: Wine bar

There's no shortage of upscale restaurants in Healdsburg these days, but if you're looking for a casual lunch or dinner, this is a good choice. The setting is a 1930s bungalow with a fireplace and wood floors and cheery colors on the walls. The menu changes daily—it's handwritten, in fact—and it's made up of lusty California cuisine, from one of the best hamburgers in the county to crab cakes and roasted poblano chili stuffed with potatoes, hominy, and cojita cheese. The wine list is small and eclectic and focused on local wineries. The prices are fair. Service can be a little casual for our taste, but casual is what Ravenous is all about.

WILLI'S SEAFOOD AND RAW BAR

707-433-9191
www.willisseafood.net
403 Healdsburg Ave., Healdsburg, CA 95448
Price: Moderate to Very Expensive
Credit Cards: AE, MC, V
Cuisine: Seafood, eclectic
Serving: Lunch, Dinner
Reservations: Recommended
Special Features: Outdoor seating

We love the energy of this place. You just want to pull up a chair or a barstool and hang out. There's a hip, industrial feel to the joint, and the best seats are the private booths on the upper level. The menu is entirely small plates, with seafood and Latino spices playing a strong role. The flavors are bold and sometimes a dish goes overboard with too many ingredients, but we're generally won over. Plates range from fresh shellfish, ceviches, and tartars and New England-style sandwich rolls to skewers. Don't miss Willi's French Fries with goat cheese ranch or the sweet corn and crab fritters. The wine list is quite small, but the prices are fair and there's a decent selection by the glass.

ZIN RESTAURANT & WINE BAR

707-473-0946
www.zinrestaurant.com
344 Center St., Healdsburg, CA 95448
Closed: Tues.
Price: Expensive
Credit Cards: AE, MC, V
Cuisine: California contemporary
Serving: Lunch, Dinner; closed Tues.
Reservations: Recommended
Special Features: Wine bar

Zin zealots converge at this restaurant, an expansive eatery that feels like an artist's loft: slabs of concrete walls beneath a high ceiling of wooden rafters. Contemporary and yet cozy, the walls are filled with colorful art. A long wine bar sweeps across one side of the restaurant, and whether you're just in for a drink or in for a full meal, you'll love this custom-made menu focused on zinfandel. Even if zinfandel isn't your thing, you'll find plenty of other wines sharing second billing, and many are available by the glass.

The menu is weighted to California cuisine and hearty American comfort food great to pair with zin. We're seldom dazzled by the kitchen, although zin has a strong following. Regular menu items include cumin-and-lime-roasted half chicken with Mexican mole sauce and zinfandel-glazed BBQ beef short ribs.

GEYSERVILLE
SANTI

707-857-1790
www.tavernasanti.com
21047 Geyserville Ave., Geyserville, CA 95441
Price: Expensive to Very Expensive
Credit Cards: AE, MC, V
Cuisine: Italian
Serving: Lunch (closed Sat.–Tues.), Dinner
Reservations: Recommended

Tucked in the sleepy town of Geyserville, just north of Healdsburg, is this storefront restaurant that makes delicious country-style Italian food. The dining room isn't much to look at, but it's always packed, probably because the food is hearty and portions are big. Standouts on the menu include *spaghettini al sugo Calabrese*—spaghetti with a rich sauce of beef and pork ribs, tomatoes, and herbs—as well as *osso buco* with a green olive and caper sauce. There's a good little wine list, focusing on local wineries plus a handful of Italian gems, and the prices are decent. The service lacks polish, but it's friendly and well intentioned.

SONOMA WEST COUNTY
APPLEWOOD INN AND RESTAURANT

707-869-909, 800-555-8509
www.applewoodinn.com
13555 Hwy. 116, Guerneville, CA 95446
Price: Expensive
Credit Cards: AE, MC, V
Cuisine: California
Serving: Dinner
Reservations: Required
Special Features: Enclosed patio dining

If you can't spend the night—Applewood is one of the best inns in Wine Country—then dinner is the next best thing. (For details on the inn, see Chapter 3, Lodging.) The main house, built in 1922, is an architectural gem done in the California Mission

Revival style. The restaurant is styled to be the estate's barn. Long and narrow with cathedral ceilings and a stone fireplace, it's handsome and masculine.

The food is excellent, and specialties include seared wild king salmon and herbs de Provence-crusted rack of lamb. Desserts often include fruit from the inn's own orchard. The wine list is impressive, highlighting Russian River Valley selections, and is generally well priced. The service is sharp and intelligent, well paced, courteous, and professional.

BAY VIEW RESTAURANT AT THE INN AT THE TIDES

707-875-2751, 800-541-7788
www.innatthetides.com/dining.asp
800 Hwy. 1, Bodega Bay, CA 94923
Price: Expensive
Credit Cards: AE, MC, V
Cuisine: Seafood, California
Serving: Dinner; closed Mon. and Tues.
Reservations: Recommended
Handicapped Access: Yes

If the hectic hum of The Tides or Lucas Wharf is too much, and if you seek something more than basic fish, the Bay View might be an alternative. Though the food is simply on par with those two popular restaurants—good, but not great—the presentation has more flair, and the view is more impressive. If these are important, you might not mind the added cost.

The menu is dominated by local seafood, and two interesting entrées are the Bodega Bay bouillabaisse and the abalone. If you prefer meat, the pistachio-crusted rack of lamb is a tasty pick. As for dessert, you won't want to miss the New York-style cheesecake.

The wine list is superbly selected, with a credible list by the glass. The decor is elegant if a bit generic, with a beamed cathedral ceiling and Scandinavian furnishings. Servers, who wear black ties and tuxedo shirts, are efficient.

THE DUCK CLUB

707-875-3525
103 Hwy. 1, Bodega Bay, CA 94923 (at Bodega Bay Lodge)
Price: Moderate to Very Expensive
Credit Cards: AE, D, DC, MC, V
Cuisine: California
Serving: Breakfast, Dinner
Reservations: Recommended
Special Features: Harbor view

This out-of-the-way restaurant—hidden amid the lush landscaping of Bodega Bay Lodge—is worth a search. It offers the best food on the Sonoma coast. The atmosphere is a bit pedestrian and the décor is strictly country club, but the views over the harbor and wetlands are gorgeous, and a blazing fire warms the room.

The menu may be too broad, with the kitchen seemingly stretched at times. Offerings range from seafood, pork chops, steaks, and chicken to pasta, hamburgers, and pizza. Presentation is pleasing but unfussy. Good picks include the Dungeness crab cakes, the marinated pork tenderloin with apple sherry sauce, and the sea bass with wild mushrooms.

Service is solid, but the wine list is a bit of a disappointment. Big names but few selections. The wine list doesn't match the ambience or the extensive menu.

FARMHOUSE INN & RESTAURANT

707-887-3300, 800-464-6642
www.farmhouseinn.com
7871 River Rd., Forestville, CA 95436
Price: Moderate to Expensive
Credit Cards: AE, MC, V
Cuisine: Contemporary California.
Serving: Dinner; closed Tues. and Wed.
Reservations: Recommended
Handicapped Access: Yes

With a kitchen that delivers one of the best food and wine experiences in Sonoma, this is one country inn that offers more than just charm. The setting is a 135-year-old farmhouse painted a pale yellow and trimmed in black and white and situated in the heart of Russian River Valley vineyards. The dining room is done in warm hues and is accented by a marble fireplace, wrought iron chandeliers, and soothing murals of harvest scenes. Guests feel as though they're at a chic dinner party, not a restaurant.

The food blends modern French with vibrant California cuisine. Specialties include something called Rabbit, Rabbit, Rabbit—rabbit done three ways: confit, bacon-wrapped loin, and roasted rack. It's delightful, as are fascinating creations such as farmhouse cassoulet with housemade rabbit sausage and duck confit. The impressive wine list takes a worldly view, with excellent selections from France, Germany, and, of course, California. Wine service is superb.

Rabbit done three ways is a specialty at the Farmhouse Inn & Restaurant in Forestville.
Courtesy Farmhouse Inn

K&L BISTRO

707-823-6614
119 S. Main St., Sebastopol, CA 95472
Price: Expensive
Credit Cards: AE, MC, V
Cuisine: French, California
Serving: Lunch, Dinner; closed Sun.
Reservations: Recommended
Handicapped Access: Yes

A small space with exposed brick walls, this casual but hectic bistro draws a crowd of locals every night. It's hard to deny the appeal of the place, but we often wonder why the fuss. The menu doesn't deliver the usual formula of large portions and good value that typically draws the devotion of locals, but the food is decent in a hearty, comforting sort of way, with a menu that includes crab cakes, mussels in white wine, a tasty hamburger, and steak frites. The wine list is modest, but the price is right.

LUCAS WHARF

707-875-3522
595 Hwy. 1, Bodega Bay, CA 94923
Price: Moderate to Expensive
Credit Cards: D, MC, V
Cuisine: Seafood
Serving: Lunch, Dinner
Reservations: No reservations on weekends
Special Features: Harbor view, outdoor deck seating, retail fish market

Ask a group of locals the best place to eat seafood on the Sonoma coast, and you're liable to start an argument. The coast isn't nearly as populated with restaurants as, say, Cape Cod—there are just a handful—and people have clear favorites. We find ourselves at Lucas Wharf more often than not. Built on piers overlooking Bodega Bay harbor, it's cozy and romantic, with a fireplace and cathedral ceiling. From your table, you'll see great sunsets and fishing boats unloading the catch of the day. Choose what's fresh off the boat, and you won't go wrong—particularly salmon when it's in season (May through September) and Dungeness crab in season (from November to May). There's also a hearty fisherman's stew in a tomato broth. The wine list and by-the-glass selection is too limited. Lucas Wharf is popular with locals and tourists alike, so be prepared to wait for a table on weekends.

MIREPOIX

707-838-0162
www.restaurantmirepoix.com
275 Windsor River Rd., Windsor, CA 95492
Price: Moderate to Very expensive
Credit Cards: MC, V
Cuisine: French
Serving: Lunch, Dinner; closed Mon.
Reservations: Recommended
Handicapped Access: Yes
Special Features: Outdoor dining

After you've been in Wine Country a few days, it's easy to get your fill of California cuisine. That's why this French-style brasserie is so appealing. The dining room is a cozy den of 24 seats with an open kitchen. The menu is the same all day, and though it evolves with the season, it's basically French comfort food: mussels in white wine, *steak au poivre,* and *coq au vin.* Chef Matthew Bousquet adds his own twist, however, creating a rich yet delicate duck confit, for example. There's a small one—hundred—wine list but it hits all the right notes and the prices are good.

THE TIDES WHARF AND RESTAURANT

707-875-3652, 800-541-7788
835 Hwy. 1, Bodega Bay, CA 94923
Price: Expensive
Credit Cards: AE, D, MC, V
Cuisine: Seafood
Serving: Breakfast, Lunch, Dinner
Reservations: Only for inn guests or parties of five or more
Special Features: Harbor view

The Tides was immortalized by Alfred Hitchcock in *The Birds*, but you wouldn't recognize it now. The current dining room has a high-raftered ceiling and stunning views of the harbor from every seat. The food is competent at best, but the catch of the day is usually a good bet: a voluminous list including red snapper, swordfish, ling-cod, and Pacific oysters. Local specialties include salmon, in season May through September, and Dungeness crab, in season from November to May. A delicious local classic is the crab cioppino: crab, prawns, scallops, mussels, and clams swimming in a shallow pool of zesty Italian sauce. The lunch menu is almost identical to dinner, but it's a few dollars cheaper. The wine list is sound; ditto the service.

UNDERWOOD BAR & BISTRO

707-823-7023
www.underwoodgraton.com
9113 Graton Rd., Graton, CA 95444
Price: Moderate to Expensive
Credit Cards: MC, V
Cuisine: Eclectic
Serving: Lunch (closed Sun.), Dinner; closed Mon.
Reservations: Recommended

If you like to eat where the winemakers hang out, this restaurant is practically a private club for the West County wine industry. The interior is a masculine blend of urban and country, and there's a long bar that's always hopping. Service is a little too laid back at times, but the food is appealing and hearty. The kitchen takes influences from all over the globe, with a menu that ranges from an eclectic selection of small plates such as crab cakes and roasted beets to a soul-warming *coq au vin,* hamburgers, and Catalan fish stew. The wine list is modest but offers lots of value; it's devoted largely to California but with a handful of selections from around the world.

WEST COUNTY GRILL

707-829-9500
www.westcountygrill.com
6948 Sebastopol Ave., Sebastopol, CA 95472
Price: Expensive to Very Expensive
Credit Cards: AE, D, MC, V
Cuisine: American, Mediterranean
Serving: Lunch, Dinner

There's a funky, urban energy in the dining room at the West County Grill in Sebastopol. Tim Fish

Reservations: Recommended
Special Features: Outdoor dining

Chef Jonathan Waxman and partner Stephen Singer arrived in Sebastopol in 2007 with impressive credentials, a combined resume that includes Chez Panisse and Domaine Chandon. They've succeeded in bringing funky, urban sophistication to this sleepy corner of Wine Country. This is a big restaurant—130 seats and 30 outside—with a warehouse feel: exposed brick walls, an open kitchen with a wood-fired oven, an open floor plan that soars two levels high, and rustic wood and metal highlights that somehow lend an overall atmosphere of warmth. There's an energy to the place that's palpable; you just want to settle in and enjoy. There's also a similar hearty passion and zest in the food. Waxman offers a seasonal menu that focuses on local ingredients, and standouts include pizzas, grilled hanger steak, and JW's grilled chicken and fries. The service seems casual at first, but it's attentive and sharp. The wine list,

though generally focused on Sonoma, has an eclectic selection from around the world and a good range of prices.

FOOD PURVEYORS

A chic restaurant isn't the only place to feast. From Mexican eateries that burn your tongue to old family delicatessens with lingering, irresistible smells of smoked meats and cheese, Napa and Sonoma have specialty food shops aplenty.

Bakeries

NAPA COUNTY

Alexis Baking Company (707-258-1827, 1517 3rd St., Napa, CA 94559) You name it, and ABC has it: bread, pastries, desserts, sandwiches, coffee, and muffins. It serves breakfast and lunch and has great wedding cakes.

Bouchon Bakery (707-944-2253, 6528 Washington St., Yountville, CA 94599) Expect sweet Parisian treats from this bakery because Thomas Keller of The French Laundry-fame is behind it. Keller opened the restaurant Bouchon in 2003, and it's now one of the most popular and flashy in Napa Valley—so why not open a bakery to boot?

The Model Bakery (707-963-8192, 1357 Main St., St. Helena, CA 94574) Everything here is baked in a big, brick oven. Sweet or sour baguettes are stacked like kindling in tall wicker baskets and scones, muffins, and croissants compete for shelf space. Behind the counter are burly loaves of rye, powdered white on top. There's a full coffee bar, and seating for 30, with lunch items—sandwiches, pizzas, and salads—offered.

SONOMA COUNTY

Artisan Bakers (707-939-1765, 750 W. Napa St., Sonoma, CA 95476) Some of the finest bread in Wine Country is made right here. Look for loaves in markets around

Pick up a loaf of bread to go with thy jug of wine at Downtown Bakery in Healdsburg. Tim Fish

Sonoma County and Napa Valley, or stop in the bakery itself. In 1996, during the baking equivalent of the Olympics, owner Craig Ponsford achieved the impossible: He baked a better baguette than the French.

Basque Boulangerie Café (707-935-7687, 460 1st St. E., Sonoma, CA 95476) You'll find some lovely loaves here as well croissants, pastries, coffee, and espresso. There are a few seats inside and out.

Downtown Bakery and Creamery (707-431-2719, 308A Center St., Healdsburg, CA 95448) There are fabulous desserts here, but it doesn't look like much as you walk in. What's the secret? The Chez Panisse connection. Owner Kathleen Stewart is a veteran of that famed Berkeley kitchen. Tortes and cakes are ungodly delicious, as are the

sticky buns, the monster Fig Newton-like cookies, and the blueberry scones. They also have great coffee and ice cream. There's no seating, but the downtown plaza is across the street.

Mom's Apple Pie (707-823-8330, 4550 Gravenstein Hwy. N., Sebastopol, CA 95472) This roadhouse makes fat pies better than most moms, served in tin pans or by the slice. The coconut cream and the fresh Gravenstein apple are to die for. Not just pies are made here; Mom's also serves lunch, offering sandwiches and salads.

Village Bakery (707-829-8101, 7225 Healdsburg Ave., Sebastopol, CA 95472; also 707-527-7654, in Santa Rosa's Town & Country Shopping Center) At both locales there are rustic, European-style breads, pastries, and pies, and elegant desserts.

Burgers, Etc.

Taylor's Refresher (707-963-3486, 933 Main St., St. Helena, CA 94574) This is a classic, old drive-in restaurant—though you have to walk to the window these days—but average Joes and gourmands alike flock to Taylor's for its updated, 1950s-style fast-food menu. (And if you're traveling with kids, it's a godsend, because Napa Valley is short on family restaurants.) Burgers, fries, and onion rings are top-notch, and you'll also find grilled chicken sandwiches and salads. There's also beer on tap and wine by the glass. Seating is strictly picnic table, but that's half the fun.

Coffeehouses

NAPA COUNTY
Calistoga Roastery (707-942-5757, 1426 Lincoln Ave., Calistoga, CA 94515) Here's a cozy and casual spot for the morning brew,

with plenty of seating inside and out. A second location is in St. Helena (707-967-0820; 677 St. Helena Hwy.). The St. Helena roastery has a pleasant outdoor court for sunny mornings. It also has a drive-up window—perfect for bleary-eyed days.

Napa Valley Coffee Roasting Co. (707-224-2233, 948 Main St., Napa, CA 94559; 707-963-4491, 1400 Oak Ave., St. Helena, CA 94574) The premier coffeehouse in the county now has two outlets. The classic old facade in downtown Napa is a popular hangout. Bags of raw, greenish beans are open in the back. The St. Helena shop is larger and sunnier, with outdoor seating. To go with the brew, there are treats galore.

San Marco Espresso and Bake Shop (707-942-0714, 1408 Lincoln Ave., Calistoga, CA 94515) This recently expanded café still makes an uncompromising cup of coffee, plus fruit and milk shakes are now offered.

SONOMA COUNTY

A'Roma Roasters (707-576-7765, 95 5th St., Santa Rosa, CA 95401) Facing historic Railroad Square, A'Roma is a touch bohemian, with exposed rafters, a copper countertop, and a coffee-bean roaster as a centerpiece. There are lots of tables, and you'll roll your eyes over goodies such as the chocolate decadent torte.

Coffee Catz (707-829-6600, 6761 Sebastopol Ave., Sebastopol, CA 95472) This funky café is like the tearoom of a Victorian train station. Breakfast and lunch are served. There's also an outdoor patio and live music about four nights a week.

The Coffee Garden (707-996-6645, 415 1st St. W., Sonoma, CA 95476) This café looks plain enough, but it's in an adobe built in the 1830s. The main draw is the lovely garden patio.

Flying Goat Coffee Roastery (707-433-9081, 324 Center St., Healdsburg, CA

94548; 419 Center St., Healdsburg, 95448) Here's a stylish spot for a cup of java. Have a muffin while you smell the roaster at work.

Wolf Coffee Co. (707-546-9653, 1810 Mendocino Ave., Santa Rosa, CA 95401) This may have the best cup of coffee in Sonoma County. The Mendocino shop is a popular take-out in the Santa Rosa Junior College area.

Ethnic Food in Wine Country

CHINESE

The best Chinese in Wine Country is found at **Gary Chu's** (707-526-5840, 611 5th St., Santa Rosa, CA 95404). The room is an elegant blend of Chinese and art deco, and the food is stylishly gourmet. Impeccable ingredients are cooked with light sautés instead of oppressive sauces. Try the spicy plum sauce pork. In Napa, **Golden Harvest** (707-967-9888, 61 Main St., St. Helena, CA 94574) offers solid Chinese fare, as does **Soo Yuan** (707-942-9404, 1354 Lincoln Ave., Calistoga, CA 94515), where a standard like kung pao chicken is competently done, hearty and mildly spicy.

JAPANESE

This close to San Francisco and the Pacific Ocean, we take our sushi seriously. A local favorite is **Sushi Mambo** (707-257-6604, 1202 1st St., Napa, CA 95449). Sonoma County has several fine Japanese restaurants. Our favorites are **Hana** (707-586-0270, 101 Golf Course Dr., Rohnert Park, CA 94928; at Doubletree Plaza) and **Osake** (707-542-8282, 2446 Patio Ct., Santa Rosa, CA 94505), which is just off busy Farmers Lane. It's a bit off the beaten path, but **Sake 'O** (707-433-2669, 505 Healdsburg Ave., Healdsburg, CA 95448) is one of the best in Wine Country. It has a sleekly upscale Asian decor and innovative cuisine.

MEXICAN

In Napa Valley there's a certain funky appeal to **Ana's Cantina** (707-963-4921, 1205 Main St., St. Helena, CA 94574), a bar with a pool table and lots of character. The food won't win awards, but it goes well with a longneck. Avoid **Armadillo's** (707-963-8082, 1304 Main St., St. Helena, CA 94574), where the atmosphere recalls a colorful village south of the border, but the food is lackluster. The atmosphere is lively at **Pacifico** (707-942-4400, 1237 Lincoln Ave., Calistoga, CA 94515), and the margaritas are knockout. The food is hearty; try the fish tacos.

In Sonoma County, chains dominate, and the results are less than impressive. The **Cantina** (707-523-3663, 500 4th St., Santa Rosa, CA 95401) is a slick, brick palace with an active bar and a heated patio, but the food is boring. A better chain experience is at **Chevys** (707-571-1082, 24 4th St., Santa Rosa, CA 95401). The food isn't authentic, but it's fresh and nicely done, especially the fajitas. The food at **La Casa** (707-996-3406, 121 E. Spain St., Sonoma, CA 95476) is adequate at best. A better choice on Sonoma Plaza is the festive **Maya** (707-935-3500, 101 E. Napa St., Sonoma, CA 95476), reviewed earlier in this chapter. Two inexpensive and low-key shops have the best Mexican in the county. Ignore the atmosphere at **Taqueria El Sombrero** (707-433-3818, 245 Center St., Healdsburg, CA 95448) and **Taqueria Santa Rosa** (two locations: 707-528-7956, 1950 Mendocino Ave., Santa Rosa, CA 95401 and 707-575-5793, 711 Stonypoint Rd., Suite 5, Santa Rosa, CA. 95403) and relish the food. Both use whole beans, not canned refrieds, and grilled meat.

ETC.

Our favorites include **Thai House** (707-526-3939, 525 4th St., Santa Rosa, CA 95401) and

Rin's Thai (707-938-1462, 139 E. Napa St., Sonoma, CA 95476). You might also try **Thai Pot** (707-829-8889, 6961 Sebastopol Ave., Sebastopol, CA 95472), **Siam Thai House** (707-226-7749, 1139 Lincoln Ave., Napa, CA 94558), and **Thai Kitchen** (707-254-9271, 1222 Trancas St., Napa, CA 94558). Another worthy Thai restaurant is **Lotus Thai** (707-433-5282, 109-A Plaza St., Healdsburg, CA 95448).

If you need an Indian fix, Wine Country offers two that will do in a pinch. Sizzling **Tandoor** (707-579-5999, 409 Mendocino Ave., Santa Rosa, CA 95401) is a sound dining room, with fiery *vindaloos* and rich curry *biryani*.

Annalien (707-224-8319, 1142 Main St, Napa, CA 94559) serves authentic Vietnamese cuisine such as savory grilled lemongrass pork. They even have a decent wine list. Don't miss it.

Deli, Gourmet Shops & Markets

NAPA COUNTY

Cantinetta Tra Vigne (707-963-8888, 1050 Charter Oak Ave., St. Helena, CA 94574) This classic stone building is primarily a wine shop, with more than one hundred wines served by the glass. There are selections of gourmet sandwiches and salads for a peaceful lunch in the quiet courtyard near the Tra Vigne restaurant.

Dean & DeLuca (707-967-9980, 607 S. St. Helena Hwy., St. Helena, CA 94574) Manhattan's upscale gourmet food shop opened an outlet in Napa Valley in 1997. It's quite a place, with all sorts of carry-out goodies such as sandwiches, cheese, fresh produce, smoked salmon, duck pâté, olives, baked goods, coffee, cookies, jams, olive oils, vinegars, cakes, and rotisserie chicken.

Genova Delicatessen (707-253-8686, 1550 Trancas St., Napa, CA 94558) You can almost smell Genova from two blocks off, so rich is the bouquet of dried salami, roasting chicken, and simmering pastas. With a history that dates to 1926, Genova is home to marbled cold cuts and glass-case treasures such as potato salad, antipasto, and olives. There are a handful of tables.

Giugni's Sandwiches (707-963-3421, 1227 Main St., St. Helena, CA 94574) A fun Italian deli with great meats, corned beef, and pastrami as well as a great chicken salad sandwich.

Napa Valley Olive Oil Manufacturing Co. (707-963-4173, 835 Charter Oak Ave., St. Helena, CA 94574) This faded white barn is a glorious time warp. The shop dates to the 1920s, when Napa Valley was largely populated by Italian farmers. You're as likely to hear Italian inside as English, and the deli counter looks like your grandmother's kitchen—if your grandmother is from Naples. There are picnic tables outside.

Oakville Grocery Co. (707-944-8802, 7856 St. Helena Hwy., Oakville, CA 94562) What looks like an old country store, with its giant red Coca-Cola sign on the side and wooden screen doors, is actually a gourmet grocery. Goodies include duck pâté, cold cuts, and even caviar. Sandwiches include turkey with pesto and a glorious *lavash*. There are also coffee by the cup, bakery treats, and local wines. It's open daily for coffee at 7 AM and food starting at 9 AM. This is a great stop before or after wine tasting. It's recently been purchased by Dean & DeLuca.

Oxbow Public Market (707-963-1345, 610 First St., Napa, CA 94559) Right next to COPIA: the American Center for Wine, Food, and the Arts, this marketplace has great appeal to foodies. Like the San Francisco Ferry building, this public market has an appealing range of food purvey

ors including Taylor's Refresher, Model Bakery, and Three Twins Organic Ice Cream. It's colossal—40,000 square feet—to showcase the wares of 30 vendors and 10 farmstands in Napa.

Olivier Napa Valley (707-967-8777, 1375 Main St., St. Helena, CA 94574) Taste Napa Valley olive oils, plus peruse some of the area's best mustards and sauces.

V. Sattui Winery (707-963-7774, 1111 White Ln., St. Helena, CA 94574; at St. Helena Hwy.) Most wineries have a picnic table tucked somewhere, but V. Sattui is Lawn Lunch Central, complete with shading oaks. The tasting room doubles as a deli shop.

SONOMA COUNTY

Basque Boulangerie Café (707-935-7687, 460 1st St. E., Sonoma, CA 95476) More than a bakery, this stylish storefront has a deli, a coffee bar, and even has some wine selections. Popular sandwiches include chicken salad and prosciutto and brie. For some reason, however, it has yet to master the classic croissant.

Dry Creek General Store (707-433-4171, 3495 Dry Creek Rd., Healdsburg, CA 95448) A few years back, Gina Gallo of Gallo of Sonoma Winery purchased this rural gathering spot, a landmark of Sonoma's rustic heritage. Keep your eye out for fancy trappings such as a wine rack and gourmet goodies amid the rustic charm. Super deli sandwiches are offered here.

The Girl & the Fig Pantry (707-933-3000, 1190 E. Napa St., Sonoma, CA. 95476) Just blocks away from The Girl & the Fig restaurant, this pantry is a lively offshoot. It has a coffee bar, gelato, wine, and gifts—tasty treats such as apricot fig chutney and fig balsamic vinegar.

Jimtown Store (707-433-1212, 6706 Hwy. 128, Healdsburg, CA 95448) An Alexander

Valley landmark for a century, this former general store and gas depot that had been abandoned for years was resuscitated in 1991 with a touch of gourmet chic. Today, Carrie Brown's Jimtown Store remains quaint yet sophisticated, drawing national attention along the way. Sandwiches are first-rate, and the aisles include old-fashioned candy, toys, and memorabilia.

Korbel Delicatessen (707-824-7313, 13250 River Rd., Guerneville, CA 95446) Under a cathedral ceiling on an acid-washed floor, five or six tables offer shady views through tall windows. Outside are plenty of additional tables. Here you can get muffins, salads, sandwiches, beer on tap, champagne and wine by the glass, and ales of all kinds (amber, pale, port, golden wheat). There are breads, jams and jellies, and vinegars, too.

Oakville Grocery, Healdsburg (707-433-3200, 124 Matheson St., Healdsburg, CA 95448) Napa Valley invaded Sonoma with this satellite of the successful upscale grocery. Goodies include duck pâté, cold cuts, cheese, olives, fresh produce, and artisan breads. Order a sandwich or pizza or a rotisserie chicken. There's even wine available by the glass. Take the food with you or eat on the patio.

Plaza Farms (106 Matheson St., Healdsburg, CA 95448) A delightful spot on the Healdsburg square with a range of tasty purveyors such as DaVero Olive Oil, Bellwether Farm Cheese, and Tandem Winery. Not to be missed is Bovolo, the café in the back, which makes everything from scratch from pizzas and gelato to its numerous pork dishes. Chef John Stewart is a self-proclaimed pork fanatic.

The Olive Press (707-939-8900, www.the olivepress.com, 24724 Hwy. 121 at Jacuzzi Family Winery, Sonoma, CA 95476) If you're tired of watching people make wine, switch to olive oil. This smart den makes and sells olive oil that rivals Italy's best. Try a complimentary taste.

Olive & Vine Marketplace and Café (707-996-9150, 14301 Arnold Dr., Glen Ellen, CA 95442) This marketplace is home base for its catering company and it has scrumptious panini sandwiches, pizzas and soups. The grilled pork loin sandwich is also a hit.

Oliver's Markets (707-537-7123, 560 Montecito Center, Santa Rosa, CA 95409; another store: 707-284-3530, 461 Stonypoint Rd., Santa Rosa, CA. 95401; Oliver's in Cotati: 707-795-9501, 546 E. Cotati Ave.) These upscale grocery stores may be bigger than others listed, but they're just as food and wine savvy. They carry high-quality food and well-chosen wines. The Cotati store has an ever-popular wine bar where people taste wines, with winemakers often there to provide running commentary. Winemaker Gina Gallo of Gallo of Sonoma is a frequent guest.

Pacific Market (at Pacific and Bryden in Santa Rosa, CA., 95401, 707-546-FOOD; Pacific Market (550 Gravenstein Hwy., Sebastopol, CA. 707-823-4916). These stores are Meccas for those who crave sophisticated cuisine. There's fresh produce, fish, meat and a great assortment of pastas, sushi and baked goods, with wine sections touting regional wines. Just order dinner – Chicken Marsala, scalloped and baked veggies – warm it up and impress your family and friends.

Sonoma Cheese Factory (707-996-1931, 2 W. Spain St., Sonoma, CA 95476) The Viviani family has made cheese in Sonoma since 1931, but this is actually no longer a factory because the cheese is made in Crescent City. Even so, this supermarket-sized deli has appeal, with its tasty grilled meats on the side-covered patio. It also has a coffee and gelato bar. Tasty samples of cheese abound, and shady Sonoma Plaza is nearby.

Traverso's Gourmet Foods (707-542-2530, 106 B St., Santa Rosa, CA 95401) Traverso's has evolved into the county's best gourmet deli and wine shop, never losing touch with its Italian roots. Dangling from the ceiling are prosciutto and flags of Italy. The deli case is a painting of salads, ravioli, and hearty meats. Sandwiches are marvelous.

Vella Cheese Company (800-848-0505, 315 2nd St. E., Sonoma, CA 95476) The dry jack is to die for. This is a Sonoma classic that dates to 1931 and is worth a visit.

Wine Country Chocolates & Truffles (707-996-1010; 14301 Arnold Dr., Glen Ellen, CA.) Chocoholics: Good news. This delightful shop has wine-infused chocolate truffles. Situated in the Jack London Village Shopping Center, it's open seven days a week from 10–5.

Cafés, Wine Bars, Etc.

NAPA COUNTY
Foothill Café (707-252-6178, 2766 Old Sonoma Rd., Napa, CA 94559) This trendy, 40-seat café is known for its savvy food. To be had here is outstanding barbecue, including wonderful baby-back ribs.

Gillwood's Café (707-963-1788, 1313 Main St., St. Helena, CA 94574) This is a great stop for breakfast and lunch. There are delicious burgers, and if you're a breakfast person, Gillwood's serves breakfast all day long.

Villa Corona (707-963-7812, 1138 Main St., St. Helena, CA 94574) Homemade flour tortillas and specialty sauces make for tasty burritos, particularly the super burrito. Some good breakfast dishes include the huevos con rancheros.

SONOMA COUNTY
Café Newsstand (707-922-5233, 301 Healdsburg Ave., Healdsburg, CA 95448) Here, there's a modern, clean feel, and the sleepy-eyed reach for their first cup of coffee and read the news of the day, although it's a worthy stop any time past morning. Peet's coffee, panini sandwiches, and

homemade ice cream are offered. The newsstand features more than two hundred different magazines and newspapers.

Healdsburg Bar & Grill (707-433-3333, 245 Healdsburg Ave., Healdsburg, CA 95448) Here you'll find great pizzas and flat breads as well as tasty burgers.

Langley's on the Green (707-837-7984, 610 McClelland Dr., Windsor, CA) This is a cozy, comfortable place where kids can romp around on the town green before chow. Here's what rates: the Manila clam chowder and ravioli when they're on the menu.

Ledson Hotel and Harmony Club Wine Bar (707-996-9779, 480 1st St. E., Sonoma, CA 95476) The wine list offers more than 30 selections, with a natural emphasis on Sonoma County, including Ledson's new Harmony Collection. There's also live piano music.

Monti's (707-568-4404, 714 Village Ct., Santa Rosa, CA 95405) Specialties revolve around a rotisserie and include prime rib for two, lavender-roasted duck, and Tuscan-styled baby back ribs. There's also an oyster bar with four different selections. Other savvy restaurants by the same owners include Willi's Wine Bar in Santa Rosa and Willi's Seafood and Raw Bar in Healdsburg.

Fish Markets

One of the joys of living on the Pacific Ocean is fresh seafood. Most prized locally are Dungeness crab and salmon. Crab season runs from mid-November to the end of May and the local salmon season runs from mid-May to September. Plus, a number of oyster farms are just south on Tomales Bay and those beefy Pacific oysters are delicious. Here are a few specialty fish markets.

Dee's Deli (707-875-8881, 595 Hwy. 1, Bodega Bay, CA 94923)

Tides Wharf Fish Market (707-875-3554, 835 Hwy. 1, Bodega Bay, CA 94923)

Produce

The bounty of Wine Country goes well beyond grapes, particularly in Sonoma County. Fine produce stands abound in Wine Country. Look for **The Fruit Basket** (707-996-7433, 18474 Hwy. 12, Sonoma, CA 95476) and **Anstead's** (707-431-0530, 428 Center St., Healdsburg Ave., Healdsburg, CA 95448).

Sonoma County Farm Trails is an informal collective of farms. Also worth seeking out is **Twin Hill Ranch** (707-823-2815, 1689 Pleasant Hill Rd., Sebastopol, CA 95472), which specializes in apples, nuts, and dried fruit. Enjoy a roaring fire on chilly days. **Kozlowski Farms** (707-887-1587, 5566 Gravenstein Hwy. N., Forestville, CA 95436) is an orchard turned down-home gourmet enterprise. This Sonoma County treasure specializes in jams and jellies, apple butter, and raspberry and other flavored vinegars as well as apples and other fresh produce.

Pizza & Pizzerias

Pizza may not be the obsession here that it is in cities such as Chicago and New York, but folks here do like their cheese pies. You know what to expect from Pizza Hut and the rest, so we've rounded up a sampling of the little guys—the independents and small chains.

Checkers Pizza & Pasta (707-942-9300, 1414 Lincoln Ave., Calistoga, CA 94515; 523 4th St., Santa Rosa, CA 95401) If you like a bit of panache in your pizza, check out Checkers. Both outlets are festive, with abstract art and polished pine and black tile. There are traditional pies of sausage and pepperoni, of course, but there's also Thai pizza, topped with marinated chicken, cilantro, and peanuts.

Pizzeria Tra Vigne (707-967-9999, 1016 Main St., St. Helena, CA 94574) In St. Helena, try this family-friendly place. Find a full review earlier in this chapter.

La Vera (707-575-1113, 629 4th St., Santa Rosa, CA 95404) For those who demand New York-style pizza, there's La Vera. The cheese stretches for a city block, and the meats are explosions of pepperoni and sausage. The crust is that perfect unison of crunchy and chewy. The atmosphere is more formal than most pizzerias, with polished brass and wood.

La Prima Pizza (707-963-7909, 1010 Adams St., St. Helena, CA 94574) makes a pleasant pie, with a puffy crust that's crisp on the bottom. The toppings are generous and of good quality. Mary's Pizza Shack (707-573-1100, 3084 Marlow Rd., Santa Rosa, CA 95403; also nine locations in Sonoma and one in Napa) is fairly safe American pizza. The crust is a tad salty and the meat toppings are rather bland, but the cheeses and veggies are top rate.

Sweets & Treats

NAPA COUNTY

Anette's Chocolate & Ice Cream Factory (707-252-4228, 1321 1st St., Napa, CA 94559) This is a dangerous place for weight watchers, offering everything from fresh chocolate turtles and truffles to jelly beans, milk shakes, and sundaes.

The Candy Cellar (707-942-6990, 1367 Lincoln Ave., Calistoga, CA 94515) Relive

Satisfy that craving at the Candy Cellar in Calistoga.
Tim Fish

your childhood as you browse this general store, with its wooden barrels stuffed with goodies such as taffy, butterscotch, fireballs, candy necklaces, gum, A&W Root Beer barrels, and the like.

Cups & Cones (707-944-2113, 6525 Washington St.Vintage 1870, Yountville, CA 94599) Stop for a treat while you browse the shops of V Marketplace. This shop offers homemade candy, Double Rainbow ice cream, and unique toys.

San Marco Espresso Co. (707-942-0714, 1408 Lincoln Ave., Calistoga, CA 94515) A small shop with a potpourri of goodies, from muffins and scones to lemon squares, fresh chocolates, decadent cakes, ice cream, and espresso.

Woodhouse Chocolate in St. Helena makes hand-crafted candy. Tim Fish

Woodhouse Chocolate (707-963-8413, 800-966-3468, 1367 Main St., St. Helena, CA 95474) This bright, airy shop specializes in European-style fresh crème chocolate with no preservatives.

SONOMA COUNTY
Chocolate Cow (707 935 3564, 452 1st St. E., Sonoma, CA 95476) These folks are "udderly" cow crazy—black-and-white heifers are everywhere, from T-shirts to

stuffed animals. The place also stocks candy, chocolates, fudge, and ice cream.

Screamin' Mimi (707-823-5902, 6902 Sebastopol Ave., Sebastopol, CA 95472) They make their own ice cream and sorbets here, and it's all wonderful.

Wine Shops

The specialty wine shops in Napa and Sonoma counties are, as you might imagine, among the finest in the nation, offering a huge variety as well as hard-to-find treasures. You'll be surprised to learn that wine is seldom cheaper at the wineries than it is at local retail shops, unless you catch a sale or buy by the case. You also run the risk, of course, of not being able to find a wine you love at the winery. It's your gamble.

NAPA COUNTY
Brix (707-944-9350, 7377 St. Helena Hwy., Yountville, CA 94558) Don't be fooled from the outside; this restaurant has an excellent wine shop just inside the front door.

Calistoga Wine Stop (707-942-5556, 1458 Lincoln Ave., Calistoga, CA 94515) Housed in an 1866 Central Pacific railroad car, this shop has a solid lineup of current Napa and Sonoma wines. Prices are average.

Dean & DeLuca (707-967-9980, 607 S. St. Helena Hwy., St. Helena, CA 94574) This gourmet food store has a large and superb selection of Napa and Sonoma wines. Prices are the going rate.

Enoteca Wine Shop (707-942-1117, 1348 B Lincoln Ave., Calistoga, CA 94515) Here you'll find great selection and a savvy staff to help you shop in a store that, surprisingly, resembles a cave.

Groezinger Wine Merchants (707-944-2331, 6484 Washington St., Yountville, CA 94599) A great selection of standards as well as collectibles and offbeat wines can be had here. It has a very hip atmosphere.

JV Wine & Spirits (707-253-2624, 301 1st St., Napa, CA 94559) This is a must stop. For starters, this place has more than 3,500 different wines and more than 450 different types of beer—a big selection with good prices. Plus, there are two sommeliers and a wine consultant on hand. Finally, here you'll find picnic supplies: cheese, bread and sausages.

St. Helena Wine Center (707-963-1313, 1321 Main St., St. Helena, CA 94574) One of Napa's oldest, dating to 1953, this shop believes in the notion of "only the best," offering few bargains. It has a small but extremely select library of current Napa and Sonoma wines. There's also a tasting bar.

St. Helena Wine Merchants (707-963-7888, 699 St. Helena Hwy., St. Helena, CA 94574) There's a giant selection of new and older vintages but no bargains here. There's also a notable assortment of large bottles and a tasting bar.

V Wine Cellar (707-531-7053, 6525 Washington St., Yountville, CA 94599) This shop focuses on cult wine: high scoring wines that are hard to find. It has about 2,500 labels and 40 different types of cigars. If you want to sit and sip, it also has a comfortable lounge area.

The Wine Garage (707-942-5332, www.winegarage.net, 1020 Foothill Blvd. #C, Calistoga, CA. 94515) This value-oriented wine shop has more than two hundred wines under $25 and a current inventory of more than three hundred bottles.

SONOMA COUNTY

Bottle Barn (707-528-1161, 3331 Industrial Dr., Santa Rosa, CA 95403) This warehouse has a huge selection, with a few hard-to-find wines and generally bargain prices.

Root's Cellar (707-433-4937, 1401 Grove St., Healdsburg, CA 95448) This small wine shop is packed with some of the top wines in Sonoma and Napa. Though it focuses on California wines, it also has a large number of imports. There are more than three hundred wines in all.

Sonoma Enoteca Wine Shop (707-935-1200, 35 E. Napa, Sonoma, CA 95476) This shop has a great selection of wines to peruse and a knowledgeable staff. It also has a great California collection.

Traverso's Gourmet Foods (707-542-2530, 3rd and B Sts., Santa Rosa, CA 95401) This Italian deli doesn't carry a huge selection of wine, but it offers only the best quality in all price ranges. Bill Traverso knows wine but is so unpretentious about it that you don't have to pretend you do. Traverso's has the best stock of Italian wines in the region.

Wine Exchange of Sonoma (707-938-1794, 452 1st St. E., Sonoma, CA 95476) There's an air of restrained refinement to this shop. You'll find few discounts, but look for the best current releases and a few vintage wines. There's also an enormous selection of specialty beers. Another plus is the wine- and beer-tasting bar in the back.

The Wine Shop (707-433-0433, 331 Healdsburg Ave., Healdsburg, CA 95448) This is an excellent wine shop right on the Healdsburg plaza. It focuses on specialty local producers and handcrafted gems.

6

WINERIES &
SPECIALTY BREWERS

Poetry Uncorked

Wineries, like the wines they make, come in different styles and qualities. You can even use the same words to describe them. Is it a sweet or sour experience? Subtle or bold? Is it friendly from the first, or does it grow on you? In compiling our list of wineries, we asked ourselves: What makes a winery worth visiting? Is it the wine? A pilgrimage to the source of your favorite cabernet sauvignon has great appeal. Is it the fame? "Wow! There's Beringer—we have to stop there." There's also the tour to consider. And is there a fee? Can you picnic? And so on.

Old-timers, of course, remember a different Wine Country. As recently as the 1960s, visitors arrived at local wineries with empty jugs and bottles in hand, ready for a fill-up right from the barrel. But as Napa and Sonoma have gained prominence in the wine world, so also has their appeal as vacation meccas. More than eight million tourists come to Napa and Sonoma counties each year. Winery hopping has become an avid pastime, and tasting rooms have evolved into bustling centerpieces—sometimes rustic, sometimes chic, but always inviting and fun. Drinking wine has always been a rich man's hobby, at least in the United States. These days, winery touring is equally expensive, with many wineries charging for tours, and a $10 fee to taste wine is not unusual anymore.

Wineries now have competition from a new generation of specialty beer brewers. These microbreweries or brewpubs are springing up all over Napa and Sonoma counties. In this edition, we devote a special section at the end of the chapter to these specialty brewers.

Fall is the favorite touring season for many—the vineyards are resplendent in rich golds and reds, the wineries and fields are hectic with the harvest, or *crush*, as it's called. Our favorite time is spring, when the mountains and fields are lush and green, the vines budding, the trees flowering, and the fields covered with the yellow of wild mustard.

We've included not only the wineries that offer tours and tastings regularly, but also those that are open by appointment only. The wineries are organized first by region, then alphabetically. Here are a few guidelines to keep in mind when winery touring and wine tasting.

1) Have a designated driver. Those small samples can creep up on you, especially if you're new to wine tasting. Also, remember that you don't have to try every wine, and wineries are not offended if you pour out a leftover sample.

2) Don't be intimidated by wine's snob-
bish image. Be yourself. Ask questions.
Have fun. A glossary is provided later in
this chapter if you need handy details.

3) Bring the right equipment. Take notes.
They don't have to be voluminous; even a
brief note—"2005 Simi Chardonnay: great"—
will jog your memory later. While touring,
take along crackers and bottled water. They
help to cleanse your palate between wineries.

4) One tour is not much different from
the next. One or two is enough. Also, try
different kinds. Korbel and Beringer are
rich in history, while Mumm and Mondavi
are technical marvels.

5) The cost of wine touring has skyrock-
eted in recent years. In the old days, tours
and tasting were free. Now most wineries
charge a fee to taste, usually $3 to $50. Often,
a souvenir glass is thrown in, and the fee
may be waived if you buy wine. Many tours
are still free, but you can pay upwards of $70
for a personalized tour and tasting at some
upscale wineries, and many wineries are
moving to a combined tasting and tour fee.

6) Don't let "open by appointment only"
scare you off. Wineries that advertise this
way are often smaller and want to discour-
age heavy traffic—and many are restricted by
recent zoning laws. If you're a casual tourist,
stick to the big wineries with the big welcome, but if you're serious about wine, these
smaller wineries are serious about you.

7) Most wineries have a picnic area. It's
courteous to buy a bottle before picnicking.

Napa County Wineries

NAPA & CARNEROS
ACACIA WINERY
707-226-9991
www.acaciawinery.com
2750 Las Amigas Rd., Napa, CA 94559
Tasting: 10–4:30 Mon.–Sat. and noon–4:30
Sun. by appointment
Tasting Fee: $5, for reserve wine

Tours: 10–4:30 Mon.–Sat., noon–4:30 Sun.
by appointment

Named for a tree that grows throughout the
area, Acacia specializes in chardonnay and
pinot noir. This winery was established in
1979 and is now owned by international
beverage giant Diageo, which also operates
Sterling, Chalone, and Beaulieu. The winery is a modern California barn that sits on
the slopes of the Carneros District, which
shoulders the top of San Pablo Bay. Acacia
uses grapes from surrounding vineyards, a
region suited to Burgundian grapes.

ARTESA VINEYARDS & WINERY
707-224-1668
www.artesawinery.com
1345 Henry Rd., Napa, CA 94559
Tasting: 10–5 daily
Tasting Fee: $10–$15
Tours: 11 and 2 daily
Special Features: Art gallery

Artesa began life in 1991 as sparkling-wine
specialist Codorniu Napa. Spain's Codorniu
has been making bubbly since 1872 but
couldn't make a go of it in California. A few
years ago, the winery changed its name and
switched to still wine: pinot noir, chardonnay, merlot, sauvignon blanc, and syrah. So
far, the wines are quite promising.

This $23-million winery is a spectacular
understatement. Covered with earth and
native grasses, the structure is an enigma
from the road, recalling a buried temple.
The mystery begins to unravel as you
approach the entrance, a long staircase with
a waterfall cascading down the center.
Inside, it seems anything but a bunker, with
elegant decor, a sunbaked atrium, and
spectacular views through grand windows.
It's a must for any student of architecture.

BOUCHAINE VINEYARDS
707-252-9065, 800-654-WINE
www.bouchaine.com
1075 Buchli Station Rd., Napa, CA 94559

Darioush Winery is styled after an ancient Persian temple. Tim Fish

Tasting: 10:30–4 daily
Tasting Fee: $5
Tours: By appointment

Well off the tourist path, on the windswept hills of southern Carneros, sits this modern, redwood winery. Built on the vestiges of a winery that dates to the turn of the 20th century, Bouchaine is a grand redwood barn that sits alone on rolling hills that lead to San Pablo Bay. A fire warms the tasting room on cool Carneros days, and a deck offers lovely views when the sun allows. Chardonnay and pinot noir are specialties, but try the crisp and spicy gewürztraminer.

FOLIO WINEMAKER'S STUDIO

707-256-2757
www.foliowinemakersstudio.com
1285 Dealy Ln., Napa, CA 94559
Tasting: 10–5 daily

Tasting Fee: $10
Tours: No
Special Features: Art gallery

Michael Mondavi spent most of his career at the house his father built: Robert Mondavi Winery. Now on his own, Michael took over the former Carneros Creek Winery and is in the process of sprucing it up considerably. He has also launched a number of new labels including I'M Wines, Oberon, Hangtime, Spellbound, and Medusa, all of which can be sampled in the "taste gallery." Believing that wine is best served with food, Mondavi typically offers food pairings with each tasting. The winery is off the beaten path, but worth checking out.

DARIOUSH WINERY

707-257-2345
www.darioush.com

4240 Silverado Tr., Napa, CA 94558
Tasting: 10:30–5 daily
Tasting Fee: $20
Tours: By appointment

Darioush Khaledi grew up in Iran's shiraz region and immigrated to the United States in the late 1970s. The passionate wine lover spent the early 1990s searching for a vineyard estate and founded Darioush Winery in 1997. Darioush, which opened in the summer of 2004, is unique in Wine Country: East meets West. The winery has classic Persian elements blended with modern European touches, and 90 percent of the stone used in building the winery came from the ancient quarries used by King Darius of ancient Persia. Darioush focuses on the Bordeaux varietals, with small lots of chardonnay, viognier, and shiraz.

DEL DOTTO VINEYARDS

707-256-3332
www.deldottovineyards.com
1055 Atlas Peak Rd., Napa, CA 94558
Tasting: By appointment
Tasting Fee: $40; includes cave tour and barrel tasting
Special Features: Cave tour, barrel tasting

Dave Del Dotto, a pop-culture icon of sorts, is best known for his real estate infomercials that aired in the 1980s. He came to Napa Valley in 1989 to create a new image, and in 1998 he opened a winery with an Italian ambience. Though varietals here include cabernet, cabernet franc, and merlot, the winery is best known for cabernet sauvignon. The tours take you through 120-year-old caves, with opera music piped in. In 2007 in St. Helena, Del Dotto opened a second visitors center, complete with an elaborate cave with Italian marble and mosaic floors.

DOMAINE CARNEROS

707-257-0101, 800-716-2788
www.domainecarneros.com.

1240 Duhig Rd., Napa, CA 94581
Tasting: 10–6 daily
Tasting Fee: $6.75–$75
Tours: 11, 1, and 3 daily
Tour Fee: $25

The Domaine Carneros winery is an exclamation point along Highway 12, towering on a hilltop surrounded by vineyards. Built in the style of an 18th-century French chateau, Domaine Carneros is no everyday winery—but then, sparkling wine isn't your everyday libation. Owned in part by champagne giant Taittinger, Domaine Carneros makes a $14-million statement about its French heritage.

The terrace of this cream-and-terracotta chateau overlooks the lovely rolling hills of the Carneros District, which has a climate similar to Champagne. Inside are marble floors and a maple interior crowned with ornate chandeliers. Behind the stylish front is a state-of-the-art winery that released its first wine in the fall of 1990.

ETUDE

707-257-5300
www.etudewines.com
1250 Cuttings Wharf Rd., Napa, CA 94559
Tasting: 11–4 Sat., weekdays by appointment
Tasting Fee: $25
Tours: 11–4 Sat., weekdays by appointment

The winery and tasting room were inaugurated with the 2003 vintage. The masonry buildings, which total about 40,000 square feet, was the former home of a brandy distillery. Founder and winemaker Tony Soter sold the winery to Foster's Group and is no longer involved, so it will be interesting to see what happens. Etude produces a full range of wines, from cabernet sauvignon to pinot gris (called pinot grigio in some other places), but it gets the most attention for its class-act pinot noir.

HAVENS WINE CELLARS

707-261-2000
www.havenswinc.com
2055 Hoffman Ln., Napa, CA 94558
Tasting: 10–4:30 daily
Tasting Fee: $5–$15
Tours: By appointment

A lot of people were convinced you could grow only pinot noir and chardonnay in the cool Carneros District, but Havens was one of the first who thought otherwise. The merlots and syrah from Havens are distinctive for their structure, subtly, and acid backbone; it's more of a European style than a California one. Established in 1984 by Michael and Kathryn Havens—the first crush was done off the back of a flatbed truck—the winery is pastoral spot on the benchlands of the Mayacamas Mountains. Visiting is a low-key affair, Napa Valley without all the bells and whistles.

THE HESS COLLECTION

707-255-1144, ext. 237
www.hesscollection.com
4411 Redwood Rd., Napa, CA 94558
Tasting: 10–5:30 daily
Tasting Fee: $10
Tours: Self-guided
Special Features: Art gallery

On the rugged slopes of Mount Veeder, Donald Hess, a Swiss mineral magnate, transformed the old Mont La Salle Winery into a showcase for his two passions: wine and art. The Hess Collection is both a winery and a museum of modern art, boasting the most impressive art collection north of San Francisco. (See chapter 4, Culture.) Up a winding road through the thick glades of Mount Veeder, the ivy-covered winery dates to 1903. It was the first Napa Valley home of Christian Brothers before Hess renovated it and opened it to the public in 1989. Inside, a towering three-story atrium with an elevator and staircase leads to two floors of painting and sculpture, a 130-piece collection that includes the works of Francis Bacon and Robert Motherwell. A self-guided tour allows you to view both art and winery. A porthole next to one painting, for example, provides views of the bottling line. Before leaving, stop in the tasting room. Hess concentrates on two wines: cabernet sauvignon and chardonnay. The chardonnays are stylish and oaky; the cabernets are well made.

JARVIS

707-255-5280, 800 255 5280
www.jarviswines.com
2970 Monticello Rd., Napa, CA 94559
Tasting and Tours: By appointment
Tasting Fee: $30
Special Features: Cave and waterfall

Jarvis boasts that it was the first winery in the world to put the entire facility underground in a cave setting. That's right—46,000 square feet of roaming caves. Jarvis is also unique because it has a waterfall streaming through its cave. When digging the cave, workers found a spring, which they decided to incorporate into the design to insure an appropriate level of humidity. If that isn't enough to pique your interest, another interesting aspect of Jarvis is that its winemaker, Dimitri Tchelistcheff, is the son of the legendary winemaker Andre Tchelistcheff, who revolutionized Napa Valley cabernet. The winery produces a full slate of wines, including mainstream cabernet as well as lesser-known petit verdot, but its best efforts are cab and chardonnay.

LUNA VINEYARDS

707-255-2474
www.lunavineyards.com
2921 Silverado Tr., Napa, CA 94558
Tasting: 10–5 daily
Tasting Fee: $12–$30
Tours: By appointment
Special Features: Gifts

In 1995 George Vare and Mike Moon launched Luna, which means "moon" in Italian, with an intent to focus on Italian varietals such as pinot grigio and sangiovese. In keeping with their Italian theme, they built their winery in the California style of Craftsman architecture, with hints of Tuscan influence. Luna also produces merlot and Canto, a red blend. Don't miss the pinot grigio; it's as tasty as pinot grigios that hail from Italy.

MASON CELLARS

707-255-0658
www.masoncellars.com
Tasting Room: 714 First St., Napa, CA 94559
Tasting: 11–5 Thurs.–Mon.
Tasting Fee: None
Tours: No

Randy Mason has been making wine in Napa Valley for years but finally struck out on his own in 1993. The house specialty is sauvignon blanc, and Mason has a genuine gift for it. His style is lush yet crisp, emphasizing fresh and lively grapefruit and fig flavors—just the thing you need after tasting one monotonous Napa chardonnay after another. Mason makes his wine miles away from this tasting room, which is a smart-looking storefront in the burgeoning Oxbox district in downtown Napa.

MONTICELLO VINEYARDS

707-253-2802, 800-743-6668
www.monticellovineyards.com
4242 Big Ranch Rd., Napa, CA 94558
Off Oak Knoll Ave.
Tasting: 10–4:30 daily
Tasting Fee: $10–$45
Tours: By appointment
Special Features: Picnic area

If the visitors center of this winery looks familiar, check the nickel in your pocket. It's modeled after Thomas Jefferson's home, Monticello. A Jefferson scholar,

owner Jay Corley paid tribute to one of America's first wine buffs. Corley began as a grape grower in the early 1970s and started making wine in 1980. Cabernet sauvignon has of late superseded chardonnay as the winery's specialty. The cabernet is generally well structured and elegant.

PATZ & HALL

707-265-7700
www.patzhall.com
Tasting Room: 851 Napa Valley Corporate Way, Suite A, Napa, CA 94558
Tasting: By appointment
Tasting Fee: $40; includes food pairing
Tours: No

One of the true stars of California wine, Patz & Hall specializes in chardonnay and pinot noir. The winery harvest grapes from top vineyards around northern California—such as Hyde and Pisoni—and the wines aren't cheap, but they're astounding for their plush and rich flavors and deep aromas. James Hall, Anne Moses, and Donald and Heather Patz got things started back in 1988, and while the wines are made in Sonoma, they established this tasting salon to better show off their wines. It's a sit-down tasting, and the atmosphere is sophisticated, like the art-filled den of a Upper West Side apartment in New York.

ROBERT CRAIG WINE CELLARS

707-252-2250
www.robertcraigwine.com
Tasting Room: 880 Vallejo St., Napa, CA 94559
Tasting: Mon.–Sat. by appointment
Tasting Fee: None
Tours: No

For most wine fans, visiting this boutique cabernet sauvignon producer was out of the question until Craig opened this tasting room in downtown Napa. Craig is a Napa veteran who launched his own label in

1992, and he makes three cabernets: a Bordeaux-style blend called Affinity and two wines made from the rocky slopes above the valley, Howell Mountain and Mount Veeder. The mountain wines are intense, concentrated, and rich. The tasting room is an intimate storefront.

SAINTSBURY

707-252-0592
www.saintsbury.com
1500 Los Carneros Ave., Napa CA 94559
Tasting: Weekdays by appointment
Tasting Fee: None
Tours: Weekdays by appointment

David Graves and Richard Ward came to Carneros in search of Burgundy. Enthused by the district's potential for Burgundian grapes chardonnay and pinot noir, in 1981 the duo formed Saintsbury, named for the author of the classic *Notes on a Cellar-Book*. With its unassuming design, weathered redwood siding, and steeply sloped roof, the winery fits snugly amid the grapevines in this rural area. We have a soft spot for Saintsbury's moderately priced Garnet pinot noir, and its Carneros pinot and chardonnay are typically lush and complex.

SIGNORELLO VINEYARDS

707-255-5990
www.signorellovineyards.com
4500 Silverado Tr., Napa, CA 94558
Tasting: 10:30–4:30 daily by appointment
Tasting Fee: $10–$35
Tours: By appointment

This small winery built in 1990 is a stylish but low-key affair that has garnered attention for its vibrant chardonnay and semillon, a cousin of sauvignon blanc. Its stable of red wines includes a powerful cabernet sauvignon as well as merlot and pinot noir. Ray Signorello's first vintage was 1985, and he prefers a low-tech, natural approach to winemaking.

TREFETHEN VINEYARDS

707-255-7700
www.trefethen.com
1160 Oak Knoll Ave., Napa, CA 94558
Tasting: 10–4:30 daily
Tasting Fee: $10–$20
Tours: By appointment

Shaded by a one-hundred-year-old oak, this winery was built in 1886 by Hamden W. McIntyre, the architect behind Inglenook and Greystone Cellars. The Trefethen family bought the winery in 1968 and restored it, painting the redwood beauty a pumpkin orange. Tours highlight the McIntyre-designed three-level, gravity-flow system in which grapes are crushed on the third floor, juice is fermented on the second, and wine is aged in barrels on the ground level. Since its first vintage in 1973, Trefethen has made its name with chardonnay.

YOUNTVILLE & STAG'S LEAP

CHIMNEY ROCK WINERY

707-257-2641, 800-257-2641
www.chimneyrock.com.
5350 Silverado Tr., Napa, CA 94558
Tasting: 10–5 daily
Tasting Fee: $15–$50
Tours: By appointment
Tour Fee: $35–$70

The design of this winery is inspired by the architecture of South Africa, which was once home to the winery's founder, the late Sheldon "Hack" Wilson. Today, the winery is owned by wine importer Tony Terlato, who has invested millions in upgrading the winery. The emphasis here is cabernet sauvignon, which prospers in the Stag's Leap District. The winery's best cabernets are sleekly structured yet age beautifully.

CLIFF LEDE VINEYARDS

800-428-2259
www.cliffledevineyards.com
1473 Yountville Cross Rd., Yountville, CA

94599
Tasting: 10–5 daily
Tasting Fee: $20
Tours: By appointment
Tour Fee: $40–$60
Special Features: Art gallery

In a few short years, Canadian Cliff Lede has made a major impact on Napa Valley. He bought the old S. Anderson Winery and practically started from scratch. Where sparkling wine had been the focus, now it's cabernet sauvignon and sauvignon blanc, and right out of the gate the wines were competing with the valley's best. Lede built a new winery and added a gracefully elegant California bungalow-style visitors center and art gallery. In the hills east of the winery, Lede opened Poetry Inn, a small, upscale, and exclusive inn that just may be the best in the valley. (See chapter 3, Lodging.)

CLOS DU VAL

707-261-5225, 800-820-1972
www.closduval.com
5330 Silverado Tr., Napa, CA 94558
Tasting: 10–5 daily
Tasting Fee: $10–$20
Tours: By appointment

Bernard Portet was raised among the casks and vines of Chateau Lafite-Rothschild, where his father was cellar master. The Bordeaux influence is strong here, in both the wines and the winery. An elegant and understated building surrounded by vineyards, Clos du Val evokes a small country winery, with red roses marking the end of each vine row, in typical French fashion. The tasting room has a vaulted ceiling and windows that open into the cellar.

Established in 1972, Clos du Val was an early Napa pioneer, and the cabernets are typically elegant and complex. The winery's roster includes a wonderfully fleshy zinfandel, but the merlot and pinot noir can be inconsistent.

DOMAINE CHANDON

707-944-2280
www.chandon.com
1 California Dr., Yountville, CA 94599
Tasting: 10–6 daily
Tasting Fee: $15
Tours: 11, 1, 3 and 5 daily
Tour Fee: $7–$30
Special Features: Restaurant

The turning point for California sparkling wine came in 1973, when Moët Hennessy built this ultramodern winery in the hills west of Yountville. If that famed French Champagne house believed in Napa's potential, then California winemaking had definitely come of age. Thus began the rush of European sparkling-wine firms to northern California.

Driving along Highway 29, you'd hardly notice the glass-and-native-stone bunker built into an oak-covered knoll. Inside is a museum with artifacts and explanations of *méthode champenoise*, the classic French process of making bubbly. The tour is thorough and takes visitors past the mechanized riddling racks, the bottling line, and so forth.

Domaine Chandon makes a variety of sparkling wines, from a round and refreshing brut to the expensive and intense Etoile. Most are available by the glass in the stylish tasting salon, where on warm days you can sit on the sun-drenched terrace. The restaurant is considered one of Napa Valley's best (see chapter 5, Restaurants & Food Purveyors.)

PINE RIDGE WINERY

707-253-7500, 800-575-9777
www.pineridgewine.com.
5901 Silverado Tr., Napa, CA 94558
Tasting: 10:30–4 daily
Tasting Fee: $15–$435
Tours: 10, 12, and 2, or by appointment
Tour Fee: $25
Special Features: Picnic area, cave tour

Pine Ridge is an unassuming winery sequestered among the hills along Silverado Trail. From the tasting room, take your glass onto the patio or explore the shady grounds. The tour begins in the vineyard and treks through the aging caves, where samples from oak barrels are offered on some tours. The winery's cabernet sauvignon is rich and focused.

ROBERT SINSKEY VINEYARDS

707-944-9090, 800-869-2030
www.robertsinskey.com
6320 Silverado Tr., Napa, CA 94558
Tasting: 10–4:30 daily
Tasting Fee: $20
Tours: By appointment
Tour Fee: $30–$40
Special Features: Cave tour

On a rise overlooking Silverado Trail, this winery blends a modern design with the warmth of stone and redwood. The ceiling of the tasting room stretches 35-feet high, wisteria entwines courtyard columns, and through a huge glass window you can get a good view of the winery at work. There are a number of tours offered, but visitors generally get an extensive trip through the cave dug into the hillside behind the winery as well as a hike through the winery's culinary garden. The pinot noir is among of the best in Napa.

SHAFER VINEYARDS

707-944-2877
www.shafervineyards.com
6154 Silverado Tr., Napa, CA 94558
Tasting: Mon.–Fri. by appointment
Tours: Mon.–Fri. by appointment
Tasting and Tour Fee: $35
Special Features: Cave tour

Dynamite is not often required to plant vineyards, but back in 1972, John Shafer was convinced that hillsides were the best place to grow cabernet sauvignon. Mountain vineyards may be the rage now, but they weren't then. The soil is shallow on the hills below the Stag's Leap palisades, so dynamite was required to terrace the vineyards. The vines struggle against the bedrock to find water and nourishment, and these stressed and scrawny vines produce intense wines.

Shafer's winery is a classic California ranch. The tasting room opens through French doors onto a second-floor veranda with an expansive view of lower Napa Valley. Under the vine-covered hill behind the winery is an 8,000-square-foot cave, carved out of solid rock. The cave—cool and immaculately clean—is the high point of the tour.

Shafer's top cabernet sauvignon is the Hillside Select, and it's typically brawny. The Stag's Leap District cab is usually blended with merlot, which makes it softer. Merlot is also bottled separately, along with chardonnay.

SILVERADO VINEYARDS

707-259-6611, 800-997-1770
www.silveradovineyards.com
6121 Silverado Tr., Napa, CA 94558
Tasting: 10:–4:30 daily
Tasting Fee: $10–$15
Tours: 10:30 and 2:30 daily by appointment
Tour Fee: $15

Built by the Walt Disney family in 1981, Silverado offers a dramatic view from its perch atop a Silverado Trail knoll. Sadly the wines have gone through a slump in recent vintages and the cabernet sauvignon, sauvignon blanc, and chardonnay are but pale examples of what this winery was once capable of producing. Still, the tasting den is a welcoming spot, with a high-pitched, raftered ceiling and plenty of seats outside to enjoy the landscape.

STAG'S LEAP WINE CELLARS

707-261-6422
www.stagsleapwinecellars.com
5766 Silverado Tr., Napa, CA 94558

Tasting: 10–4:30 daily
Tasting Fee: $15–$40
Tours: By appointment
Tour Fee: $40

Stag's Leap Wine Cellars falls into the select pilgrimage category. In 1976 it achieved instant fame when its 1973 cabernet won the famous Paris tasting, which changed the way the world looked at California wine. Hidden within an oak grove, Stag's Leap is an ever-growing village of buildings. Founded by the Winiarski family in 1972, the winery has an unassuming charm, despite its fame. The tasting room is merely a table tucked among towering wooden casks in one of the aging cellars.

A handful of wines are offered for tasting every day and, regrettably, the quality of the wines has been declining somewhat in recent years. Don't expect to sample the winery's premier bottling Cask 23. The winery was purchased in late 2007 by Washington-based Ste. Michelle Estate and Italian vintner Piero Antinori, so expect changes in the future.

OAKVILLE & RUTHERFORD
BEAULIEU VINEYARD
707-967-5230, 800-264-6918
www.bvwines.com
1960 St. Helena Hwy., Rutherford, CA 94573
Tasting: 10–5 daily
Tasting Fee: $5–$25
Tours: By appointment
Special Features: Gifts

If you could sum up the early history of Napa Valley winemaking with a single bottle of wine, it would be the Georges de Latour Private Reserve cabernet sauvignon by Beaulieu. Though no longer the best cabernet in the valley, it has been the yardstick against which all other cabernets have been measured.

Pronounced bowl-YOU and called BV for short, Beaulieu is one of Napa's most distinguished wineries, dating back to 1900, when Frenchman Georges de Latour began making wine. In 1938 Latour hired a young Russian immigrant, Andre Tchelistcheff, who went on to revolutionize California cabernet. Today, though, Beaulieu struggles to maintain that rich tradition.

Built of brick and covered with ivy, the winery isn't particularly impressive, but a tour can be an eye-opener, particularly when it passes the forest of towering redwood tanks. A video in the visitors center briefs guests on Beaulieu's past and present. Three or four wines are offered; sip as you browse through the museum of old bottles and memorabilia.

CAKEBREAD CELLARS
707-963-5221, 800-588-0298
www.cakebread.com
8300 St. Helena Hwy., Rutherford, CA 94573
Tasting: By appointment
Tasting Fee: $10–$20
Tours: By appointment

The Cakebread clan runs this winery set in prime cabernet sauvignon territory. Jack and Dolores Cakebread began making wine in 1973 and have won a loyal following. This striking winery looks like a modern rethinking of a historical California barn and is surrounded by gardens and vineyards. While you're in the tasting room, try the melony sauvignon blanc—one of the best. Cakebread's cabernet sauvignons and chardonnay, lean and crisp on release, bloom after a few years.

CAYMUS VINEYARDS
707-967-3010
www.caymus.com
8700 Conn Creek Rd., Rutherford, CA 94573
Tasting: 10–4 daily by appointment
Tasting Fee: $25
Tours: No

No American wine is more highly regarded than the Caymus Special Selection cabernet sauvignon. Okay, you could argue in favor of cabernets by Screaming Eagle or Harlen Estate, but few wines make the annual "best of" lists of critics and wine lovers as often as Caymus SS. At release, people crowd the winery for the honor of paying $130 a bottle.

Caymus remains a low-frills family outfit and tampers little with its wines. The main 40-acre vineyard lies east of the Napa River, in the heart of Napa Valley's cabernet country a blessed location. The tasting room is in a modern winery made of sturdy fieldstone. Wines are poured at a seated tasting, and in addition to the cabernets, the winery samples its zinfandel and sauvignon blanc, sold only at the winery.

CHAPPELLET WINERY

707-963-7136, 800-4-WINERY
www.chappellet.com
1581 Sage Canyon Rd., St. Helena, CA 94574
Tasting and Tours: By appointment
Tasting and Tour Fee: $15

Styled like a pyramid, this winery would make a striking statement along Highway 29. Instead, it's hidden among the rustic hills east of the valley. Built in the late 1960s by Donn and Molly Chappellet, the winery was only the second to open in the county after Prohibition. The vineyards are steeply terraced and produce a firm cabernet sauvignon as well as something called Old Vine Cuvée, a classic white blend made mostly from chenin blanc.

FRANCISCAN OAKVILLE ESTATE

707-963-7111, 800-529-9463
www.franciscan.com
1178 Galleron Rd., Rutherford, CA 94574
Tasting: 10–5 daily
Tasting Fee: $10–$30
Tours: Limited, by appointment
Special Features: Gifts

Franciscan used to be one of our favorite stops along Highway 29, but the wines just haven't inspired us as they used to. Icon Estates, the wine giant that owns Franciscan, has expanded production of the cabernet sauvignon, merlot, and chardonnay—and it shows. Still, the visitors center is big and roomy and sets a classy tone, and you can also taste the burly cabernets from sister winery, Mount Veeder.

FROG'S LEAP WINERY

707-963-4704, 800-959-4704
www.frogsleap.com
8815 Conn Creek Rd., Rutherford, CA 94573
Tasting: By appointment
Tasting Fee: None
Tours: By appointment
Special Features: Retail, 10–4 Mon.–Sat.

It's rare to find a winery with a sense of humor as well oiled as Frog's Leap. Printed on every cork is the word *ribbit,* and the weather vane atop the winery sports a leaping frog. The name, a takeoff on Stag's Leap Wine Cellars, was inspired by the winery's original site, an old St. Helena frog farm. Founders Larry Turley and John Williams parted ways in 1994, and Williams moved Frog's Leap south and restored a winery that dates to 1884. All five wines—cabernet sauvignon, zinfandel, merlot, chardonnay, and sauvignon blanc—are reliable and often superb. Tasting takes place in the vineyard house behind the winery.

GRGICH HILLS CELLARS

707-963-2784, 800-532-3057
www.grgich.com
1829 St. Helena Hwy., Rutherford, CA 94573
Tasting: 9:30–4:30 daily
Tasting Fee: $10
Tours: 11 and 2 daily by appointment
Tour fee: $15

French wine lovers worship the land, but in California, the winemaker is king. Cult followings have a way of developing—as with Mike Grgich, one of Napa Valley's best-known characters. The scrappy immigrant from the former Yugoslavia became a star in 1976 when, as winemaker at Chateau Montelena, his 1973 chardonnay beat Burgundy's best whites in the famous Paris tasting. Later, Grgich joined with Austin Hills and opened this winery.

An ivy-covered stucco building with a red-tiled roof, Grgich's winery remains a house devoted to chardonnay. Elegant and rich, it's consistently among the finest in California. Grgich also makes a graceful fumé blanc and has considerable luck with zinfandel and cabernet sauvignon. All this can be sampled in Grgich's modest tasting room, where the smells of oak and wine float in from the barrel-aging room nearby. You might see a feisty old fellow with a black beret—that's Grgich.

GROTH VINEYARDS AND WINERY

707-754-4254
www.grothwines.com
750 Oakville Cross Rd., Oakville, CA 94562
Tasting: 10–4 Mon.–Sat. by appointment
Tasting Fee: $10
Tours: 11 and 2 Mon.–Fri., 11 Sat.

This California Mission-style winery is a grand sight along the Oakville Cross Road. It's also home to a top-notch cabernet sauvignon, the Groth Reserve. A former

Mumm Napa Valley Winery in Rutherford specializes in sparkling wine. Courtesy Mumm Napa Valley Winery

executive with Atari—the hallway near the barrel room is lined with video games—Dennis Groth began making wine in 1982, and his graceful winery was completed a few years later.

The tour is enlightening, beginning on a terrace that overlooks the vineyards, continuing past the bottling line and the cavernous barrel-aging room, and ending at the tasting bar. Groth cabernets typically have a lush elegance married to a firm backbone.

MINER FAMILY VINEYARDS

707-945-1270, 800-366-9463
www.minerwines.com
7850 Silverado Tr., Oakville, 94562
Tasting: 11–5 daily
Tasting Fee: $10
Tours: By appointment

Miner is making some impressive cabernet sauvignons and zinfandels. David Miner, a former software salesman, purchased a 60-acre vineyard high above the valley in 1989. A winery, situated above Silverado Trail, is a smart-looking edifice, done in a rich golden hues and a modern, Mediterranean style. The tasting room, sleek in its polished-wood tones, offers a grand view of the valley. Visitors can watch the winery in action through wide windows that overlook the barrel and fermentation rooms.

MUMM NAPA VALLEY

707-967-7770, 800-MUM-NAPA
www.mummnapa.com
8445 Silverado Tr., Rutherford, CA 94573
Tasting: 10–5 daily
Tasting Fee: $5–$20
Tours: On the hour, 10–3 daily
Special Features: Patio, gifts

Mumm Napa Valley may have a French pedigree, but it's a California child through and through. The winery is a long, low ranch barn with redwood siding and a green slate roof. Mumm blends traditional French

méthode champenoise with the distinctive fruit of Napa Valley, and the result is some of California's best sparkling wines.

The winery tour offers a detailed look at the French way of making sparkling wine. Guides first lead you inside a football field of a room housing giant tanks in which the grape juice is fermented. Then they continue through long hallways, allowing gallery views of the winemaker's lab, bottling plant, aging cellars, and so on.

Brut Prestige is the main release, a snappy blend of pinot noir and chardonnay, and Blanc de Noirs is a zesty rosé. The salon is *quaint* and country, with sliding glass doors that allow easy views of the Rutherford countryside. There's also an outdoor patio when the day's weather begs a seat in the sun.

Visiting the tasting room at Nickel & Nickel is like stepping back in time. Tim Fish

NICKEL & NICKEL

707-967-9600
www.nickelandnickel.com
8164 St. Helena Highway, Oakville, CA 94562
Tasting: 10–3 Mon.–Fri., 10–2 Sat.
Tours: By appointment
Tasting and Tour Fee: $40

Nickel & Nickel was established by the partners of Far Niente, and the winery opened in July 2003. The idea was to produce 100 percent single-vineyard wines that best express the personality of each vineyard and varietal. Visiting the tasting room is like stepping back in time. It's housed in a building that dates back to 1882. Nickel & Nickel produces high-end chardonnay, merlot, syrah, cabernet, and zinfandel, but it's best known for cab—and these cabs, in the $65 to $125 range, are typically well worth the price.

OPUS ONE

707-944-9442
www.opusonewinery.com
7900 St. Helena Hwy., Oakville, CA 94562
Tasting: 10–4 daily
Tasting Fee: $25
Tours: 10:30 daily by appointment
Tour Fee: $30, includes tasting

A joint venture between Robert Mondavi and France's Chateau Mouton-Rothschild, Opus One is an elegant temple, a cross between a Mayan palace and *Battlestar Galactica*. With the $1.36-billion buyout of the Robert Mondavi Winery by Constellation Brands of New York, insiders suspect Mouton-Rothschild may buy Mondavi's stake and take sole ownership.

Designed by the firm that created San Francisco's Transamerica Pyramid, the winery opened in 1991 but was largely inaccessible to the public until 1994. Built of Texas limestone and untreated redwood, the building is partially buried by an earthen berm. The courtyard entrance is a circular colonnade, and above is an open-air pavilion that looks out over a sea of vines. The interior blends classic French antiquity with warm California hues.

It's apropos that the winery makes a vivid architectural statement. Opus One has been one of Napa Valley's highest-profile wines since its first vintage in 1979.

The wine—a blend of cabernet sauvignon, cabernet franc, and merlot—is a classic: rich, oaky, and elegant. As the tour reveals, few wineries treat their grapes and juice as delicately as Opus One. Arriving in small bins, grapes are sorted by hand—an arduous task—and the juice flows by gravity, not by pump, to the tank room below. The system is advanced in its simplicity. The tasting room fee is extravagant (what do you expect for a $160 bottle of wine?), but the pour is generous.

PEJU PROVINCE

707-963-3600, 800-446-7358
www.peju.com
8466 St. Helena Hwy., Rutherford, CA 94573
Tasting: 10–6 daily
Tasting Fee: $10
Tours: Self-guided
Special Features: Garden, sculpture collection

The grounds of this family-owned estate are lovely. There's good reason: Tony Peju ran a nursery in Los Angeles before coming north in the early 1980s. A row of beautiful sycamores leads to the French provincial winery, which is enveloped in white roses and other flowers. There is also a fine collection of marble sculptures. The tour doesn't take long; it's a small place. Cabernet sauvignon and chardonnay are the specialties.

PLUMPJACK WINERY

707-945-1220
www.plumpjack.com
620 Oakville Cross Rd., Oakville, CA 94562.
Tasting: 10–4 daily
Tasting Fee: $10
Tours: No

PlumpJack, founded by San Francisco mayor Gavin Newsom, is named for the roguish spirit of Shakespeare's Sir John Falstaff. In the mid-1990s the company bought a century-old

Napa Valley vineyard property renowned for producing cabernet of exceptional quality. Cabernet is still PlumpJack's flagship wine. The tasting room has Shakespearean whimsical touches, an uneven wavering fence outside, and iron decanters filled with flowers inside.

PROVENANCE VINEYARDS
707-968-3633
www.provenancevineyards.com
695 St. Helena Hwy., Rutherford, CA 94573
Tasting: 10:30–5:30 daily
Tasting Fee: $10–$20
Tours: No

Provenance Vineyards makes appealing cabernet and merlot, and it gets particularly high marks for the latter. It's no wonder: Winemaker Tom Rinaldi cut his teeth at Duckhorn Vineyards as founding winemaker, and he spent 22 vintages at the winery that exemplifies the best in merlot. Ironically, Rinaldi wanted to be a veterinarian, but because he worked with so many dissatisfied doctors who wanted to be winemakers, he opted for the latter. The modern-looking winery has a tasting room that's known for its French and American oak flooring constructed from strips of barrels—quite a conversation piece at the horseshoe-shaped tasting bar.

QUINTESSA
707 967-1601
www.quintessa.com
1601 Silverado Trail, Rutherford, CA 94573
Tasting and Tours: By appointment
Tasting Fee: $35

This winery is somehow both inconspicuous and dramatically styled. Arching like a crescent moon from a wooded knoll in Rutherford, most of the winery is underground. The facade is rugged stone, and inside is a state-of-the-art, gravity-flow winery in which the grapes arrive on the roof and end up as wine in oak barrels in the underground cellar. On the rolling hills surrounding the winery are 170 acres of vineyards, mostly cabernet, and owners Valeria and Agustin Huneeus produce just one wine: Quintessa, the elegant red Bordeaux-style blend.

ROBERT MONDAVI WINERY
888-RMONDAVI
www.robertmondaviwinery.com
7801 St. Helena Hwy., Oakville, CA 94562
Tasting: 10–5 daily
Tasting Fee: $15–$45
Tours: 10–4 daily, several types offered
Tour Fee: $25–$60
Special Features: Art gallery, gifts

We never thought we'd see it in our lifetime: Robert Mondavi without a winery. Of course, Mondavi began to loosen his grip when the winery went public in 1993, but he and his family lost ownership interest with the $1.36-billion buyout by Constellation Brands of New York.

Robert Mondavi, now in his 90s, has been such an innovator, such a symbol of the "new" Napa Valley, that it's hard to believe he founded his winery in 1966. Once too flamboyant for conservative Napa County, the Spanish Mission-style winery now seems as natural as the Mayacamas Mountains. Since first setting out on his own from family-owned Charles Krug, Mondavi has been the most outspoken advocate for California and its wines.

Few Napa wineries are busier on a summer day than Mondavi, which offers one of the most thorough tours in the valley. Several different tours are offered, from a general trip through the winery to an advanced wine-growing tour. The basic tour leads visitors into the vineyards for a lecture on how grapes are grown and harvested, then to the grape presses and a view of all the latest wine wizardry. The tour ends in the tasting room, where a selection of wines is offered, along with a mini-course on tasting wine.

Learn about wine and olive oil at Round Pond Winery in Rutherford. Courtesy Round Pond Winery

Mondavi bottles one of the most extensive lists of wines in the valley. Reds seem to be the winery's strong suit. The reserve cabernet sauvignons and pinot noirs become more magnificent every year—and so do the prices. Of course, the regular bottlings are hardly slackers.

ROUND POND WINERY

707-302-2575
www.roundpond.com
875 Rutherford Rd., Rutherford, CA 94573
Tasting: 11–4 Thurs.–Mon.
Tasting fee: $25–$35
Tours: By appointment
Special Features: Olive oil press, luncheons by appointment

The MacDonnell family has been selling cabernet sauvignon to the likes of Beaulieu and Franciscan for two decades and today owns more than 400 acres in the Rutherford area. A few years ago they decided to build their own winery and start making wine. The early results are promising: The cabernets are polished yet concentrated. The winery is a showplace and there are a number of tastings and tours available, including an exploration of the olive oil press.

RUBICON ESTATE

707-968-1161
www.rubiconestate.com
1991 St. Helena Hwy., Rutherford, CA 94573
Tasting: 10–5 daily
Entrance Fee: $25; includes basic tour, tasting, and valet parking
Tours: 10:30–3:30 daily; basic tours on the half hour
Special Tour Fee: $15–$50, in addition to entrance fee; appointment required
Special Features: Wine history museum, gifts

Francis Ford Coppola, famed director of *The Godfather* series of films and *Apocalypse Now*, rescued the Inglenook chateau from potential oblivion in the mid 1990s and lovingly restored the chateau, the romantic ideal of what a Napa Valley winery should look like: a sturdy stone castle, shrouded in ivy and enveloped by vineyards. Visitors approach the winery through a long, tree-lined driveway.

Coppola's affections for Inglenook date to the mid-1970s, when he bought the former home of Inglenook's founder, Gustave Niebaum, which is next to the winery. Coppola released his own wine, Rubicon, a stout yet elegant Bordeaux-style blend, beginning with the 1978 vintage. The history of the chateau is on display inside. Scottish for "cozy corner," Inglenook originated in 1880 when Niebaum, a Finnish sea captain, came to Rutherford and spent some of the fortune he made in the fur trade on building this towering Gothic structure. Coppola's movie memorabilia, formerly on display at Rubicon, is finding a new home at his latest winery addition: Rosso & Bianco in Sonoma County.

RUDD WINERY AND VINEYARDS

707-944-8577
www.ruddwines.com
500 Oakville Cross Rd., Oakville, CA 94562
Tasting and Tours: Tues.–Sat. by appointment
Tasting and Tour Fee: two tours–$35 and $60
Special features: Cave tour

Leslie Rudd knows a thing or two about luxury. He owns upscale retailer Dean & DeLuca, several restaurants around the country, and even a high-end gin distillery. In the mid-1990s Rudd came to Napa and transformed an underperforming winery into a showpiece. He replanted the vines on the 55-acre estate and created a stone winery with a 22,000-square-foot cave. Cabernet is the star attraction and the wines are powerful and polished. The tour is an extensive affair, offering a thorough overview of Rudd and ending with a seated tasting.

RUTHERFORD HILL WINERY

707-963-1871, 800-637-5681
www.rutherfordhill.com
200 Rutherford Hill Rd., Rutherford, CA 94573
Tasting: 10–5 daily
Tasting Fee: $10
Tours: 11:30, 1:30, and 3:30 daily
Tour Fee: $15, including tasting
Special Features: Picnic area, gifts, cave tour

The winery here is a mammoth barn, albeit a stylishly realized barn covered in cedar and perched on the hills overlooking Rutherford. Carved into the hillside behind are among the largest man-made aging caves in California, snaking a half mile into the rock. The titanic cave doors are framed by geometric latticework that recalls the work of Frank Lloyd Wright. A trek through the cool and humid caves is the tour highlight. Merlot is the star here, and it's typically fleshy with a tannic backbone.

ST. SUPÉRY VINEYARDS AND WINERY

707-963-4507, 800-942-0809
www.stsupery.com
8440 St. Helena Hwy., Rutherford, CA 94573
Tasting: 10–5:30 daily May–Oct., 10–5 daily Nov.–Apr.
Tasting Fee: $15–$20
Tours: Guided and self-guided
Tour Fee: $20 for guided, by appointment
Special Features: Interactive wine museum, gifts

Wineries, on the whole, aren't the best places to take kids. St. Supéry is the exception. It adds a touch of science-museum adventure, with colorful displays, hands-on activities, and modern winery gadgetry.

St. Supéry was established in 1982, when French businessman Robert Skalli bought Edward St. Supéry's old vineyard and built a state-of-the-art winery next door to St. Supéry's original Queen Anne Victorian. A second-floor gallery shows off the day-to-day activities. Windows reveal the bottling line, the barrel-aging room,

and the like. A highlight is the "smell station," where noses are educated on the nuances of cabernet sauvignon and sauvignon blanc. Ever hear cabernet described as cedar or black cherry? Hold your nose to a plastic tube, and smell what these descriptions mean. Another display gives you a peek under the soil to see the roots of a grapevine. St. Supéry offers a solid cabernet sauvignon and an exceptional sauvignon blanc, among other wines.

SEQUOIA GROVE WINERY

707-944-2945, 800-851-7841
www.sequoiagrove.com
8338 St. Helena Hwy., Napa, CA 94558
Tasting: 10:30–5 daily
Tasting Fee: $10–$15
Tours: 12 and 2 daily
Tour Fee: $30

Dwarfed by century-old sequoia trees, this winery is easy to overlook along Highway 29, but the cabernet sauvignons are worth the stop. Wine was made in the redwood barn before Prohibition, but the wine and the winery had been long forgotten when the Allen family began making wine here again in 1980. Samples are offered from a small table in a corner of the winery, surrounded by giant puncheons, or upright wooden casks. The chardonnay is solid, but the regular and reserve cabernets can achieve greatness.

SILVER OAK CELLARS

707-944-8808, 800-273-8809
www.silveroak.com
915 Oakville Cross Rd., Oakville, CA 94562
Tasting: 9–4 Mon.–Sat
Tasting Fee: $10
Tours: By appointment

Not many wineries can live off one wine, but then Silver Oak isn't just any winery. Here, cabernet sauvignon has been raised to an art form. Low-profile by Napa Valley standards, Silver Oak is known to cabernet lovers around the country, and that's all that

Grapes ripen on the vine. Tim Fish

matters. The Alexander Valley cabernet is typically more accessible than the Napa Valley bottling, but both are velvety and opulent and done in a distinct California style. Silver Oak was established in 1972 on the site of an old Oakville dairy. A fire destroyed much of the original cellar in 2006 and the winery is rebuilding from scratch, hoping to pay tribute to the past while looking toward the future.

SWANSON VINEYARDS

707-967-3504
www.swansonvineyards.com
1271 Manley Ln., Rutherford, CA 94573
Tasting: Wed.–Sun. by appointment
Tasting Fee: $25–$55
Tours: No

The Swanson family moved to Napa Valley after Clarke Swanson realized that wine had

more allure than banking and journalism. The winery produces a cabernet blend, merlot, and pinot grigio. The syrah is great, but it's not produced every year, and when it is, it's made in small batches. On the upside, there's a great supply of Alexis, the cab blend, so keep your eye out for that. The tasting room is extravagant, inspired by the sumptuous salons of 18th-century Paris.

TURNBULL WINE CELLARS

707-963-5839, 800-887-6285
www.turnbullwines.com
8210 St. Helena Hwy., Oakville, CA 94562
Tasting: 10–4:30 daily
Tasting Fee: $10
Tours: By appointment

This small, redwood winery in the heart of cabernet sauvignon territory was designed by award-winning architect William Turnbull, a former partner in the winery, which originated in 1979. The cabernet is known for its distinct minty quality.

ZD WINES
707-963-5188, 800-487-7757
www.zdwines.com
8383 Silverado Tr., Napa, CA 94558
Tasting: 10–4:30 daily
Tasting Fee: $10–$15
Tours: By appointment

Chardonnay, pinot noir, cabernet sauvignon: ZD has a way with all three. The winery began life in 1969 in Sonoma Valley and transplanted to Napa 10 years later. Crowned with a roof of red tile, the winery was expanded a few years back by the de Leuze family. The star is chardonnay, an opulent beauty, while cabernets are dense and powerful. The pinots are light but intensely fruity.

St. Helena
ANDERSON'S CONN VALLEY VINEYARDS
800-946-3497
www.connvalleyvineyards.com
680 Rossi Rd., St. Helena, CA 94574
Tasting and Tours: By appointment
Tasting Fee: None

A small winery in the foothills east of the valley, it's well off the beaten path, but its cabernet sauvignon is already one of Napa's rising stars. The 1987 vintage was the first for the Anderson family, and their cabernet is intense yet elegant. The Andersons are down-to-earth folks who welcome serious cab fans, although this isn't an extravagant venture, and refreshingly so.

BERINGER VINEYARDS
707-963-8989, ext. 2222
www.beringer.com.
2000 Main St., St. Helena, CA 94574
Tasting: 10–5 daily
Tours: 10:45, 1:30, 2:00 daily for basic tour;

others by appointment
Tasting and Tour Fee: $5–$35
Special Features: Gifts

There's something almost regal about the Rhine House, the circa-1874 mansion that forms the centerpiece of Beringer Vineyards. Sitting amid manicured lawns and meticulously restored, the Rhine House suggests that Beringer doesn't take lightly its past or its reputation.

This is one of the few wineries that has it all. A prime tourist attraction with a historical tour, it's also one of Napa's most popular makers of cabernet sauvignon and chardonnay. The oldest continually operated winery in Napa Valley, Beringer was founded by German immigrants Jacob and Frederick Beringer. The tour offers a few juicy details about the early days.

For a quick taste of wine, go past the Rhine House and up the walk to the Old Bottling Room, where you can take in vino and history. The room is decorated with artifacts such as a photo of Clark Gable visiting and a dusty bottle of sacramental wine produced during Prohibition. To taste Beringer's top wines, climb the staircase of the Rhine House to the reserve tasting room. The reserve cabernet is stunning. Of course, there's an additional fee.

Beringer offers a number of winery tours, ranging from history lessons to wine and food pairings. The general tour takes visitors through the original aging cellar, a stone-and-timber building built by Chinese laborers. If you want to see a working winery, though, you'll be disappointed. The real action takes place across Highway 29, and it isn't open to the public.

BUEHLER VINEYARDS
707-963-2155
www.buehlervineyards.com
820 Greenfield Rd., St. Helena, CA 94574
Tasting and Tours: 10–4 Mon.–Fri. by appointment
Tasting Fee: None

"We're not at the end of the world," John Buehler Jr. likes to say, "but you can see it from here." The winery, a complex of handsome, Mediterranean buildings, is not that remote, although it is secluded above the rocky hills that overlook Lake Hennessey. The bread and butter here is zinfandel, both a ripe and tannic red and a dry white. Buehler, in fact, makes one of Napa's best white zinfandels. The cabernet sauvignon is rather inconsistent.

BURGESS CELLARS

707-963-4766, 800-752-9463
www.burgesscellars.com
1108 Deer Park Rd., St. Helena, CA 94574
Tasting and Tours: 10–4 daily by appointment
Tasting Fee: None

Built atop the vestiges of a stone winery that dates to the 1880s, Burgess has a low profile and likes it that way. High on the western slopes of Howell Mountain, the two-story, stone-and-redwood winery is not one that tourists happen upon. Tom Burgess began it in 1972 and built a reputation for cabernet and merlot.

CHARLES KRUG WINERY

707-963-5057, 888-747-5784
www.charleskrug.com
2800 Main St., St. Helena, CA 94574
Tasting: 10:30–5 daily
Tasting Fee: $10–$20
Tours: No.
Special Features: Picnic area

After working under Agoston Haraszthy in Sonoma, Charles Krug built Napa Valley's first winery in 1861. This massive stone winery was gutted by fire the day after it was finished, but Krug rebuilt. When the Mondavi family bought Krug in 1943, another Napa dynasty began. Robert Mondavi began his own winery in 1966 after a family feud.

In disrepair for many years, the historic winery building has recently regained much of its former glory. The winemaking now takes place in a facility just behind the first site. The tour is one of the most thorough and educational in the valley, leading visitors into the vineyards and through the winery. Beginning wine tasters are put at ease here. The winery bottles one of the valley's most exhaustive wine menus, and its cabernet sauvignons have recently regained their former stature.

CORISON WINERY

707-963-0826
www.corison.com
987 Hwy. 29, St. Helena, CA 94574
Tasting: 10–5 daily by appointment
Tasting Fee: $10–$25
Tours: By appointment

Corison Winery was built in 1999, but like many Napa Valley success stories, the label dates back further—in this case to 1987. Winemaker Cathy Corison is a pioneer, among the first women winemakers in the valley. She's been making wine for close to 30 years, and her background includes a decade as winemaker for Chappellet Vineyards. At Corison the specialty is cabernet, and stylistically they're complex yet elegant. The winery resembles a 19th-century barn with gables, and the modest tasting room is in the middle of the cellar, with temperatures ranging from 55 degrees to a high of 70 degrees—quaint and chilly.

DUCKHORN VINEYARDS

888-354-8885
www.duckhornvineyards.com
1000 Lodi Ln., St. Helena, CA 94574
Tasting: 10–4 daily
Tasting Fee: $20
Tours: One daily by appointment
Tour Fee: $30, includes tasting

Duckhorn has long reigned as the king of merlot in Napa and the winery's cabernet sauvignon and sauvignon blanc are first-rate as well. The tasting room, set in the majestic

Corison Winery is a well-regarded cabernet producer in St. Helena. Courtesy Corison Winery

estate house, is a chic den with a fireplace, done with polished wood and granite. Since its first release in 1978, Duckhorn has been a major presence on restaurant wine lists around the country. In late 2007, the winery was purchased by an investment firm, so big changes could be in store.

FLORA SPRINGS WINE COMPANY

707-967-8032
www.florasprings.com
Tasting Room: 677 St. Helena Hwy., St. Helena, CA 94574

Tasting: 10–5 daily
Tasting Fee: $5–$12
Tours: By appointment
Tour Fee: $20

This tasting room on the heavy tourist path of Highway 29 is a comfortable space, decorated with humorous murals, and there's a garden in the back where you can sip from a glass on a sunny day. The winery itself on Zinfandel Lane is a handsome stone edifice that dates to 1888, and current owners Jerome and Flora Komes arrived in 1977. After some shaky years, the wines are coming into their own, with a lineup that includes several solid chardonnays, an exotic sauvignon blanc named Soliloquy, and an intriguing red blend dubbed Trilogy.

FREEMARK ABBEY WINERY

707-963-9694, 800-963-9698
www.freemarkabbey.com
3022 St. Helena Hwy., St. Helena, CA 94574
Tasting: 10–5 daily
Tasting Fee: $10–$20
Tours: By appointment
Special Features: Picnic area, gifts

Freemark Abbey was a leader in the 1960s and 1970s, with its Bosche vineyard cabernet sauvignon. But the wine floundered in the '80s and early '90s and only recently regained some of its stature. An undisputed success is Edelwein Gold, a sweet Johannisberg Riesling that's one of California's top dessert wines. Winemaking on the site dates to 1886, when Josephine Tychson-likely the first woman to build a winery in California-constructed a wood winery. The present stone winery was built in 1895, and the tasting room is a lovely space with a wood-beamed ceiling.

HALL WINERY

707-967-2620, 866-667-4255
www.hallwines.com
401 St. Helena Hwy., St. Helena, CA 94574
Tasting: 10–5:30
Tasting Fee: $10–$15
Tours: 11, 1, and 3 by appointment
Tour Fee: $25

This tasting room offers a glimpse into the lives of Kathryn Walt Hall, former U.S. ambassador to Austria, and her husband, Craig Hall, a Texas businessman. They've made headlines in Wine Country with their $100-million Hall Winery project because of their fiercely unconventional architect, Frank Gehry. Some have argued that Gehry—known for dramatic, ultramodern buildings in metal and glass such as Guggenheim Bilbao in Bilbao, Spain, and the Walt Disney Concert Hall in Los Angeles—isn't a good fit for rural Napa Valley and will congest the area with curious tourists.

Wine Classes on the Run

If you consider learning an adventure, one great getaway is a two-to-five-day course at the Profesfftsional Wine Studies Program, which is held on the West Coast campus of the Culinary Institute of America in St. Helena. The program's faculty is the best and the brightest in Wine Country. Its director is Karen MacNeil, author of *The Wine Bible* and host of the new PBS show *Wine, Food & Friends with Karen MacNeil*, and heavyweight instructors include wine critic Robert Parker Jr., publisher of the *Wine Advocate*, and celebrity chef John Ash, award-winning cookbook author.

In addition to choice instructors, the program has state-of-the-art accommodations at the Rudd Center. Once the distillery of the old Christian Brothers winery, the remodeled center has two tasting theaters, an air-filtration system, spit sinks at each tasting area, and inset lighting. Each seat is also equipped with buttons so that a computer can quickly tally votes in blind tastings. Wine has never been so pampered!

To acquaint yourself with the in-depth course offerings, visit www.ciaprochef.com or call 800-888-7850.

The couple, who own Kathryn Hall Vineyards in Napa Valley and T-Bar-T Ranch in Sonoma County, began construction on the new winery in mid-2007 on a prime piece of Highway 29 real estate. As for the wines, Hal has had good success with cabernet sauvignon, merlot, and sauvignon blanc.

HEITZ WINE CELLARS

707-963-3542
www.heitzcellar.com
436 St. Helena Hwy. S., St. Helena, CA 94574
Tasting: 11–4:30 daily
Tasting Fee: None
Tours: By appointment

Driving along Highway 29, you'd never know that a redwood shack on the outskirts of St. Helena is home to one of Napa's historically collectible wines—but the wine faithful do, and they line up every year to buy Heitz Martha's Vineyard Cabernet Sauvignon.

Curmudgeon and maverick Joe Heitz worked at Beaulieu before going his own way in 1961. Within a few years, he'd refurbished a stone winery in the hills of the valley's east side, keeping the old winery on Highway 29 as a tasting room. Joe died in 2000, but the winery keeps plugging along. The modest tasting room features a library of old wines for sale, and typically two or three current wines are poured—though seldom the good stuff. Heitz also produces a chardonnay, and grignolino, a stout Italian varietal, has considerable charm.

JOSEPH PHELPS VINEYARDS

707-963-2745
www.jpvwines.com
200 Taplin Rd., St. Helena, CA 94574
Tasting: By appointment
Tasting Fee: $20–$30
Tours: No

This winery pioneered Bordeaux blends in California with its Insignia bottling, and it remains among the best of the breed. Bordeaux blends use the traditional grapes of that region: cabernet sauvignon, merlot, petit verdot, and the like. Phelps built his large and elegant redwood barn in 1973 and drew immediate attention. The current offerings include a toasty chardonnay and some of the best cabernets in Napa Valley. We're also fans of the winery's syrah and viognier, two lesser-known Rhone-style wines that merit a taste.

LONG MEADOW RANCH

707-963-4555
www.longmeadowranch.com
1775 Whitehall Lane, St. Helena, CA 94574
Tasting: Several types offered, by appointment
Tasting Fee: Varies
Tours: Several types offered, by appointment
Tour Fee: Varies
Special Features: Tours in all-terrain vehicles; tour of working ranch with olive orchards, olive press, wine caves, cattle and gardens

Long Meadow Ranch is not just a winery, it's an agricultural experience. Nestled on 650 acres atop the Mayacamas Mountains, the ranch has a history that dates to the 1870s. Today, it's owned by the Hall family, and they're devoted to organic farming and produce a little of everything: eggs, olive oil, grass-fed beef, organic produce and—of course—wine. Cabernet is the main selection, and it's a burly red that usually requires a few years in the cellar. The Halls offer and number of different tours, tastings, and excursions, some of them in Hummer-like all-terrain vehicles.

LOUIS M. MARTINI WINERY

707-968-3361, 800-321-WINE
www.louismartini.com
254 St. Helena Hwy. S. Helena, CA 94574
Tasting: 10–6 daily
Tasting Fee: $8–$15

The tasting room of Louis Martini Winery is a comfortable den. Tim Fish

Tours: By appointment.
Tour Fee: $30, includes tasting
Special Features: Picnic grounds

Run by the third generation of Martinis, but owned since 2002 by the wine behemoth E&J Gallo, this large but unostentatious winery is one of Napa Valley's best known. That's one of the charms of visiting Wine Country: You know the label; why not visit the source? Martini is one of the valley's great overachievers, producing a voluminous roster that runs from cabernet sauvignon to sherry and other dessert wines. They're all capable and good values. Its top cabernet, Monte Rosso, has recently regained much of its glory. Originating in Kingsburg, California, in 1922, Martini moved to St. Helena in 1933. Napa's first post-Prohibition success story, the winery flourished under founder Louis M. Martini, one the valley's great characters. Son Louis P. Martini brought the winery into the modern era.

MARKHAM WINERY

707-963-5292
www.markhamvineyards.com
2812 St. Helena Hwy. N., St. Helena, CA 94574
Tasting: 10–5 daily
Tasting Fee: $5–$15
Tours: No
Special Features: Art gallery, gifts

Founded in 1978, Markham quietly went about its business until the Japanese firm Sanraku took over in 1988. Since then, the wines have been on a roller coaster ride of quality. Once known for its elegant merlot, the winery has had more recent success with whites such as chardonnay and sauvignon blanc. Following a multimillion-dollar facelift in the early 1990s, the winery became a popular tourist attraction. Beyond large fountains out front is an expansive and affluent tasting room.

MERRYVALE VINEYARDS

707-963-7777
www.merryvale.com
1000 Main St., St. Helena, CA 94574
Tasting: 10–6:30 daily
Tasting Fee: $5–$20
Special Features: Gifts, gourmet foods

As Sunny St. Helena Winery, this historic stone cellar was the first winery built here after Prohibition, and in 1937 it was the Mondavi family's first venture in Napa Valley. It became home to Merryvale in 1985, when the building was renovated, updating its wine technology while retaining much of its historic charm. Done in rich wood, the tasting room feels like a large cabin, and behind the iron gates, you'll see the cask room with its massive 100-year-old cask. Profile, a cabernet blend that's the winery's flagship, is a wine to watch.

NEWTON VINEYARD

707-963-9000
www.newtonvineyard.com
2555 Madrona Ave., St. Helena, CA 94574
Tasting: 11 Thurs.–Mon. by appointment
Tours: 11 Thurs.–Mon. by appointment
Tasting and Tour Fee: $30
Special Features: Garden, cave tour

Perched high on Spring Mountain, this is one of the most spectacular wineries to visit in the valley, offering an eclectic mix of elaborate English gardens, Chinese red lanterns, and gates and vineyards carved into steeply terraced hillsides. A tank room sits at the bottom of a three-story pagoda; because of the building's shape, square tanks were required—which is highly unusual. Beneath all of this is an extensive cave system that extends several stories beneath the surface of the earth. As part of the tour, tastings are offered in a barrel-

aging corridor deep inside one cave. The merlot and chardonnays are worth a taste.

PHILIP TOGNI VINEYARD

707-963-3731
www.philiptognivineyard.com
3780 Spring Mountain Rd., St. Helena, CA 94574
Tasting and Tours: By appointment
Tasting Fee: None

Creating a name for himself as winemaker for Mayacamas, Chappellet, Chalone, and *Cuvaison*, Togni began making his own wine in 1983. His cabernet sauvignon is an assertive beauty that has a legion of fans. His sauvignon blanc is rather unusual, lean and too astringent for our tastes. Togni is a meticulous and hands-on winemaker, and the winery is a modest affair.

PRAGER WINERY AND PORT WORKS

707-963-7678, 800-969-7678
www.pragerport.com
1281 Lewelling Ln., St. Helena, CA 94574
Tasting: 10:30–4:30 daily
Tasting Fee: $10
Tours: By appointment

Bored with plain chocolate (cabernet sauvignon) and vanilla (chardonnay)? Try this small family winery that produces six styles of port, including two whites. Port is a slightly sweet wine fortified with brandy. Prager also makes small amounts of cabernet and zinfandel, and all the wines are organic. The winery is small, and the atmosphere is low key.

PRIDE MOUNTAIN VINEYARDS

707-963-4949
www.pridewines.com
4026 Spring Mountain Rd., St. Helena, CA 94574
Tasting and Tours: By appointment
Tasting fee: $5

Some 2,100 feet high on the crest of the Mayacamas Mountains, this estate straddles Napa and Sonoma counties. In fact, the county line is laid out on the crush pad so visitors can stand with one foot in each county. That image is appropriate because Pride Mountain has one foot in the past and the other in the cutting-edge present. Vines were planted at Pride Mountain as early as 1869 and the ruins of the old Summit Ranch winery built in 1890 are still there. The current winery may just be a modest wood-beam affair, but the wines produced inside are exceptional. Bob Foley is a true talent when it comes to cabernet sauvignon, merlot, and chardonnay.

SPOTTSWOODE WINERY

707-963-0134
www.spottswoode.com
1902 Madrona Ave., St. Helena, CA 94574
Tasting and Tours: 10 Tues. and Fri. by appointment
Tasting Fee: None

The first Spottswoode wines were made in 1982 in the basement of this estate's 1882 Victorian. Intense and impeccably balanced, Spottswoode's cabernet sauvignon was quickly regarded as among the best in the 1980s, a stature it still retains. The cabernet's success is nearly matched by the sauvignon blanc, a wine that's typically intense in citrus and mineral character. Run by the Novak family, Spottswoode is a small enterprise that welcomes devotees of fine cabernet.

ST. CLEMENT VINEYARDS

800-331-8266
www.stclement.com
2067 St. Helena Hwy. N., St. Helena, CA 94574
Tasting: 10–5 daily
Tasting Fee: $10–$25
Tours: 10:30 and 2:30 daily by appointment
Tour Fee: $20
Special Features: Picnic area

Built in 1878, St. Clement's exquisite Gothic Victorian was one of the earliest bonded wineries in the valley. Wine is no longer produced in the stone cellar; in 1979 a modern winery made of fieldstone was built in the hill behind the mansion, which now serves as a stately visitors center. The wide wooden porch offers a soothing view of the valley below, and wines are poured in a small parlor. It's so traditional and homespun, it's hard to fathom that St. Clement is owned by wine and beer giant Foster's. The winery has an excellent record with chardonnay and cabernet sauvignon.

SUTTER HOME WINERY

707-963-3104, 800-967-4663
www.sutterhome.com
277 St. Helena Hwy., St. Helena, CA 94574
Tasting: 10–5 daily
Tasting Fee: None
Tours: Self-guided, garden only

Who'd have thought back in the 1970s that a simple, sweet rosé would become the Holy Grail—some would say Unholy Grail—of California wine? Since white zinfandel became one of Wine Country's hottest commodities, Sutter Home has grown from one of Napa Valley's smallest wineries to one of its biggest.

Sutter Home's winery dates from 1874; since 1946 it has been owned and operated by Italian immigrant brothers John and Mario Trinchero. Until 1970, Sutter Home specialized in wine in bulk. Its motto was: If you can carry it or roll it through the front door, we'll fill it with wine. In 1972 winemaker Bob Trinchero began tinkering with a rosé-style zinfandel. Sutter Home called it white zinfandel, and it became one of the best-selling varieties in America. There's no tour here—the wine is made elsewhere—but Sutter Home's tasting room is an expansive space that doubles as a folksy museum of wine and Americana. Visitors should try the red zinfandel as well as the white; it's sturdy and tasty.

V. SATTUI WINERY

707-963-7774, 800-799-2337
www.vsattui.com
1111 White Ln., St. Helena, CA 94574
Tasting: 9–6 daily summer, 9–5 daily winter
Tasting Fee: None
Tours: Self-guided
Special Features: Deli, picnic area, gifts

Just about every winery has a picnic table
tucked somewhere, but V. Sattui is Lawn
Lunch Central. The tasting room doubles as a
deli shop. The front lawn is shaded by tall oaks
and filled with frolicking kids. Picnickers
won't find a heartier welcome in Napa Valley.

While some wineries prefer simply to
make wine and not deal with the public, V.
Sattui is just the opposite. Its wines are
available only at the winery. It's a busy
place, yet the atmosphere is cordial, not
frantic. Though completed only in 1985, the
Italian Romanesque winery looks like an
old monastery.

V. Sattui is named for Vittorio Sattui,
who founded a winery at a different location in 1885. It didn't survive Prohibition,
but Vittorio's great-grandson Daryl revived
the label in 1976. The winery produces
solid chardonnays and zinfandels, but for
good picnic wines, try the light and fruity
Johannisberg Riesling and Gamay Rouge.

WHITEHALL LANE WINERY

707-963-9454, 800-963-9454
www.whitehalllane.com
1563 St. Helena Hwy., St. Helena, CA 94574
Tasting: 11–5:45 daily
Tasting Fee: $5–$10
Tours: No

This handsomely modern winery, seemingly designed with geometric building
blocks, is on its third owner since it opened
in 1980 and has changed winemakers a
number of times, but now the Leonardini
family seems to have a firm hand on things.
The winery produces first-rate cabernet
sauvignon and merlot.

Calistoga
CASTELLO DI AMOROSA WINERY

707-967-6272
www.napavalleycastle.com
4045 St. Helena Hwy. N., St. Helena, CA
94574
Tasting: 9:30–6 daily Mar.–Nov., 9:30–5
daily Dec.–Feb.
Tasting and Tour Fees: $10–$40
Tours: Daily, by appointment

The wineries of Napa have often been called
"castles," but in the case of Castello di
Amorosa, it's true. Daryl Sattui, who owns
the tourist-friendly V. Sattui Winery, spent
14 years and $30 million building this
extravagant, 121,000-square-foot,
medieval style fortress. With 107 rooms on
eight levels, it even has towers, turrets, a
moat, and a dungeon! The tour is exhaustive but fascinating, rich with colorful fres-
cos and a barrel cellar with a dramatically
arched ceiling.

CHATEAU MONTELENA

707-942-5105
www.montelena.com
1429 Tubbs Ln., Calistoga, CA 94515
Tasting: 9:30–4 daily
Tasting Fee: $15–$25
Tours: Two daily by appointment
Tour Fee: $25

"Not bad for a kid from the sticks," was all Jim
Barrett said when Chateau Montelena jolted
the wine world by winning the legendary Paris
tasting in 1976. A Who's Who of French wine
cognoscenti selected Chateau Montelena's
1973 chardonnay in a blind tasting over the
best of Burgundy. Chateau Montelena's star has
been shining brightly ever since.

No serious wine lover would think of
leaving Chateau Montelena off the tour list.
The wines are first-rate, and the winery is
an elegant and secluded old estate at the
foot of Mount St. Helena. Alfred Tubbs
founded the original Chateau Montelena in
1882, and its French architect used the

V. Sattui Winery is as popular for picnicking as it is for its wines. Tim Fish

great chateaux of Bordeaux as inspiration. The approach isn't too impressive, but walk around to the true facade, and you'll discover a dramatic stone castle.

During Prohibition the winery fell into neglect, but in 1958, a Chinese immigrant, Yort Franks, created the Chinese-style Jade Lake and the surrounding garden. It's shaded by weeping willows, with swans and geese, walkways, islands, and brightly painted pavilions.

CLOS PEGASE

707-942-4981
www.clospegase.com
1060 Dunaweal Ln., Calistoga, CA 94515
Tasting: 10:30 5 daily
Tasting Fee: $10
Tours: 11:30 and 2 daily
Special Features: Art collection, cave tour

Clos Pegase is architecturally flamboyant, a postmodern throwback to the Babylonian temple—a shrine to the gods of art, wine,

Clos Pegase offers a treasury of art along with its wines. Tim Fish

and commerce. This commanding structure of tall pillars and archways, in hues of yellow and tan, is the work of noted Princeton architect Michael Graves.

The name Clos Pegase derives from Pegasus, the winged horse which, according to the Greeks, gave birth to art and wine. Owner Jan Shrem is an avid art collector. The tour offers a glimpse of the collection, including 17th- and 18th-century French statuary artfully displayed in the winery's massive underground cave. A casual browse through the visitors center reveals great treasures, with a sculpture garden featuring the works of Henry Moore, Richard Serra, Mark Di Suvero, and Anthony Caro. Pegase's wines include a ripe and complex cabernet sauvignon and a chardonnay that's typically refined but with plenty of forward fruit.

CUVAISON WINERY

707-942-6266
www.cuvaison.com
4550 Silverado Tr. N., Calistoga, CA 94515
Tasting: 10–5 daily
Tasting Fee: $10–$15
Tours: 10:30 and 11:30 daily
Tour Fee: $15
Special Features: Picnic area, gifts, cave tour

Cuvaison is a French term that describes the period in which the juice of grapes soaks with the skins and seeds to develop color and flavor. It's an appropriate name because Cuvaison's wines are often boldly flavored. Though the winery is in northern Napa, the grapes for its plush chardonnay come from Carneros vineyards in the south valley. Be sure to try the cabernet sauvignon and merlot as well. A white Mission-style building with a red-tiled roof, Cuvaison is bordered by vineyards and a splendid landscaped picnic area. The tasting room is busy but retains a friendly tone.

SCHRAMSBERG VINEYARDS

www.schramsberg.com

707-942-4558
1400 Schramsberg Rd., Calistoga, CA 94515
Tasting and Tours: 10, 11:30, 1, and 2:30 daily by appointment
Tasting and Tour Fee: $25
Special Features: Cave tour

No winery symbolizes the rebirth of Napa Valley better than Schramsberg. Jack and Jamie Davies were the quintessential post-Prohibition wine pioneers. When they bought the old Schramsberg estate in 1965, it was rich in history but near ruin. Jacob Schram had established Napa's first hillside vineyard and winery in 1862 and, with the help of Chinese laborers, built a network of underground cellars. After a few years of sweat equity, Jack and Jamie Davies became the country's premier producers of *méthode champenoise* sparkling wine, and they remain one of the finest to date. They're also making a Diamond Mountain cabernet called J. Davies that's worth trying.
The grounds of Schramsberg are lovely. The tour offers insight into the winery's history and the art of making bubbly, but it's rather a lecture at times. The highlight is the old cellar caves lined with walls of bottles.

STERLING VINEYARDS

707-942-3344, 800-726-6136
www.sterlingvineyards.com
1111 Dunaweal Ln., Calistoga, CA 94515
Tasting: 10:30–4:30 daily
Visitor Fee: $15 weekdays, $20 Sat. and Sun., $10 for ages 20 and younger
Tours: Self-guided
Special Features: Aerial tramway to winery

Sterling isn't just a winery, it's an experience. A modern white villa perched atop a tall knoll, it just may be Napa Valley's most dramatic visual statement. Sure, there's a touch of Disneyland—you ascend on an aerial tramway—but that's Sterling's appeal, and from the top the view is unsurpassed.

Sterling retains such a contemporary look that it's hard to believe it was built in

1973. A well-marked, self-guided tour allows a leisurely glimpse of the winery's workings and leads you ultimately to one of Napa's most relaxing tasting rooms. After picking up a glass at the counter—usually a sample of sauvignon blanc—visitors sit at tables inside or on the balcony. Once you're seated, the wines come to you. A varying selection is poured, and most are solid efforts. Sterling can achieve greatness occasionally, particularly with its Reserve Cabernet, but can be inconsistent.

STORYBOOK MOUNTAIN VINEYARDS

707-942-5310
www.storybookwines.com
3835 Hwy. 128, Calistoga, CA 94515
Tasting and Tours: By appointment
Tasting Fee: None

With a dramatic gate along Highway 128 and tucked amid rolling hills, Storybook Mountain earns its romantic name. The winery devotes itself to one wine: zinfandel. The regular and the reserve bottlings are typically powerful and long lived. Jacob and Adam Grimm—the brothers Grimm, thus the Storybook name—made wine on the property back in the late 19th century. Jerry Seps restored it in 1976, and this small and unpretentious winery remains his baby. The wines reveal a hands-off attitude: The vineyards are organic, and Seps tinkers little with the wine in the cellar.

VON STRASSER WINERY

707-942-0930
www.vonstrasser.com
1510 Diamond Mountain Rd., Calistoga, CA 94515
Tasting and Tours: Daily by appointment
Tasting Fee: $20

Its first release arrived in 1993, and since then von Strasser has caught the eye of cabernet sauvignon fans. Rudy and Rita von Strasser own prime vineyard space on Diamond Mountain, a stone's throw from the famous Diamond Creek Vineyards. The cab is intensely built and production is small, but the von Strassers are immersed, tending the vineyards and hand-sorting the grapes.

Sonoma County Wineries

SONOMA VALLEY

ARROWOOD VINEYARDS & WINERY

707-935-2600, 800-938-5170
www.arrowoodvineyards.com
14347 Sonoma Hwy., Glen Ellen, CA 95442
Tasting: 10–4:30 daily
Tasting Fee: $5–$10
Tours: 10:30 and 2:30 daily by appointment
Tour Fee: $20–$30

Richard Arrowood was one of the first high profile winemakers in Sonoma County. After toiling at a number of wineries over the years, Arrowood and wife Alis opened this winery in 1986, and the wines are among the best in California. The visitors center features a dramatic two-story limestone fireplace and views of the vineyard. The winery, a gray-and-white farmhouse with a wide porch, looks deceptively small from the outside. A tour includes the usual crushing facilities, bottling line, and barrel room, ending with a tasting. The king here is chardonnay, rich and complex. Cabernet sauvignon and merlot are also first-rate.

Beginning in 2000, the winery changed hands a number of times and is now owned by Jess Jackson of Kendall-Jackson. The Arrowoods have remained on board the entire time, but it's hard to know the fate of winery at this point.

BENZIGER FAMILY WINERY

888-490-2739
www.benziger.com
1883 London Ranch Rd., Glen Ellen, CA 95442
Tasting: 11–5 daily
Tasting Fee: $5–$10
Tours: Daily

Tour Fee: $10
Special Features: Motorized tram tour, picnic area, art gallery

If this winery seems familiar, there's a reason. Millions know this spot along the gentle slope of Sonoma Mountain as Glen Ellen Winery, the king of the $5 bottle of vino. From a run-down grape ranch purchased from a naked hippie doctor in 1981, the Benziger clan built a multimillion-dollar Goliath. Weary, they sold the Glen Ellen brand in 1994 but kept the ranch, which dates to 1860, and now concentrate on their premium Benziger label.

The Benzigers may have downsized, but the winery grounds are more beautiful than ever and are now entirely organic. Past an old farmhouse and down the hill is the wooden ranch barn that serves as aging cellar and tasting room. The extensive tour is largely by motorized tram, leading visitors through the vineyards and grape-crushing facilities, with a final stop at the tasting room. The Benziger cabernet sauvignons can be a knockout in a good vintage, and the citrusy sauvignon blanc is usually a winner.

BLACKSTONE WINERY

707-833-1999, 800-955-9585
www.blackstonewinery.com
8450 Sonoma Hwy., Kenwood, CA 95452
Tasting: 10–4:30 daily
Tasting Fee: $5
Tours: No

With the cost of wine rising so quickly, it's good to see that some winemakers still have value on their mind. Blackstone is part of the giant beverage company Constellation, and it offers a wide range of wines at decent prices. The house style is ripe and fruit forward, and the merlot is particularly reliable. Real winemaking is limited in Kenwood, but the tasting room is in a small cottage, and it's as easy going and laidback as the wines.

B. R. COHN WINERY

707 938 4064, 800 330 4064
www.brcohn.com
15000 Sonoma Hwy., Glen Ellen, CA 95442
Tasting: 10–5 daily
Tasting Fee: $10
Tours: By appointment
Tour Fee: $15
Special features: Picnic area, gourmet foods

Manager for the Doobie Brothers and other rock bands, Bruce Cohn began a second career in wine when he bought Olive Hill Ranch in 1974. Cohn sold his grapes until 1984, when he bottled his first cabernet sauvignon. Ripe and concentrated, it was an immediate hit. Subsequent vintages have fared similarly, but his chardonnay and merlot are more routine. The tasting room has a handsome mahogany bar and marble fireplace and sits on a knoll covered with olive trees. Olive oil is Cohn's latest passion.

BUENA VISTA WINERY

707-938-1266, 800-926-1266
www.buenavistawinery.com
18000 Old Winery Rd., Sonoma, CA 95476
Tasting: 10–5 daily
Tasting Fee: $5–$20
Tours: By appointment

This is where it all began: California's oldest premium winery. Buena Vista is where Agoston Haraszthy, known as the Father of California Wine, started his experiments in 1857. Though others had made wine in Sonoma before this, they had used only the coarse mission variety grapes brought north by Spanish missionaries for Mass wine. Haraszthy was the first to believe that the noble grapes of Bordeaux and Burgundy could thrive in California.

Visitors to Buena Vista stroll down a gentle, quarter-mile path, past thick blackberry bushes and tall eucalyptus trees, to the tasting room set inside the thick stone Press House, built in 1863. The wine is made a few

The historic press house at Buena Vista Winery Courtesy Buena Vista Winery

miles away. Buena Vista's reputation has varied widely over time, but the wines have improved significantly in recent years.

CHATEAU ST. JEAN

707-833-4134, 800-543-7572
www.chateaustjean.com
8555 Sonoma Hwy., Kenwood, CA 95452
Tasting: 10–5 daily
Tasting Fee: $10–$15
Garden Tours: 11 and 2 daily
Tour Fee: $15
Special Features: Picnic area, deli, gifts

Surrounded by luxuriant lawns and tall trees, with Sugarloaf Ridge in the distance, Chateau St. Jean—a modern version of a medieval French castle—is a visual treat. Opening in 1973, Chateau St. Jean drew immediate acclaim for its white wines, particularly the Robert Young Vineyard chardonnay, a luscious and oaky beauty that helped set the standard for chardonnay. Today, Chateau St. Jean is owned by wine and beer giant Foster's, which also runs Beringer, Souverin, and other wineries. Ironically, its red wines are now drawing attention. Its cabernet sauvignons and merlots are lush and well structured.

There's a spacious visitors center behind the chateau. Buy a bottle of the melony Johannisberg Riesling or a chardonnay or sauvignon blanc to pour with a picnic; the winery has one of Sonoma's best picnic grounds.

CLINE CELLARS

707-940-4000, 800-546-2070
www.clinecellars.com
24737 Arnold Dr., Sonoma, CA 95476
Tasting: 10–6 daily
Tasting Fee: None–$5
Tours: 11, 1, and 3 by appointment
Special Features: Picnic area

Cline was Rhone before Rhone was popular. Fred Cline got started in the East Bay in 1982, preferring unsung Rhone-style grapes such as carignane and mourvedre.

Cline then took up shop in Sonoma's Carneros District in 1991. The tasting room is inside an 1850s farmhouse with a wraparound porch; the pleasant grounds have duck ponds and rose gardens. Nearby, viognier and syrah, Cline's latest Rhone passions, are newly planted. The winery has also had great success with zinfandel.

GLORIA FERRER CHAMPAGNE CAVES

707-933-1917
www.gloriaferrer.com
23555 Carneros Hwy., Sonoma, CA 95476
Tasting: 10:30–5 daily
Tasting Fee: $2–$10
Tours: Daily by appointment
Special Features: Gourmet food, gifts, cave tour

If you've had the pleasure of paying a mere $10 for Cordon Negro, the simple but tasty little sparkling wine in the ink-black bottle, then you already know the people behind Gloria Ferrer. Freixenet of Spain is the world's largest producer of sparkling wine, and it was drawn to the great promise of California. Gloria Ferrer, named for the wife of Freixenet's president, makes consistently good bubbly at fair prices. It also makes admirable still wines: merlot, syrah, pinot, and chardonnay.

The Carneros location places Gloria Ferrer away from the high-traffic areas. Sitting dramatically on the gentle slope of a hill, the winery, done in warm tones of brown and red, is a bit of Barcelona. The tasting room fireplace glows in the winter, and during the summer the terrace doors are pushed open to the cool breezes from nearby San Pablo Bay. Gloria Ferrer's tour also has great appeal, particularly tours of the caves carved from the hillside where the sparkling wine ages.

GUNDLACH-BUNDSCHU WINERY

707-939-3015

The winery at Chateau St. Jean has old-world charm. Tim Fish

www.gunbun.com
2000 Denmark St., Sonoma, CA 95476
Tasting: 11–4:30 daily
Tasting Fee: $5–$15
Tours: By appointment
Special Features: Picnic area, cave tour on summer weekends

Passionate about wine and the Sonoma Valley, Jim Bundschu doesn't take himself seriously. At a wine auction a few years back, he dressed as *Batman*, and his winery's humorous posters are classic. He even hijacked the Napa Valley Wine Train and—gasp!—handed out samples of Sonoma Valley wine. Behind all this frivolity is great wine and rich history. Since 1858, six generations have tended the winery's home vineyard, Rhinefarm—but wine wasn't bottled from Prohibition until Jim restored the original stone winery in the early 1970s. Located down a winding road, it's worth the trek. Take time to tour the winery's 10,000-square-foot cave.

HANZELL VINEYARDS
707-996-3860
www.hanzell.com
18596 Lomita Ave., Sonoma, CA 95476
Tasting and Tours: By appointment
Tasting and Tour Fee: $45

The original boutique winery, Hanzell has greatly influenced California winemaking. The late ambassador James Zellerbach, who founded the winery in 1956, patterned it after the chateaux of Burgundy. The winery, with its dark wood and pitched roof, was modeled after Clos de Vougeot, and Hanzell was first in California to barrel-ferment chardonnay and use French oak barrels for aging. The winery went through a few rough years, but the pinot noir and chardonnay are now up to the old standards.

IMAGERY ESTATE WINERY
707-935-4500, 877-550-4278
www.imagerywinery.com
14335 Hwy. 12, Glen Ellen, CA 95442

Napa Valley Collectives

If you want to sip and swirl variety, collective tasting rooms are the way to go: You'll find many wineries under one roof. Each may not have its own tasting room, or the winery may have one in a remote area. Either way, you win; you'll get to taste boutique wines, and their limited supply makes them nearly impossible to find elsewhere.

Dozen Vintners (707-967-0666, 3000 N. Hwy. 29, St. Helena, CA 94574; www.adozenvintners.com) Inside this cream-colored building is an art-deco-style tasting room with some top names in Napa Valley wine. The notables include Howell Mountain Vineyards and Fife.

Napa Wine Merchants (707-257-6796, www.napawinemerchant.com, 1146 1st St., Napa, CA 94559) This collective, in the historic Gordon building, has about 75 different offerings. You typically come across some of these wines on restaurant wine lists. Wineries include Gustavo Thrace, Mandolin, and Waterstone.

Vintners Collective (707-255-7150, www.vintnerscollective.com, 1245 Main St., Napa, CA 94559) This is the crème de la crème of collectives. It's housed in a historic building and offers a range of sought-after wines, including those by Skowket, Ahnfeldt, and Philippe Melka.

Wineries of Napa Valley (707-253-9450, www.napavintages.com, 1285 Napa Town Center, Napa. CA 94559) This tasting room is next door to Napa's visitors center and includes Goosecross Cellars, Girard Winery, and Burgess Cellars.

Kunde Winery's barrel-aging caves are hidden beneath a hillside vineyard. Tim Fish

Tasting Fee: None
Tours: No
Special Features: Gifts

Don't let Kenwood Vineyards fool you. The tasting room might be in a rustic little barn, but behind the simple charm is a savvy winery, one of Sonoma County's largest. Here's a homey and relaxed tasting room with wines that will please everyone in your group. Built by the Pagani brothers in 1906, the winery is now owned by Gary Heck, who also runs Korbel Champagne Cellars. Kenwood doesn't really have a specialty. Whites or reds, they have luck with both. There's no better wine with fresh oysters than Kenwood's lemony sauvignon blanc. Try Kenwood's cabernet sauvignons, particularly the expensive but outstanding Artist Series—big wines with great aging potential.

KUNDE ESTATE WINERY
707-833-5501
www.kunde.com
10155 Sonoma Hwy., Kenwood, CA 95452
Tasting: 10:30–4:30 daily
Tasting Fee: $5–$10
Tours: By appointment
Special Features: Picnic area, gifts

Since 1904, five generations of Kundes have grown grapes. Stopping production during World War II, the clan began making wine again in the late 1980s. The Kundes have 2,000 acres of vineyards, and they know the personality of each varietal grape and put that to use. They also brought in a fine winemaker, David Noyes, who worked at Ridge for 10 years. The strengths so far are chardonnay, typically elegant and creamy, and a muscular zinfandel made from one-hundred-year-old vines. The winery is a stylish white barn. In the hillside beyond, the Kundes have carved out a $5-million cave to age their wine. Visitors to the tasting room can watch the winery in action through picture windows.

Tasting: 10–4:30 daily winter, 10–5:30 daily summer
Tasting Fee: $5–$10
Tours: Self-guided art gallery and varietal walk
Special Features: Art gallery, bocce court, picnic area

Art and single-vineyard wines are the focus of this energetic winery run by the Benziger family. The artist collection series features boldly designed labels and offbeat varietals such as tempranillo and sangiovese, while the vineyard collection features distinctive cabernets, merlots, and other grapes from one unique place. The wines are sold almost exclusively at the winery, so you know you'll be able to taste a wine you'll never be able to buy back home.

KENWOOD VINEYARDS
707-833-5891
www.kenwoodvineyards.com
9592 Sonoma Hwy., Kenwood, CA 95452
Tasting: 10–4:30 daily

LANDMARK VINEYARDS

707-833-0218
www.landmarkwine.com
101 Adobe Canyon Rd., Kenwood, CA 95452
Tasting: 10:30–4:30 daily
Tasting Fee: $5–$10
Tours: By appointment
Special Features: Gifts, picnic area, bocce court, horse-drawn wagon tours

This attractive Mission-style winery, in the shadow of Sugar Loaf Ridge, is a house of chardonnay. Landmark began in Windsor in 1974, but suburban squeeze forced a move south in 1989, when Damaris Deere Ethridge assumed control. The menu includes two impressive chardonnays and a pinot noir. The tasting room is an appealing space, with a cathedral ceiling, fireplace, and granite bar. The cloistered courtyard looks onto the eastern slopes.

LEDSON WINERY AND VINEYARD

707-537-3810.
www.ledson.com
7335 Sonoma Hwy., Kenwood, CA 95409
Tasting: 10–5 daily
Tasting Fee: $10–$15
Tours: By appointment
Special Features: Gifts, gourmet foods

From the road, this winery looks a bit like Wayne Manor in the old *Batman* TV show. Originally designed as the Ledson family

Ledson Winery is a showplace in Sonoma Valley. Tim Fish

home, the 16,000-square-foot gothic "castle" turns heads on Sonoma Highway. Make your way up the long drive and through the vines, enter through the portico, and you'll see that the interior is just as extravagant as the outside. The wines are good but not great, with sauvignon blanc and chardonnay generally leading the pack.

MATANZAS CREEK WINERY

707-528-6464, 800-590-6464
www.matanzascreek.com
6097 Bennett Valley Rd., Santa Rosa, CA 95404
Tasting: 10–4:30 daily
Tasting Fee: $5
Tours: 10:30 and 2:30 Mon.–Fri., 10:30 Sat. by appointment

Lavender as well as grapes are harvested at Matanzas Creek Winery. Courtesy Matanzas Creek Winery

Special Features: Estate garden and lavender field

If you forgo the beaten path for this winery, you won't regret it. Matanzas Creek is one of the few wineries in Bennett Valley, a quiet, untouched fold of land west of Kenwood. The first wines were made in 1978 in a converted dairy barn, but these days, if you continue down the long driveway to the foot of the Sonoma Mountains, you'll find a state-of-the-art facility with a modest tasting room. Jess Jackson, of Kendall-Jackson fame, bought the winery in 2000. Matanzas Creek focuses on three wines: chardonnay, sauvignon blanc, and merlot. The wines haven't been up to their past glory in recent vintages, but only time will tell.

MAYO FAMILY WINERY

707-938-9401
www.mayofamilywinery.com
13101 Arnold Dr., Glen Ellen, CA 95442
Tasting: 10:30–6:30 daily
Tasting Fee: $6–$12
Special Features: Picnic area

Owner Henry Mayo had a career in real estate, but in 1990 he decided to forsake his business for grapes. It all began with a property in Kenwood he transformed into Laurel Hill Vineyards. By 1993 the Mayo family was bottling wine. The tasting room opened in July 2003, a more accessible location than the main winery nearby in the hills. Mayo produces more than a dozen varietals, but zinfandel and pinot steal the limelight. Mayo also maintains several other tasting rooms around the county.

RAVENSWOOD WINERY

707-933-2332, 888-669-4679
www.ravenswood-wine.com
18701 Gehricke Rd., Sonoma, CA 95476
Tasting: 10–4:30 daily
Tasting Fee: $10–$15
Tours: 10:30 daily by appointment

Tour Fee: $10
Special Features: Picnic area, gifts

Cabernet sauvignon may be a passion, but zinfandel is an obsession. Cursed with a shady reputation by its evil twin, white zinfandel, red zinfandel was once a second-class citizen. Not anymore. At its best, zinfandel is luscious and jammy, equal to cabernet in most ways and at half the price. Zin lovers have long been wise to Ravenswood.

Ravenswood is now part of the Icon Estates, a conglomerate that owns Simi Winery and Franciscan. It's an unassuming stone winery built into the side of a hill—and the location fits the label: a classic image of a circle of ravens. The old tasting room is a busy spot but made soothing by a crackling fire. If you're lucky, Ravenswood will pour one of its top zinfandels. Cooke, Old Hill, Dickerson. A sure way to sample the good stuff is to visit in the late winter and spring, when the zins are still in the barrel.

Ravenswood's tour typically includes a walk through the vineyard and a barrel tasting. Because the winery is small, the tour is brief, but guides are detailed in their discussion of Ravenswood's natural approach to winemaking.

ROCHE WINERY

707-935-7115, 800-825-9475
www.rochewinery.com
28700 Arnold Dr., Sonoma, CA 95476
Tasting: 10–5 daily
Tasting Fee: None–$5
Tours: Horseback tours, covered wagon—all by appointment

On the southernmost edge of Sonoma County, in the cool and foggy Carneros District, Roche occupies a lonely spot near San Pablo Bay. The long porch of the white, ranch-style winery has an expansive view. Joe and Genevieve Roche planted wines in the early 1980s, even though popular wis-

dom said the area was too cold. Chardonnay and pinot noir, they discovered, thrive quite nicely and have become the house specialties. The merlot and syrah are also worth a taste.

ST. FRANCIS WINERY AND VINEYARD

707-833-4666, 888-675-9463
www.stfranciswine.com
100 Pythian Rd., Kenwood, CA 95409
Tasting: 10–5 daily
Tasting Fee: $10–$45
Tours: By appointment
Special Features: Gifts

Merlot is the current popular flavor, and St. Francis makes two of the best, a regular and a reserve. Both are gorgeous and full bodied, with enough muscle to age a few years. Another success story for St. Francis is its chardonnay, done in a lean and fruity style. Its old-vine zinfandel packs a punch of brilliant fruit. They can all be sampled at the lovely mission-style visitor's center located near the winery.

SCHUG CARNEROS ESTATE WINERY

707-939-9363, 800-966-9365
www.schugwinery.com
602 Bonneau Rd., Sonoma, CA 95476
Tasting: 10–5 daily
Tasting Fee: Reserve wines only
Tours: By appointment

Nestled against a windswept hill on the western edge of Carneros is a little bit of Germany. Architecturally, Schug's winery would be more at home along the Rhine, where the winemaker was raised. His wines, too, reflect his European heritage. Schug established his impressive credentials at Joseph Phelps, where he was winemaker from 1973 to 1983. His current wines, poured in a cozy tasting room, are distinctive and more European in style than those produced by most California wineries.

St Francis Winery in Kenwood is a popular tourist destination. Tim Fish

Visitors take the tour at Sebastiani Vineyards in Sonoma. Courtesy Sebastiani Sonoma Cask Cellars

SEBASTIANI SONOMA CASK CELLARS

707-938-5532, 800-888-5532
www.sebastiani.com
389 4th St. E., Sonoma, CA 95476
Tasting: 10–5 daily
Tasting Fee: $5–$10
Tours: 11, 1, and 3 daily
Tour Fee: $5–$7.50
Special Features: Picnic area, gifts, trolley tour

For many people, Sebastiani is another way to spell Sonoma. It's the epitome of the county's wine tradition: an unpretentious family winery—big, old, and Italian. Once among Sonoma County's largest wineries, Sebastiani trimmed production considerably a few years back to focus on quality. It remains one of Sonoma's most popular tourist attractions.

The winery dates to 1896, when Samuele Sebastiani crushed his first grapes—zinfandel, to be precise—and the press he used is still on display in the tasting room. Samuele's son August, a man with an affinity for bib overalls and stout, simple wines, built the winery's reputation on inexpensive jug wines. Since his death in 1980, the family has concentrated on premium wines.

Tours offer a thorough look behind the scenes, from the wine presses to the aging tanks. The highlight is the collection of intricately hand-carved wine casks. The spacious tasting room—renovated and modernized in 2001—is partly crafted from old wine tanks. Visitors can taste Sebastiani's wide range of wines. Try the Sonoma County cabernet sauvignon and merlot, delightful wines and excellent bargains.

VALLEY OF THE MOON WINERY

707-939-4500
www.valleyofthemoonwinery.com
777 Madrone Rd., Glen Ellen, CA 95442
Tasting: 10–4:30 daily
Tasting Fee: Free–$2
Tours: 10:30, 2 daily
Special Features: Gifts, picnic area

It's not every day that a winery starts over from scratch. Brands such as Beaulieu

While strolling around the Healdsburg plaza, stop in for a taste at Cellar 360. Tim Fish

Valley of the Moon Winery is an easy stop along Sonoma Valley's wine roads. Courtesy Valley of the Moon

Vineyards and Charles Krug Winery have received makeovers in recent years, but those were just tummy tucks and face-lifts compared to that of Valley of the Moon Winery. When Gary Heck—who owns Korbel and Kenwood Vineyards—bought this winery a few years back, it was run down, and the wines had a nasty reputation. Just about the only thing left from the old days is the winery's original 110-year-old foundation. The new tasting room is sleek and modern, and so is the winery's bottle design, a stark yet dramatic etched bottle. But what about the wines? They're good and getting better, particularly the zinfandel and syrah.

VIANSA WINERY AND ITALIAN MARKET PLACE

707-935-4700, 800-995-4740
www.viansa.com
25200 Arnold Dr., Sonoma, CA 95476
Tasting: 10–5 daily
Tasting Fee: $5
Tours: 11, 2, and 3 daily
Special Features: Deli, gourmet foods, gifts, picnic area

This tribute to Tuscany is situated high atop a knoll in the Carneros District. Done in warm shades with a terra-cotta tile roof and Italian opera music in the background, Viansa is one of Wine Country's most festive spots. Even the stainless-steel wine tanks are adorned with colorful faux marble frescoes. The marketplace offers sumptuous picnic fare, plus a picnic area with a dramatic view. (See chapter 5, Restaurants & Food Purveyors). Viansa is concentrating increasingly—and with considerable success—on Italian-style wines such as barbera and nebbiolo and blends that recall a hearty Chianti.

RUSSIAN RIVER
ARMIDA WINERY

707-433-2222
www.armida.com
2201 Westside Rd., Healdsburg, CA 95448
Tasting: 11–5 daily
Tasting Fee: None
Tours: By appointment
Special Features: Bocce court, picnic area

Three unique geodesic domes comprise this winery, which occupies the border of the Dry Creek and Russian River valleys. Wines include zinfandel, chardonnay, and pinot noir, all nicely done. Buy a bottle to share on the wooden deck, which offers an expansive view of Sonoma County.

CELLAR 360

707-433-2822
www.cellar360.com
308B Center St., Healdsburg, California 95448
Tasting: 11–6 daily
Tasting Fee: $5–$10
Tours: No
Special Features: Gifts

Talk about one-stop shopping. This attractive tasting room on the Healdsburg plaza features more than 150 wine labels from 40 wine regions around the world. Some of the names are familiar—Beringer, Souverain, Penfolds—while others are more obscure. All are owned by Australian wine and beer giant Foster's.

Chalk Hill Winery in Sonoma County offers verdant hills. Courtesy Chalk Hill Winery

On any given day, up to 10 wines are available to taste, ranging from a bargain zinfandel from Cellar. No 8 to a pricey cabernet from Chateau St. Jean.

CHALK HILL WINERY

707-657-4837
www.chalkhill.com
10300 Chalk Hill Rd., Healdsburg, CA 95448
Tasting: 10–3 Mon.–Fri. by appointment
Tasting Fee: $10
Tours: 10, 1, and 3, Mon.–Fri. by appointment
Tour Fee: $15

The white soil gives the Chalk Hill area its name—even though it's really volcanic ash, not chalk. Fred and Peggy Furth established this winery well off the beaten path in 1980 and hired a series of talented winemakers. White wines thrive in the area, and chardonnay is the winery's specialty; it ranges from average to excellent. The sauvignon blanc is consistently a beauty.

DAVIS FAMILY VINEYARDS

707-433-3858
www.davisfamilyvineyards.com
Tasting Room:52 Front St., Healdsburg CA 95448
Tasting: 11–4:30 Thurs.–Sun.
Tasting Fee: None

Tours: By appointment
Special Features: Bocce ball court, picnic area

When you drink his wines, you can almost taste the passion Guy Davis has for winemaking. He produces a little of everything but seems particularly apt at cabernet, zinfandel, and pinot noir. Most of the grapes come from the nearby Russian River, but Davis is savvy enough to turn to Napa for his cabernet grape source. The winery isn't much to look at but you get to taste the wines right in the barrel room, the staff is laid back and friendly, and the picnic area overlooks the Russian River.

DE LOACH VINEYARDS

707-526-9111
www.deloachvineyards.com
1791 Olivet Rd., Santa Rosa, CA 95401
Tasting: 10–4:30 daily
Tasting Fee: $5–$10
Tours: By appointment
Special Features: Picnic area

After the French wine company Boisset bought this winery from Cecil De Loach in 2003, people didn't know what to expect. The De Loach family had been making wines since the mid-1970s but fell on hard financial times and the wines began to suffer. In just a few years, Boisset has turned things around dramatically. The chardonnays and pinot noirs are classic Russian River: supple, rich, and elegant. All of the De Loach wines are available in the tasting room located in the handsome and grand redwood building at the end of a long drive embraced by vineyards.

FOPPIANO VINEYARDS

707-433-7272
www.foppiano.com
12707 Old Redwood Hwy., Healdsburg, CA 95448
Tasting: 10–4:30 daily
Tasting Fee: None
Tours: Self-guided through vineyard

Five generations of Foppianos have tended vines here. John Foppiano arrived from Genoa in 1896 and planted a vineyard. Wine was sold in bulk and, later, in jugs. The family began moving into premium wine in the 1970s. The winery is unabashedly utilitarian, and the tasting room is in an unassuming wood cottage. The self-guided vineyard tour is worth a few minutes. Foppiano's stars are zinfandel and a beefy petite sirah made from old vines.

GALLO TASTING ROOM

707-433-2458
www.galloofsonoma.com
320 Center St., Healdsburg, CA 95448
Tasting: 11–5 Sun.–Wed.; 11–7 Thu.; 11–10 Fri.–Sat.
Tasting Fee: $7–$15
Tours: By appointment

Gallo of Sonoma, a division of wine giant E. & J. Gallo, set up a winery in Dry Creek Valley in the late 1970s, and its award-winning wines have steadily improved Gallo's image, which was formerly based solely on inexpensive brands. Many of the Sonoma wines are poured at this handsome salon on Healdsburg plaza. While Gallo's large Dry Creek winery isn't open to the public, it does offer an extensive tour of its Barrelli Creek Vineyard in Alexander Valley. It begins in the tasting room, and then guests head north for an in-depth exploration of grape-growing that finishes with a tasting of limited-release wines and local artisan cheeses lakeside at the vineyard.

GARY FARRELL WINES

707-473-2900
www.garyfarrellwines.com
10701 Westside Rd., Healdsburg, CA 95448
Tasting 11–4 daily
Tasting Fee: $5
Tours: By appointment
Tour Fee: $15–$25

Don't let Gary Farrell's quiet demeanor fool you. He's one of the best winemakers in the business. While the winery is now owned by Beam Wine Estates, which runs Clos du Bois, Geyser Peak, and other area wineries, Farrell remains involved in the winemaking for now. The Farrell style is elegant, complex, and fruit-forward, and the winery has a knack for pinot noir, chardonnay, and zinfandel. Situated like a mission-style chapel on a hill above Russian River, the tasting room offers wide and glorious views of the surrounding landscape.

HARTFORD FAMILY WINERY

707-887-8010
www.hartfordwines.com
8075 Martinelli Rd., Forestville CA 95436
Tasting: 10–4:30 daily
Tasting Fee: $5
Tours: By appointment

If you've ever dreamed of retiring to some grand estate in wine country, Hartford is the sort of place you might have in mind. Hidden amid the lush canyons of West County, this stately mansion produces pinot noir, zinfandel, and chardonnay that are deeply flavored and intense. The winery is part of the Jess Jackson family of wineries, which means it has access to top vineyards in Sonoma County. Inside, the tasting room has the venerable atmosphere of a private club.

HOLDREDGE WINES

707-431-1424
www.holdredge.com
51 Front St., Healdsburg, CA 95448
Tasting: 11–4:30 Sat.–Sun., or by appointment
Tasting Fee: $5
Tours: 11–4 Sat.–Sun., or by appointment
Tour Fee: None

Hop Kiln Winery in the Russian River Valley has a distinctive facade. Tim Fish

What started as a hobby for John Holdredge turned into a second job. A Santa Rosa attorney by day, he's a winemaker, grape grower, and wine salesman during what's left of his 24 hours. Wife Carri at first indulged him and then joined the winery when he launched in 2001. Tasting is a low-key affair amid the barrels in the winery, a historic old redwood barn on the outskirts of Healdsburg. Pinot noir is the main focus, but Holdredge makes a little zinfandel and syrah, and stylistically the wines are graceful in their complexity.

HOP KILN WINERY

707-433-6491
www.hopkilnwinery.com
6050 Westside Rd., Healdsburg, CA 95448
Tasting: 10–5 daily
Tasting Fee: None–$5
Special Features: Gourmet foods, picnic area, lake

Hop Kiln began life as an ode to beer, not wine. Hops were a major crop along Sonoma County's Russian River at the turn of the 20th century. This is one of the few remnants from that era. Built in 1905, the unusual stone barn is topped with three pyramid towers. The tasting room inside is rustic but pleasant, warm with wood and history. Tasters can choose from any number of wines and the winery specializes in blends such as the soft and fragrant white, Thousand Flowers, and the hearty Rushin' River red. Both are delightful, especially for a picnic. Outside, a small lake is bordered by a sunny patch of picnic tables—be prepared to share your lunch with the ducks.

IRON HORSE VINEYARDS

707-887-1507
www.ironhorsevineyards.com
9786 Ross Station Rd., Sebastopol, CA 95472
Tasting: 10–3:30 daily
Tasting Fee: $10
Tours: 10 Mon.–Fri. by appointment

This winery amid the undulating hills of Green Valley is one of Sonoma County's most respected producers of sparkling wine. Barry and Audrey Sterling bought the estate, a former railroad stop, in 1976. Elegant in its sheer simplicity, the winery stretches throughout a series of wooden barns and is surrounded by vineyards and gardens. The tour reveals the classic *méthode champenoise* process used in making French-style bubbly. In addition to its line of opulent sparkling wine, Iron Horse produces chardonnay and pinot noir, both fine examples.

JOSEPH SWAN VINEYARDS

707-573-3747
www.swanwinery.com
2916 Laguna Rd, Forestville, CA 95436
Tasting: 11–4:30 Sat. and Sun.; weekdays by appointment.
Tasting Fee: None
Tours: No

Hardly more than a bungalow, this modest structure belies Joseph Swan's near-legendary status in Wine Country. Beginning in 1969, Swan was a pioneer of zinfandel, crafting heroically ripe and long-lived wines. Pinot noir became Swan's star in the 1980s. Swan died in 1989, and son-in-law Rod Berglund is now winemaker. Although the zins are no longer legendary, they remain fine and authentic creations.

J VINEYARDS AND WINERY

707-431-5400
www.jwine.com
11447 Old Redwood Hwy., Healdsburg, CA 95448
Tasting: 11–5 daily
Tasting Fee: $20–$45, food pairing included
Tours: By appointment

Wine and food pairing at most wineries is a cracker with a smear of something but J does it right. Wines are always sampled with small bites of things—for example, Brut Rose may come with blue claw crab *alla pescatora*. The tasting room is a stylish café, with angular concrete walls and bold modern art, and the winery produces a steely Brut as well as first-rate still wines such as pinot noir and pinot gris (sometimes known as pinot grigio). Visitors tour the winery along a concrete balcony that overlooks the entire plant, where the *méthode champenoise*, the French technique of making sparkling wine, is detailed.

KENDALL-JACKSON WINE CENTER

707-571-8100
www.kj.com
5007 Fulton Rd., Fulton, CA 95439
Tasting: 10–5 daily
Tasting Fee: $25, food pairing included
Garden Tours: 11, 1, and 3 daily
Special Features: Picnic area, gifts

Kendall-Jackson is a major force in California wine, particularly in its home base of Sonoma County. K-J, as it's known, operates several wineries in the area and uses this faux chateau as a visitor center. It's rather Disney-like in its notion of grandeur, but the garden is lovely. Inside, you can taste a wide range of K-J wines. Be sure to try the fleshy yet crisp sauvignon blanc.

KORBEL CHAMPAGNE CELLARS

707-824-7000
www.korbel.com
13250 River Rd., Guerneville, CA 95446
Tasting: 9–5 daily May–Sept., 9–4:30 daily Oct.–Apr.
Tasting Fee: None
Tours: Daily on the hour, 10–3:45 summer, 10–3 winter; garden tours 11, 1, and 3 daily in summer
Special Features: Picnic area, gifts, garden, deli, microbrewery

As you drive through the gorgeous redwood forests of the Russian River area, you'll see this century-old, ivy-covered stone wine cellar rising nobly from a hillside. Korbel is one of Wine Country's most popular destinations, offering romance, history, and beauty.

To avoid the crowds in summer, arrive early in the morning or late in the afternoon. The half-hour tour is great fun. The Korbel brothers from Czechoslovakia came to Guerneville for the trees, which were perfect for cigar boxes. When the trees were cleared, they planted grapes and made wine using *méthode champenoise*, the traditional French method of making champagne. You'll poke your nose in large wood aging tanks and learn the mystery of the riddling room, where sediment is slowly tapped from each bottle. The tasting room is one of the friendliest, and any or all of the winery's dependable sparklers are offered. During the summer, Korbel's prized antique garden is also available for touring.

LA CREMA WINERY

707-431-9400
www.lacrema.com
Tasting Room: 235 Healdsburg Ave., Healdsburg, CA 95448
Tasting: 10:30–5:30 daily
Tasting Fee: None
Tours: No

La Crema has a long history in Sonoma County and has seen good times and bad, but the winery is now making some of its best wines to date. Pinot noir and chardonnay dominate the lineup. Both are typical plush and fruit-forward wines, and while prices have been creeping up in recent vintages, the cost-versus-quality ratio remains good. Part of the Jess Jackson family of wines, La Crema has a winery in West County but runs this smart-looking tasting room just off the Healdsburg plaza.

LONGBOARD VINEYARDS

707-433-3473
www.longboardvineyards.com
5 Fitch St., Healdsburg, CA 95448

Tasting: 11–7 Thurs.–Sat., 11–5 Sun.
Tasting Fee: $5
Tours: No

A surfer tried and true, Oded Shakked named his winery after his surfboard of choice. In his mind, both surfing and wine-making require balance, harmony, and a respect for nature. A beach bum born near Tel Aviv, Shakked studied winemaking in California and for many years made bubbly at J Wine Co. before launching his own winery a few years back. The tasting room, inside a warehouse near downtown, is a hangout for surfer and wine drinkers alike. Merlot and cabernet are the specialties, but Shakked also makes a tasty syrah and sauvignon blanc.

MARIMAR TORRES ESTATE

707-823-4365
www.marimarestate.com
11400 Graton Rd, Sebastopol, CA 95472
Tasting: 11–4:30 daily
Tasting Fee: None
Tours: By appointment

Marimar Torres's family in Spain has been making wine for generations, so when she came to Sonoma County in the mid-1970s, she was beginning her own wine legacy. In 1992 she built this Catalan farmhouse-inspired winery amid the isolated, rolling hills of West Sonoma, and planted 60 acres of pinot noir and chardonnay vineyards. The wines reflect a European passion for refinement and elegant complexity. The tasting room hardly seems like one. It's more like you've stopped in for a glass of wine at a neighbor's place down the road.

MARTINELLI WINERY

707-525-0570
3360 River Rd., Windsor, CA 95492
Tasting: 10–5 daily
Tasting Fee: None
Tours: No
Special Features: Picnic area, gifts

This historic hop barn painted a vivid red is home to a prized zinfandel called Jackass Hill. The wine comes from the steepest hillside vineyards in Sonoma County, planted in 1905. Like many old-vine zins, it grabs your taste buds like a two-horse team. The winery also makes a tasty chardonnay and pinot noir, and they're all lush and complex. Legendary winemaker Helen Turley is a consultant, and it shows. Four generations of Martinellis have been farming, and the tasting room is a feast of apples, dried fruit, and other goodies.

MILL CREEK VINEYARDS

707-431-2121
www.millcreekwinery.com
1401 Westside Rd., Healdsburg, CA 95448
Tasting: 10–5 daily
Tasting Fee: Free–$5
Tours: No
Special Features: Picnic area

It's hard to miss this tasting room, a red-wood barn with a waterwheel. The Kreck family has been growing grapes since 1965 and bottled their first wine with the 1974 vintage. Mill Creek helped pioneer merlot but is not among the masters. Sauvignon blanc is the winery's best effort, and it's a delightful companion for a picnic on the winery's deck. Other wines include cabernet, zinfandel, and chardonnay.

ROCHIOLI VINEYARDS & WINERY

707-433-2305
6192 Westside Rd., Healdsburg, CA 95448
Tasting: 11–4 daily
Tasting Fee: None
Tours: No
Special Features: Picnic area, art gallery

The pinot noir vineyards of Rochioli are the envy of all winemakers. The top pinots in the business—Gary Farrell, Williams Selyem, and, of course, Rochioli (pronounced *row-key-OH-lee*)—begin here. Three generations of Rochiolis have been growing grapes along the Russian River.

They stay close to the land, and because of that, they make great wine. In the modest tasting room, which looks out across vineyards toward the river, every wine is a winner. The chardonnay is ripe and buttery and the sauvignon blanc, flowery and complex.

RODNEY STRONG VINEYARDS

707-431-1533, 800-678-4763
www.rodneystrong.com
11455 Old Redwood Hwy., Healdsburg, CA 95448.
Tasting: 10–5 daily
Tasting Fee: None–$10
Tours: 11 and 3 daily
Special Features: Art gallery, picnic area

A dramatic pyramid of concrete and wood, this winery has weathered many incarnations and owners over the years but it seems to be coming into its own again. The wines are reliable and frequently superb, with cabernet sauvignon, chardonnay, and pinot noir among the standouts. Balconies outside the tasting room overlook the tanks and oak barrels, so a tour may be academic.

ROSENBLUM CELLARS

707-431-1169
www.rosenblumcellars.com
250 Center St., Healdsburg, CA 95448
Tasting: 10–6 daily
Tasting Fee: None–$5
Tours: No
Special Features: Art gallery

Rosenblum Cellars makes some of the richest, most full-bodied, no-holds-barred wines in California. While the winery is located in Alameda, across the bay from San Francisco, Rosenblum relies on a number of vineyards in Sonoma County and opened this tasting room just off the Healdsburg plaza. The winery releases dozens of different wines a year—20 different zinfandels alone—but it manages to

produce everything from chardonnay and viognier to syrah and rosé with remarkable panache.

SEGHESIO WINERY

707-433-3579
www.seghesio.com
14730 Grove St., Healdsburg, CA 95448
Tasting: 10–5 daily
Tasting Fee: $5
Tours: No.
Special Features: Picnic area, bocce courts

Moving into its fourth generation, the great-grandsons of Italian immigrant Edoardo Seghesio are continuing the legacy that he began in 1895. The family owns more than 400 acres in Sonoma County, and the winery produces many Italian-style varieties such as sangiovese, barbera, pinot grigio, and arneis, but its known for it's supple yet intense zinfandel. The Tuscan-style tasting room is shaded by an old cork tree.

SIDURI WINES

707-578-3882
www.siduri.com
980 Airway Ct., Suite C, Santa Rosa, CA. 95403
Tasting and Tours: 10–3 daily by appointment
Tasting Fee: None

The name Siduri comes from the Babylonian goddess of wine. Adam and Dianna Lee, two wine lovers, thought it was a fitting name for their house of pinot noir. They began modestly with a small quantity of pinot from the 1994 vintage and now produce pinot from vineyards as far north as Oregon's Willamette Valley and as far south as Santa Barbara County. These lush pinots are pricey but well worth the *dinero*. Siduri is a gravity-flow winery that operates out of a no-frills warehouse, and it's interesting to tour. A footnote: Siduri also produces a label called Novy, a nonpinot, family venture. Varietals include syrah, zin, and grenache.

SONOMA-CUTRER VINEYARDS

707-528-1181
www.sonomacutrer.com
4401 Slusser Rd., Windsor, CA 95492
Tasting and Tours: By appointment
Tasting Fee: None

Harvest is called "crush," yet crush is a crude way to describe how Sonoma-Cutrer makes chardonnay. Pampering is more like it. Grapes arrive in small boxes and are then chilled to 40 degrees in a specially-designed cooling tunnel. Then they are hand sorted and, left in whole clusters, are put through a gentle, membrane press. A tour reveals the entire process as well as an underground aging cellar.

Once the leader in California chardonnay, Sonoma-Cutrer now has keen competition. Brice Cutrer Jones, a jet fighter pilot in the Vietnam War, founded the winery in 1981 and built an ultramodern facility that blends into the hills. (Sonoma-Cutrer also has two world-class croquet courts.) In 1999 the winery was purchased by conglomerate Brown-Forman, which owns Fetzer Vineyards and other well known consumer brands such as Jack Daniels and Southern Comfort.

ALEXANDER VALLEY
ALEXANDER VALLEY VINEYARDS

707-433-7209, 800-888-7209
www.avvwine.com
8644 Hwy. 128, Healdsburg, CA 95448
Tasting: 10–5 daily
Tasting Fee: None–$10
Tours: By appointment
Special Features: Picnic area

Cyrus Alexander, who lent his name to this beautiful valley, built his homestead here. His 1840s adobe remains. The Wetzel family planted vines in the early 1960s; in 1975 they built a winery with a cool cellar carved into a hill and a gravity-flow system that's less stressful to wine. The tasting room is homey, with chairs gathered around a fireplace. The cabernet sauvignons are elegant and easy to drink.

ROSSO & BIANCO WINERY

707-857-1400
www.ffcwinery.com
300 Via Archimedes, Geyserville, CA 95441
Tasting: 11–5 daily
Tasting Fee: Free–$10
Tours: 12:30 and 2:30 daily
Special Features: Restaurant, gifts

This dramatic chalet, inspired by the old hop kilns that once spread across the Russian River Valley, was once Chateau Souverain but is now home to Francis Ford Coppola's new winery. The name Rosso & Bianco—Italian for red and white—pays tribute to his Italian heritage, and the tasting room offers a selection of easy-drinking, food friendly wines. Coppola, the director of *The Godfather* and other classic films, bought the winery in 2006 and has big plans that will take several years to come to fruition. So for now, as they say in the movies: to be continued.

CLOS DU BOIS

707-857-3100, 800-222-3189
www.closdubois.com
19410 Geyserville Ave., Geyserville, CA 95441
Tasting: 10–4:30 daily
Tasting Fee: $5
Tours: No
Special Features: Gifts, gourmet foods, covered picnic area

Clos du Bois, one of Sonoma's largest and most prominent wineries, seems to do everything well and a few things superbly. They may not produce big flashy wines, but their offerings are seldom disappointing—which is surprising, considering the larger roster of wines that range from values to collectibles.

Enjoy a mesmerizing view of the Alexander Valley from Rosso & Bianco Winery. Tim Fish

Vineyards are key to this success; the winery has access to some 1,000 prime acres in Alexander and Dry Creek valleys. The Calcaire chardonnay is lush and steely, though we often prefer the straightforward character of the regular chardonnay. The cabernet sauvignons and merlots are generally impressive. The tasting room is a friendly spot, and the staff is knowledgeable, yet they never roll an eye over novice questions.

MOSAIC VINEYARDS & WINERY

800-546-7718
www.mosaicvineyards.com
2001 Hwy. 128, Geyserville, CA 95441
Tasting: 10–4:30 daily
Tasting Fee: $5–$10
Tours: By appointment

Set amid a sea of vines in the north end of Alexander Valley, this winery—a modern barn with brown shingles—is well off the beaten path. It dates to 1986, when surgeon Alfred de Lorimier decided to make wine with the grapes he'd been growing for years. The biggest successes are sauvignon blanc and a crisp and elegant white blend called Spectrum.

FIELD STONE WINERY & VINEYARDS

707-433-7266, 800-54 GRAPE
www.fieldstonewinery.com
10075 Hwy. 128, Healdsburg, CA 95448
Tasting: 10–5 daily
Tasting Fee: None
Tours: By appointment
Special Features: Picnic area

Cozy inside an Alexander Valley knoll, this winery takes its name from the rugged stone that decorates the facade. Open the wide wooden door, and amble past the oak barrels to the tasting room—and you've pretty much taken the tour. A house specialty is petite sirah from circa-1894 vines. It's a ripe bruiser. The cabernet sauvignon is also recommended. The picnic grounds are superb.

GEYSER PEAK WINERY

707-857-9400, 800-255-9463
www.geyserpeakwinery.com
22281 Chianti Rd., Geyserville, CA 95441
Tasting: 10–5 daily
Tasting Fee: $5–$10
Tours: No
Special Features: Picnic area, gifts

This winery went through a golden era in the 1990s, but production has expanded, and in recent vintages the wines have been good but not up to the old standards. Founded in 1880 by Augustus Quitzow, the winery is a complex of buildings both old and new. The main, ivy-covered building has a commanding view of Alexander Valley. In the tasting room, the staff pours selections from Geyser Peak's large repertoire. Don't miss the shiraz and merlot.

HANNA WINERY

707-431-4310
www.hannawinery.com
Tasting Room: 9280 Hwy. 128, Healdsburg, CA 95448; additional tasting room (10–4 daily), 707-575-3371, 5355 Occidental Rd., Santa Rosa CA 95401
Tasting: 10–4 daily
Tasting Fee: $5–$10

Noted cardiac surgeon Elias Hanna went into the wine business in 1985. Since the winery is well off the tourist path, Hanna opened a tasting room in the heart of its Alexander Valley vineyard. The building—a Frank Lloyd Wright-style pagoda—makes for a striking image among the rolling hills. Hanna owns prime vineyard space around Sonoma County, and the best wines to date are an elegant and sleek pinot noir plus a solid chardonnay and sauvignon blanc. Other wines in the lineup include cabernet and merlot.

JORDAN VINEYARD & WINERY

707-431-5250.
www.jordanwinery.com.
1474 Alexander Valley Rd., Healdsburg, CA 9544
Tasting and Tours: By appointment
Tasting Fee: None

This spectacular French-style chateau rose from a former prune orchard in the mid-1970s to become one of Sonoma County's premier wineries. Covered in ivy, the chateau seems like a grand classic, but inside it's a state-of-the-art winery. The forest of towering wood tanks in its aging room is an impressive sight. Jordan's cabernet sauvignon is elegant and ready to drink on release—one reason it's such a popular wine in restaurants. The tour explores the lush gardens and the winemaking facility.

MURPHY-GOODE ESTATE WINERY

707-431-7644
www.murphygoodewinery.com

4001 Hwy. 128, Healdsburg, Geyserville, CA
95441
Tasting: 10:30–4:30 daily
Tasting Fee: None
Tours: No
Special Features: Gifts

Murphy-Goode has access to some of the best
vineyards in Alexander Valley, and it shows in
their wines. The house specialty is a crisp and
complex fumé blanc, but Murphy-Goode—
which is now owned by Kendall-Jackson—
manages with finesse every wine, from an
elegant cabernet sauvignon to a fruity zin.
Step away from the polished-wood bar in the
tasting room and peer through the picture
window that overlooks the barrel room.

PEDRONCELLI WINERY

707-857-3531, 800-836-3894
www.pedroncelli.com
1220 Canyon Rd., Geyserville, CA 95441
Tasting: 10–4:30 daily
Tasting Fee: None
Tours: By appointment
Special Features: Art gallery

One of Sonoma County's oldest wineries—
its origins date to 1904—Pedroncelli is also
an old reliable. The winery and tasting
room are agreeable but not elaborate. The
wines are solid, though modestly scaled,
and the prices are fair. Two generations of
Pedroncellis tend the place. Try the cabernet sauvignon, sauvignon blanc, and zinfandel—all nicely done.

ROBERT YOUNG ESTATE WINERY

707-431-4811
www.ryew.com
4960 Red Winery Road, Geyserville, CA
95441
Tasting: 10–4:30 daily
Tasting Fee: $5
Tours: By appointment

Back in the early 1960s, many people
thought Robert Young was crazy for planting

a 14-acre cabernet vineyard in an old prune
orchard, but he did it anyway and helped
revive Alexander Valley as a wine region.
These days, the Young family has 300 acres
of vines, and after watching wineries such
as Chateau St. Jean win medals with their
grapes, they started making their own in
1997. The winery, appropriately, is in an old
prune barn, and the tasting room is little
more than a simple counter, but the
chardonnay and cabernet are wonderful
examples of how some places are uniquely
suited for grape growing.

SAUSAL WINERY

707-433-2285, 800-500-2285
www.sausalwinery.com
7370 Hwy. 128, Healdsburg, CA 95448.
Tasting: 10–4 daily
Tasting Fee: None
Tours: No
Special Features: Picnic area

Zinfandel is the top dog at this small
winery. The Demostene family bought the
ranch back in 1956 and inherited a plot
of zinfandel that was planted before 1877.
They began bottling in 1974, and the zin
is full-bodied yet smooth. The tasting
room sits snugly among the vineyards,
and the vine-covered patio is a soothing
spot to sip.

SILVER OAK CELLARS

707-857-3562, 800-273-8809
www.silveroak.com
24625 Chianti Rd., Geyserville, CA 95441
Tasting: 9–4 Mon.–Sat.
Tasting Fee: $10
Tours: 1:30 Mon.–Fri. by appointment

Cabernet sauvignon specialist Silver Oak
considers Napa home, but it made its
reputation on Alexander Valley cabernet.
Consider this Silver Oak West. The winery, with its steeply pitched roof and
flagstone courtyard, remains an elegant
spot. While only the Alexander Valley

bottling is produced here, all of Silver Oak's wines are poured when available. (For the full scoop on Silver Oak, see Oakville & Rutherford earlier in this chapter.)

SIMI WINERY

707-433-6981
www.simiwinery.com
16275 Healdsburg Ave., Healdsburg, CA 95448
Tasting: 10–5 daily
Tasting Fee: $2–$5
Tours: 11 and 2 daily
Special Features: Gifts, picnic area

If we had to choose only one winery to visit—akin to limiting yourself to one glass of champagne on New Year's Eve—that would be a tough call, but we vote for Simi, an alluring combination of history and high-tech. You never feel you're being herded through a factory, even though the winery is hardly small. The staff knows wine but doesn't lord it over you. And best of all: The wines are first-rate.

Hidden in a shady grove of trees on the northern outskirts of Healdsburg, Simi has had a history as shaky as it is long. Italian immigrants Pietro and Giuseppe Simi built the original stone winery in 1890 and called the spot Montepulciano. Over the years, changes in ownership brought good times and bad, until French giant Moët Hennessy bought Simi in 1981 and restored its former glory. Simi changed hands again and is now owned by wine giant Icon Estates.

Simi gives one of the best tours, offering peeks at everything from the oak-barrel aging room to the bottling line. The tasting room is a cordial spot. Try the sauvignon blanc, always delightful, and the impressive cabernet sauvignons.

TRENTADUE WINERY

707-433-3104
www.trentadue.com
19170 Geyserville Ave., Geyserville, CA 95441
Tasting: 10–5 daily
Tasting Fee: Free–$5
Tours: By appointment
Special Features: Gondola tour of vineyards, picnic area, gifts, gourmet food

Trentadue makes Arnold Schwarzenegger wines: massive, muscular reds that won't be taken lightly. The Trentadue family has been making wine since 1969, favoring hearty classics such as carignane and sangiovese. After a spotty history, wine quality here took a leap in the 1990s. The tasting room is packed with gifts and picnic supplies, which you can put to fine use on the trellis-covered picnic patio. A fun feature is the tractor-powered gondola tour of the property. You can even taste wines along the way.

DRY CREEK

ALDERBROOK WINERY

707-433-9154
www.alderbrook.com
2306 Magnolia Dr., Healdsburg, CA 95448
Tasting: 10–5 daily
Tasting Fee: None–$5
Tours: No
Special Features: Picnic grounds

With its wraparound porch, bleached-pine interior, and fireplace, Alderbrook's tasting room is a touch of New England in Wine Country—not that Alderbrook specializes in stout reds perfect for cool Vermont nights. White wine is the house forte, and the sauvignon blanc and chardonnay are consistently solid. Nevertheless, the zinfandel, syrah, and pinot noir are increasingly impressive.

A. RAFANELLI WINERY

707-433-1385
www.arafanelliwinery.com
4685 W. Dry Creek Rd., Healdsburg, CA 95448
Tasting and Tours: By appointment
Tasting Fee: None
Special Features: Picnic area

If you want to try one of the best zinfandels in Wine Country, a trip to this small, folksy redwood barn is a requirement. The wines are nearly impossible to find otherwise. Rafanelli epitomizes old-school Sonoma County: good wine, no fuss. The Rafanellis have been growing grapes for generations and began making wine in 1974, believing their vineyards, not a winery with high-tech gadgets, did the talking. The winery makes great merlot and cabernet. The hospitality at the winery, once a bit snooty, has improved over the years.

BELLA VINEYARDS

707-473-9171
www.bellawinery.com
9711 West Dry Creek Rd., Healdsburg, CA 95448
Tasting: 11–4:30 daily
Tasting Fee: $5
Tours: By appointment
Special Features: Cave tour

Situated at the far end of a country road, Bella isn't the sort of winery you stumble onto but it's well worth the trek. Scott and Lynn Adams are a passionate young couple who decided to live the dream and started Bella. The focus is zinfandel and syrah, mostly from 80- or 100-year-old vines, and the wines are supple yet full of character. While you're tasting, be sure to check out the wine cave.

DRY CREEK VINEYARDS

707-433-1000, 800-864-9463
www.drycreekvineyard.com
3770 Lambert Bridge Rd., Healdsburg, CA 95448
Tasting: 10:30–4:30 daily
Tasting Fee: $5–$10
Tours: No
Special Features: Picnic area, gifts

Dry Creek Valley, we've always imagined, is what Napa Valley used to be: small, quiet, and unaffected by it all. It was a land of prunes and pears when Dave Stare, a former railroad engineer, arrived. The winery marked its 30th year in 2002. Designed after the small country wineries of France, Dry Creek has

---

Sonoma County Collectives

These tasting rooms offer a broad range of boutique wines—labels made in such small quantities that they typically aren't found in retail shops—so drink these rare offerings.

Cornerstone Place (707-933-3010, 23570 Hwy. 121, Sonoma, CA 95476, www.cornerstone place.com) A one-stop shop for tasting some of Sonoma County's best wines. The line-up includes Artesa, Roshambo, Larson Family Winery, and Ridgeline. The collective is a rare find because it's also an eye-catching hub of interesting shops such as Artefact Design & Salvage and 20 plots of gardens.

The Cellar Door (707-938-4466; www.sonomacellardoor.com; 1395 Broadway, Sonoma, CA 95476) A group of Sonoma Valley vintners banded together in this co-op to show their latest releases in this. Wineries include Mayo Family, Sunset Cellars, and Richardson Vineyards.

The Wine Room (707-833-6131; www.the-wine-room.com; 9575 Sonoma Hwy., Kenwood, CA 95452) When his career slowed in the 1970s, comedian Tommy Smothers bought a Kenwood ranch and planted grapes. Smothers Brothers wines soon followed, depending on how distracted Tom was by comedy. Dick Arrowood makes the bulk of the wine—now called Remick Ridge-and recent vintages have been impressive. These days, Smothers shares the tasting room with a number of other Sonoma Valley wineries, including Moondance, Sonoma Valley Portworks, and Family Dog Winery.

always reminded us of a simple country chapel: ivy-covered, with a pitched roof, and set amid a lush lawn and shady trees.

It only adds to the pleasure that Dry Creek's wines are consistently fine, often exceptional, as you'll discover in the tasting room. The atmosphere is laid-back, and the staff is chatty. Visitors can choose four samples from the winery's impressive list—not an easy task. Dry Creek has made its name with fumé blanc, a marvelous, crisp wine that dominates the winery's production. The chenin blanc is so fruity and distinctive that we prefer it over many chardonnays. As for reds, the zinfandel is always one of the best, and the cabernet sauvignon has fine character and can be exceptional in a good vintage. The picnic area, shaded mostly by tall trees, is one of the best in Wine Country.

FERRARI-CARANO VINEYARDS & WINERY

707-433-6700
www.ferrari-carano.com
8761 Dry Creek Rd., Healdsburg, CA 95448
Tasting: 10–5 daily
Tasting Fee: $5–$15
Tours: By appointment
Special Features: Gifts, garden

Ferrari-Carano seems to be on every restaurant wine list in America. The chardonnay is its flagship, a big, lush, complex wine. The fumé blanc is also impressive in its own right, while the cabernet sauvignon and merlot are both solid efforts.

Don and Rhonda Carano own the Eldorado Hotel and Casino in Reno, so their arrival in Wine Country has been a dramatic one. Situated in northern Dry Creek Valley, Ferrari-Carano is a bold statement. Villa Fiore, the winery's visitor's center, was completed in late 1994, and it's an extravagant Mediterranean palace surrounded by brushy lawns, flowers (more than 18,000

tulips bloom every spring), and vineyards. The tasting room has a faux marble floor and a mahogany and black-granite tasting bar. Visitors descend the limestone staircase to what is possibly the most opulent underground cellar in Wine Country.

J. FRITZ WINERY

707-894-3389, 800-418-9463
www.fritzwinery.com
24691 Dutcher Creek Rd., Cloverdale, CA 95425
Tasting: 10:30–4:30 daily
Tasting Fee: $5
Tours: By appointment
Special Features: Picnic area, gifts

This winery, in the farthest reaches of northern Sonoma wine country, is built like a bunker into the side of hill. Well off the road and hidden amid the scrub trees, J. Fritz blends into the countryside. J. Fritz takes zinfandel quite seriously, and it relies on gnarly old vines to make a burly yet graceful zin. Chardonnay and sauvignon blanc, too, are generally fine examples; try the melon, a white that's easy to quaff.

LAMBERT BRIDGE WINERY

707-431-9600, 800-975-0555
www.lambertbridge.com
4085 W. Dry Creek Rd., Healdsburg, CA 95448
Tasting: 10:30–4:30 daily
Tasting Fee: $10–$25
Tours: No
Special Features: Picnic area

Quaint is a woefully abused word, but we can't think of a better way to describe Lambert Bridge. Open since 1969, Lambert Bridge has maintained a low profile. This romantic little winery, with redwood siding and a porch shaded by wisteria, is a comfortable fit among the oaks and vines covering the hillsides overlooking Dry Creek. Inside, it's a comfortable space done in rich, dark wood. Merlot and chardonnay are specialties. There's a delightful picnic area out front, making this one of the best wineries around for a casual lunch.

MAZZOCCO VINEYARDS

707-431-8159, 800-501-8466
www.mazzocco.com
1400 Lytton Springs Rd., Healdsburg, CA 95448
Tasting: 10–5 daily
Tasting Fee: $5
Tours: No
Special Features: Picnic area

This winery is hardly a visual treat, but it occupies prime zinfandel land. Founded by Tom Mazzocco in 1984, the winery has weathered ups and downs, but one constant has remained: great zinfandel—big and spicy, yet with considerable finesse. Cabernet sauvignon and chardonnay also have charm.

PAPAPIETRO PERRY WINERY

707-433-0422
www.papapietro-perry.com
Tasting Room: 4791 Dry Creek Rd., Healdsburg, CA 95448.
Tasting: 11–4:30 daily
Tasting Fee: $5
Tours: No

The winery name may be a little hard to pronounce, but you'll have no trouble drinking the wines. Ben Papapietro and Bruce Perry were bitten by the bug way back in the 1970s, when they used to help out at harvest at Williams Selyem Winery. After making their own homemade wine for years, they started the winery in 1998. Zinfandel and pinot noir are their passions, and these wines are ripe and richly structured. The winery and tasting room are located just off Dry Creek Road amid a rural complex of small producers.

PRESTON OF DRY CREEK

707-433-3372, 800-305-9707
www.prestonvineyards.com

9206 W. Dry Creek Rd., Healdsburg, CA 95448
Tasting: 11–4:30 daily
Tasting Fee: $5
Tours: By appointment
Special Features: Picnic area, gifts, bakery

On the northern edge of Dry Creek Valley, this out-of-the-way winery has been quietly redefining itself in recent years. Lou and Susan Preston began as growers in 1973, specializing in grapes cherished by old Italian farmers: zinfandel and barbera. A winery followed two years later, and Preston made its name with zinfandel and sauvignon blanc, but Rhone varietals have taken on importance in recent years. The tasting room of this grand California barn was expanded a few years back, and there's a plush lawn for picnicking just off the tasting room porch. An olive oil and bread fanatic, Lou Preston has his own bakery on the property and olive trees are scattered around the site.

QUIVIRA VINEYARDS

707-431-8333, 800-292-8339
www.quivirawine.com
4900 W. Dry Creek Rd., Healdsburg, CA 95448
Tasting: 11–5 daily
Tasting Fee: $5
Tours: 10 Tues.–Sat.
Tour Fee: $10
Special Features: Picnic area, gifts

Quivira was a wealthy kingdom of legend that explorers believed was hidden in what is now Sonoma County. Though the name belongs to antiquity, this Quivira is a modern winery inside and out. The winery changed hands a few years back, and the wines seem to be struggling for an identity. That said, Quivira's zinfandel and sauvignon blanc are worth checking out.

RIDGE VINEYARDS

707-433-7721
www.ridgewine.com

650 Lytton Springs Rd., Healdsburg, CA
Tasting: 11–4 daily
Tasting Fee: Free–$5
Tours: No

This Sonoma County outpost of the popular Santa Cruz Mountain producer was once exclusively a destination for zinfandel lovers but now the winery has become part of the attraction. Environmentally friendly ,it has a smooth, contemporary construction that was done with recycled lumber and hay bale-insulated walls. Solar panels produce up to 75 percent of the winery's energy. Ridge produces most of its zinfandels on the property, and there's a range offered for tasting. Be sure to sip the Lytton Springs bottling as you gaze out the window to the thick-fingered, year-old vines that produced it.

UNTI VINEYARDS

707-433-5590
www.untivineyards.com
4202 Dry Creek Rd., Healdsburg, CA 95448
Tasting: By appointment
Tasting Fee: None
Tours: No

One of the charms about driving through the back roads of Sonoma County is discovering a small winery such as Unti that sells most of its wine out the door. The Unti family began growing grapes in 1990 and started making wine in 1997. The winery is as basic as it gets—the "tasting room" is a plywood counter topped by polished stainless steel. Unti lets the wine do the talking, and the wines are intense and authentic. The zinfandel is elegant in the classic Dry Creek Valley style, and the grenache and barbera are full of personality. This place is a gem.

WILSON WINERY

707-433-4355
www.wilsonwinery.com
1960 Dry Creek Rd. Healdsburg, CA 95448

Tasting: 11–5 daily
Tasting Fee: $5–$10
Tours: By appointment

The Wilson family owns more than 220 acres of prime Dry Creek hillside vineyards, and that's part of the key to the winery's success. Wilson makes a wide range of wines but zinfandel is the strong suit, as you might expect, because that's Dry Creek's specialty. The zins here are powerful and peppery. The winery is in an old tin barn, a local landmark, and the tasting room in the backside of the barn offers a soothing view of the surrounding vineyards.

SPECIALTY BREWERS

Watch out, wine connoisseurs: Beer lovers are getting serious, too. Microbreweries and brewpubs are cropping up all over Wine Country. It's a return to the days when any city of size had a brewery or two, bottling suds for the local area. (The San Francisco Bay Area is a leader in brewpubs.) It also harks back to England and Germany, where beers still have character. Also, beer hops were once an important crop in Sonoma County near the turn of the 20th century.

NAPA COUNTY
CALISTOGA INN & BREWERY

707-942-4101
www.napabeer.com
1250 Lincoln Ave., Calistoga, CA 94515

With its shady beer garden, this is one of our favorite destinations on a warm summer day. If you have lunch while sipping a brew, stick with the basics: a salad or a sandwich. When the weather cools, the action moves inside the historic Calistoga Inn. Come evening, the dining room is not our first choice in Calistoga for dinner, but stop in the pub for a beer before or after

Fans stand guard in vineyards to ward off frost in the spring. Tim Fish

you dine. The beers are all solid, particularly the pilsner and the red ale.

DOWNTOWN JOE'S MICROBREWERY

707-258-2337
www.downtownjoes.com
902 Main St., Napa, CA 94559

Some great beer—plus a comfortable wooden bar and a patio along the Napa River—can be found at this stylish and historic storefront in downtown Napa. The copper brew kettles are in plain sight, so you can watch the brewmaster do his stuff. The food is solid pub fare.

SILVERADO BREWING CO.

707-967-9876
www.silveradobrewingcompany.com
3020 St. Helena Hwy., Suite A, St. Helena, CA 94574

We like the atmosphere of this spot. The hand-hewn stone building, built in 1895, was once a winery, but now it's a popular hangout for tourists and locals alike. The beers, however, are unexciting, and, sadly, the food is a perfect match.

SONOMA COUNTY
BEAR REPUBLIC BREWING CO.

707-433-BEER
www.bearrepublic.com
345 Healdsburg Ave., Healdsburg, CA 95448

This may be Healdsburg's hottest nightspot, featuring food, live music, and some excellent handcrafted beers. The Scottish-style Red Rocket Ale is a specialty, and they also make a yummy Hefeweizen (pronounced *HEF-ay-vite-zen*), a light German brew perfect for a warm summer day. The atmosphere is lively, and from your table or the bar, you can watch brewing at work. As for the food, stick with the basics—burgers and so forth—and you won't go wrong.

DEMPSEY'S ALE HOUSE

707-765-9694
www.dempseys.com
50 E. Washington St., Petaluma, CA 94953

This is Wine Country's best brewpub—period. From the outside, Dempsey's doesn't look like much—it's in a generic shopping center—but it offers a handsome interior plus outdoor seating right along the Petaluma River. Peter Burrell brews superior ales, particularly his Red Rooster, and the food is better than you'll find at any pub. Chef Bernadette Burrell worked in the kitchen at Mustards Grill, so expect pork chops, wood-fired pizzas, and roasted half chickens.

RUSSIAN RIVER BREWING COMPANY

707-545-2337
www.russianriverbrewing.com
725 4th St., Santa Rosa, CA. 95404

The Russian River Brewing Company has 10 specialty brews on tap, ranging from Damnation, a Belgian-style ale, to Pliny the Elder, a double IPA. Brewmaster Vinnie Cilurzo is passionate about what he does. Eats include thin-crusted pizza, calzones, and salads, and the atmosphere of the pub is big, roomy, and energetic.

THIRD STREET ALEWORKS

707-523-3060
www.thirdstreetaleworks.com
610 3rd St., Santa Rosa, CA 95404

A popular downtown hangout, this brewpub has a stylish, almost industrial atmosphere, with polished-metal highlights and an open balcony. Third Street makes some great beer, including the Annadel pale ale. The food is better than most pubs, particularly the pizza and the spicy Cajun selections. If the weather is good, there's plenty of room on the patio, and in the balcony there are two pool tables and large communal tables.

Learning the Lingo: A Wine Glossary
No one expects you to be an expert when you're wine-tasting, but just in case, here's a crash course in the words of wine, how to say them, and what they mean.

Appellation: A legally defined grape-growing region. Alexander Valley, for example, is an appellation.

Blanc de Blancs (blonc deh blonc): A sparkling wine made from white grapes, usually chardonnay. Delicate and dry.

Blanc de Noirs (blonc deh nwahr): A sparkling wine made from red grapes, usually pinot noir. Sometimes faintly pink. Fruity but dry.

Blush: A pink or salmon-colored wine made from red grapes. Juice from red grapes is actually white. Red wine derives its color from juice left in contact with the grape skin. The longer the contact, the darker the wine.

Brut (broot): The most popular style of sparkling wine. Typically a blend of chardonnay and pinot noir. Dry.

Cabernet Franc (cab-er-NET fronc): Red wine of Bordeaux, similar to cabernet sauvignon, but lighter in color and body. Often used in blends.

Cabernet Sauvignon (cab-er-NET so-vin-YON): Red, fragrant, and full-bodied wine of Bordeaux. Dry and usually tannic. Can age in the bottle 5 to 10 years.

Chardonnay (shar-do-NET): California's most popular white grape, famed in France as the essence of white burgundy. Produces wine that's fruity, with hints of citrus or butter.

Chenin Blanc (shen-nin blonc): A white grape that produces a wine that's more delicate and less complex than chardonnay. Slightly sweet.

Crush: Harvesting and pressing of grapes. The beginning of the winemaking process.

Estate Bottled: Wines made from vineyards owned or controlled by the winery.

Fermentation: The conversion of grape juice into wine, using yeast to change sugar into alcohol.

Fumé Blanc (fu-may blonc): Same as sauvignon blanc. The name has traditionally been used to describe a dry-style sauvignon blanc.

Futures: Wines sold prior to release, usually at a discount, and delivered later.

Gewürztraminer (geh-VURZ-trah-me-ner): A white grape that yields a medium-bodied, semi-sweet, and lightly spicy wine.

Johannisberg Riesling (jo-HAHN-is-berg reesling): A white grape that produces a delicate wine, medium bodied and semisweet, with a melony fruit taste.

Late Harvest: Sweet dessert wine made from grapes left on the vine longer than usual. *Botrytis cinerea* mold forms, dehydrating the grapes and intensifying the sugar content.

Malolactic Fermentation: A second fermentation that converts malic acids (which have a tart-apple quality) to softer lactic acids (which lend a buttery quality).

Merlot (mer-LOW): Increasingly popular red grape from Bordeaux. Similar to cabernet sauvignon, but softer and more opulent.

Méthode Champenoise (meh-thowd SHAM-pen-nwas): Traditional French champagne-making process. Still wine is placed with sugar and yeast into a bottle, which is then sealed. The yeast devours the sugar, creating bubbles. The wine then "sits on the yeast," or ages in the bottle, several years. Finally, the yeast is extracted, and the sparkling wine—never once removed from its original bottle—is ready to drink.

Oak: Wine aged in oak barrels picks up some of the smell and taste of the wood. Also contributes to tannins and long aging. Example: "That chardonnay has too much oak for my taste."

Petite Sirah (peh-teet syr-AWH): Dark, rich, intense red wine.

Pinot Noir (pe-no nwahr): Silky, fruity, dry red grape that is also used to produce French Burgundy.

Reserve: A term traditionally used to mean wine held back or reserved for the winery owners, but the meaning has become vague in recent years. It's now sometimes used to mean better-quality grapes or wine aged longer in oak barrels.

Residual Sugar: Unfermented sugar that remains in the wine. Wine is considered sweet if it contains more than 0.5 percent residual sugar by weight.

Riddling: Process used to extract yeast from sparkling wine. A laborious process that slowly shakes deposits to the neck of the bottle, where they can be removed without disturbing the wine.

Sangiovese (san-jo-VEY-ze): The sturdy and often spicy red grape used in Chianti.

Sauvignon Blanc (so-vin-YON blonc): A crisp, light white wine with hints of grass and apples.

Semillon (sem-me-YAWN): A cousin to sauvignon blanc; the two are often blended together.

Sparkling Wine: Generic term for champagne. Technically, real champagne can come only from the Champagne region of France.

Syrah (syr-AWH): Ruby-colored grape of the Rhone region in France. Smooth, yet with rich and massive fruit.

Tannic: The puckery sensation caused by some wines, particularly young reds. Comes from the skin and stalk of the grapes as well as oak barrels. It's thought to further a wine's ability to age.

Varietal: A wine named for the grape variety from which it's made. Example: Chardonnay is a varietal; Bordeaux is not. (Bordeaux is a region in France—but Bordeaux wine can contain a number of varietals: cabernet sauvignon, merlot, etc.)

Vintage: The year the grapes for a particular wine are harvested. Nonvintage wines can be blends of different years.

Viognier (vee-own-YAY):This highly perfumed white wine is surprisingly dry on the palate. Native to the Rhone area of France, it's increasingly chic in California.

Viticultural Area: A wine-growing region. The Russian River Valley, for example, is a viticultural area of Sonoma County.

Zinfandel (ZIN-fan-dell): A spicy and jamlike red wine. A California specialty. Used also to make a blush wine called white zinfandel.

Golfers tee up at Meadowood in St. Helena. Tim Fish

7

RECREATION

The Great Outdoors

In Wine Country, a casual drive down the road is considered recreation. It's that beautiful. Rolling hills laced with vineyards, fertile valleys, a breathtaking coastline, and a mild climate: No wonder so many people are drawn to Napa and Sonoma—but there's more here than just wine and landscapes. If you crave something more physical, you'll keep busy. From long hikes through a gentle wilderness to rides above it all in hot-air balloons, there are recreational adventures to fit every style, taste, and budget.

Auto Racing

Yes, auto racing in Wine Country. It's our version of the Indianapolis 500, where you can experience the thrill of watching the fastest cars in the world. Sears Point International Raceway (707-938-8448, 800-733-0345, www.espnrus sellracing.com, Hwys. 37 and 121, Sonoma, CA 95476)offers speed aplenty during its season from April to August, which includes races featuring the hottest factory-backed sports cars, warp-speed dragsters, motorcycles, and even vintage cars.

Ballooning

Soaring silently above the vineyards and rolling hills of Wine Country in a hot-air balloon is an experience you won't quickly forget. Rides start early in the day, before surface winds interfere with the launch, and each ride is unique, dependent on the whim of the winds.

Some balloon companies provide pickup at your lodging; most provide continental breakfast and a champagne brunch following the ride. Prices vary, but expect to spend about $200 per person. Reservations are necessary.

For a real balloon extravaganza, each June take in Sonoma County's **Hot Air Balloon Classic**, when 50 balloons fill the sky over the vineyards in Windsor.

NAPA COUNTY

Napa Valley Aloft (707-944-8638, www.nvaloft.com, P.O. Box 2290, Yountville, CA 94599) Owners Carol Ann and Nielsen Rogers operate three Yountville balloon companies that share a reputation for personalized attention, unsurpassed service, experienced professional pilots, and special amenities: **Above the West** (800-627-2759) offers pickup from San Francisco and Napa Valley hotels, champagne breakfast, and daily flights. **Adventures Aloft** (800-944-4408), Napa's oldest balloon company, offers champagne flights daily,

Up, Up, and Away!

It's 6 AM. A group of early risers fends off the chilly dawn air with hot coffee, waiting for their ballooning adventure to begin. Though the balloon isn't in the air yet, anticipation soars as the balloon pilot and helpers unroll expanses of magnificent colored fabric onto the open field. Before long, giant fans are steadily blowing air into a flat balloon held open by the pilot. There are signs of life as the balloon grows slowly, like a whale rising above the water's surface—but it's still earthbound. Only when the pilot lights his propane burner and begins to heat the trapped air does the balloon rise.

The heated air, lighter than the cold air around it, lifts the weight of the fireproofed nylon fabric gradually, and within 15 minutes, the balloon is standing inflated on the open field—enormous, beautiful. Six or seven passengers hop into the basket with the pilot, and the lines are released.

Slowly, the balloon heads skyward—and slowly, the perspective of the passengers is changed until they can see the other balloons below them on the field, then buildings around the field, then hills in the distance. There is no sensation of movement, because the balloon moves with the wind; there is no sound except for the barking of a dog below or an occasional whoosh from the pilot's burner to keep the air heated.

The balloon follows the wind effortlessly, drifting over the countryside with the pilot's gentle guidance; he can "find" different currents to ride, like a canoeist on a fast-moving stream, but he can't change direction at will. He can turn the balloon in a circle, by opening flaps in the balloon with pulleys, but can't choose his landing place.

After about an hour's flight, the pilot allows the air to cool, and the balloon descends slowly. The pilot maneuvers it to avoid trees while he finds an open field for landing. The balloon lands gently; usually, there's no more than a gentle bump, though passengers will occasionally get tumbled out of the basket—an undignified though not harmful way to return to earth. The company's vans or trucks have followed the trip from below, and they are immediately on hand to secure and empty the balloon and load everyone in for the ride back.

The disappointment of returning to earth is diminished by a glass or two of champagne and a gourmet brunch designed to complete a memorable experience.

---

shuttle service, and a minister who's available for in-flight weddings. Sunrise launches daily from parking lot of V Marketplace in Yountville. **Balloon Aviation of Napa Valley** (800-367-6272) offers flights daily.

Napa Valley Balloons (707-944-0228, 800-253-2224, www.napavalleyballoons.com, P.O. Box 2680, Yountville, CA 94599) This highly regarded hot-air balloon company was founded in 1978. It offers a champagne brunch following flight.

SONOMA COUNTY

A Balloon Over Sonoma (707-546-3360, www.aballoonoversonoma.com ,109 Wikiup Meadows Dr., Santa Rosa, CA 95403) Offers daily flights for small groups. Balloons typically fly through the Russian River Valley. Champagne breakfast at a restaurant is included.

Above the Wine Country Ballooning (707-829-9850, 888-238-6359, www.winecountry balloons.com, 2508 Burnside Rd., Sebastopol, CA 94572) Offers romance flights for two, champagne, and custom videos.

Bicycling

Want to slow the pace of your Wine Country tour? Try a bike. With terrain that varies from meandering valleys to steep mountains and a spectacular coastline, there are roads and trails to satisfy everyone from the most leisurely sightseer to ambitious cycling fanatics.

Mountain bicycling, which started in Marin County just to the south, is extremely popular in Wine Country. **Annadel State Park** (707-939-3911) at times has more mountain bikes than runners on its trails, and **Austin Creek** is also a favorite spot in Sonoma county. Mountain cyclists in Napa County head for **Skyline Park** and **Mount St. Helena**.

Serious enthusiasts race in a number of annual events, including the **Cherry Pie Race** (a Napa tradition) and the **Terrible Two** (a grueling 208-mile course through Sonoma and Napa Counties). Charity races are popular in both counties. Most bike shops have information.

Many local parks have extensive bike trails, including **John F. Kennedy Park** in Napa (707-257-9529), **Skyline Wilderness Park** in Napa (707-252-0481), **Ragle Regional Park** in Sebastopol (707-823-7276), and **Spring Lake County Park** in Santa Rosa (707-539-8092).

Bicyclists of every level are welcome to join the weekend jaunts of the **Santa Rosa Cycling Club** (707-544-4803). The club meets every Saturday and Sunday (weather permitting) for different rides around the county. Call for times and meeting places or pick up specific ride information at local bike shops.

So rent a bicycle, pack a picnic lunch, and explore a park—or point your wheels toward the nearest country road, and enjoy the scenery you would miss from your car. Two excellent guides for specific trails are *Sonoma County Bike Trails* and *Rides In and Around the Napa Valley*.

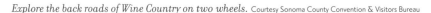

Explore the back roads of Wine Country on two wheels. Courtesy Sonoma County Convention & Visitors Bureau

BIKE RENTALS

Many inns offer bikes for casual day trips, and most bike shops rent two-wheelers for the day. Also, **Getaway Adventures** (707-942-0332, 800-499-2453, www.getawayadventures .com, 1718 Michael Way, Calistoga, CA 94515 and 2228 Northpoint Pkwy., Santa Rosa, CA 95407) organizes tours through Napa and Sonoma counties, suggests routes, and includes helmets and the like. They also offer wine tours called "Sip and Cycle" for $125.

Napa County
Calistoga Bike Shop (707-942-9687, 1318 Lincoln Ave., Calistoga, CA 94515)

St. Helena Cyclery (707-963-7736, www.sthelenacyclery.com, 1156 Main St., St. Helena, CA 94574)

Sonoma County
Rincon Cyclery (707-538-0868, 800-965-BIKE, www.rinconcyclery.com, 4927 Sonoma Hwy., Suite H, Santa Rosa, CA 95409)

Sonoma Valley Cyclery (707-935-3377, www.sonomavalleycyclery.com, 20091 Broadway, Sonoma, CA 95476)

Spoke Folk Cyclery (707-433-7171, www.spokefolk.com, 201 Center St., Healdsburg, CA 95448)

Boating and Watersports

The dry summer season may be crucial to growing great grapes, but it also means Napa and Sonoma are anything but wetlands. Humans, as usual, devised a way around nature, creating reservoirs for community water supplies and the delight of watersport fans.

Napa County
LAKE BERRYESSA

The largest man-made lake in the area, Lake Berryessa is about 15 miles east of Rutherford along Highway 128. About 26 miles long, it's one of northern California's most popular water recreation areas. **Lake Berryessa** (www.lakeberryessa.com) features seven resorts that offer complete facilities: full-service marinas, boat rentals for the avid fisherman, sailboats, water-ski and Jet Ski equipment, and overnight accommodations from tent and RV camping to top-quality motels.

Markley Cove has houseboats available for rent for leisurely overnights on the water.

Willi's Water Ski Center at Steele Park Resort (707-966-5502, 1605 Steele Canyon Rd., Napa, CA 94558) Offers water-ski instruction for beginners through competitive-level skiers run by German champion Willi Ellermeier.

Lake Berryessa Marina Resort (707-966-2161, 5800 Knoxville Rd., Napa, CA 94558) Offers boat launching, cabins, a full-service store and snack bar, campsites, RV hookups, boat rentals, and Jet Skis.

Markley Cove Resort (707-966-2134, 7521 Hwy. 128, Napa, CA 94558) offers boat launching and a store, but no camping.

Putah Creek Park & Store (707-966-2116) Offers boat launching, campsites, RV hookups, boat rentals, and a motel.

Rancho Monticello Resort (707-966-2188, www.ranchomonticelloresort.com, 6590 Knoxville Rd., Napa, CA 94558) Offers boat launching, campsites, and RV hookups.

Spanish Flat Resort (707-966-7700; www.spanishflatresort.com; 4290 Knoxville Rd., Napa, CA 94558) Offerings include boat launching, campsites, boat rentals, and water-ski and Jet Ski rentals.

Steele Park Resort (707-966-2123, 800-522-2123, www.steelepark.com; 1605 Steele Canyon Rd., Napa, CA 94558) Offers boat launching, RV hookups, wave runner and patio boat rental, water-ski school, and a motel.

SONOMA COUNTY
LAKE SONOMA
Sonoma County's Lake Sonoma, 11 miles north of Healdsburg on Dry Creek Road, offers 3,600 surface acres of scenic recreational waters. There are many secluded coves for the quiet boater or angler, while water-skiers and Jet Skiers are allowed in designated areas. Facilities include a public boat ramp, full-service marina, campsites (both drive-in and those accessible only by boat), hiking trails, swimming areas, and a visitors center and fish hatchery near the Warm Springs Dam. For information, try the **Lake Sonoma Recreation Area** (707-433-9483, ext. 27, 3333 Skaggs Rd., Geyserville, CA 95441) or **Lake Sonoma Marina** (707-433-2200), which offers boat rentals—including fishing boats, paddleboats, canoes, and water skis and Jet Skis.

RUSSIAN RIVER
Because the Pacific Ocean is chilly and the surf is a bit rugged (see The Coast later in this chapter), the Russian River is a good alternative for a leisure day on the water. During the hot summer, riverside beaches are popular with families who enjoy swimming in the refreshing water while canoes glide past. Canoes and kayaks can be rented near Healdsburg or Guerneville for a leisurely trip, with stops to relax or swim along the way. Don't be surprised if you spot a few nude sunbathers. The county doesn't condone it, but the freewheeling '60s still live in West County.

Bodega Bay Kayak (707-875-8899, www.bodegabaykayak.com, 1580 East Shore Dr., Bodega Bay, CA 94923) Offerings include rental, sales, and tours at $45 for four hours.

Burke's Canoe Trips on the Russian River (707-887-1222, www.burkescanoetrips.com, P.O. Box 602, Forestville, CA 95436; at River Rd. at Mirabel, 1 mile north of Forestville) Burke's offers a leisurely 10-mile trip to Guerneville through the redwoods. A return shuttle service is available. Reservations are required, $58 per canoe. Closed from mid-October to April.

River's Edge (800-345-0869, www.riversedgekayakandcanoe.com, 13840 Healdsburg Ave., CA 95488) Offers two-day, full-day and half-day trips down the river. Its Web site details each trip.

OTHER SITES
Lake Ralphine (707-543-3424, Howarth Park, Santa Rosa, CA 95409) This is a popular spot for water activities, from boating to feeding ducks. Stocked with fish, this small man-made lake has a city-run boat rental where rowboats, canoes, and paddleboats are available for a minimal fee. Powerboats are not permitted.

Spring Lake (707-539-8092, off Montgomery Dr., Santa Rosa, CA 95409) This lovely 75-acre lake is open only to canoes, rowboats, and kayaks—all of which can be rented during the summer. Windsurfing and rafting are also allowed. There's a separate lagoon for swimming. For boat rentals, call 707-538-3608.

Camping

Wine Country campgrounds and RV parks are plentiful for the adventurous who like to "rough it." Camping may be a low-key affair, but don't be laid back about reserving a spot. Campsites fill up quickly in the summer months. Reservations, in fact, are mandatory at most California state parks and beaches and are accepted up to eight weeks in advance or as late as 48 hours prior to the first day of the reservation if space is available. State campgrounds are noted with an asterisk (*) in the following listing.

Camping fees in Wine Country state parks vary with the season and the park. (Fees range from $17 to $32 per night per campsite—which includes a $7 reservation-processing fee plus an additional $3–$5 for the peak-season rate.) As a rule, campgrounds described as "developed" have flush toilets, hot showers, drinking water, improved roads, and campsites with a table and stove or fire ring. Primitive campsites usually have chemical or pit toilets, tables, and a central water supply. Environmental campsites are primitive sites in undisturbed natural settings. Enroute campsites are day-use parking areas where self-contained trailers, campers, and motor homes may park overnight. To make reservations at state campgrounds, phone 800-444-7275.

Fees at privately operated parks and resorts are generally $15–$24 per night for tent camping, and from $27 to $30 per night for RV sites with hookups.

NAPA VALLEY

*Bothe-Napa Valley State Park (707-942-4575, 3801 St. Helena Highway North, Calistoga, CA 94515; midway between St. Helena and Calistoga, off Hwy. 29) This 1,920-acre state park has 50 developed campsites. Campers up to 31 feet and trailers to 24 feet can be accommodated; no sanitation station is provided. Services include horseback-riding trails, hiking, swimming pool, picnic area, and exhibits. Handicapped accessible in all areas.

Putah Creek Resort (707-966-0794, 7600 Knoxville Rd., Napa, CA 94558; Highway 128 to Knoxville Road at Lake Berryessa) This is a full-service resort with 200 campsites, 55 RV sites, and a 26-unit motel. Offerings include a grocery store, a restaurant and lounge, a delicatessen, and a snack bar. There's also a marina with fishing supplies and a bait shop.

Rancho Monticello Resort (707-966-2188, www.ranchomonticelloresort.com, 6590 Knoxville Rd., Napa, CA 94558; on Knoxville Road, about 4.5 miles off Highway 128) The resort includes waterfront cabins, travel trailer and camping sites with RV hookups, vacation rentals of three- to four-room mobile homes, a restaurant, a beer garden, a grocery, and a snack bar.

Spanish Flat Resort (707-966-7700, www.spanishflatresort.com, 4290 Knoxville Rd., Napa, CA 94558; Highway 128 to Knoxville Road, on Lake Berryessa) This establishment includes 120 lakeside tent and RV sites, a sanitation station, a restroom with showers, a convenience store, and a snack bar.

SONOMA COUNTY

Austin Creek State Recreation Area (707-869-2015, Armstrong Woods Rd., Guerneville, CA 95446; 3 miles north of Guerneville) This is a rugged, natural setting of 5,683 acres with just three primitive, hike-in campsites and 24 car-camping sites. Trailers and campers longer than 20 feet are prohibited.

Casini Ranch Family Campground (707-865-2255, 800-451-8400, 22855 Moscow Rd., P.O. Box 22, Duncans Mills, CA 95430; off Highway 116 at Duncan Mills, 0.5 mile east on Moscow Road) This family campground on the Russian River has 250 pull-through spaces, many of them riverfront sites. Offerings include boat, kayak, and canoe rentals; fishing; swimming; a playground; a general store; Laundromat; and cable TV.

KOA San Francisco North (707-763-1492, 20 Rainsville Rd., Petaluma, CA 94952; Old Redwood Highway exit off Highway 101, west to Stony Point Road, north to Rainsville Road) This 60-acre, rural, farm setting has 312 tent and RV sites with full hookups. Also offered are a swimming pool, a hot tub, a convenience store, Laundromats, a playground, camping cabins, a petting zoo, and daily San Francisco tours.

River Bend RV & Campground (707-887-7662, 11820 River Rd., Forestville, CA 95436; about 11 miles west of Highway 101 on River Road) This full service campground has hookups, river access, and a general store. Pets on leash are allowed, and there's 24-hour, on-site security.

*Salt Point State Park (707-865-2391, 707-847-3221, 25050 Coast Hwy. 1, Jenner, CA 95450; 20 miles north of Jenner on Highway 1) Here you'll find 30 developed campsites (no showers), 20 hike-in tent sites, and 30 enroute sites on 6,000 acres. Trailers and campers longer than 31 feet are prohibited. There's no sanitation station.

*Sugarloaf Ridge State Park (707-833-5712, 2605 Adobe Canyon Rd., Kenwood, CA 95452; 7 miles east of Santa Rosa on Highway 12, north on Adobe Canyon Road) This 2,500-acre park offers 50 developed campsites, an observatory, 25 miles of nature trails, hiking, horseback riding trails, and exhibits. Trailers and campers up to 28 feet long are permitted.

*Sonoma Coast State Beach (707-875-3483; 3905 Hwy 1, Bodega Bay, CA 94923; between Jenner and Bodega Bay) This site encompasses 5,000 acres, with two developed campgrounds (**Bodega Dunes** and **Wrights Beach**) and two primitive sites (**Willowcreek** and **Pomo**).

Bodega Dunes Campground (707-875-3483, Bodega Bay, CA 94923; 0.5 mile north of Bodega Bay on Highway 1) This is the larger of the two state beach campgrounds, with 99 developed campsites. Trailers and campers up to 31 feet are permitted. Included are showers, picnicking, hiking, fishing, and horseback riding. A sanitation station is provided, but there are no hookups. Most facilities are wheelchair accessible.

Wrights Beach Campground (707-875-3483, Bodega Bay, CA 94923; 6 miles north of Bodega Bay on Highway 1) Here you'll find 28 developed campsites. Trailers and campers up to 27 feet are allowed. Picnicking, hiking, and fishing are included, but there are no showers. Some facilities are wheelchair accessible.

Willowcreek Campground (707-875-3483, Jenner, CA 95450; Willowcreek Rd., 1.5 miles off Highway 1) There are 11 undeveloped camping sites a short hike from your car at this campground. Also provided are picnic tables and fire rings. There are no showers, and there are chemical toilets. The policy: first come, first served—no reservations.

Pomo Environmental Campground (707-875-3483, Jenner, CA, 95450; Willowcreek Rd., 3 miles off Highway 1) Here there are 21 undeveloped camping sites a short hike from your car. Picnic tables and fire rings are provided, but there are no showers and there are chemical toilets. The policy: first come, first served—no reservations.

Ft. Ross Reef Campground (707-847-3286, 10 miles north of Jenner on Highway 1) Here you'll find 21 campsites, flush toilets, running water. The site accepts tents and trailers, and offers fishing and abalone diving. The limitation on trailers: only 18 feet, bumper to bumper.

The Coast

Sonoma County's 62-mile coastline has a rustic beauty that's scarcely changed from the days when the Miwok and Pomo Indians were the only inhabitants in the area. The white man has left his mark, however. Early Russians settlers in the 1800s decimated the sea otter population for the creature's highly prized pelt. Now under government protection, the sea otter is slowly making a comeback—although much to the distress of abalone divers, who compete for the otter's favorite food. The Americanization of California, along with the population surge after the Gold Rush, created a need for timber, so the giant redwoods near the coast were harvested heavily. Lush forests remain, however.

Enjoy spectacular views on the Sonoma coast. Tim Fish

Visitors flock to the Sonoma coast to enjoy some of the most spectacular views in all of California. The rugged cliffs, continually battered by the wild Pacific Ocean, afford a set ting of breathtaking beauty. Thanks to the foresight of those who fought to preserve public access to the coast, there are many outlets from which to view the ocean along Highway 1. Particularly popular is the stretch **between Bodega Bay and Jenner,** where several beaches offer a variety of topography and vistas for hiking, picnicking, wetsuit diving, surfing, or just relaxing.

Whatever your activity, it's important to remember at all times that the Pacific Ocean can be dangerous. Every year, deaths are caused by unpredictable waves and the strong undertow. Be cautious.

Bodega Bay harbor offers protection from the rough Pacific surf and serves as the home port for many commercial fishing boats. After gaining fame as the setting of Alfred Hitchcock's *The Birds*, the town of **Bodega Bay** has now become a well-known stopover and destination spot for California residents and visitors alike. Sportfishing, harbor cruises, and whale-watching trips can be arranged from **Porto Bodega Marina**, off Highway 1 on Bay Flat Road. The gentle beaches on the west side of the harbor afford a perfect spot for windsurfing or sea kayaking.

BEACHES

Here are some of the beaches along the coast, listed from north to south. For detailed information, call the **Sonoma County Tourism Program** (800-576-6662). Some of the beaches have a day-use fee.

Bodega Headlands (707-875-3483, at the end of Bay Flat Road, off Highway 1, Bodega Bay, CA 94923) Originally part of the Sierra Nevadas, the headlands stretch like a curved arm out to sea. For 40 million years, they have ridden the Pacific Plate northward, out of step with the land on the other side of the San Andreas Fault. The cliffs of the headlands provide a spectacular vista of the Pacific Ocean coast. They provide the best spots to watch for whales in the winter and early spring. It's not a bad idea to bring binoculars and a jacket. Also of interest at the headlands is the **Bodega Marine Lab** (707-875-2211, www.blm.ucdavis.edu, 2099 Westside Rd., Bodega Bay, CA 94923), open to the public on Friday from 2 to 4 PM. It's educational, and kids will love it.

Doran Regional Park (707 875 3540, Doran Beach Rd., off Highway 1, south of Bodega Bay, CA 94923) This is a popular family spot because of its level, sandy beach and overnight camping facilities. An annual sand castle competition is held every August. There's a day-use fee.

Salt Point State Park (707-847-3221, 800-444-7275, 25050 Hwy. 1, 95450, north of Timber Cove) Here you'll find 4,114 acres along 5 miles of shore, offering picnicking, fishing, skin diving, and hiking. More than 14 miles of trails wind through tall forests, windswept headlands, a stunted Pygmy forest, and grassy valleys along the San Andreas Fault. Camping is available. Adjacent to the park is Kruse Rhododendron State Reserve. In May and June the brilliant pink blossoms of native rhododendrons brighten the forest along the path.

Goat Rock Beach (707-875-3483, 3905 Bodega Bay, CA 94923, off Highway 1, south of Jenner) Named for the huge beach rock that bears a resemblance to the hunched back of a grazing goat, the beach extends from the sandbars along the mouth of the Russian River, where sea lions and their young exit the waters of the river at certain times of the year. They're fun to watch, but please don't disturb them.

Sonoma Coast State Beach (707-875-3483, Salmon Creek, Bodega Bay, CA 94923) This is actually a chain of many beaches along 18 miles of coastline, from Goat Rock to Bodega Head. Each has its own personality and invites different activities, whether it's tide pooling or a serious game of volleyball. Wildflowers brighten the cliffs in the spring. The coast is always cool in the summer, supplying an escape from inland heat.

Bodega Dunes (707-875-3483; 2485 Hwy. 1, Bodega Bay, CA 94923) Here you'll find a boardwalk and 5 miles of trails through the dunes. No dogs are allowed on the beach, trails, or dunes because of endangered western snowy plover in these areas, but dogs are allowed in the campground, which has 98 sites for tents and RVs up to 31 feet long.

SCUBA DIVING & OTHER SURF EQUIPMENT

The Sonoma coast is Wine Country's busiest recreational spot. Whatever water sport you prefer—scuba diving, abalone diving, surfboarding, kayaking—there's plenty to do on the coast. The water temperatures range from 40 to 55 degrees, making a full wetsuit a minimum requirement, with many divers preferring drysuits for added comfort. Diving is a year-round activity, as long as the sea is calm. Divers must respect the power of the ocean.

Abalone can be harvested from April to December (excluding July). Scuba equipment is not allowed while hunting these succulent creatures, and there's a limit of four abalone per person. You'll also need a license to harvest them.

Pinnacles Dive Center (707-542-3100, 2112 Armory Dr., Santa Rosa, CA 95401) Offers diving courses, rentals, equipment sales, and diving trips.

Bodega Bay Surf Shack (707-875-3944, www.bodegabaysurf.com, 1400 Hwy. 1, Bodega Bay, CA 94923) Here you'll find instruction and tips, and rentals and sales, including kayaks.

Bodega Bay Kayak (707-875-8899, www.bodegabaykayak.com) Offers rentals, sales, and tours at $45 for four hours.

TIDE POOLING

The Sonoma coastline has its own wildlife preserve: the tide pool. Here, the rocky coast is as productive as a tropical rain forest. As the tide goes out twice daily, small oases are left behind among the rocks—shelters for starfish, snails, sea anemones, and a multitude of other visible and almost invisible life-forms.

In these tide pools there's little movement at first glance, but with a bit of patience, you'll find there's much to discover. Follow a hermit crab as it creeps out of its turban shell and maneuvers over a rock. Watch the sea anemone's green tentacles entwine a mussel. Track the Crayola-green fish or sculpins as they dart in and out of the rocks. Search out the starfish playing dead. Tide pools are full of old-timers. Snails may be 20 to 30 years old, and a starfish may be 10 years old.

Remember: Please don't remove anything from the pools; even an empty shell might be a hermit crab's mobile home. Tide poolers are advised to wear waterproof boots for the best exploration. Be cautious. Crabs pinch, octopuses bite, and sea urchin spines are prickly. Also, beware of sleeper waves—those unexpectedly large waves that sneak up and sweep away beachcombers.

The rocky Sonoma coast provides the perfect environment for tide pools as well as secluded beaches. Tim Fish

For additional insight into the world of the tide pool, visit the **Bodega Marine Laboratory** (707-875-2211, www.bml.ucdavis.edu/index/html, 2099 Westside Rd., P.O. Box 247, Bodega Bay, CA 94923). The laboratory is open to the public on Friday from 2 to 4 PM.

Where are the best places to tide pool? Nearly any rocky place along Sonoma Coast State Beach, which stretches between Bodega Bay and Jenner. The Bodega Marine Lab recommends two: Try the north end of **Salmon Beach**, which is accessible from any Highway 1 pull-off north of the Salmon Creek Bridge. **Shell Beach**, a few miles south of Jenner on Highway 1, is more remote, requiring a trip down steep stairs, but it's worth it.

Family Fun

Wine Country isn't just a playground for adults. Kids and kids at heart can find all sorts of fun, from pony rides and water slides to a planetarium show guaranteed to stretch the imagination. Also see Swimming and Boating and Water Sports in this chapter for other family activity suggestions.

Napa County

Old Faithful Geyser (707-942-6463, www.oldfaithfulgeyser.com, 1299 Tubbs Ln., Calistoga, CA 94515; 1 mile north of Calistoga) One of just three regularly erupting geysers in the world, it shoots steam and vapor 40 to 50 feet into the air for three minutes, and repeats this feat every 40 minutes. Because seismic activity influences the frequency of the eruptions, many believe Old Faithful predicts earthquakes. Open daily, the site includes picnic grounds. Admission: $7 for per family with AAA, $8 adult, $3 children 6-12, children under 6 free.

Petrified Forest (707-942-6667; 4100 Petrified Forest Rd., Calistoga, CA 94515; 5 miles west of Calistoga) Here you'll find remains of a redwood forest turned to stone by molten lava from the eruption of Mount St. Helena three million years ago. The Petrified Forest was discovered in 1870 and immortalized by Robert Louis Stevenson in *The Silverado Squatters.* Included here are picnic grounds and a gift shop, and the site is open daily. Admission: 60-plus, $5; $6 adults, $5 youths 12–17, $3 children 6–11, children under 6 free.

SONOMA COUNTY

Maxwell Family Fun Center (707-996-3616, 19171 Sonoma Hwy., Sonoma, CA 95476) This game arcade and miniature golf course features scale models of historic Sonoma landmarks.

Howarth Park (707-543-3425, Montgomery and Summerfield Rds., Santa Rosa, CA 95409) This popular, city-run park offers a merry-go-round; pony rides; a petting zoo; a small railroad; play and picnic areas; paddleboats, canoes, and rowboats to rent; and ducks to feed on Lake Ralphine. Activities are open on the weekends in the winter.

Planetarium (707-527-4465, 800-616-2695, Santa Rosa Junior College, Room 2001 Lark Hall, 1501 Mendocino Ave., Santa Rosa, CA 95401) This excellent planetarium is open to the public on weekends during the school year. Shows are offered at 7 and 8:30 PM Friday and Saturday, and 1:30 and 3 PM Sunday during the fall and spring academic year. There are no reservations, so arrive early to park. Admission: $4 general, $2 students and seniors, no children under 5 admitted.

Safari West (707-579-2551, www.safariwest.com, 3115 Porter Creek Rd., Santa Rosa, CA 95404) This 400-plus acre park features 150 species, including 400 rare and endangered animals. Not a drive-through animal park, this is a 2.5-hour tour that's comparable to a real African safari. You even get to feed a giraffe. Admission: $62 adults, $28 children age 3–12.

Scandia Family Fun Center (707-584-1361, www.scandiafunland.com, 5301 Redwood Dr., Rohnert Park, CA 94920) Here you'll find little Indy racers, miniature golf, baseball batting cages, bumper boats, and a game arcade. This is a favorite recreation center for kids and families and is packed on summer weekends. There's even a Fika Pizza inside. Separate fees for each activity; hours vary.

Traintown (707-938-3912, www.traintown.com, 20264 Broadway, Sonoma, CA 95476; 1 mile south of Sonoma Plaza) Take a 20-minute ride on a scale-model steam train around 10 acres of beautifully landscaped park, through a 140-foot tunnel, over bridges, and past historic replica structures. Also offered: a petting zoo, exhibits, and amusement rides. Traintown is open daily June–Sept., weekends the rest of the year. Admission: $3.75 adults, seniors, and children; amusement rides additional.

PLAYGROUNDS

If you're touring Wine Country with tykes, they need their share of fun, too. Sometimes 30 minutes on a playground can go a long way. Grab a picnic or a snack, and head to one of these parks. Best of all: It's all free.

NAPA COUNTY

One of the best playgrounds in Napa Valley is in **Yountville City Park**, just off Madison Street on the north edge of town. It's a modern and well-maintained playground, and the park offers plenty of shade for Mom and Dad. Other Napa County playgrounds: In the heart

Howarth Park in Santa Rosa is one of the most family friendly spots in Wine Country. Tim Fish

of St. Helena is a modest little playground in **Lyman Park**, off Main Street near Adams. In Calistoga there's a pleasant little playground in **Pioneer Park**, on Cedar Street just off Lincoln Avenue. In the city of Napa, head to **Klamath Park**, on the north edge of town just off Highway 29 at Trower Avenue.

SONOMA COUNTY

In Sonoma Valley you can't ask for a more convenient playground than **Sonoma Plaza**. A beautiful spot with lots of shade, there's even a duck pond to keep the kids busy. Best of all, Mom and Dad can take turns shopping while the kids blow off steam. In Healdsburg head for **Giorgi Park** on University Street, and Sebastopol has one of the best playgrounds around in **Libby Park**, on Pleasant Hill Road just north of Highway 12.

Santa Rosa has two excellent playgrounds. On the east side of town is a new, highly creative playground at **Howarth Park**. It's on Summerfield Road; from Highway 12, take Mission Boulevard south to Montgomery, and then make a quick left on Summerfield. On the west side is **Finley Park**, which has a modern playground that will keep kids busy for hours. To find it, take College Avenue west from Highway 101, and then turn south on Stony Point Road.

Fishing

For the expert or the novice, Wine Country offers a fine variety of fishing opportunities. Where else could you hook a giant salmon in the Pacific in the morning, and then snag a trophy bass in one of California's largest man-made lakes in the afternoon of the same day?

Remember to pick up a fishing license through a local sporting supply or department store. See Boating and Water Sports in this chapter for additional information.

NAPA COUNTY

Lake Berryessa (www.lakeberryessa.com, 5800 Knoxville Rd., Napa, CA 94558) is a designated trophy lake, boasting trout, bass (both largemouth and black), crappie, bluegill, and catfish. With seven resorts, camping, and full-service marinas, there are unlimited facilities for every type of fishing. For more information, see Boating and Water Sports in this chapter.

There's plenty to do at Lake Ralphine in Santa Rosa. Tim Fish

Lake Hennessey (4 miles east of Rutherford on Highway 128, closest town: Rutherford, CA 94543) This is a water source for the city of Napa. Fishing and boating are allowed, though the only facilities are a car-top launch ramp and picnic grounds.

Napa River can be fished for stripers or sturgeon year-round. **Kennedy Park** (707-257-9529, 2291 Streblow Dr., off Highway 121, Napa CA 94558) Provides a boat-launch ramp and is a good spot for fishing off the riverbank.

Napa Sea Ranch (707-252-2799, 3333 Cuttings Wharf Rd., Napa CA) Offers a boat-launch ramp as well as a bait-and-tackle store and 1,800 feet of river frontage.

SONOMA COUNTY

Lake Sonoma (Visitor Center & Hatchery: 707-433-9483, Marina: 707-433-2200; 11 miles north of Healdsburg on Dry Creek Road, Sonoma, CA 95448) Offers 53 miles of shoreline and secluded coves for the quiet angler as well as a boat-launch ramp and a full-service marina for boat rentals. Fish include bass, Sacramento perch, channel catfish, red-ear perch, and blue catfish. Of interest is the fish hatchery, where visitors can watch tanks full of lively young salmon and steelhead, which are released into Dry Creek when they reach 6 to 7 inches long.

Lake Ralphine (707-543-3424, Howarth Park, Santa Rosa, CA 95409) and Spring Lake (707-539-8092, off Montgomery Dr., Santa Rosa, CA 95409) are popular family destinations for low-key fishing expeditions. Both lakes are stocked with catfish, black bass, trout, and bluegill and practically guarantee beginners a catch. Both lakes also offer boat rentals.

The Russian River offers smallish runs of steelhead trout and salmon fishing Nov. through Mar. The Russian River can be fished from its banks or from canoes and other nonpower boats.

Bodega Bay is home port for sportfishing boats, offering all-day trips on the Pacific Ocean. Leaving daily, weather permitting, 40- to 65-foot boats search out 200 species of rock and bottom fish and, between Apr. and Nov., prized salmon. The cost is about $50–$150 a person. You can also take the ride just for fun.

Bodega Bay Sport Fishing Center (707-875-3344, 1410 Bay Flat Rd., Bodega Bay, CA 94923) Offerings include daily charter boats, equipment rentals, sportfishing for many species of rock and bottom fish and salmon, and whale-watching tours.

The Boathouse (707-875-3495, 1445 Hwy. 1, Bodega Bay, CA 94923) This establishment has three boats: the 65-foot *Sea Angler,* the 50-foot *Profishn't,* and the 40-foot *Predator.* It offers daily trips for salmon, rockfish, and Dungeness crab.

Galvin Park (Bennett Valley, Santa Rosa CA) Fly-fishing enthusiasts will appreciate the fly-casting practice pond constructed by the city of Santa Rosa and the Russian River Flyfishers Club. Fly-fishing clinics are held Thursday from 4 to 6 PM. To reserve a spot call **Western Sport Shop** (707-542-4432, 2790 Santa Rosa Ave., Santa Rosa, CA 95407).

Flying
You won't need a pilot's license to zoom low over Wine Country. Take a scenic flying tour above vineyards and mountains or try aerobatics in a 1940 biplane. For those whose psyches crave an extra thrill, there's hang gliding and paragliding by the cliffs near Jenner or Mount St. Helena.

Vintage Aircraft (707-938-2444, www.vintageaircraft.com, Sonoma Valley Airport, 23982 Arnold Dr., Sonoma, CA 95476) Red Baron, move over. These scenic tours of Napa Valley and Sonoma County are in vintage biplanes that have been meticulously restored. Aerobatic flights are also available, offering loops, rolls, and "kamikaze" flights. Not for the faint of heart.

Golf

Golf courses cover the rich valleys and rolling hills of Wine Country as eagerly as vine-yards. One of the region's favorite recreational activities, golf can be played year-round in this mild climate. Where to play? Stay at a premier resort with its own course, such as Silverado or Meadowood, or at accommodations with courses close at hand, such as Doubletree Inn and Sonoma Mission Inn. Or sample a variety of public and semiprivate courses (private clubs that also allow the public to play). Many private clubs allow members of other clubs to enjoy the benefits of their own members.

Greens Fees Price Code

Inexpensive: Under $25

Moderate: $25 to $50

Expensive: More than $50

NAPA COUNTY

Aetna Springs (707-965-2115, www.aetnasprings.com, 1600 Aetna Springs Rd., Pope Valley, CA 94567) This public course was established in the 1890s. Here you'll find 9 holes, par 35; a driving range; a pro; lessons; and snacks. Price: inexpensive.

Chardonnay Golf Club (707-257-1900, 800-788-0136, www.chardonnaygolfclub.com, 2555 Jamieson Canyon Rd., P.O. Box 3779, Napa, CA 94558) This is a semiprivate course offering three 9-hole championship courses, par 72, Scottish links style; a driving range; three pros; a shop; and a clubhouse. Price: expensive.

Napa Municipal Golf Course (707-255-4333, www.playnapa.com, Kennedy Park, 2295 Streblow Dr., Napa, CA 94558) This public course offers 18 holes, par 72; a driving range; instruction; a cocktail lounge; and reserve tee time seven days in advance. Price: moderate.

Meadowood Resort (707-963-3646, 800-458-8080, www.meadowood.com, 900 Meadowood Ln., St. Helena, CA 94574) This course is private to members and guests. It offers 9 holes, par 31, on a tree-lined, narrow course. Price: moderate to expensive.

Mount St. Helena Golf Course (707-942-9966, 2025 Grant St., Calistoga, CA 94515) This course is private for hotel members and guests. It offers 9 holes, par 34, and a snack bar. Price: inexpensive.

Napa Valley Country Club (707-252-1114, 3385 Hagen Rd., Napa, CA 94558) This private course offers 18 holes, par 72; a shop; a pro; and lessons that are open to the public. Price: moderate to expensive.

Silverado Country Club and Resort (707-257-5460, 800-362-4727, www.silverado resort.com, 1600 Atlas Peak Rd., Napa, CA 94558) This club is private to members and guests. It offers two 18-hole championship courses, par 72; a pro; and a shop. Many consider it to be the best course in northern California. Price: expensive.

SONOMA COUNTY

Adobe Creek Golf Course (707-765-3000, www.adobecreek.com, 1901 Frates Rd.,
Petaluma, CA 94954) This public course offers 18 holes, par 72; a driving range; a putting
green; and a lounge and restaurant. Price: inexpensive to moderate.

Bennett Valley Golf Course (707-528-3673, 3330 Yulupa Ave., Santa Rosa, CA 94505) This
municipal course offers 18 holes, par 72; three pros; a shop; a driving range; a putting
green; and a restaurant and lounge. Reserve one week ahead. Price: inexpensive.

Bodega Harbour Golf Links (707-875-3538, 21301 Heron Dr., Bodega Bay, CA 94923)
This semiprivate course designed by Robert Trent Jones offers 18 championship holes, par
69; two pros; a shop; lessons; a restaurant and lounge; and spectacular ocean views from
all holes. Price: expensive.

Fountaingrove Golf & Athletic (707-579-4653, 1525 Fountaingrove Pkwy., Santa Rosa, CA
95403) This private course designed by Ted Robinson offers 18 championship holes, par
72; a pro; a shop; a restaurant; and tennis courts. Price: expensive.

Foxtail Golf Club (707-584-7766; 100 Golf Course Dr., Rohnert Park, CA 94928) This
public club offers two 18-hole championship courses, par 72; a pro; a shop; a driving
range; a putting green; and a restaurant and lounge. Price: inexpensive to moderate; two
courses, price varies.

Oakmont Golf Club (707-539-0415, 7025 Oakmont Dr., Santa Rosa, CA 95409) This club
comprises two private and public 18-hole championship courses, par 72, designed by Ted
Robinson; four pros; two shops; a driving range; and lessons. Reservations are suggested.
Price: inexpensive to moderate.

Sea Ranch Golf Links (707-785-2468, 4200 Hwy. 1, Sea Ranch, CA 95497) This Scottish
links style public course designed by Robert Muir Graves offers 18 holes, par 72; a pro; a
shop; a driving range; lessons; a snack bar; and ocean views from every hole. Price: moderate to expensive.

Sebastopol Golf Course (707-823-9852, 2881 Scott's Right-Of-Way, Sebastopol, CA
95472) This public course offers 9 holes, par 31; a pro; a shop; a snack bar; and picnic
facilities. Price: inexpensive.

Sonoma Golf Club (707-996-0300, 707-939-4100, www.sonomagolfclub.com, 17700
Arnold Dr., Sonoma, CA 95476) This is a private course—an individual can play only if he
or she is a guest at the Fairmont Sonoma Mission Inn. It offers 18 championship holes, par
72; a driving range; a putting green; and a restaurant. Price: moderate to expensive.

Hiking & Parks

Whether you choose a trail through sand dunes or redwoods, grassy valleys or mountain
forests, there's no better way to appreciate the natural beauty of Wine Country than to pack
a snack and leave the roads behind you. Each season has its own personality: brilliant
wildflowers in the spring, dry heat and golden grass in summer, colored foliage in the fall,
cool breezes and green hills in winter. A number of state and county parks await you,
whether you're toting a baby for his first hike or you're ready for serious backpacking. For
help with the details of your trip, see Bob Lorentzen's *The Hiker's Hip Pocket Guide to Sonoma
County* (which includes some hikes in Napa County).

Hike some Wine Country trails to appreciate the natural beauty of the area.
Tim Fish

Remember, though you're not likely to find bears, mountain lions are seen occasionally, and rattlesnakes and ticks are common in the backcountry. Stay away from poison oak, and don't forget to take your own water on summer hikes. **Getaway Adventures** (800-499-2453, www.getawayadventures.com) offers organized hikes through Robert L. Stevenson, Bothe-Napa Valley, and Skyline parks.

NAPA COUNTY

Bothe-Napa Valley State Park (707-942-4575, 3801 St. Helena Hwy. North, Calistoga, CA 94515) Originally home to the Wappo Indians, this land became a country retreat for San Francisco's wealthy Hitchcock family in the 1870s. The History Trail passes a pioneer cemetery to Bale Grist Mill, a partially restored 1846 grist mill. Here you'll find 1,917 acres and 10 miles of hiking trails. Day-use fee.

John F. Kennedy Park (707-257-9529, 2291 Streblow Dr., Napa CA; off Hwy. 121) This 340-acre park features hiking trails along the Napa River and plenty of undeveloped open space as well as softball fields, playgrounds, and boat-launch ramps.

Robert Louis Stevenson State Park (707-942-4575, 7 miles north of Calistoga on Highway 29) Composed of ancient lava, Mount St. Helena rises 4,343 feet to provide the highest landmark in Wine Country. In 1841 Russian settlers from Fort Ross scaled the peak, naming it for their commandant's wife, Elena. In 1880 Robert Louis Stevenson spent two months near the mountain, recovering from tuberculosis. It made a lasting impression on him, and he renamed it Spyglass Hill in his most famous work, *Treasure Island*. Located here are 3,300 acres, including 10- and 6.5-mile round-trips to two summits, past the once-prosperous Silverado Mine. The area is undeveloped except for the trails, and it's open daily during daylight hours.

Skyline Wilderness Park (707-252-0481, 2201 E. Imola Ave., Napa CA) This is 900 acres of wilderness close to downtown Napa, with 35 miles of hiking, mountain bike, and horse trails. Its oak-wooded hills are ideal for hiking. On a clear day, enjoy spectacular views of San Francisco from the park's ridges. A small lake offers bass fishing. It's open daily year-round. Day-use fee.

Westwood Hills Wilderness Park (707-257-9529, Browns Valley Rd., Napa CA; at Laurel Street) This city-owned, 111-acre park has hiking trails, a nature museum, and native flora and fauna.

White Sulphur Springs (707-963-8588, 3100 White Sulphur Springs Rd., St. Helena CA) This secluded countryside is located 3 miles west of St. Helena. You'll find hiking trails throughout and a year-round creek and waterfalls. Day-use fee.

SONOMA COUNTY

Annadel State Park (707-539-3911, 6201 Channel Dr., Santa Rosa CA; off Montgomery Drive) Surrounded by an increasingly developed Santa Rosa, Annadel offers 5,000 acres of hills, creeks, woodlands, and meadows accessible through 40 miles of trails used by hikers, horseback riders, and mountain bikers. Annadel visitors enjoy a small central lake created by the last owner, Joe Coney, and named for Joe and his wife, Ilsa: Lake Ilsanjo. Day-use fee.

Armstrong Redwoods State Reserve (707-869-2015, 17000 Armstrong Woods Rd., Guerneville CA) In the late 1800s Colonel James Armstrong sought to preserve this ancient 5000-acre grove of redwoods he had come to love. Because of his efforts and those of his family, Sonoma is fortunate to be able to enjoy this virgin stand of thousand-year-old trees stretching 300 feet high-one of the largest of which is named after the colonel. Walk among these giants, where even on the hottest day, you'll feel their cool serenity. You'll find hiking trails, picnic sites, and an outdoor theater. The area is open year-round until sunset. Day-use fee.

Austin Creek State Recreation Area (707-869-2015, 17000 Armstrong Woods Rd., Guerneville CA) Adjacent to Armstrong Grove, this undeveloped park of 4,200 acres offers miles of trails for hikers and equestrians through canyons, enormous glades, and dark, cool forests. Twenty-four campsites are also available. Day-use fee.

Hood Mountain Regional Park (707-565-2041, 3000 Los Alamos Rd., Santa Rosa CA) Accessible by car from Alamos Road or by a 4-hour hike from Sugarloaf Ridge State Park, Hood Mountain (elevation 2,730 feet) commands an imposing view of the Mayacamas Mountains. Located here are challenging trails. The area is closed Tues.–Thurs. Day-use fee.

Lake Sonoma (707-433-9483, 3333 Skaggs Spring Rd., Healdsburg CA; near Dry Creek Road) Forty miles of trails wind through the 3,600 acres of redwood groves and oak woodlands surrounding Sonoma's newest man-made lake. A visitors center is located at the base of the dam. There are also camping, boating, swimming, and a fish hatchery.

Jack London State Historic Park (707-938-5216, 707-939-6191 (kiosk), 2400 London Ranch Rd., Glen Ellen CA; off Arnold Drive) Writer Jack London fell in love with the Valley of the Moon and began buying land there in 1905. By the time he died in 1916, he was immersed in the innovative projects of his Beauty Ranch. Visitors can traverse these 800 acres, seeing the remains of the Londons' Wolf House mansion, hiking 7 miles of trails, and taking in a scenic 3.5-mile climb with breathtaking views of the Valley of the Moon. The area is open daily, and no dogs are allowed. Day-use fee: $6; $5 for seniors.

Ragle Ranch Regional Park (707-823-7262, 500 Ragle Rd., Sebastopol CA; off Bodega Highway) This 156-acre former ranch offers trails through a rugged wilderness of oak woodlands and creeks, baseball fields, playgrounds, and picnic areas.

Sugarloaf Ridge State Park (707-833-5712, 800-444-7275, 2605 Adobe Canyon Rd., Kenwood, CA 95452; off Highway 12) The Wappo Indians lived in this beautiful area before many were decimated by European diseases in the 1830s. Purchased by the state in 1920 as a site for a dam that was never built, Sugarloaf Ridge (2,700 acres) now offers more than 25 miles of trails through a varied landscape including ridges surrounding Bald Mountain and meadows along Sonoma Creek. Camping is also offered, but no dogs are allowed. Day-use fee.

Horseback Riding

Wine Country adamantly maintains its rural flavor, despite its growing population and worldwide tourist appeal. With an estimated 26,000 horses in Sonoma County alone, there is plenty of interest in horse breeding, competition, and riding. Some 50 horse events take place annually at the Sonoma County Fairgrounds, including top shows such as the California State Horse Show, which attracts visitors from all over the West.

Like Jack London, who was described by one biographer as the "sailor on horseback," many Wine Country residents and visitors take to the hills on horseback to explore the countryside as the early California settlers did before them. Bridle paths and trails can be found at these parks: **Annadel, Armstrong Redwoods, Austin Creek, Bothe-Napa Valley, Jack London, Salt Point, Skyline,** and **Sugarloaf Ridge.** For those without their own steeds, the following stables rent horses for the day. Trail-ride packages start as low as $50 and can go as high as $150 for the more experienced riders.

NAPA COUNTY

Northbay Natural Horsemanship (707-479-8031, www.northbaynaturalhorsemanship.com, Napa, CA) These stables offer training and lessons. Camping involves staying in tents, riding horses, working on horsemanship, and enjoying nature.

SONOMA COUNTY

Armstrong Woods Pack Station (707-887-2939, Armstrong Redwoods State Park, 17000 Armstrong Woods Rd., P.O. Box 287, Guerneville, CA 95446) Offers rentals for trail rides through Armstrong Redwoods State Reserve and Austin Creek State Recreation Area. Also offers trail rides.

Chanslor Guest Ranch and Horse Stables (707-875-3333, www.chanslor.com, 2660 Hwy. 1, Bodega Bay, CA 94923) Offers scenic guided trail rides for riders of all levels. Rides include one- or two-hour treks on the ranch and dunes. Open year-round.

Horse Racing

Horse-racing fans converge each summer at the **Sonoma County Fair** (707-545-4200, 1350 Bennett Valley Rd., Santa Rosa, CA 95404) to watch California's fastest horses vying for a purse of nearly $2 million. During the rest of the year, the fairgrounds offer **The Jockey Club** (707-524-6340), with simultaneous broadcasting of races at Golden Gate Fields, Bay Meadows, and Hollywood Park.

Rock Climbing

For those who like to live on the edge, rock climbing has become a sport with built-in adventure, but it's important to do it right. **Sonoma Outfitters** (707-528-1920; www.sonoma outfitters.com; 145 3rd St., Santa Rosa, CA 95401) offers a complete selection of shoes, gear, and camping equipment.

When you're ready for the real thing, favorite climbing spots in the area are **Sunset Boulder** at Goat Rock on the Sonoma coast and **Mount St. Helena** in Napa. Check out the book *Bouldering in the Bay Area* for other possible challenges.

Running

Joggers of all ages, sizes, and shapes can be seen on park trails and roadsides in Sonoma and Napa counties. The fresh air and rural countryside of Wine Country, along with its mild climate, have made running an extremely popular year-round activity for the health conscious.

For serious runners looking for competition, several events take place each year, including the **Napa Valley Marathon,** which is run from Calistoga to Napa on the second Sunday in March. Another demanding event is the **International Vineman Triathlon,** combining running, bicycling, and swimming competitions. Many races in both counties, such as Sonoma County's **Human Race,** benefit local causes. Get specific schedules from the **Sonoma County Tourism Program** (800-5-SONOMA) or the **Napa Valley Conference and Visitors Bureau** (707-226-7459, 1310 Napa Town Center, Napa, CA 94559).

Skating
ICE SKATING

The late famed cartoonist and ice-skating buff Charles Schulz built the **Redwood Empire Ice Arena** (707-546-7147, 1667 W. Steel Ln., Santa Rosa, CA 95403) in 1969, and it's one of Sonoma County's most popular spots. The rink, surrounded by walls painted with Alpine scenes, is the site for recreational and would-be Olympic skaters, birthday parties, and holiday ice shows with professional figure skaters. Next door is **Snoopy's Gallery & Gift Shop** (707-546-3385), filled with every conceivable item relating to Snoopy and the *Peanuts* gang as well as skating gear, including high-tech in-line skates.

ROLLER SKATING

It's still a fun-time favorite with kids, teens, and adults. After all, they say it's the best aerobic exercise around. Find the fun at **Cal Skate** (707-585-0500, www.calskate.com, 6100 Commerce Blvd., Rohnert Park, CA 94928).

Spas

Long before pioneers came to settle northern California, Native Americans knew the locations of hot springs, and used the steamy pools, volcanic mud, and mineral waters to heal and
soak away pains. Calistoga remains the most popular destination for mud, mineral baths, and
professional massage, but health spas are beginning to dot all of Wine Country. Many spas are
a part of resorts or other places to stay; check chapter 3, Lodging, for more information.
Credit Cards

The following abbreviations are used for credit card information.
    AE: American Express
    DC: Diner's Club
    CB: Carte Blanche
    MC: MasterCard
    D: Discover Card
    V: Visa

Napa County
AUBERGE DU SOLEIL
707-963-1211
180 Rutherford Hill Rd., Rutherford, CA 94573
Open: 8–8 daily
Credit Cards: AE, D, MC, V

What would Napa Valley's most luxurious resort be without an excellent spa? The facility is
top–notch—but then, so is everything at this inn hidden in the mountains above Napa
Valley. Auberge du Soleil offers a variety of treatments, from aromatherapy and facials to
foot massages and ayurveda, an ancient East Indian healing system that uses massage and
curative oils. If you're staying at the inn, many treatments can be done in your room. One-
hour massage: $180.

CALISTOGA SPA HOT SPRINGS
707-942-6269
www.calistogaspa.com
1006 Washington St., Calistoga, CA 94515
Open: 8:30 AM–9 PM Fri.–Mon., 8:30–4:30 Tues. and Thurs.
Credit Cards: MC, V

Stylishly designed, with high-tech masonry, polished-metal accents, and glass-block
walls, this is one of Calistoga's most pleasant spa experiences. Massage rooms are
equipped with skylights—a nice touch. Mud baths use a traditional blend of volcanic ash,
peat moss, and hot-spring water. The staff is extremely attentive. Massage is generally
Swedish technique. This is one of the best pool destinations in Napa, with four naturally
heated outside pools, varying from an 80-degree lap pool to a huge, 104-degree, covered
whirlpool. The wading pool signals that kids are welcome here. Pools are open to the public for day use and are surrounded by pleasant and private landscaping. Steam rooms and
the exercise room are large. Mud bath, mineral whirlpool, and half-hour massage:
$40–$199 packages.

CALISTOGA VILLAGE INN AND SPA

707 942 0991
www.greatspa.com
1880 Lincoln Ave., Calistoga, CA 94515
Credit Cards: AE, D, MC, V

A small facility removed from the bustle of the downtown strip, this was once known as the French Spa. The name has changed, but the French-style spa equipment remains. Changing rooms are makeshift, but the spa rooms are pleasantly adorned with blue-and-white tiles. The mud treatment is one of best in town; it uses a pleasant mix of peat moss and white clay that's mildly heated by mineral water before you enter. French steam cabinets—contraptions that cover everything except your head—substitute for steam rooms, an enjoyable change. Specialties include herbal wraps and an invigorating salt scrub. Outside mineral pools have a magnificent view of the surrounding mountains. There's a wading pool for kids, and the pool house has a whirlpool and sauna. Mud bath, mineral whirlpool, organic facials, body wraps, scrubs, foot treatments and 50-minute massage for $80 and 80-minute massage for $125.

DR. WILKINSON'S HOT SPRINGS

707-942-4102
www.drwilkinson.com
1507 Lincoln Ave., Calistoga, CA 95415
Open: 7:30 AM—11 PM daily
Credit Cards: AE, MC, V

John "Doc" Wilkinson was a young chiropractor when he gave his first spa treatment in 1946. One of the most popular spas on Calistoga's main drag, Dr. Wilkinson's remains a no-frills outfit. The concrete-block walls of the spa area create a utilitarian atmosphere, the steam room is closet sized, and the mineral baths are simple claw-foot tubs—but the staff is first rate. Mud baths use a traditional blend of volcanic ash, peat moss, and hot-spring water. One of the best massages in Calistoga is found here; both Swedish and Shiatsu techniques are used. The salon offers six different types of facials. Outdoor pools are not open for day use. Mud bath, mineral whirlpool, and half-hour massage: $55.

EUROSPA AND INN

707-942-6829
www.eurospa.com
1202 Pine St., Calistoga, CA 9451.
Open: 8 AM—10 PM daily
Credit Cards: AE, D, MC, V

Eurospa takes its lead, as its name suggests, from century-old Continental traditions. Located in the Eurospa Inn, the spa sets an intimate yet airy mood. Spa rooms have pleasant views of the grounds, and after treatments, guests are free to roam outside to use the pool and Jacuzzi. Treatments include various body wraps, aromatherapy facials, body scrubs, and Swedish massage. Mud wrap and one-hour massage: $180.

Playing with Mud

Along with all its other striking features, Wine Country is blessed with a little extra something: geothermal activity from down under. The most popular signs of hot steam and bubbling mineral water are the SPA signs along Lincoln Avenue in downtown Calistoga, where salvation is offered to the body and soul in the form of mud and mineral baths.

What exactly is a mud-bath treatment? First, you immerse yourself in a thick, warm, black mass of volcanic ash and/or peat moss, mixed with naturally heated mineral water. It's like a warm cocoon enveloping you, so just lie back and go with it. The benefits? Relaxed muscles and joints and soft, renewed skin. There are drawbacks, of course. Some may find the mud too warm, and others may feel claustrophobic being engulfed in so much earth. Also, the mud sticks like glue as you wash it off in a lukewarm shower.

Afterward, soak in warm mineral water, and then open your pores in a eucalyptus-scented, geyser-heated steam room. Finish up with a cooling blanket wrap. Ahhhh. If you can handle additional pleasure, expert masseuses will work your body into a Silly-Putty state.

GOLDEN HAVEN HOT SPRINGS SPA AND RESORT

707-942-6793
www.goldenhaven.com
1713 Lake St., Calistoga, CA 94515
Open: 8 AM—11 PM daily
Credit Cards: AE, MC, V

Situated in a residential neighborhood three blocks from Calistoga's downtown, the Golden Haven isn't fancy but has been drawing a following since the 1950s. Service is pleasant and the atmosphere is low key. This is one of the few spas to offer mud baths and mineral baths for couples—a cozy touch. Mud baths use a mix of peat moss, clay, and mineral water. Specialties include an inch-reducing European body wrap and oatmeal facial scrubs. Massage is Swedish, along with Esalen, acupressure, and deep tissue. Spa guests have access to an outside Jacuzzi and a large 80-degree pool. Mud bath, mineral whirlpool, and half-hour massage: $125.

LINCOLN AVENUE SPA

707-942-2950
www.lincolnavenuespa.com
1339 Lincoln Ave., Calistoga, CA 94515
Open: 10—6 Sun.–Fri., 10—8 Sat.
Credit Cards: AE, MC, V

Housed in a sturdy, rock building—originally Calistoga's first bank—this spa is in the heart of downtown. Although you won't find any ink pens on chains, the spa has done a good job of preserving the bank's interior, even retaining the vault. Lincoln Avenue offers a few unusual treatments. If being buried in mud isn't your cup of tea, try the herbal wrap: A balm of warm herbs is applied to your skin—a soothing steam treatment. The mud comes in different "flavors," as well, including seaweed and mint. Other treatments include facials and massages, and all treatments are for singles or couples. No pools or whirlpools are offered. Body mud and half-hour massage: $129.

MEADOWOOD

707-963-3646, 800-458-8080
www.meadowood.com
900 Meadowood Ln., St. Helena, CA 94574
Open: 7 AM–8 PM daily
Credit Cards: AE, D, DC, MC, V

Want to be pampered? The health spa at Meadowood Resort is the place. One of Napa Valley's best spas, it comes at a price, yet a basic massage is priced competitively. Meadowood specializes in face and body treatments as well as fitness programs. The set ting alone soothes the soul. The spa is set in the lush foothills of Howell Mountain, and the outside pool and Jacuzzi are surrounded by towering trees. Treatments include something called a citrus salt glow as well as facials, waxing, and various therapeutic combinations of all individual treatments. Massage rooms are darkly lit, and light music is piped in. Treatments are available to resort guests and members only. Sixty-minute massage with use of steam room, sauna, and pools: $135.

MOUNT VIEW SPA

707-942-5789, 800-816-6877
www.mountviewspa.com
1457 Lincoln Ave., Calistoga, CA 94515
Open: 9–9 daily
Credit Cards: AE, MC, V, D

If you're turned off by the communal locker room atmosphere of many Calistoga spas, this spa has the solitude you crave. Private treatment rooms have lockers, steam rooms, and two-person Jacuzzi tubs for both singles and couples. Part of the newly restored Mount View Hotel, the spa is elegant yet unpretentiously appointed. Mud treatments come in two forms: Moor Mud, a light, warm chocolate–milklike blend of mineral water, herbs, and concentrated volcanic ash; and Grapeseed Rosehip Mud that infuses the body with power-ful antioxidants and vitamins E and C before it's wrapped in warm blankets. Other treat-ments include a variety of hydrotherapy baths, facials, and Swedish and reflexology massage. Choice of hydrotherapy bath with 50-minute massage: $130.

OASIS SPA

707-942-2122
1300 Washington St., Calistoga, CA 94515
Open: 9–5 Tues. and Wed., 9–9 Thurs.–Mon.
Credit Cards: MC, V

A bungalow next to the Roman Spa Motel, Oasis offers a variety of treatments from tradi-tional mud, mineral baths, and massage to herbal facials, foot reflexology, and seaweed baths and wraps. All treatments are for singles or couples. Massage is Swedish and Esalen. Mud bath, mineral whirlpool, and a 25-minute massage: $115.

SOLAGE

866-942-7442
755 Silverado Trail, Calistoga, CA 94515
Open: 8–8 daily
Credit Cards: AE, DC, MC, V

The Solage Spa has five buildings with warm tones and natural stones. In addition to the treatment center, other key buildings include a bath house, a fitness center, and a movement studio. The spa offers massages, facials, and body scrubs and it also has a full service nail lounge. At the bath house it offers a "mud slide" treatment, which involves baking in mud for twenty minutes, then resting in a geothermic water tub, and finally sitting in a vibrational healing chair developed by NASA. The movement center offers yoga and spinning classes. The one-hour Swedish-style Solage Massage: $115.

SPA TERRA OF THE MERITAGE RESORT

707-251-3000
www.themeritage.com
875 Bordeaux Way, Napa, CA 94558
Open: 8–8 daily
Credit Cards: AE, D, MC, V

This underground spa is undeniably unique. It's not often you get a massage in a cave setting with a wine tasting bar within reach. The spa is part of a 22,000-square-foot underground space, and it has 12 treatment rooms, two reserved for couples. It offers massages, facials and manicures. Perhaps the most decadent is the Solo Vino, which begins with a grape seed scrub, followed by a jet shower, and then application of a wine mud mask before a 50-minute Swedish massage. The $235 treatment includes a cheese tray and a glass of red or white wine.

SONOMA COUNTY
A SIMPLE TOUCH

707-433-6856
239C Center St., Healdsburg, CA 95448
Open: 10–6 daily
Credit Cards: MC, V

An intimate spot just off the Healdsburg square, this spa is a welcome addition to northern Sonoma County. With a large tub room, one couple's room, and two treatment rooms, Simple Touch offers individualized care. The lobby welcomes you with warm tones, a bit of Tuscany. Mud baths are fango style—a light and warm chocolate-milklike blend of mineral water and powdered mud. There are champagne baths as well as rose-petal wraps, herbal facials, Swedish deep tissue massage, sports massage, and hot rocks massage. Mud bath and one-hour massage: $130.

FAIRMONT SONOMA MISSION INN AND SPA

707-938-9000, 800-862-4945
www.fairmont.com
100 Boyes Blvd., Hot Springs, CA 95416
Open: 8 AM–9 PM Sun.–Thurs., 8 AM–10 PM Fri. and Sat.
Credit Cards: AE, DC, MC, V

Who's that lounging in the mineral pool? Billy Crystal? The waters at this Wine Country favorite for the rich and famous have made this site a destination since Native Americans first considered it a healing ground. It's also Wine Country's most expensive spa. The inn has recently tapped into a new source of mineral water, and the soft and lightly green liquid warms the pool and Jacuzzi. The spa house is a stylish combo of Mission and Art Deco, and the pool area is in a peaceful grove of trees. The array of treatments is mind-boggling, from Swedish and sports massage to seaweed body wraps, hair and foot care, waxing, color analysis, and nearly a dozen different facials. There's also a fitness center. Sonoma Lavender Kur, a bubble bath, a body wrap, and a 55-minute massage: $255.

OSMOSIS

707-823-8231
www.osmosis.com
209 Bohemian Hwy., Freestone, CA 95472
Open: 9 AM–8 PM daily
Credit Cards: AE, MC, V

A truly unique experience, Osmosis is the only place in the Western world to offer Japanese-style enzyme baths. The baths are similar to mud baths in only one way: You're covered from neck to toe. In this case, though, it's not mud but a sawdustlike mix of fragrant cedar, rice bran, and more than six hundred active enzymes. The concoction ferments and generates gentle and natural heat. Guests don kimonos and begin their treatment in a Japanese sitting room, sipping enzyme tea as they gaze through shoji doors into the Japanese garden. Baths can be taken solo or with a friend. The treatment concludes with a shower and a 30-minute blanket wrap or Swedish massage. Enzyme bath with 75-minute massage: $170.

SONOMA SPA

707-939-8770
www.sonomaspaontheplaza.com
457 1st St. W., Sonoma, CA 95476
Open: 9–9 daily
Credit Cards: AE, D, MC, V

This spa has brought a much-needed dose of indulgence to downtown Sonoma. The Greek Revival storefront looks out onto historic Sonoma Plaza. There are no traditional mud baths here, but treatments are available for singles and couples. They include Swedish and Esalen massage as well as rose-petal body masques, cooling body mud, herbal wraps, facials, and foot reflexology. Mud and wrap treatments include an herbal sauna. A body mud treatment and a one-hour massage: $149.

THE SPA AT HOTEL HEALDSBURG

707-433-4747
www.hotelhealdsburg.com
327 Healdsburg Ave., Healdsburg, CA 95448
Open: 9–8 daily
Credit cards: AE, D, DC, MC, V

There's an understated sophistication to this spa, which is secluded deep inside this downtown hotel. There are six treatment rooms, and the decor blends soothing colors with plantation shutters and pecan wood floors. Guests have access to a whirlpool tub and pool. Treatments range from pedicures and facials to hot stone massages and detoxifying seaweed wraps. Fifty-minute massage: $105.

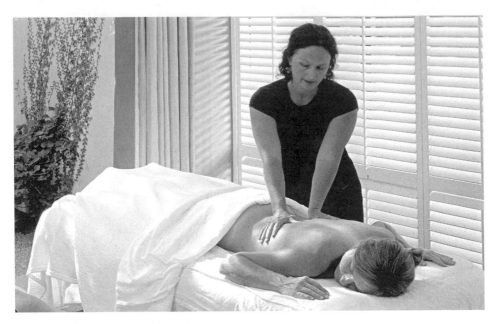

Be pampered at the spa at Hotel Healdsburg. Courtesy Hotel Healdsburg, Cesar Rubio

Swimming

Summer in Wine Country brings day after day of blue skies—that is, after the sun breaks through the morning fog. It does get hot in the summer, and a dip in cool water is luscious relief. Remember, the Pacific Ocean—with year-round temperatures around 50 degrees and dangerous undercurrents—is not a good choice. For those whose swimming is more for exercise than for fun, indoor pools with lap lanes are also available year-round. In Calistoga some spas open their pools to the public for day use for a nominal fee.

NAPA COUNTY

Bothe-Napa Valley State Park (707-942-4575, 3801 Hwy. 29, 5 miles north of St. Helena) The swimming pool is open mid-June through Labor Day. Day-use fee.

Lake Berryessa Marina Resort (707-966-2161, 5800 Knoxville Rd., Napa, CA 94558; west of Rutherford on Highway 128) Miles of clear blue water with temperatures up to 75 degrees make this an ideal summer destination.

Several resorts, including **Putah Creek, Spanish Flat,** and **Steele Park,** offer swimming areas. (See Boating and Water Sports in this chapter for specific information on resorts.)

St. Helena Community Pool (707-963-7946, 1401 Grayson Ave., St. Helena, CA 94574) Open all summer.

SONOMA COUNTY

Lake Sonoma (707-433-9483, 3333 Skaggs Rd., Geyserville, CA 95441; 11 miles north of Healdsburg on Dry Creek Road) Beaches, along with picnic, hiking, and boating facilities, can be found at **Lake Sonoma Marina** and **Yorty Creek**.

Morton's Warm Sonoma Springs Resort (707-833-5511, 800-551-2177, www.sonoma springs.com, 1651 Warm Springs Rd., Kenwood, CA 95452) Here you'll find two large pools and one wading pool, picnic grounds, volleyball, baseball, and bocce. Now open year-round, this location is perfect for group outings.

Russian River residents and visitors alike enjoy swimming in the slow-flowing, deep-green Russian River. Swimming areas are at **Veterans Memorial Beach** in Healdsburg (707-433-1625, Healdsburg Ave.), and **Monte Rio Beach** and **Johnson's Beach** in Guerneville (707-869-2022), both just off River Road, where canoes can be rented.

Spring Lake (707-539-8092, 5585 Newanga Ave., Santa Rosa, CA 95409; off Summerfield Road) The 3-acre swimming lagoon—separated from the lake's boating and fishing areas—is filled with kids and their families every hot day in summer. A gentle, sandy shoreline with water floats to mark depth; rafts and tubes to rent; and lifeguards help make this a great swimming experience for beginners. Admission $6 per vehicle.

YMCA (707-545-9622, 1111 College Ave., Santa Rosa, CA 95404) The Y's indoor heated pool is open daily, year-round, for laps, exercise, instruction, and family fun. Day and evening hours.

Tennis

In an area where the climate is mild and it rains only six months out of the year, you would expect any who play tennis to pursue it avidly. Do they ever! With a variety of both public and private tennis courts offering competition and teachers offering instruction, Wine Country gives the tennis enthusiast plenty of action.

NAPA COUNTY

Calistoga Public Courts (707-942-2838, Stevenson and Grant Sts., Calistoga, CA) Open year-round, the facility includes four lit courts. There's city-run instruction in summer.

Meadowood Resort (707-963-3646, 900 Meadowood Ln., St. Helena, CA 94574) The courts are open to members and guests, and a pro is on-site.

Napa Public Courts (707-257-9529) are available during the summer at **Napa Valley College** (Vallejo Hwy., Napa CA), **Vintage High School** (1375 Trower Ave., Napa, CA), **Napa High School** (2475 Jefferson St., Napa, CA), and **Silverado Middle School** (1133 Coombsville Rd., Napa, CA). City-run instruction can be found at these sites.

Napa Valley Country Club (707-252-2299, www.napavalleycc.com, 3385 Hagen Rd., Napa, CA 94558) The courts are private. A pro is on-site, and lessons are open to the public. This is an active spot.

St. Helena Public Courts (707-963-5706) are available at **Robert Louis Stevenson School** (1316 Hill View Pl., St. Helena CA) and **St. Helena High School** (1401 Grayson Ave., St. Helena, CA). City-operated courts can be found at **Crane Park** (off Crane Avenue, St. Helena, CA). There's an active women's city league program for A and B players.

Silverado Country Club and Resort (707-257-0200, www.silveradoresort.com, 1600 Atlas Peak Rd., Napa, CA 94558) The courts are open to members and guests. Altogether, there are 14 courts, three of them lit, and there's a pro on-site.

SONOMA COUNTY

La Cantera Racquet and Swim Club (707-544-9494, 3737 Montgomery Dr., Santa Rosa, CA 95405) Courts are open to members and guests. Altogether, there are 12 courts, four of them lit. There's an on-site pro, leagues, and tournaments.

Montecito Heights Health and Racquet Club (707-526-0529, 2777 4th St., Santa Rosa, CA 95405) Courts are open to members and guests. There are five unlit courts, an on-site pro, leagues, and tournaments.

Rohnert Park Public Courts (707-588-3456) are available at nine parks in Rohnert Park (Rohnert Park, CA 94928): **Alicia** (400 Santa Alicia Dr.), **Dorotea** (895 Santa Dorotea Circle), **Eagle** (1115 Emily), **Golis** (1450 Golf Course Ln.), **Honeybee** (1170 Golf Course Dr.), **Ladybug** (8517 Liman Way), **Magnolia Park** (1401 Middlebrook Way), **Rainbow Park** (1345 Rosana Way), and **Sunrise** (5201 Snyder Ln.). The Recreation Department offers instruction and sponsors the Rohnert Park Tennis Club, a group that draws players from Sonoma, Napa, and Marin counties.

Santa Rosa Public Courts (707-543-3282, Santa Rosa, CA 94928) are available at **Howarth, Finley** and **Galvin Parks, Burbank Playground, Santa Rosa Junior College,** and **Santa Rosa** and **Montgomery high schools.**

Whale-Watching

One of the great attractions in California is the opportunity to watch gray whales in their annual round-trip migration between summer feeding grounds in the Bering Sea and their breeding and birthing waters off Baja California. From late May to October, the gray whales feed in the cold Pacific waters to build up fat for their 12,000-mile pilgrimage. Then, beginning in late November, they head south, passing close enough to shore to navigate by sight as well as to avoid killer whales in the deeper waters. Their return usually starts in late February and lasts until early June.

The **Point Reyes Lighthouse** (415-669-1534) at the tip of the **Point Reyes National Seashore** in Marin County—about a 1.5-hour drive from Santa Rosa—offers one of the best vantage points in the state for whale-watching. The lighthouse is open from 10 to 4:30 daily except Tuesday and Wednesday, but parking is limited and extremely crowded on weekends. Call ahead to find out if there's any visibility, because the lighthouse sits on the windiest and rainiest spot on the entire Pacific Coast.

Sonoma County offers good whale-watching sites, including **Gualala Point, Stillwater Cove, Fort Ross,** and **Bodega Head.** On a clear day, you'll have plenty of company to share sightings—everyone bundled against the sea breezes, toting binoculars and picnic lunches, and ready to spend several hours searching for the telltale white spouts shooting above the blue Pacific waters.

For a close-up view, reserve a place on a whale-watching boat out of Bodega Bay. Remember that it's typically 15 degrees colder on the water, so wear plenty of warm clothes. Law prohibits boaters from harassing whales, but the large mammals have little fear of man and often approach boats at sea. All boats leave from **Porto Bodega Marina** on Bay Flat Road, off Highway 1. The boating season is January through April, and boats run weather permitting.

Bodega Bay Sport Fishing Center (707-875-3344, 1410 Bay Flat Rd., Bodega Bay, CA 94923)

The Boathouse (707-875-3495, 1445 Hwy. 1, Bodega Bay, CA 94923)

This and That

Napa Valley Wine Train (707-253-2111, 800-427-4124, 1275 McKinstry St., Napa, CA 94559) This is one of the biggest disappointments in Wine Country. The train itself is a gloriously restored, vintage beauty, and the trip through Napa Valley is a charming and scenic adventure—but oh, the price! A dinner excursion tops $97, and the food is adequate at best. A safer bet is riding the deli lunch.

River Rock Casino (707-857-2777, 3250 Hwy. 128, Geyserville, CA 95441) This Indian casino is in the hills just above Alexander Valley's prime vineyards. The facility isn't fancy, but it's well maintained, and all the usual games are available, including slots, blackjack, and three-card poker.

Six Flags Marine World (707-643-6722, www.sixflags.com/marineworld, 2001 Marine World Pkwy., Vallejo, CA 94589; off I-80) This isn't in Napa or Sonoma counties, but it's only a short drive. This 160 acre facility includes whale and seal shows, elephant rides, and the usual wild creatures. Walk through a glass tunnel surrounded by sharks or see robotic dinosaurs in action. It also has some first-class rides and roller coasters. Open daily; closed November–March. Admission: $45.99 adults, seniors, and disabled; $24.99 children 4–12; children 2 and under free.

In Healdsburg it's shops, shops, and more shops. Tim Fish

8

Shopping

For the Sport of It

Shopping is sporting, an exercise in endurance, an exhausting workout, a test of willpower, and pure capitalistic fun. Just start your day with a shot of espresso, catalog your credit cards, and set off on a great marathon through Wine Country.

This chapter is organized by city, detailing eight shopping areas. These burgeoning meccas of retail sales are growing at a furious rate, thanks to affluent, latte-drinking tourists and locals with expensive tastes. This chapter will serve as your compass; it will guide you to both traditional and offbeat stores. Some will be within easy reach; others will be off the beaten path.

Some antiques stores listed will make you feel as though you're prowling an attic. Some furniture stores reveal a new breed of artist-designers who create both comfort and style in one sitting. You could lose a day or two wandering through the bookstores listed here. All are user friendly and equipped with beautiful books, classical music, and for the most part—helpful clerks. As for clothing, we list shops both conservative and chic. Indeed, if you take our tour of clothing stores, you will come across—perhaps for the first time in your life—a pair of silk boxer shorts priced at $58. We were naturally befuddled. Just when did it begin costing more to undress than to dress?

So hit an ATM, harvest some cash, and pick a city—any city: Napa, Yountville, St. Helena, Calistoga, Sonoma, Santa Rosa, Sebastopol, or Healdsburg. You'll find as a rule that Sonoma County stores tend to be funkier than their Napa County counterparts.

Shopping in Napa County

NAPA

While the restaurant scene is heating up, the shopping in Napa lags behind. Most tourists still find their way to St. Helena or Calistoga. That said, shopping has picked up from years past.

If the downtown storefronts in Napa don't seem bustling, it's because some of the shopping has shifted to **Napa Town Center,** a concentrated area in the city's core, and to **Napa Premium Outlets,** just on the other side of Highway 29.

Napa Town Center is bordered by 1st Street, Pearl Street, Franklin Street, and Main Street. It's an upscale, outdoor mall with a brick path that meanders conveniently by the **Napa Valley Visitors Bureau.** Shoppers stroll past outdoor cafés, ice cream parlors, and storefronts that boast the best in consumer goods.

McCaulou's (707-255-9375, 1380 Napa Town Center, Napa, CA 94559) is a department store offering shoes, clothes, cosmetics, housewares, kidswear—one-stop shopping. The **Mustard Seed Clothing Co.** (707-255-4222, 1301 Napa Town Center, Napa, CA 94559) carries upscale weekend and sportswear for women, with lines that include Flax, Eileen Fisher, and Gotcha Covered. **Napa Valley Jewelers** (707-224-0997, 1317 Napa Town Center, Napa, CA 94559) sells gold and diamond jewelry and has a designer on-site to customize jewelry.

Outside Napa Town Center you'll find a range of other interesting stores. **Oxbow Public Market** (707-963-1345, 610 1st. St., Napa CA 94559.) is right next to COPIA: The American Center for Wine, Food, and the Arts. This public market has great appeal to foodies. Like the San Francisco Ferry building, it has an appealing range of food purveyors that include Taylor's Refresher, Model Bakery, and Three Twins Organic Ice Cream. It's colossal—40,000 square feet—to showcase the wares of 30 vendors and 10 farmstands in Napa. The kid in you will be drawn to the **Learning Faire** (707-253-1024, 1343 Main St., Napa, CA 94559), a playful shop that includes infant toys, dolls, puppets, games, puzzles, wooden trains, and even arts and crafts for kids. At **The Beaded Nomad** (707-258-8004, 1238 1st. St., Napa, CA 94559) you don't have to be a child of the '60s to relish the wares. This bead shop features jewelry and imported items such as masks and bronze statues. The offbeat will look forward to perusing **Napa Coin & Jewelry** (888-239-2370, 3053 Jefferson St., Napa, CA 94558), which features unique jewelry, watches, and keepsakes such as Harry Potter coins and the Year of the Horse coins.

Bookends Book Store (707-224-1077, 1014 Coombs St., Napa, CA 94559) is a bookstore with a serious, smart feel to it. The store boasts the valley's largest magazine selection as well as an extensive map and travel section and music CDs. **Copperfield's** (707-252-8002, 3900 Bel Aire Plaza, Napa, CA 94558) is an all-purpose bookstore and a fun stop for folks who like to peruse books.

Splash (707-254-0767, 1403-A Lincoln St., Napa, CA 94559) caters to beach fanatics, with a variety of swimwear and accessories. You can even sport a tan after shopping here because it has 10 tanning rooms. **Napa Valley Traditions** (707-226-2044, 1202 Main St., Napa, CA 94559) is a quaint shop full of gift baskets and spa products, lotions, hand therapies, and the like. **The Napa Valley Emporium** (707-253-7177, 1225 Napa Town Center, Napa, CA 94559) sells customized apparel, from T-shirts and aprons to caps, as well as grape-related gifts such as wine racks and corkscrews.

Finally, at **Napa Premium Outlets** (707-226-9876, 629 Factory Stores Dr., Napa, CA 94558), there's a maze of 40 stores including **Mikasa, Kenneth Cole, Cole Haan, J. Crew, Liz Claiborne, Tommy Hilfiger, Jones New York, Ann Taylor, Timberland, Nine West, Book Warehouse**, and **Levi's**.

YOUNTVILLE

The predominant shopping area is **V-Marketplace** (6525 Washington St., Yountville, CA 94599), and it plays to tourists. The historic complex was once the Groezinger Winery, and it has stone flooring, brick walls, and wooden rafters. Here's a glance at some of the shops.

Hansel & Gretel Clothes Loft (707-944-2954) outfits babies, girls up to 16, and boys up to 12. The clothes are great clothes, the toys are inventive, and the service is friendly. If you're on a crusade to make your house home, another delightful shop is **Domain Home & Garden** (707-945-0222, 6525 Washington St., Yountville, CA 94599), where you'll find everything from fountains and furniture to wine racks.

Yountville is a retail mecca. Tim Fish

Some engaging stores are just a stone's throw from V-Marketplace. **Antique Fair** (707-944-8440, 6512 Washington St., Yountville, CA 94599) has large, stately French walnut pieces: huge armoires, tables, bookcases, carved bed frames, and more. **Overland Sheepskin Co.** (707-944-0778, 6505 Washington St., Yountville, CA 94599) was the Yountville Railroad Depot; today the shop is devoted to fighting Mother Nature's cool winters in Wine Country. Great coats, hats, rain gear, gloves, and luggage. If you're furniture shopping, stop in **Venika International** (707-944-8944, 6774 Washington St., Yountville, CA 94599). This shop has mahogany reproductions of French country-style furniture.

Just a footnote: Though it's not in Yountville, one tasty stop up the road in Rutherford is the **St. Helena Olive Oil Company** (707-967-1003, 8576 St. Helena Hwy., Rutherford, CA 94573). This shop, which showcases local artisans, has Napa Valley bottled extra-virgin olive oils, balsamic vinegars, mustards, and jams.

Downtown St. Helena offers some of the best shopping in Napa Valley. Tim Fish

ST. HELENA

You'd better schedule a good 12-hour day of shopping in this quaint yet cosmopolitan Main Street, USA. St. Helena has some of the best shopping in all of Wine Country.

Consider **St. Helena St. Helena Antiques & Collectibles** (707-963-5878, 1231 Main St., St. Helena, CA 94574)-"St. Helena" stated twice in the store name hints that this shop is a bit unusual. Step inside and you'll confirm it as you meander past a large collection of corkscrews and 18th- and 19th-century antiques, including some lovely French armoires.

Chic and refreshing, **Jan de Luz** (707-963-1550, 1219 Main St., St. Helena, CA 94574) is a rare find. Frenchman Jan de Luz has a store in Carmel and has ventured up to Wine Country to feature his custom-designed linens. His store also carries chandeliers, fountains, and everything you can imagine to outfit a kitchen and bathroom.

Main Street Books (707-963-1338, 1315 Main St., St. Helena, CA 94574) is a small, quaint bookstore with a few comfortable chairs for the weary. It offers used books and some children's books and claims to be the smallest used bookstore in California. **River House Books** (707-963-1163, 1234 Adams St., St. Helena, CA 94574) is a high-end, general bookstore. It's a great place to hunt for a range of books, with categories that include humanities, sciences, bestselling fiction, travel guides, and wine books.

Mario's Great Clothes for Men (707-963-1603, 1223 Main St., St. Helena, CA 94574) carries designer clothes by Jhane Barnes and Zanella, with attire from casual to elegant. It also sells Michael Toschi shoes. When the great outdoors beckons, it's best to be prepared. **Sportago** (707-963-9042, 1224-B Adams St., St. Helena, CA 94574) is an authorized Patagonia dealer, and it also carries upscale casualwear. **Identity** (707-963-0486, 1219 Main St., St. Helena, CA 94574) features high-end men's and women's clothing for people in their mid-twenties and up. Lines for women include Synthia Steffe and Susana Monaco, and lines for men include Ted Baker and Arnold Zimberg. It also carries handbags and accessories for women. **Twenty-six** (707-963-0495, 1219-B Main St., St. Helena, CA 94574) focuses on casual clothes for the younger set, both men and women. One hot seller is jeans. The store includes many brands.

A great find for the upscale female shopper is **Pearl** (707 963 3236, 1428 Main St., St. Helena, CA 94574). This is a boutique with class. Lines include Mark Jacobs, Megan Park, and Rozae Nichols. **Pearl Too** (707-967-9594, 1422 Main St., St. Helena, CA 94574), a spin-off of the original Pearl, focuses on casual, relaxed weekend wear. Lines include Stewart Brown and Vince. Pearl Too also carries some shoes and jewelry. At **Cricket** (707-963-8400, 1234 Main St., St. Helena, CA 94574) you'll find wool sweaters, hats, dresses, and more—women's clothing with the emphasis on casual. Imelda Marcos would like **Amelia Claire** (707-963-8502, 1230 Main St., St. Helena, CA 94574), which carries upscale shoes from makers such as Donald Pliner and Taryn Rose and even Aquatalia—100 percent water-proof shoes. Another upscale shoe mecca is **Foot Candy** (707-963-2040, 1239 Main St., St. Helena, CA 94574), whose lines include Jimmy Choo, Mark Jacobs, and Pucci. **Reeds** (707-963-0400, 1302 Main St., St. Helena, CA 94574) is a good shop for professional and eveningwear and carries lines such as Harari, Three Dot, and Fabrizio Gianni.

Vanderbilt & Co. (707-963-1010, 1429 Main St., St. Helena, CA 94574) is brimming with the smart and artsy accessories you might find while flipping through a glossy home and garden catalog. From bedding and kitchenware to patio suites, it has everything you need to warm up your home with a little country mirth or cool it off with contemporary savvy. **Napa Valley Vintage Home** (707-963-7423, 1201 Main St., St. Helena, CA 94574) offers European-inspired home accessories and antiques. The shop is best known for its handmade print ceramics. **Pennaluna** (707-963-3115, 1220 Adams St., St. Helena, CA 94574) is an eclectic home-accessories store that's a "must see" shop. This is the place to find offbeat treasures such as an Eiffel Tower ornament and a colorful hammock. Walling in to **Flying Carpets** (707-967-9192, 1152 Main St., St. Helena, CA 94574) is like visiting a traveling exhibit. You'll find a display of handmade Oriental carpets, wool and silk rugs, masks, and art, aside from rugs from 14 different countries. **Calla Lily** (707-963-8188, 1222 Main St., St. Helena, CA 94574) is the consummate bed-and-bath shop, offering fur-niture, jewelry, unusual items from local artisans, linens, lotions, towels, and the like. It's a refreshing stop. Just north of downtown is the **Campus Store and Marketplace of the Culinary Institute of America at Greystone** (707-967-2309, 2555 Main St., St. Helena, CA 94574), which has a superb collection of cookbooks and professional kitchenware.

David's (707-963-0239, 1343 Main St., St. Helena, CA 94574) is essentially a designer's showcase for jewelry. Virtually every piece is handcrafted, with styles from traditional to contemporary. Another great place to shop for jewels is **Palladium Fine Jewelry** (707-963-5900, 1339 Main St., St. Helena, CA 94574). The store specializes in fine and custom jewelry, such as engagement and wedding sets.

Fideaux (707-967-9935, 1312 Main St., St. Helena, CA 94574) is where PetSmart meets Fifth Avenue, an appealing place for the discriminating pet owner, with nifty stuff for dogs, cats, and people. You'll find practical items such as flea collars and litter pans as well as the avant garde: wine-barrel doghouses and a full line of European coats and sweaters for dogs. **Baksheesh** (707-968-9182, 1327 Main St., St. Helena, CA 94574) is committed to trading fairly with artists in the developing world and the United States. It guarantees fair wages to artists for their work. Popular items include jewelry from Kenya, scarves from Bolivia, and toys from India.

For type-A domestics, a practical discovery is **Pennyweight** (707-963-3198, 1337 Main St., St. Helena, CA 94574). Here you'll find stationery, fine gifts, and hostess goods. **Woodhouse Chocolate** (800-966-3468, www.woodhousechocolate.com, 1367 Main St., St. Helena, CA 94574) is a bright and airy house of chocolate that resembles a highbrow jewelry store, but with chocolates under glass. It specializes in European-style fresh crème chocolate with no preservatives. Don't miss this savvy shop.

Just north of town is **St. Helena Premium Outlets** (707-963-7282, 3111 N. St. Helena Hwy., St. Helena, CA 94574), which features 10 upscale stores, including **Brooks Brothers, Coach, Jones New York, Escada**, and **Sunglass Outfitters.**

CALISTOGA

The hot springs have brought visitors to Calistoga for more than 130 years. You'll be tempted to do nothing but take in a spa, but with soothing shops, Calistoga caters to a growing population of relaxed shoppers. Offerings include fun lotions and potions as well as offbeat, whimsical gifts. It won't take you too long to cover the strip—a string of four blocks, with the majority of stores on the north side of the street.

A must stop is **Casa Design** (707-942-2228, 1419 Lincoln Ave., Calistoga, CA 94515). Included here are lovely custom furniture, linens, mirrors, original art work, jewelry, and other accessories. A store with both whimsy and wit is **Zenobia** (707-942-1050, 1410 Lincoln Ave., Calistoga, CA 94515). This shop has it all, from candles to cards, clothing to purses—but most intriguing are the inspirational wall hangings.

Copperfield's Books (707-942-1616, 1330 Lincoln Ave., Calistoga, 94515) is a local favorite, the only bookstore in town. Its approach is general, and it also carries candles and calendars and has authors come and speak.

Browse the shops in downtown Calistoga. Tim Fish

At **Evens Designs Gallery** (707-942-0453, 1421 Lincoln Ave., Calistoga, CA 94515) ceramics sell for 40 percent to 90 percent off retail prices. Among the decorative pieces—such as plates, bowls, bases, and candlestick holders—you'll find Raku ceramics, blown glass, and slumped glass. **Mr. Moon's** (707-942-0932, 1365 Lincoln Ave., Calistoga, CA 94515) features nifty products such as candles, cards, scarves, and soap—but usually with a twist. If you're in Healdsburg, stop by that branch, as well. **Hurd Beeswax Candles & Hurd Gift & Gourmet** (707-963-7211, 1255 Lincoln Ave., Calistoga, CA 94515) attracts a lot of tourists, but it's fun and worth the trip. All the candles are handcrafted from sheets of pure beeswax, and there are hundreds of designs.

At **Mud Hens** (707-942-0210, 1348-C Lincoln Ave., Calistoga, CA 94515) you can pick up plenty of personal care supplies, including lotions, massage oils, all-natural body products, and aromatherapy paraphernalia.

A Man's Store (707-942-2280, 1343 Lincoln Ave., Calistoga, CA 94515) is called a man's store for work and play. It features rugged and casualwear for men, including clothes and shoes. One perk: it also carries fine cigars. **Attitudes** (707-942-8420, 1333-B Lincoln Ave., Calistoga, CA 94515) focuses on women's lifestyle clothing, from business to yoga wear. It also carries accessories such as shoes and jewelry. **Chateau Ste. Shirts** (707-942-5039; 1355 Lincoln Ave., Calistoga, CA 94515) has stylish swimwear and sportswear and even sells the Ugg line of shoes. **Bella Tootsie Shoes & More** (707-942-8821, 1373 Lincoln Ave., Calistoga, CA 94515) is a shoe store for women. It also offers purses, hats and glasses. **Mud Puddles** (707-942-5925, 1443 Lincoln Ave., Calistoga, CA 94515) carries upscale children's clothing and accessories. It also has puzzles, games, and toys.

Shopping in Sonoma County

SONOMA

The Old World-style Sonoma Plaza is a large park with a duck pond, a rose garden, a swing set, and a slide. This family-friendly downtown has charm, and buildings such as the Sebastiani Theatre, circa 1933, speak of a less complicated time. A closer look reveals that Sonoma is quickly becoming gentrified. A few years ago, the downtown square was home to some country shops and some mundane food purveyors. Today, it has high-style clothing stores, gourmet food shops, and ethnic stores, and it can get plenty crowded on weekends. Expect to jockey for a parking spot.

A not-to-be-missed gallery is **Lisa Kristine** (707-938-3860, 452 1st. St. E., Sonoma, CA 95476). Kristine spends most of her time traveling the world, snapping pictures of people from unique cultures, and she has a gift for capturing stunning places such as the Great Wall of China. She was recently honored by the United Nations for her work.

Artifax International Gallery & Gifts (707-996-9494, 450-C 1st St. E., Sonoma, CA 95476) is a true sensory experience. Here you'll see Asian imports, Chinese baskets, soaps, exotic textiles, beads, and jewelry. You'll smell burning incense and hear tapes of evocative world music. The shop also carries kitchenware, linens, and cookbooks. Equally interesting is **Baksheesh** (707-939-2847, www.vom.com/baksheesh, 423 1st. St. W., Sonoma, CA 95476). Baksheesh is Persian for "gift," and this store, which vows fair trading practices, is full of pieces made by artists who live in developing countries. It has an interesting mix of clothing, jewelry, toys, games, and even musical instruments.

Tiddle E. Winks (707-939-6933, 115 E. Napa St., Sonoma, CA 95476) is a shop full of fun retro items. Owner Heidi Geffen says she rounds up her old toys, tins, and pendants by traveling back in time—boarding a Pan Am flight back to the 1950s. **The Laughing Queen** (707-935-6611, 122 E. Napa St., Sonoma, CA 95476) is a kick. It has funny cards, irreverent gifts, costumes, and accessories. It also has an adult section with sexy gifts such as the book *Naughty Crosswords* and the "Inflatable Husband," which according to promotional material, is quiet and always keeps the toilet seat down.

If you like to sip and shop, stop in at the **Mayo Family Tasting Room** (707-996-9911)on Sonoma Plaza inside the **Corner Store** (707-996-2211, 498 1st. St. E., Sonoma, CA 95476). The Mayo family wines make this a worthy destination. Try the zin from Ricci Vineyard and the chardonnay from Laurel Hill Vineyard. The **Corner Store** has linens, purses, books, clocks, mirrors, and more.

Sign of the Bear (707-996-3722, 435 1st St., Sonoma, CA 95476) is for Wine Country gourmands as well as Wine Country gourmand-wannabes. It features kitchenware, linens, and cookbooks. There are vegetable roasters, herb grills, bagel containers, and upscale All-Clad pans.

A unique find is **The Candlestick** (707-933-0700, 38 W. Spain St., Sonoma, CA 95476), which is full of clever specialty candles, oil lamps, and even whimsical nightlights. It has a full line of beeswax candles, as well as Palm and Yankee candles.

Nesters will appreciate **Harvest Home Stores** (707-933-9044, 107 W. Napa St., Sonoma, CA 95476), a shop with lovely custom furniture, sofas, and leather chairs. Another find is **Sonoma Home** (707-939-6900, 497 1st St. W., Sonoma CA 95476), which has great ideas for home decor and garden, from furniture and books to pillows.

While **Readers' Books** (707-939-1779, 127 E. Napa St., Sonoma, CA 95476) may not be the City Lights of Sonoma County, it has the reputation of being urbane and very literary. Expect great classics and fiction, an expansive cookbook section, and myriad books for children. **Sonoma Bookends Bookstore** (707-938-5926, 201 W. Napa St., Suite 15, Sonoma, CA 95476) is a general bookstore catering to the tourist, with expanded travel and wine sections. It also features local authors.

Half Pint (707-938-1722, 450 1st St. E., Sonoma, CA 95476) outfits newborns to kids up to age 14, and it does it with style. Some toys can be found here, but the shop sells mostly clothes and accessories.

Uniquely California (707-939-6768, 28 W. Spain St., Sonoma, CA 95476) features artwork and gourmet foods. Gift baskets brimming with California products are a hot item here. **North Bay Gallery** (707-996-3453, 407 31 E. Napa St., Sonoma, CA 95476) has a gallery as well as a collection of fine glassware. **Kaboodle** (707-996-9500, 453 1st St. W., Sonoma, CA 95476) emphasizes silk flowers and has lots of unique items—candleholders, picture frames, and pillows, with a horde of other items sandwiched in between. You may never find your way out of this clever maze.

Great women's clothing and accessories for the chic are found at **Chico's** (707-933-0100, 29 E. Napa St., Sonoma, CA 95476). This chain, with hundreds of stores in the U.S., has its own design department and appeals to everyone from teens to seniors. **Eraldi's Men's Wear & Shoes** (707-996-2013, 475 1st St. W., Sonoma, CA 95476) carries casual men's clothing with lines such as Tommy Bahama, Levi's, and Wrangler as well as sports coats, dress slacks, and shoes.

If you're shopping for an artist, step in to **Spirits In Stone** (707-938-2200, www.spirits instone.com, 452 1st St. E., Suite A, Sonoma, CA 95476). Here you'll find an exhibit of Zimbabwe's Shona stone sculpture and African paintings, masks, and crafts available for purchase. Another artistic shop is **Kokopelli Gallery** (707-933-1750, 11 E. Napa St., Sonoma, CA 95476), a playful shop full of authentic Native American art and contemporary jewelry.

Cornerstone Jewelers (707-996-6635, 416 1st St. E., Sonoma, CA 95476) is a direct importer of diamonds and fine jewelry. It also offers an assortment of watches and stopwatches, among other products. **Santa Fe Connection** (707-938-8703, 481-A 1st St. W., Sonoma, CA 95476) is a good place to peruse Indian jewelry, pottery, and artifacts. The store features handcrafted goods from American Indians of the Southwest. Everything here is sold at wholesale prices. You have to admire **Sonoma Silver Co.** (707-933-0999, www.sonomasilver.com, 491 1st St. W., Sonoma, CA 95476) for selling sterling silver toe rings. This shop has upscale and less expensive items, including cubic zirconia rings.

An important footnote: Some of the best shops are found in the courtyards and lanes off the main square. The most hip gathering is called the **Sonoma Court Shops** off East Napa Street, where you'll find clothing stores, spa shops, and so forth. One of the most whimsical shops in this courtyard is **Three Dog Bakery** (707-933-9780, 526 Broadway, Sonoma, CA. 95476). Nearly 50 canines stop in every weekend, and their favorite treat is carrot cake. The shop is also human-friendly and offers a bi-species cookie.

PETALUMA

Though Petaluma has a distinctive downtown, tourists typically find **Petaluma Village Premium Outlets** (707-778-9300, 2200 Petaluma Blvd. N., Petaluma, CA 94952) more appealing. It has more than 50 top-name stores, including **Off 5th, Saks Fifth Avenue Outlet, Reebok, Mikasa, Kitchen Collection, Jones New York, Nine West, Brooks Brothers Factory Store, Book Warehouse, OshKosh B'Gosh,** and **Bass.**

SANTA ROSA

Santa Rosa's downtown is on the cusp of a revival, thanks in part to Barnes & Noble bookstore, which made its home in the old Rosenberg department store. What was once just a cozy mix of bookstores and coffeehouses is now filling in with interesting gift shops and clothing stores—stores that appear to have staying power.

Barnes & Noble (707-576-7494, 700 4th St., Santa Rosa, CA 95404) appeals to the tourist with expanded sections on local authors, local travel, and local wineries. **Treehorn Books** (707-525-1782, 625 4th St., Santa Rosa, CA 95404) has an extensive collection of children's books, cookbooks, and books on Western Americana. Most of the books are used, with some rare books in the mix. If you want to keep current, step into **Sawyers News** (707-542-1311, 733 4th St., Santa Rosa, CA 95404), which sells newspapers from all over the world. The emphasis here, however, is on magazines, with more than 2,500 titles offered.

If you're an artist without a medium, try **The Pottery Studio** (707-576-7102, 632 4th St., Santa Rosa, CA 95404). Here you select a ceramic piece, paint it, and fire it in the kiln. Ceramic pieces are varied and include vases, birdhouses, and watering cans.

At **Corrick's** (707-546-2423, 637 4th St., Santa Rosa, CA 95404), you can peruse upscale gift items and office supplies in one shop. Corrick's also carries china, with upscale lines such as Lenox and Gorham.

At **Skeeters** (707-523-1651, 626 4th St., Santa Rosa, CA 95404), look for a broad range of items, including women's clothing, pottery, and jewelry. You can even order custom-made maple and cherry cabinets. **Positively Fourth Street** (707-526-3588, 628 4th St., Santa Rosa, CA 95404) focuses on local artists but also has international appeal: art deco pens, teapots from China, and jewelry from Bali. Practically an heirloom, **E. R. Sawyer** (707-546-0372, 638 4th St., Santa Rosa, CA 95404) was established in 1879. It sells fine jewelry and watches—even waterproof watches. It also does custom-design work. **Hampton Court Essential Luxuries** (707-578-9416, 631 4th St., Santa Rosa, CA 95404) carries obscure European fragrances, bath and body lotions, and even romantic clothing. **California Luggage Co.** (707-528-8600, 609 4th St., Santa Rosa, CA 95404) carries a broad range of luggage plus convenient travel necessities. It also does repairs for travelers passing through.

   The Last Record Store (707-525-1963, 1899-A Mendocino Ave., Santa Rosa, CA 95401) sells CDs, cassettes, and records, and its eclectic inventory includes rock, jazz, classical, world music, blues, and Celtic music.

   Aside from Santa Rosa's downtown, a quaint place to shop nearby is **Railroad Square**, a shopping area built around a park with a historic train depot. (Check out the depot and the tourist information stocked there.) Most shops in the square sell antiques, but keep your eyes open. Plenty of other shops are worth your while.

   Whistle Stop Antiques (707-542-9474, 130 4th St., Santa Rosa, CA 95401) is a collective with some 35 dealers. Sift through the collectibles and general line of furniture, and note the handy section devoted to supplies for refurbishing furniture. At **Old Town Furniture** (707-575-8287, 110 4th St., Santa Rosa, CA 95401), check out the spanking new furniture, replicas of Victorian, Mission, and traditional styles for the home and office. **Furniture Depot** (707-575-3198, 100 4th St., Santa Rosa, CA 95401) carries an eclectic mix of cherry and pine furniture for the bedroom, office, and dining room.

   At **Sonoma Outfitter** (707-528-1920, 145 3rd St., Santa Rosa, CA 95401), you can answer the call of the wild in high style. There's clothing for men and women, with lines such as Patagonia and Sigrid Olsen. Outdoor gear includes kayaks and camping equipment.

   Searching for a new look? **Hot Couture** (707-528-7247, 101 3rd St., Santa Rosa, CA 95401) has vintage clothing that dates back to the early 1900s up through the 1960s. It also offers rentals year-round. **Disguise the Limit** (707-575-1477, 100 4th St., Santa Rosa, CA 95401) carries theatrical goods, gag gifts, and clothing for the avant garde. It's the most popular shop in town during Halloween season.

   While few tourists find their way there, **Montgomery Village** in Santa Rosa has become a popular place for locals to shop for clothing, home and garden accessories, and gifts. The outdoor shopping center encompasses about four blocks, so the best way to shop it is to stroll through it. Upbeat shops include the ultimate gadget store, **The Sharper Image**; **Ireko,** an upscale home and garden shop; and clothing stores such as **J. Jill** and **Chico's** for the hip yet professional woman.

HEALDSBURG

Taking a stroll at Healdsburg's town plaza is like stepping into a Norman Rockwell print. Healdsburg may just be the town that time forgot. Once you take a closer look, however, you realize that Healdsburg is an interesting mix: countrified chic, cosmopolitan, yet down to earth—more Land Rover than BMW. Here's a look at Healdsburg's quaint town square-primo shopping.

   Copperfield's Books (707-433-9270, 104 Matheson St., Healdsburg, CA 95448). There's a large "Wines and Vineyards" section at the front of this general-interest bookstore. Specialties include self-help and spiritual awareness as well as a good selection of

Peruse the many shops and restaurants along the Healdsburg plaza. Tim Fish

cookbooks, mysteries, and new fiction. **Levin & Co.** (707-433 1118, 306 Center St., Healdsburg, CA 95448) is a lively shop that caters to the book and music lover. In books, it specializes in the classics and quality fiction. The music collection focuses on jazz and international music, and also carries classical and pop.

    Plaza Farms (707-433-2345, 106 Matheson St., Healdsburg, CA 95448) is a delightful spot on the Healdsburg square with a range of tasty purveyors such as DaVero Olive Oil, Bellwether Farm Cheese, and Tandem Winery. Not to be missed is Bovolo, the café in the

Plaza Farms in Healdsburg is an open market of food and wine retailers. Tim Fish

back, which makes everything from scratch from pizzas and gelato to its numerous pork dishes. Chef John Stewart is a self-proclaimed pork fanatic.

As for clothing and accessories, Healdsburg is teeming with options. There's even a shop based entirely on the little black bag: Practical yet chic, **Clutch** (707-433-8189, www.clutchhealdsburg.com, 307 Healdsburg Ave., Healdsburg, CA 95448) features men's and women's accessories to carry. **M Clothing** (707 431 8738, 381 Healdsburg Ave., Healdsburg, CA 95448) has hip, smart clothing for women, with lines that include Nanette Lepore and Diane Von Furstenberg. **Circe** (707-433-8482, 311 Healdsburg Ave., Healdsburg, CA 95448) was an enchantress in Greek mythology, and this upscale woman's clothing store has lines that include Luna Luz, Ivan Grundahl, and Isabel de Pedro. **Susan Graf Limited** (707-433 6495, 100 Matheson St., Healdsburg, CA 95448) is a shop that carries upscale women's clothing, with lines such as Kate Spade, Delman, and Agnona. **Rainsong Shoes** (707-433-8058, 117 Plaza St., Healdsburg, CA 95448) is a well-heeled shop that emphasizes comfort as well as style, with prices ranging from $30 to $280. Lines include Reiker and Arche.

Saint Dizier Home (707-473-0980, 259 Center St., Healdsburg, CA 95448) features Ralph Lauren Collection furnishings, with some Henredon furniture in stock. Francophiles will want to step into **Myra Hoefer Design** (707-433-2166, 309 Healdsburg Ave., Healdsburg, CA 95448). Hoefer is the designer owner and this shop carries mostly French or French-inspired antiques and accessories. Hoefer does about one third of her design work in Paris and the remainder in North Bay. **Midnight Sun** (707 431 7085, 355 Healdsburg Ave., Healdsburg, CA 95448) is a bed-and-bath place that sells all the fixings for a luxurious bedroom and bath: jammies, sheets, towels, bath oils, and creams—even iron beds and pine armoires.

Fideaux (707-433-9935, 43 North St., Healdsburg, CA 95448) is a shop that caters to cats and dogs with whimsical items that include wine-barrel dog houses and breed-specific clocks. It also carries pillows, beds, note pads, and picture frames.

Powell Sweet Shoppe (707-431-2784, 322 Center St., Healdsburg, CA 95448) has the feel of an old-time candy store, but it also carries toys and gelato. More celebrated retro candy includes Slicks, Zotz, Necco Wafers, and Wacky Packages.

Healdsburg is rich with antiques shops. **Antique Harvest** (707-433-0223, 225 Healdsburg Ave., Healdsburg, CA 95448) has items that range from country pine to Victorian, with lamps, brass, and art deco furnishings to boot. Meander through the wares of more than 20 dealers. **Healdsburg Classic Antiques** (707-433-4315, 226 Healdsburg Ave., Healdsburg, CA 95448) is an enormous shop that spans two Quonset huts and includes about 20 dealers. You'll find furniture here from Victorian through art deco.

Custom design is the signature style at **Ann Marie** (707-433-5053, 122 Matheson St., Healdsburg, CA 95448), and all the work is done on-site. Popular pieces include jewelry made with Murano glass, which hails from an island outside of Venice. The shop also sells Chinese, South Seas, and Tahitian freshwater pearls. **Options** (707-431 8861, 126 Matheson St., Healdsburg, CA 95448) has a clear sense of style, and it's stocked with one-of-a-kind items and sophisticated collectibles. Look for jewelry, furniture, baskets, pottery, and ceramics.

The designer in you could linger for hours in **Galeria Two-O-Six** (707-431-1234, 111 Mill St., Healdsburg, CA 95448). This shop carries the work of more than 80 local artists and offers custom-designed furniture, with a focus on the kitchen and bathroom. **Plaza Gourmet** (707-433 7116, 108 Matheson St., Healdsburg, CA 95448) could outfit Martha

Stewart's kitchen. It has a wide range of kitchenware, tableware, books, and candles. **Mr. Moon's** (707-433-6666, 105 Plaza St., Healdsburg, CA 95448) coaxes in window shoppers with festive displays of cards, candles, clothes, soaps and lotions, and stuffed animals. There's another location in Calistoga.

Fabrications (707-433-6243, 116 Matheson St., Healdsburg, CA 95448) will inspire those who love sewing, with its exotic collection of natural fabrics from Guatemala, Bali, Africa, and other international locales. Dark batik fabrics and unusual silks are specialties. **Virginia Carol** (707-431-1297, 120 Matheson St., Healdsburg, CA 95448) focuses on "Sonoma-wear" for women, and the casual clothing lines include Eileen Fisher, Tribal, and Isda. The folks at **Out of Hand** (707-431-8178, 333 Healdsburg Ave., Healdsburg, CA 95448) say the emphasis at this store is on "Wine Country wear"—casual yet fashionable. You'll find plenty of handcrafted leather handbags, plus smart-looking casual clothing and fancier items. Main lines include Three Dot and Cambio.

Toy Chest (707-433-4743, 401 Center St. B, Healdsburg, CA 95448) is a refreshing toy store of yore. Peruse the goodies: globes, kites, puzzles, and even kits for building your own magic show. **Midnight Sun Children's Shoppe** (707-433-3800, 107 Plaza St., Healdsburg, CA 95448) features great apparel for packaging your kid in smart and whimsi- cal styles. The store outfits babies to boys and girls size 14. **Papitre** (707-431-8665, 353 Healdsburg Ave., Healdsburg, CA 95448) emphasizes personalized invitations; you'll also find distinctive frames, cards, and stationery.

SEBASTOPOL

Sebastopol is a pretzel of a town. A series of one-way streets downtown make navigating a bit of a chore, but shopping here is interesting nonetheless. This tiny West County metropolis seems to have a style of its own: New Age Vintage Coastal Funk. You'll have to search out traditional shops, which tend to be overshadowed by the offbeat.

Buddies (707-823-2109, 415 S. Main St., Sebastopol, CA 95472) looks like a gallery, with wearable art displayed on clean, white walls. It carries handcrafted, one-of-a-kind clothing—wearable art—and ethnic pieces. **Dressers** (707-829-8757, 141 N. Main St., Sebastopol, CA 95472) is an upscale store with stylish clothes and nifty accessories. Main brands include Tianello and Theory. **Global Village** (707-829-4765, 172 N. Main St., Sebastopol, CA 95472) is truly an international affair. Women's clothes come from Bali, Peru, and India—to name just a few countries—and there's also jewelry and some men's and unisex clothing, too. The clothing in **Shards & Remnants** (707-823-1366, 130 S. Main St., Suite 103, Sebastopol, CA 95472) spans from the '50s to the present day. You'll find some real antiques, as well, such as a 1915 black velvet dress with a hobble skirt, plus feather boas and fake furs. Look for fun stuff in **East of Eden** (707-829-1968, 103 Main St., Sebastopol, CA 95472). It carries new fashions, wedding gowns, and accessories, with a few vintage items.

Country Home and Sonoma Fine Furniture (707-829-1793, 195 N. Main St., Sebastopol, CA 95472) is two shops in one: Sonoma Fine Furniture provides the backdrop with furniture—arts and crafts, Mission, and traditional style in oak, pine, and cherry. Country Home provides the accessories—candles, cookie jars, bath lotions, and baskets. It's one of the few traditional shops in Sebastopol. Stepping inside is like walking through a *Country Living* magazine.

Wild Things (707-829-3371, 130 S. Main St., Suite 102, Sebastopol, CA 95472) is one of the most hip nature shops you'll ever come across. Inventory includes finger puppets, screen-painted T-shirts, and beautiful cards. At **Toyworks** (707-829-2003, 6940 Sebastopol Ave., Sebastopol, CA 95472) peruse the goodies: globes, kites, puzzles, and even kits for building your own volcano.

Copperfield's Books (707-823-2618, 138 N. Main St., Sebastopol, CA 95472) is a large bookstore that seems to have a New Age state of mind. It bills itself as a general-purpose bookstore with specialties in fiction, metaphysics, and alternative health.

Devlin Jewelry Design (707-823-9152, 139 N. Main St., Sebastopol, CA 95472) offers custom design with a bonus: a goldsmith on the premises. Original designs tend to be contemporary, incorporating gold, gemstones, and diamonds. **Milk & Honey** (707-824-1155, 123 N. Main St., Sebastopol, CA 95472) celebrates the goddess, featuring the feminine in art, music, jewelry, literature, gifts, and body care. **Rosemary's Garden** (707-829-2539, 132 N. Main St., Sebastopol, CA 95472) is an herbal apothecary and gift store that's well stocked with products to soothe the soul, including Chinese herbs, tea blends, and massage oils.

Sebastopol is Antiques Central in Wine Country. **Antique Society** (707-829-1733, 2661 Gravenstein Hwy. S., Sebastopol, CA 95472) is Sonoma County's largest antiques collective, with more than one hundred dealers. Naturally, you'll find a wide assortment of antiques and collectibles, from estate jewelry to furniture, including oak, country, and primitive. **Ray's Trading Co.** (707-829-9726, 3570 Gravenstein Hwy. S., Sebastopol, CA 95472) is a salvage company recognized as an important resource for Bay Area people restoring Victorian homes. Ray's stock bins are full of antique doorknobs and drawer pulls, and the company is even a source for windows and doors.

Adventure in Wine Country is just a phone call away. Tim Fish

9

INFORMATION

Facts on File

A little peace of mind goes a long way when you want to savor Wine Country. The information compiled in this chapter covers emergencies as well as everyday practical matters. It caters to both the tourist and newcomer, with information running the gamut from weather reports and visitors bureaus to real estate services and school listings. So acquaint yourself with Napa and Sonoma. You may decide to stretch your vacation into a lifetime.

AMBULANCE, FIRE, POLICE, COAST GUARD

Simply dial 911 in both Napa and Sonoma counties. You'll reach an operator who will swiftly put you through to the right agency: fire and rescue, ambulance, local police, sheriff, California Highway Patrol, or Coast Guard Search and Rescue.

To report rape and sexual assault, call **Napa Emergency Women's Services** (707-255-6397) or **United Against Sexual Assault** of Sonoma County's Rape Crisis (707-545-7273).

For the **Poison Control Center,** call 800-523-2222.

Area Codes, Zip Codes & City Halls

Area Codes

Napa and Sonoma counties	707
San Francisco	415
Oakland and Berkeley	510

Area codes for adjacent counties

Marin	415
Mendocino	707
Alameda and Contra Costa	510
Lake County	707
Solano	707
Yolo	916, 530

Zip Codes & City Halls

Napa County

Calistoga	94515	707-942-2754
St. Helena	94574	707-967-2792
Yountville	94599	707-944-8851
Napa	94588, 94559, 94581	707-257-9503

Sonoma County

Bodega Bay	94923	
Healdsburg	95448	707-431-3317
Sebastopol	95742, 95473	707-823-1153
Santa Rosa	95401-95409	707-543-3010
Sonoma	95476	707-938-3681
Petaluma	94952-94954, 94999, 94975	707-778-4345

Banks

If you have a bank card, you're the king of cash in the age of the automated teller. Hungry for a few more traveler's checks? The following is a sampling of regional and national banks. Each branch office is equipped with at least one ATM. Note the systems to which each bank is electronically linked.

Bank of America (707-542-4433, 800-441-6437) Linked to Plus, Star, and Interlink. Locations:

    1429 Lincoln Ave., Calistoga
    2 Financial Plaza, Napa
    1700 1st St., Napa
    2355 California St., Napa
    1001 Adams St., St. Helena
    35 W. Napa St., Sonoma

19181 Sonoma Hwy., Sonoma
502 Healdsburg Ave., Healdsburg
1155 W. Steele Ln., Santa Rosa
2420 Sonoma Ave., Santa Rosa
10 Santa Rosa Ave., Santa Rosa
7185 Healdsburg Ave., Sebastopol
939 Lakeville Hwy., Petaluma
200 Kentucky St., Petaluma
9022 Brooks Rd. S., Windsor

Wells Fargo Bank (800-869-3557) Linked to Star, Plus, Interlink, Cirrus, and MasterCard.
Locations:
1115 Vine St., Healdsburg
2960 Cleveland Ave., Santa Rosa
200 B St., Santa Rosa
6585 Oakmont Dr., Santa Rosa
480 W. Napa St., Sonoma
5 Padre Pkwy., Rohnert Park
1107 Main St., St. Helena
125 Western Ave., Petaluma
6484 Washington St., Yountville
3255 Jefferson St., Napa

West America Bank (800-848-1088) Linked to Star, Cirrus, Plus, Explore, Maestro, and MasterCard.
Locations:
1 Financial Plaza, Napa
1400 Clay St., Napa
1221 Imola Ave., Napa
6470 Washington St., Yountville
1000 Adams St., St. Helena
1110 Washington St., Calistoga
129 N. Cloverdale Blvd., Cloverdale
105 N. Main St., Sebastopol
655 1st St., Santa Rosa
2498 Guerneville Rd., Santa Rosa
300 Rohnert Park Hwy., Rohnert Park
300 Crawford Way, American Canyon
511 Healdsburg Ave., Healdsburg
200 Washington St., Petaluma
203 S. McDowell Blvd., Petaluma
16265 Main St., Guerneville

BIBLIOGRAPHY

Browse through our bookshelves. Wine Country can be a curious place, what with the specter of ghost wineries and the mystique of winemaking. Consider the two lists compiled: Books You Can Buy and Books You Can Borrow.

Books You Can Buy lists titles generally available in Sonoma and Napa bookstores, nationally, or from the publishers. Books You Can Borrow are those that are generally found in Napa and Sonoma local libraries and in most public libraries elsewhere. They are typically no longer for sale.

For wine books, two helpful—and free—sources are the **Napa Valley Wine Library** (707-963-5244; St. Helena Public Library, 1492 Library Ln., St. Helena, CA 94574) and the **Sonoma County Wine Library** (707-433-3772; Healdsburg Public Library, 139 Piper St., Healdsburg, CA 95448). For more information, see Libraries in chapter 4, Culture.

Books You Can Buy

WINE AND FOOD

Ash, John, with Sid Goldstein. *From the Earth to the Table: John Ash's Wine Country Cuisine.* New York: Dutton, 1995.

——. *American Game Cooking.* New York: Addison-Wesley, 1991.

Asher, Gerald. *Vineyard Tales: Reflections on Wine.* San Francisco: Chronicle Books, 1996.

Bailey, Lee. *California Wine Country Cooking.* New York: Potter, 1991.

Bernstein, Leonard S. *The Official Guide to Wine Snobbery.* New York: Quill Press, 1982.

Cass, Bruce. *The Oxford Companion to the Wines of North America.* Oxford: Oxford University Press, 2000.

Chappellet, Molly. *A Vineyard Garden.* New York: Viking Studio Books, 1991.

DeCarlo, Tessa, and Lynne Tuft. *The Grapes Grow Sweet.* Napa, Calif.: River Press, 1996.

Fisher, M. F. K. *Here Let Us Feast: A Book of Banquets.* San Francisco: North Point Press, 1996.

Fisher, M. F. K., with Joan Reardon. *Art of Eating.* Simon & Schuster/Macmillan Co., 1990.

Immer, Andrea. *Great Wine Made Simple.* New York: Broadway Books, 2000.

Johnson, Hugh. *World Atlas of Wine.* New York: Simon & Schuster, 1994.

——. *Vintage: The Story of Wine.* New York: Simon & Schuster, 1989.

Jordan, Michele Anna. *A Cook's Tour of Sonoma.* New York: Addison-Wesley, 1990.

Kramer, Matt. *Making Sense of Wine.* New York: William Morrow, 1989.

MacNeil, Karen. *The Wine Bible.* New York: Workman, 2001. Everyone should own this wine book, the ultimate resource to wine.

MacNeil, Karen. *Wine, Food & Friends with Karen MacNeil.* Des Moines: Oxmoor House, 2006. This book is full of great ideas for hosts who love to entertain.

McCarthy, Ed, and Mary Ewing-Mulligan. *Wine for Dummies.* New York: IDG Books, 1995.

Robinson, Jancis. *The Oxford Companion to Wine.* 2nd edition. Oxford: Oxford University Press, 1999.

Roby, Norman S., and Charles E. Olken. *The New Connoisseurs' Handbook of California Wine.* New York: Alfred A. Knopf, 1995.

Steiman, Harvey. *California Kitchen.* San Francisco: Chronicle Books, 1990.

Sterling, Joy. *A Cultivated Life.* New York: Villard Books, 1993.

Sullivan, Charles. *A Companion to California Wine: An Encyclopedia of Wine and Winemaking from the Mission Days to the Present.* Berkeley: University of California Press, 1998.

Taber, George. *The Judgment of Paris.* New York: Scribner, 2005. This book chronicles the Paris Tasting of 1976 and how that pivotal event changed the wine world.

Thompson, Bob. *The Wine Atlas of California and the Pacific Northwest.* New York: Simon & Schuster, 1993.

Wine Spectator Magazine. *Ultimate Guide to Buying Wine.* New York: Wine Spectator Press, 2004.

LITERARY WORKS

London, Jack. *Call of the Wild and Selected Stories.* New York: Penguin Books, 1960.

Stevenson, Robert Louis. *The Works of Robert Louis Stevenson.* London: Octopus Pub. Group, 1989.

BIOGRAPHIES

Dreyer, Peter. *A Gardener Touched with Genius: The Life of Luther Burbank.* Berkeley: University of California Press, 1985.

London, Joan. *Jack London and His Daughters.* Berkeley: Heyday Books, 1990.

McGinty, Brian. *Strong Wine: The Life and Legend of Agoston Haraszthy.* Stanford, Calif.: Stanford University Press, 1998.

LOCAL HISTORIES

Conaway, James. *Napa: The Story of an American Eden.* Boston: Houghton Mifflin, 1990.

Heintz, William F. *Wine Country: A History of Napa Valley, the Early Years 1838 to 1920.* Santa Barbara, Calif.: Capra Press, 1990. A study of winemakers through Napa history.

LeBaron, Gaye, Dee Blackman, Joann Mitchell, and Harvey Hansen. *Santa Rosa: A Nineteenth-Century Town.* Santa Rosa, Calif.: Historia Ltd., 1985.

LeBaron, Gaye, and Joann Mitchell. *Santa Rosa: A Twentieth Century Town.* Santa Rosa, Calif.: Historia Ltd., 1993.

Lukacs, Paul. *American Vintage: The Rise of American Wine.* New York: Houghton Mifflin, 2000.

Wilson, Simone. *Sonoma County: The River of Time.* Chatsworth, Calif.: Windsor Publications, 1990.

RECREATION

Emmery, Lena. *Wine Country Bike Rides.* San Francisco: Chronicle Books, 1997.

Lorentzen, Bob. *The Hiker's Hip Pocket Guide to Sonoma County.* Mendocino, Calif.: Bored Feet Publications, 1990.

Powers, Peter. *Touring California's Wine Country by Bicycle.* Eugene, Ore.: Terragraphics, 1990.

Books You Can Borrow

Darlington, David. *Angel Visits: An Inquiry into the Mystery of Zinfandel.* New York: Henry Holt, 1991.

Dutton, Joan Parry. *They Left Their Mark: Famous Passages Through the Wine Country.* Illuminations Press, 1983. A historical look at the famous people who traveled through Wine Country and the influence they had on the region.

Haynes, Irene W. *Ghost Wineries of Napa Valley.* Sally Taylor & Friends Publishing, 1980. Take an eeric tour of old and abandoned wineries if you dare.

Issler, Anne Roller. *Stevenson at Silverado.* Caldwell, Id.: Caxton Printers, 1939. Follows Stevenson as he roams through Napa Valley. The book gives insight into his work *The Silverado Squatters.*

Johnson, Rheta Grimsley. *Good Grief: The Story of Charles M. Schulz.* Pharos Books, 1989. An intimate portrait of Charles Schulz, the Santa Rosan behind the comic strip *Peanuts.*

King, Norton L. *Napa County: A Historical Overview.* Self-published, 1967. Geographic, topographic, and geologic origins of Wine Country.

Kraft, Ken and Pat. *Luther Burbank: The Wizard and the Man.* Des Moines: Meredith Press, 1967. Burbank was as famous as Henry Ford in 1915, and this book chronicles his life in Santa Rosa.

Lundquist, James. *Jack London: Adventures, Ideas & Fiction*. Ungar, 1987. A biography of the
man who wrote *The Sea Wolf* and *The Call of the Wild*.

CHILD CARE

Child care spells relief for some parents who want to roam Wine Country without their
teetotaler tots. For travelers and newcomers alike, here's a sampling of licensed child care
centers. Parents can find out more about licensed day care providers by studying
providers' files at Community Care Licensing in the California State Building, 50 D Street,
Santa Rosa. The following organizations make free child care referrals.

Community Child Care Council of Sonoma County (707-544-3077)

Community Resources for Children, Napa (707-253-0366)

   In the following sections are a few specific options.

NAPA COUNTY
Hopper Creek Montessori School (707-252-8775, Napa, CA 94559)

SONOMA COUNTY
Alphabet Soup Pre-School & Day Care Center (707-829-9460, Sebastopol, CA 95472)

Happy Time Christian Pre-School & Day Care (707-527-9135, Santa Rosa, CA 95405)

Healdsburg Montessori School (707-431-1727, Healdsburg, CA 95448)

CLIMATE & WEATHER REPORTS

Climate

The late Luther Burbank, known as the plant wizard, called Napa and Sonoma counties
"the chosen spot of all the earth as far as nature is concerned."
   The moderate weather is a blessing for those who have suffered midwestern and north-
eastern blizzards. In Napa and Sonoma the winter is cool, with temperatures dipping down
to the 40s. Rainy season begins in late December and lingers until April. Of course, the
droughts in recent years have made the season somewhat unpredictable, and the locals
count raindrops with good cheer. Rain makes for a lush countryside and hillsides ribbed
with green vineyards.

Temperature and Precipitation

AVERAGE TEMPERATURES

	NAPA	SONOMA
October	62.0	62.2
January	47.6	47.2
April	56.6	56.6
July	67.4	70.0

AVERAGE ANNUAL TOTAL PRECIPITATION

	NAPA	SONOMA
Rain	24.64	29.94
Snow	o	o

Weather Reports

NAPA COUNTY
Calistoga: 707-942-2828

SONOMA COUNTY
Healdsburg: 707-431-3360

GUIDED TOURS

Looking for some packaged fun? Consider our list of tours. They'll take you on a Wine Country adventure via a stretch limo, a horse-drawn wagon, or even a cable car.

Getaway Adventures (707-942-0332, 800-499-2453, www.getawayadventures.com, 1117 Lincoln Ave., Calistoga, CA 94515) Day trips priced at $115 per person have bikers pedaling to five or six wineries, with a gourmet lunch to boot. The company also books two- and six-day bike trips. Adventurers will find the Pedal and Paddle Tour invigorating. It features a half day of canoeing and a half day of bicycling. Rentals are available.

Viviani, Inc. Destination Management (707-265-1940, www.viviani.com, 2800 Jefferson St., Napa, CA 94558) This is highbrow travel at its best. Viviani specializes in corporate, incentive, and exclusive events in California's Wine Country, offering private, customized tours that make you an insider. You'll meet winemakers, hike in private vineyards, and learn the art of *méthode champenoise* that monks perfected so long ago in Champagne. Among its many offerings are half-day winery tours, full-day tours with lunch, and a tour of Napa for those departing from San Francisco.

Wine & Dine Tours (707-963-8930, 800-946-3868, www.wineanddinetour.com, P.O. Box 204, St. Helena, CA 94574) This tour is for the discriminating traveler who would like to stop in at small boutique wineries in Napa Valley and Sonoma Valley. Most of the wineries are private or by appointment only.

HANDICAPPED SERVICES

Wine Country is accessible—even in a wheelchair. Napa and Sonoma offer a number of easy solutions to help anyone with a handicap get to and fro.

Handyvan-Calistoga (707-963-4229) The vans are wheelchair accessible.

The Vine (707-255-7631) The Valley Intracity Neighborhood Express has five routes in the city of Napa. All buses are wheelchair accessible.

Volunteer Wheels of Sonoma County (707-573-3377) Here you'll find transportation for senior citizens and disabled riders.

The Hiker's Hip Pocket Guide to Sonoma County (Bored Feet Publications; see Bibliography) includes a special section for the handicapped indicating which scenic trails are accessible.

HOSPITALS

Healdsburg District General Hospital (707-431-6500, 1375 University Ave., Healdsburg) 24-hour emergency care, with a physician on duty. Call the general number and ask for the Emergency Room.

Petaluma Valley Hospital (707-778-1111, emergency room: 707-778-2634, 400 N. McDowell Blvd., Petaluma) 24-hour emergency care.

Queen of the Valley Hospital (707-252-4411, emergency room: 707-257-4038, 1000 Trancas St., Napa) 24-hour emergency care, with a physician on duty.

Santa Rosa Memorial Hospital (707-546-3210, emergency room: 707-525-5207, 1165 Montgomery Dr., Santa Rosa) 24-hour emergency care, with a physician on duty.

Sonoma Valley Hospital (707-935-5000, emergency room: 707-935-5105, 347 Andrieuxe St., Sonoma) 24-hour emergency care.

St. Helena Hospital (707-963-3611, emergency room: 707-963-6425, 650 Sanitarium Rd., Deer Park)

Sutter Medical Center of Santa Rosa (707-576-4000, emergency room: 707-576-4040, 3325 Chanate Rd., Santa Rosa) 24-hour emergency care.

LATE-NIGHT FOOD & FUEL

Insomnia after too much gourmet food or wine? Or perhaps you're just a weary traveler looking for a place to gas up. Whatever the case, here are some options for night birds.

NAPA COUNTY
Lucky (707-255-7767, 1312 Trancas St., Napa, CA 94558)

Bel Aire Shell Service (707-226-1720, 1491 Trancas St., Napa, CA 94558)

SONOMA COUNTY
Flamingo Shell (707-542-4456, 2799 4th St., Santa Rosa, CA 95405)

Safeway (707-522-1455, 2751 4th St, Santa Rosa, CA 95405)

Safeway (707-996-0633, 477 W. Napa St., Sonoma, CA 95476)

MEDIA

Magazines & Newspapers

Healdsburg Tribune (707-433-4451, 5 Mitchell Ln., Healdsburg, CA 95448; Wed.) This Sonoma County paper, born in 1953, still has the flavor of the '50s.

Napa Valley Register (707-226-3711, 1615 2nd St., Napa, CA 94559; daily) The paper made its first run in 1865 and, over the years, has proved to give a good local account of Napa County.

North Bay Biz (707-575-8282, 3565 Airway Dr., Santa Rosa, CA 95404; monthly) Covers business and industry in Sonoma County well. It delves into the "politics" of business.

North Bay Business Journal (707-579-2900, 5464 Skylane Blvd., Suite B, Santa Rosa, CA 95403; twice-monthly in Sonoma and Marin counties, monthly in Napa and Solano counties) The region's rendition of the *Wall Street Journal,* with news on the deals and the players and profiles on key business leaders.

North Bay Bohemian (707-527-1200, 216 E St., Santa Rosa, CA 95404; Wed.) Edgy alternative weekly with strong—and liberal—views on politics in northern California.

Press Democrat (707-546-2020, 427 Mendocino Ave., Santa Rosa, CA 95401; daily) Purchased by the *New York Times* in the 1980s, the *Press Democrat* is the largest newspaper in the North Bay. It emphasizes Sonoma County, with newly expanded coverage of the Napa food and wine scene.

San Francisco Chronicle (415-777-7000, 901 Mission St., San Francisco, CA 94103; daily) This metro is not impressive to look at, but it's a good source for national and international news. There are often good Wine Country articles in the food and people sections.

Savor (707-521-5464, 427 Mendocino Ave., Santa Rosa, CA 95401) Published by the *New York Times*-owned *Press Democrat,* this slick magazine is a smart insider's guide to what's happening in Napa, Sonoma, and Mendocino counties.

Sonoma Index-Tribune (707-938-2111, 117 W. Napa St., Sonoma, CA 95476; twice weekly) This is a community paper that focuses exclusively on life in Sonoma Valley.

St. Helena Star (707-963-2731, 1328 Main St., St. Helena, CA 94599; weekly) This is a folksy weekly that covers this town in the heart of Napa Valley.

Wine Country This Week (707-938-0780, P.O. Box 92, El Verano, CA 95433; weekly) This is a good magazine for tourists, with articles on winemakers, inns, and restaurants. There are helpful maps included in each issue. Free.

Radio Stations

KFGY 92.9 and 103.1 FM (707-543-0100, Santa Rosa) Country
KGRP 100.9 FM (707-588-0707, Santa Rosa) Adult contemporary
KJZY 93.7 FM (707-528-4434, Santa Rosa) Light jazz
KMHX 104.1 FM (707-584-1595, Rohnert Park) Modern adult
KNOB 96.7 FM (707-588-0707, Santa Rosa) Adult hits from the 1960s to the present
KRCB 90.9 FM and 91.1 FM (707-585-8522, Rohnert Park) National Public Radio and classical and eclectic music
KRPQ 104.9 FM (707-584-1058, Rohnert Park) Country
KRSH 95.5 and 95.9 FM (707-588-0707, Healdsburg) Adult album alternative
KSRO 1350 AM (707-543-0100, Santa Rosa) News and talk
KSXY 98.7 FM (707-588-0707, Middletown/Santa Rosa) Contemporary
KVON 1440 AM (707-252-1440, Napa) News, talk, sports
KVRV 97.7 FM (707-543-0100, Santa Rosa) Classic rock
KVYN 93.3 FM (707-258-1111, Napa) Adult contemporary
KXFX 101.7 FM (707-543-0100, Santa Rosa) Rock
KZST/100.1 FM (707-528-4434, Santa Rosa) Adult contemporary

Television

There's only one local TV station in all of Wine Country. **KFTY, Channel 50** (707-526-5050), broadcasts from 533 Mendocino Ave., Santa Rosa, CA 95401. Depending on your location, San Francisco and Oakland stations are often within range as well.

Both counties have access to cable television that offers most Bay Area and Sacramento TV channels as well as the usual cable fare such as CNN, HBO, and the USA Network. **ATT Broadband** (877-722-3755) services most of the cities within Napa and Sonoma counties.

REAL ESTATE

Buying a piece of the American Dream—real estate—is downright costly for Californians. In fact, for some it's a nightmare. But if you come to Wine Country and decide to stay, here's information that may help you.

Housing costs in Sonoma and Napa are among the highest in the country. The median price for a 3-bedroom, 1.5-bath, 1,800-square-foot house in Napa County, for instance, is $488,210. Whatever the case, most natives won't dicker over price endlessly. They know they're purchasing not just real estate; they're also buying rights to the nearby ocean, the steep mountains, and a tapestry of vineyards in the countryside—a rare combination.

For information on real estate matters, consult "Real Estate Agents" in the yellow pages in Napa and Sonoma phone books. For insight into the real estate market, call the **Napa Chamber of Commerce** (707-226-7455), the **North Bay Association of Realtors, Napa Chapter** (707-255-1040), and the **North Bay Association of Realtors** (707-542-1579). The latter two organizations compile statistics on area real estate. You can also follow the local newspapers. *The Press Democrat,* for instance, has a complete real estate section published every Sunday (see Media earlier in this chapter).

RELIGIOUS SERVICES & ORGANIZATIONS

The best sources for information about church and synagogue services are the Saturday editions of the *Napa Register* and the *Press Democrat.* The Napa and Sonoma County phone books have comprehensive lists of all mainstream religious organizations, along with specific church and synagogue phone numbers. You can also consult pamphlets put out by the Napa and Sonoma visitors bureaus. For nontraditional groups, keep an eye on community bulletin boards at colleges such as Sonoma State University and Napa Valley College.

ROAD SERVICE

Puncture your tire on a broken bottle of 1995 Rafanelli zinfandel? Stranger things have happened. For emergency road service from AAA anywhere in Napa or Sonoma counties, call 800-222-4357. Listed below are other 24-hour emergency road services.

NAPA COUNTY
Calistoga Towing (707-942-4445)
Grapevine Towing (707-226-3780)

SONOMA COUNTY
ABC Towing (707-433-1700, Healdsburg)
Sebastopol Towing (707-823-1061)
Santa Rosa Towing: (707-542-1600)

SCHOOLS

Public School Districts

NAPA COUNTY
Calistoga Joint Unified School District (707-942-4703, Calistoga)
Napa County School District (707-253-6800, Napa)
St. Helena Unified School District (707-967-2708, St. Helena)

SONOMA COUNTY
Cotati–Rohnert Park Unified School District (707-792-4700, Cotati)
Healdsburg Unified School District (707-431-3117, Healdsburg)
Piner-Olivet Union School District (707-522-3000, Santa Rosa)
Roseland School District (707-545-0102, Santa Rosa)
Santa Rosa School District (707-528-5373, Santa Rosa)
Sonoma Valley Unified School District (707-935-6000, Sonoma)

Private and Religious Schools

NAPA COUNTY
Highlands Christian Preschool (707-942-5557, Calistoga)
Kolbe Academy (707-255-6412, Napa)
St. Helena Montessori School (707-963-1527, St. Helena)

SONOMA COUNTY
Brush Creek Montessori (707-539-7980, Santa Rosa)
Sebastopol Christian School (707-823-2754, Sebastopol)
St. Luke Lutheran Preschool & Day Care Center (707-545-0512, Santa Rosa)
Ursuline High School (707-524-1130, Santa Rosa)

Colleges

NAPA COUNTY
Napa Valley College (707-253-3000, Napa)

SONOMA COUNTY
Empire College, Business School and Law School (707-546-4000, Santa Rosa)
Santa Rosa Junior College (707-527-4011, Santa Rosa)
Sonoma State University (707-664-2880, Rohnert Park)

TOURIST INFORMATION

NAPA COUNTY

Calistoga Chamber of Commerce (707-942-6333, www.calistogafun.com, 1458 Lincoln Ave., Suite 9, Calistoga, CA 94515)

Napa Valley Conference and Visitors Bureau (707-226-7459, www.napavalley.com, info@napavalley.org, 1310 Napa Town Center, Napa, CA 94559

St. Helena Chamber of Commerce (707-963-4456, www.sthelena.com, 1010 Main St., Suite A, St. Helena, CA 94574)

Yountville Chamber of Commerce (707-875-3866, www.yountville.com, 6516 Yount St., P.O. Box 2064, Yountville, CA 94599)

SONOMA COUNTY

Bodega Bay Area Visitors Center (707-875-3422, www.bodegabay.com, 850 Hwy. 1, Bodega Bay, CA 94923)

Healdsburg Chamber of Commerce and Visitors Bureau (707-433-6935, www.healds burg.org, hbgchamb@pacbell.net, 217 Healdsburg Ave., Healdsburg, CA 95448)

Petaluma Area Chamber of Commerce (707-762-2785, www.petaluma.org, pacc @petaluma.org, 800 Baywood Dr., Suite B, Petaluma, CA 94954)

Russian River Chamber of Commerce and Visitors Center (707-869-9000, www.russian river.com, info@russianriver.com, 16209 1st St., Guerneville, CA 95446)

Santa Rosa Chamber of Commerce (707-545-1414, www.santarosachamber.com, keithw @santarosachamber.com, 637 1st St., Santa Rosa, CA 95404)

Sebastopol Chamber of Commerce (707-823-3032, www.sebastopol.org, apples @sebastopol.org, 265 S. Main St., Sebastopol, CA 95472)

Sonoma County Tourism Bureau (707-522-5800, www.sonomacounty.com, info@sonoma county.com, 520 Mendocino Ave., Suite 210, Santa Rosa, CA 95401)

Sonoma Valley Visitors Bureau (707-996-1090, www.sonomavalley.com, svvb@verio.com, 453 1st St. E., Sonoma, CA 95476; a second office is now open below Viansa Winery: 707-935-4747, 25200 Arnold Dr., Sonoma, CA 95476)

10

If Time Is Short

Ideally, your visit to Wine Country should be long enough to include visits to several of the attractions in each category—but if time is of the essence, and you find yourself forced to choose just one restaurant for dining or one winery to visit, then perhaps we can help. Here are our personal favorites—with emphasis on the personal. Not everyone might pick these particular spots, but we feel confident that you will enjoy them as much as we do.

Inns

Oak Knoll Inn (707-255-2200, oakknollinn.com, 2200 E. Oak Knoll Ave., Napa, CA 94558) This is an intimate and luxurious inn just north of the city of Napa. The hospitality is exceptional and the breakfasts are among the best in Wine Country.

Inn at Occidental (707-874-1047, 800-522-6324, www.innatoccidental.com, 3657 Church St., Occidental, CA 95465) This is well off the beaten path but worth it. Perched on a hill overlooking the quiet village of Occidental, this Victorian inn is a jewel.

Cultural Attractions

The Hess Collection (707-255-1144, 4411 Redwood Dr., Napa, CA 94558) This stylish winery has one of the most impressive art collections north of San Francisco. Plus, the wine is superb.

Mission San Francisco Solano (707-938-9560, corner of Spain St. and 1st St. E., Sonoma Plaza, Sonoma, CA 95476) Wine Country history doesn't get any richer than this. Built before 1841, this white adobe with a red-tiled roof was the last mission built in California.

Restaurants

Bouchon (707-944-8037, 6534 Washington St., Yountville, CA 94599) Bouchon has the authentic feel of an upscale brasserie in Paris, and it has a menu to match. The man behind it is Thomas Keller of The French Laundry. What a find—Paris in Napa Valley.

Deuce (707-933-3823, 691 Broadway, Sonoma, CA 95476) Set in a charming, 110-year-old Victorian farm house, this is one of the most popular restaurants in Sonoma Valley, and rightly so. The menu offers comfort and adventure.

Wineries

For Beginners
Korbel Champagne Cellars (707-824-7000, 13250 River Rd., Guerneville, CA 95446) No mystery why visitors flock here. It has everything: rich history, a beautiful locale, a great tour, and lots of bubbly.

For Wine Buffs
Opus One (707-963-1979, www.opusonewines.com, 7900 St. Helena Hwy., P.O. Box 106, Oakville, CA 94562) This distinctive winery was largely inaccessible to the public until 1994. You'll still need an appointment. It makes one wine: a blockbuster red.

Recreation

Lazy Fun
A spa treatment is a must. A one-hour massage with whirlpool bath is Nirvana. (Mud baths, though, aren't for everyone.) Our favorite spas include **Calistoga Spa Hot Springs**; **Meadowood Resort** outside St. Helena; and the unique, Japanese-style **Osmosis** in Occidental.

Real Adventure
A **hot-air balloon ride** over Wine Country is beautiful and exhilarating. See Ballooning in chapter 7, Recreation, for details and suggested companies.

INDEX

Dining by Cuisine

Dining by Price

Inexpensive: Up to $20
Moderate: $20 to $30
Expensive: $30 to $40
Very Expensive: $40 and up

Calistoga (Napa County)

Moderate
Boskos Trattoria, 128

Moderate to Expensive
Wappo Bar and Bistro, 128–29

Expensive
All Seasons Bistro, 127–28
Brannan's Grill, 128

Geyersville (Sonoma County)

Expensive to Very Expensive
Santi, 139

Healdsburg (Sonoma County)

Moderate to Expensive
Bovolo, 136–37

Moderate to Very Expensive
Willi's Seafood and Raw Bar, 138–39

Expensive
Bistro Ralph, 136
Dry Creek Kitchen, 137–38
Ravenous, 138
Zin Restaurant & Wine Bar, 139

Very Expensive
Barn Diva, 135–36
Cyrus, 137
Madrona Manor, 138

Napa (Napa County)

Moderate
Pizza Azzurro, 117
Ubuntu Restaurant and Yoga Studio, 118

Moderate to Expensive
Bistro Don Giovanni, 114
Boon Fly Cafe (at the Carneros Inn), 114–15
Bounty Hunter Wine Bar, 115
Tuscany, 117–18

Expensive
Angele, 117
Celadon, 116

Very Expensive
Cole's Chop House, 116–17
Farm (at the Carneros Inn), 117
Julia's Kitchen, 117

Oakville/Rutherford (Napa County)

Moderate to Expensive
Rutherford Grill, 124

Very Expensive
Auberge Du Soleil, 123–24
La Toque, 124

Santa Rosa (Sonoma County)

Moderate to Expensive
Flavor, 134

Expensive
Syrah, 134–35
Willi's Wine Bar, 135
Zazu, 135

Very Expensive
John Ash & Company, 134

Sonoma Valley (Sonoma County)

Moderate
Cafe Citti, 129
Della Santina's, 130

Moderate to Expensive
Maya, 133
Saddles, 133

Expensive
Cafe La Haye, 129–30
Carneros Bistro and Wine Bar, 130
Deuce, 130–31
The General's Daughter, 131
The Girl & the Fig, 131
Glen Ellen Inn, 132
Harvest Moon Cafe, 132
Kenwood Restaurant and Bar, 132

Very Expensive
Sante-Fairmont Sonoma Mission Inn, 133

Sonoma West County (Sonoma County)

Moderate to Expensive
Farmhouse Inn & Restaurant, 140–41
Lucas Wharf, 141
Underwood Bar & Bistro, 142

Lodging by Price

Inexpensive:	Up to $100
Moderate:	$100 to $150
Expensive:	$150 to $250
Very Expensive:	$250 and up

Calistoga (Napa County)

Moderate to Expensive
Brannan Cottage Inn, 58
Carlin Cottages, 58–59

Moderate to Very Expensive
Hideaway Cottages, 61

Expensive
Chanric Inn, 59–60
Chelsea Garden Inn, 59

Expensive to Very Expensive
Chateau De Vie, 59
Christopher's Inn, 59
Foothill House, 60–61
Garnett Creek Inn, 61
Meadowlark, 61
Mount View Hotel, 61–62
The Pink Mansion, 62

Very Expensive
Calistoga Ranch, 58
Cottage Grove Inn, 60
Solage Calistoga, 62

Calistoga Spa Lodging (Napa County)

Inexpensive to Expensive
Golden Haven Hot Springs and Resort, 63
Roman Spa, 63

Moderate
Calistoga Spa Hot Springs, 62

Moderate to Expensive
Calistoga Village Inn and Spa, 62–63
Eurospa & Inn, 63

Expensive
Dr. Wilkinson's Hot Springs, 63

Expensive to Very Expensive
Indian Springs Spa and Resort, 63

Geyersville (Sonoma County)

Moderate to Expensive
Hope-Merrill House and Hope-Bosworth House, 76

Healdsburg (Sonoma County)

Inexpensive to Expensive
Dry Creek Inn, Best Western, 73

Moderate to Expensive
Camellia Inn, 72–73

Moderate to Very Expensive
Haydon Street Inn, 74

Expensive to Very Expensive
Belle De Jour Inn, 71–73
Grape Leaf Inn, 73
Honor Mansion, 74
Hotel Healdsburg, 74–75, 246
Les Mars, 75
Madrona Manor, 76

Very Expensive
Healdsburg Inn on the Plaza, 74

Napa (Napa County)

Moderate to Expensive
Elm House Inn, Best Western, 43–44

Moderate to Very Expensive
Hennessey House, 44–45
River Terrace Inn, 48

Expensive
Stahlecker House, 49
The Westin Verasa Napa Residences, 50

Expensive to Very Expensive
Beazley House, 42
Candlelight Inn of the Dunn Lee Manor, 42–43
Churchill Manor, 43
Cottages of Napa Valley, 43
Embassy Suites, Napa Valley, 44
La Belle Epoque, 45
La Residence Country Inn, 45
The Magnolia Napa, 45–46
Meritage, 46
Milliken Creek Inn and Spa, 46–47
Napa River Inn, 46–47
Napa Valley Marriott, 47
The Old World Inn, 48

Very Expensive
Carneros Inn, 43
The Poetry Inn, 47–48
Silverado Resort, 48–49

Motels (Sonoma County)

Inexpensive
Bodega Harbor Inn, 80

Inexpensive to Moderate
Fairview Motel, 81

Inexpensive to Expensive
Geyersville Inn, 81
Holiday Inn Express, 81
Wine Country Travel Lodge, 81

Inexpensive to Very Expensive
El Pueblo Inn, 80

Moderate to Expensive
Santa Rosa Courtyard by Marriott, 81

Moderate to Very Expensive
Bodega Coast Inn, 80
Timber Cove Inn, 81